A Handbook of Wisdom

A topic ignored in mainstream scientific inquiry for decades, wisdom is beginning to return to the place of reverence that it held in ancient schools of intellectual study. *A Handbook of Wisdom* explores wisdom's promise for helping scholars and lay people to understand the apex of human thought and behavior. At a time when poor choices are being made by notably intelligent and powerful individuals, this book presents analysis and review on a form of reasoning and decision making that is not only productive and prudent but also serves a beneficial purpose for society.

A Handbook of Wisdom is a collection of chapters from some of the most prominent scholars in the field of wisdom research. Written from multiple perspectives, including psychology, philosophy, and religion, this book provides the reader with an in-depth understanding of wisdom's past, present, and possible future direction within literature, science, and society.

Robert J. Sternberg is IBM Professor of Psychology and Education at Yale and Director of the PACE Center at Yale. He was the 2003 President of the American Psychological Association. He is the author of more than 1,000 publications on topics related to cognition and intelligence. He has won numerous awards from professional associations and holds five honorary doctorates.

Jennifer Jordan is an advanced doctoral student in psychology at Yale University. She has studied wisdom under the guidance of both Robert Sternberg at Yale and Paul Baltes at the Max Planck Institute for Human Development in Berlin, Germany. She is the recipient of a John F. Enders Grant and an American Psychological Association Award for her dissertation, which examines moral awareness and business expertise.

A Handbook of Wisdom

Psychological Perspectives

Edited by

ROBERT J. STERNBERG

Yale University

JENNIFER JORDAN

Yale University

CAMBRIDGE UNIVERSITY PRESS
Cambridge, New York, Melbourne, Madrid, Cape Town, Singapore, São Paulo

Cambridge University Press
40 West 20th Street, New York, NY 10011-4211, USA

www.cambridge.org
Information on this title: www.cambridge.org/9780521834018

First published 2005

Printed in the United States of America

A catalog record for this publication is available from the British Library.

Library of Congress Cataloging in Publication Data

A handbook of wisdom : psychological perspectives /
edited by Robert J. Sternberg, Jennifer Jordan.
p.   cm.
Includes bibliographical references and index.
ISBN 0-521-83401-5 (hardcover) – ISBN 0-521-54182-4 (pbk.)
1. Wisdom.   2. Conduct of life.   I. Sternberg, Robert J.   II. Jordan, Jennifer, 1982-
III. Title.
BJ1595.H29   2005
150′.1 – dc22   2004024337

ISBN-13   978-0-521-83401-8 hardback
ISBN-10   0-521-83401-5 hardback

ISBN-13   978-0-521-54182-4 paperback
ISBN-10   0-521-54182-4 paperback

Contents

List of Contributors

Monika Ardelt
University of Florida
Gainesville, FL

Paul B. Baltes
Max Planck Institute of Human Development
Berlin, Germany

James E. Birren
University of California
Los Angeles, CA

Susan Bluck
University of Florida
Gainesville, FL

Warren S. Brown
Fuller Theological Seminary
Pasadena, CA

Mihaly Csikszentmihalyi
Claremont Graduate University
Claremont, CA

Jessica Dörner
International University Bremen
Bremen, Germany

Lloyd S. Etheredge
Yale University
New Haven, CT

Howard Gardner
Harvard Graduate School of Education
Cambridge, MA

Judith Glück
University of Vienna

Jennifer Jordan
Yale University
New Haven, CT

Ute Kunzmann
Max Planck Institute of Human Development
Berlin, Germany

Joel J. Kupperman
Harvard Graduate School of Education
Cambridge, MA

Paula Marshall
Harvard Graduate School of Education
Cambridge, MA

Charlotte Mickler
International University Bremen
Bremen, Germany

Jeanne Nakamura
Claremont Graduate University
Claremont, CA

Lisa M. Osbeck
State University of West Georgia
Carrollton, GA

Willis F. Overton
Temple University
Philadelphia, PA

M. Pasupathi
University of Utah
Salt Lake City, UT

M. J. Richardson
University of Utah
Salt Lake City, UT

Daniel N. Robinson
Philosophy Faculty, Oxford University, UK
Distinguished Professor Emeritus, Georgetown University

Jeffrey L. Solomon
Harvard Graduate School of Education
Cambridge, MA

Ursula M. Staudinger
International University Bremen
Bremen, Germany

Robert J. Sternberg
Yale University
New Haven, CT

Cheryl M. Svensson
California State University
Fullerton, CA

Masami Takahashi
Northeastern Illinois University
Chicago, IL

Foreword

Monika Ardelt

Back in 1990, when I was a graduate student at the University of North Carolina at Chapel Hill, I decided to investigate predictors of life satisfaction in old age as my dissertation topic. I was not convinced by the traditional sociological explanation that well-being in old age depended mostly on the conditions older people encountered, such as physical health, finances, socioeconomic status, social involvement, and residential situation. I was searching for a concept that would represent the internal strength of older adults, which enabled some older people to be satisfied with their life despite adverse circumstances. After studying the literature on lifelong psychosocial growth, it occurred to me that the acquisition of wisdom might hold the key to subjective well-being in old age. Although I now had the concept, I had no idea how to define and much less how to measure wisdom.

I remember going to the library to pick up another book on the life course and aging when, right next to it, I saw the edited book by Sternberg (1990) on *Wisdom: Its Nature, Origins, and Development*. It felt like a book sent by heaven, and it became instantly my "bible" on wisdom. Up to this point I had no idea that wisdom was actually a topic of modern scientific inquiries and that respected researchers had tackled this somewhat esoteric topic. Not that it made my life much easier at first. As Birren and Svensson mention in this *Handbook*, the 13 chapters in the 1990 edited *Wisdom* book resulted in 13 different definitions of wisdom. However, the 1990 book introduced me to the contemporary wisdom research at that time and led me to the wisdom studies by Vivian Clayton (e.g., Clayton & Birren, 1980), whose model of wisdom as an integration of cognitive, reflective, and affective personality qualities has been the basis of my own wisdom research ever since (e.g., Ardelt, 2003).

The 1990 edited *Wisdom* book was not called a handbook, and rightly so. Contemporary empirical research on wisdom was in its infancy, and there just was not enough research to summarize and synthesize to justify the title of "Handbook." Yet, times have changed and the publication of the present *Handbook of Wisdom* was sorely needed. In fact, wisdom research has grown tremendously during the past 15 years. A search in PsycINFO (via EBSCO Host Research Databases) under the subject or key concept of "wisdom" yielded 12 entries of published articles, books, chapters, or dissertation abstracts before 1980, 10 entries between 1980 and 1984, 18 entries between 1985 and 1989, 40 entries between 1990 and 1994, 71 entries between 1995 and 1999, and 146 entries between 2000 and the present. Although such a search is not necessarily precise because not all relevant literature is listed and some listed items are unrelated to wisdom research, it still is an, albeit crude, indicator for the exponential progress in wisdom research. It appears that between 1980 and 2004, published entries on the subject or key concept of "wisdom" have doubled approximately every 5 years.

Whereas the 1990 edited *Wisdom* book was able to present almost the entirety of contemporary wisdom research, this is no longer possible in a single volume. Yet, the *Handbook of Wisdom* comes close to this task. It provides an extensive overview of the state of the art of modern inquiries and debates in the study of wisdom.

After more than a quarter century of ever-growing wisdom research, does a uniform definition of wisdom exist? The answer is still no, but we might be getting closer to a common and generally agreed-upon definition of wisdom, although measuring wisdom is a different matter. In fact, the authors in Part I of the *Handbook of Wisdom* – the largest section of the volume – address the questions of what wisdom is; how the answer varies across time, culture, and peoples; and why wisdom disappeared until recently from modern psychological and philosophical research. Birren and Svensson investigate how the concept of wisdom evolved historically, starting with the ancient Sumerians and ending with modern psychological sciences. Both Birren and Svensson and Takahashi and Overton unearth the roots of contemporary definitions of wisdom. Takahashi and Overton focus particularly on the difference between Western and Eastern wisdom traditions and introduce a culturally inclusive developmental model of wisdom that integrates the (Western) analytic mode with the (Eastern) synthetic mode of wisdom.

Robinson and Osbeck examine wisdom from the perspective of classical Greek philosophy. How did the ancient Greeks fathom the acquisition of wisdom and why did they consider the possession of wisdom desirable? What is the distinction between Aristotle's concepts of practical and theoretical wisdom, and how is this distinction relevant for our contemporary lives? How is wisdom dependent on the perception of an objective truth?

Bluck and Glück explore people's implicit (or lay) theories of wisdom and ask how those theories are assessed, how they are used in everyday life, how they vary by culture and age, how they differ from explicit (or expert) theories of wisdom, and why it is necessary to distinguish between implicit and explicit wisdom theories. After reviewing five implicit wisdom theories, Bluck and Glück identify five aspects that they deem essential for wisdom: cognitive ability, insight, reflective attitude, concern for others, and real-world skills.

Explicit theories are the theories of an elite group of experts in the field. Yet, if wisdom is considered a highly advanced stage of human development that only very few individuals attain, wisdom experts might be extremely rare. Hence, one might argue that most wisdom theories are implicit theories since not many people, even among wisdom researchers, might be genuine experts in wisdom and an externally verifiable criterion of wisdom does not exist. That would mean that "explicit wisdom theories" are simply the implicit theories of wisdom researchers. Most explicit theories of wisdom researchers, however, show considerable overlap with implicit (lay) theories of wisdom.

Kunzmann and Baltes introduce the Berlin wisdom paradigm, an explicit theory of wisdom developed by Baltes and colleagues at the Max Planck Institute of Berlin and probably the most widely known contemporary model of the empirical study of wisdom to date. According to this paradigm, wisdom can be defined as expert knowledge in the meaning and conduct of life and in the fundamental pragmatics of life (i.e., life planning, life management, and life review). Wisdom-related knowledge is assessed according to five wisdom criteria: rich factual knowledge, rich procedural knowledge, life-span contextualism, value relativism, and uncertainty. Kunzmann and Baltes also give an overview of the antecedents, correlates, and consequences of wisdom-related knowledge.

The authors in Part II of the *Handbook* investigate the development of wisdom across the life span, using the Berlin wisdom paradigm. The questions that are addressed are (a) when and how does wisdom-related knowledge develop and (b) what is the relation between wisdom-related knowledge and age in adulthood? Pasupathi and Richardson report that wisdom-related knowledge increases during adolescence as the result of normative developmental changes in cognitive abilities, self/identity development, and personality development. In adulthood, however, Jordan does not find any evidence that wisdom-related knowledge changes with age. Rather, the relation between wisdom-related knowledge and age appears to support the crystallized model of wisdom in adulthood: Wisdom-related knowledge tends to neither increase nor decrease during the adulthood years but remains relatively stable.

Because this result is based on cross-sectional data alone and on the assessment of wisdom as general wisdom-related knowledge, the evidence is not conclusive at this point. On the one hand, it supports the generally held assumption that wisdom does not *automatically* increase with age. On the other hand, longitudinal studies have shown that wisdom tends to increase during adulthood for people who might be particularly interested and motivated to pursue the attainment of personal wisdom (Helson & Srivastava, 2002; Wink & Helson, 1997).

The authors in Part III of the *Handbook* analyze the connection between wisdom and the person. Staudinger, Dörner, and Mickler start with the question whether wisdom is (a) a personality characteristic, (b) the result or correlate of specific personality characteristics, or (c) both. To answer the question, Staudinger, Dörner, and Mickler differentiate between general and personal wisdom, based on their notion that one can have general wisdom without being wise (personal wisdom). General wisdom (i.e., insight into life in general) is considered a precursor for personal wisdom (i.e., insight into one's own life). Even though not all researchers might agree with this distinction (Ardelt, 2004; Moody, 1986), it is useful to highlight some of the existing differences in the theoretical and empirical approaches to the study of wisdom.

Whereas Staudinger, Dörner, and Mickler believe that general wisdom precedes personal wisdom, Csikszentmihalyi and Nakamura argue that a wise person is an individual who has sought and found general wisdom. Csikszentmihalyi and Nakamura are particularly interested in the emotions that accompany the pursuit and acquisition of wisdom-related knowledge. They conclude that both the pursuit and realization of wisdom bring forth positive emotions of joy and serenity through the transcendence of self-centeredness. This finding, however, is in direct contradiction to Staudinger, Dörner, and Mickler's viewpoint that personal wisdom does not result in subjective well-being because the development of wisdom has its costs. The question remains whether seeing reality more clearly is intrinsically rewarding and enjoyable or leads to the somber realization that life is suffering. A third possibility is that the mental clarity that accompanies wisdom illuminates not only the reality of human suffering but also the path to the cessation of suffering (e.g., Nanamoli, 2001).

Part IV deals with wisdom in society. Kupperman discusses the difference between knowing-how (e.g., to live) and knowing-that (e.g., knowledge and theories about the good life or the fundamental pragmatics of life). He argues that the "knowing-that" of wisdom by itself is meaningless unless it is applied in "knowing-how" to live a life that is good for oneself, good for others, and good for the larger society. In other words, wisdom is knowing how to live a good life, which must be exhibited in the life of a wise person. To develop wisdom, scholarly learning is less important than the realization of wisdom, which requires a personal transformation and good role models. Kupperman demonstrates that moral and ethical choices necessitate the knowing-how of wisdom.

Gardner, Solomon, and Marshall give an overview of their study on generative wisdom. They define generative wisdom as work (i.e., products, outcomes, and initiatives) by professionals that is intended to maximize the benefit and welfare of present and future generations. Gardner, Solomon, and Marshall present six case studies that illustrate the development of generative wisdom through three mental models of boundary crossing: (a) going beyond conventional knowledge or understanding, (b) seeing beyond the here and now, and (c) going beyond traditional professional boundaries.

Etheredge states that wisdom in public policy includes good judgment and commitment to the well-being of all present and future members of society and, in international politics, also to members of other nations. He defines wise policies by eight values for human betterment: power, enlightenment (education and personal growth), wealth, (physical and mental) well-being, skill, affection, rectitude, and respect. Theoretically, political wisdom should lead to a better world, but as Etheredge shows, it is not necessarily clear how political wisdom might be implemented and how a better world might be attained.

The *Handbook* concludes in Part V with a discussion of the absence of wisdom. Sternberg opens the last chapter with the observation that "smart people can be foolish." Hence, intelligence and knowledge by themselves do not protect against foolishness. Sternberg introduces an imbalance theory of foolishness, which is a mirror image of his balance theory of wisdom (Sternberg, 1998). Five fallacies in thinking increase the likelihood of foolish behavior: unrealistic optimism, egocentrism, and illusions of omniscience, omnipotence, and invulnerability. Sternberg argues that the study of foolishness is important, because the costs of foolishness to the individual, others, and/or society can be great.

The different wisdom perspectives presented in the *Handbook of Wisdom* might remind the reader of Buddha's story of the blind men and the elephant. According to the story, a king gathered several men who were blind from birth around an elephant and told them to describe the animal to him. Each of the blind men gave a different definition of the elephant, depending on the part of the elephant he was investigating (Nanamoli, 2001). In some sense, this might still be the stage of current wisdom research. We concentrate on certain aspects of wisdom, depending on the focus of our research interests, but the whole meaning of wisdom escapes us. Interestingly, Takahashi and Overton report in the *Handbook* that people's implicit theories of wisdom tend to correspond to an ideal self, which varies in different cultures. Could it be that lay persons' and wisdom researchers' theories of wisdom represent an ideal and desired image of (their own) perfect development? Yet, if wisdom (the "elephant") exists and is not just in the head of the beholder, it is to our advantage to describe and investigate as many of its parts as possible until a coherent and complete picture of wisdom emerges. I believe that the *Handbook of Wisdom* does just that; it contributes essential pieces to the overall puzzle of wisdom.

April 2004

References

Ardelt, M. (2003). Development and empirical assessment of a three-dimensional wisdom scale. *Research on Aging, 25,* 275–324.

Ardelt, M. (2004). Wisdom as expert knowledge system: A critical review of a contemporary operationalization of an ancient concept. *Human Development, 47,* 257–285.

Clayton, V. P., & Birren, J. E. (1980). The development of wisdom across the life-span: A reexamination of an ancient topic. In P. B. Baltes & O. G. Brim, Jr. (Eds.), *Life-span development and behavior* (Vol. 3, pp. 103–135). New York: Academic Press.

Helson, R., & Srivastava, S. (2002). Creative and wise people: Similarities, differences and how they develop. *Personality and Social Psychology Bulletin, 28,* 1430–1440.

Moody, H. R. (1986). Late life learning in the information society. In D. A. Peterson, J. E. Thornton, & J. E. Birren (Eds.), *Education and aging* (pp. 122–148). Englewood Cliffs, NJ: Prentice Hall.

Nanamoli, B. (2001). *The life of the Buddha. According to the Pali Canon.* Seattle, WA: BPS Pariyatti Editions.

Sternberg, R. J. (Ed.). (1990). *Wisdom: Its nature, origins, and development.* Cambridge: Cambridge University Press.

Sternberg, R. J. (1998). A balance theory of wisdom. *Review of General Psychology, 2*, 347–365.

Wink, P., & Helson, R. (1997). Practical and transcendent wisdom: Their nature and some longitudinal findings. *Journal of Adult Development, 4*, 1–15.

PART I

THEORIES OF WISDOM ACROSS TIME, CULTURE, AND PEOPLES

1

Wisdom in History

James E. Birren and Cheryl M. Svensson

Wisdom is not a new concept that originated in the technologically advanced information age of today. Rather, wisdom bears the connotations of "ancient" and seemingly transcends time, knowledge, and even culture. All peoples, whether primitive or civilized, have sought to pass their *wisdom* on to following generations by means of myths, stories, songs, and even cave paintings that date back 30,000 years. Will Durant (1935) defined civilization as a social order that promotes cultural creation and that contains four elements: economic provision, political organization, moral traditions, and pursuit of knowledge and the arts. Civilizations and the written records thereof will be the basis for our explorations as we trace the concept of wisdom throughout history. This is not a definitive review of wisdom since that has been well documented by previous authors (Bates, 1993; Brugman, 2000; Csikszentmihalyi & Rathunde, 1990; Robinson, 1990). Rather, it is a brief overview of the ways in which the concept of wisdom has been interpreted over time and its relevance to contemporary studies of wisdom.

Even though wisdom is an ancient topic, our perceptions and definitions have not remained static and unchanged over the years. This chapter begins with the early references to wisdom and explores how the definitions and understanding have evolved over the ages. Next, we consider the history of wisdom in the psychological sciences. Following that, we explore the development of empirical studies of wisdom beginning in the late 1970s. Finally, we examine new research on wisdom and suggest directions for the development of wisdom research in the future.

Ancient History

Among the oldest known civilizations are the Sumerians, who lived along the fertile valley of the Tigris and Euphrates rivers in an area then known as Mesopotamia, now Iraq. More than 5,000 years ago, the Sumerians set up organized states, built cities, and invented writing (Durant, 1935). Sumerian writings were preserved on clay tablets and formed the basis of the earliest "wisdom literature." The wisdom literature consisted of philosophical reflections, such as, "We are doomed to die; let us spend," and "He who possesses much silver may be happy" (Readers Digest Association [RDA], 1973). In this context, wisdom referred to practical advice for daily living. The Sumerian culture was the foundation for the Greek and Roman cultures. The transfer of culture and "wisdom" is evidenced by the fact that in one of the Sumerian epic tales, "Gilgamesh," king of Uruk, met the survivor of a "great flood." One passage of this tale is so similar to the story of Noah and the flood told in Genesis in the Old Testament of the Bible that it is believed that the writers of the Old Testament may have drawn upon these ancient Sumerian texts (Kramer, 1959).

The Egyptian civilization flourished from 3200 B.C. to 300 A.D. Some of the earliest written teachings on wisdom are attributed to the Egyptians. Ptah-hotep in the 5th dynasty of the Pharaoh of Issi (2870–2675 B.C.) wrote texts on wisdom that concerned proper behavior (Brugman, 2000). The Egyptian wisdom literature contained universally popular precepts for good behavior and wisdom such as "Be not puffed up with thy knowledge, and be not proud because thou are wise" (RDA, 1973). It is believed that these and other writings from the early Egyptians were a source of Hebrew wisdom familiar to many Christians and Jews in the books of the Old Testament.

Of all the ancient philosophers, the Greeks, the "lovers of wisdom," are best known to modern man. They were the first philosophers who sought to understand the world by using reason rather than by relying on religion, authority, or tradition (Magee, 1998). This was a major step forward in the intellectual development of mankind and formed the basis for rational thinking. One of the early Greek philosophers, often referred to as the father of philosophy, was Thales, active in the 6th century B.C. Along with his followers, he started the Milesian school (Magee, 1998). Thales was advanced in his thinking and believed that everything in the world was reducible to one element, but he mistakenly believed that element to be water. There were a number of other important philosophers prior to Socrates, but they all shared the common goal of understanding the nature of the world and to what all things could be reduced (Durant, 1926). Wisdom did not refer to precepts for living but, rather, to an investigation into the laws and constituents of the natural world. These broad theories from the early Greek philosophers paved the way for our later attempts to understand how our world functions.

Socrates (470–399 B.C.) was born in Athens. Following the *Sophists*, traveling teachers of wisdom, he changed the focus of the questions from what we need to know regarding the natural world to what we need to know to conduct a "good life" (Durant, 1926). Socrates focused on questions such as: "What is good?" and "What is just?" The answers to these questions would have a profound influence on how people lived. His method of questioning became known as the "Socratic method" and usually showed that those who thought they knew the answer to a given question did not. He taught people to question everything. Certain fundamental beliefs underlie Socrates' teaching and one of those is that no one knowingly does wrong. That is, if a person fully understood that it was wrong to do something, then he or she would not do it. If, however, someone did it, then it was because that individual had not fully and completely grasped that it was the wrong thing to do (Magee, 1998). For Socrates, the wise did not seek wisdom, but the lovers of wisdom were somewhere between the wise and the ignorant. He believed only God to be wise and refused to call any man wise, rather, men could be "lovers of wisdom" (Adler, 1952).

Socrates left no written records, but his pupil Plato (428–348 B.C.) did and these have survived intact. Plato believed that Socrates was the best, most wise, and just of all men (Magee, 1998). Plato's early dialogues concerned the problems of moral and political philosophy as well as problems of the natural world. Two primary components of his philosophy concern his belief that the only real harm that could be done to a person is harm to his soul and also that people should think for themselves and never take anything for granted (Magee, 1998). For Plato, wisdom was the virtue of reason and not only contemplated the truth but also directed conduct (Adler, 1952). Thus wisdom was concerned with the ultimate meaning of life and the nature of both the physical universe and mankind.

Aristotle (384–322 B.C.) was a student of Plato, and like him, considered wisdom to be one of the most basic human virtues (Adler, 1952). According to Aristotle, wisdom belonged to philosophical knowledge, especially to the speculative brand of theology. Thus, a distinction was made between "practical" and "speculative" wisdom; practical wisdom was referred to as "prudence" and speculative wisdom as simply "wisdom." For Aristotle, wisdom connoted the highest form of knowledge and was thus more aptly applied to speculative rather than to practical wisdom. The writings of Plato and his students continued to dominate philosophy in the West for 600–700 years.

It is believed that the Hebrew people migrated from Ur in Sumeria to Palestine in about 2200 B.C. (Durant, 1935). The Hebrews added a theological component to the Greek's treatment of wisdom and wisdom became a divine enlightenment and revelation of truth from God (Bates, 1993). References to wisdom abound in the Bible's Old Testament, particularly in the books of Job, Proverbs, and Ecclesiastes. The Bible is a model for behavior for many contemporary people. The book of Proverbs includes statements about wisdom that are intended as guides to behavior.

Proverbs 8

1. Does not wisdom call,
and does not understanding raise her voice?
10. Take my instructions instead of silver
and knowledge rather than choice gold
11. For wisdom is better than jewels,
and all that you may desire
cannot compare with her.
12. I, wisdom, live with prudence and discretion.

Proverbs 9

1. Wisdom has built her house,
she has hewn her seven pillars.
9. Give instructions to the wise, and
they will become wiser still;
teach the righteous and they will
gain in learning.
10. The fear of the Lord is the
beginning of wisdom,
and the knowledge of the
Holy One is insight.
    (Proverbs 8: 1, 10–12, and
    Proverbs 9: 1, 9–10. *Holy Bible:*
    New Standard Revised Version)

In these selections from Proverbs we see several important elements. Wisdom is referred to as "she," presumably a legacy from the early Greeks, who designated Athena as the goddess of wisdom. These Proverbs also describe qualities of wisdom, including the fact that "The fear of the Lord is the beginning of wisdom."

With the emergence of Christianity, a clearer distinction was made between earlier philosophic wisdom as human wisdom at its highest, and the concept of religious wisdom as a gift from God. For the Jewish people, wisdom arises from a relationship with God (Bates, 1993). King Solomon, in the 9th century B.C., was considered wise and his wisdom was thought to be a Divine gift from Yahweh, an exercise of justice, political wisdom, technical wisdom, intelligence, and knowledge (Brugman, 2000). Yahweh promised Solomon wisdom that surpassed all men before and after him (1 Kings 3:12).

After the fall of the Roman Empire, Christianity ruled for a thousand years. The writings of the Greek philosophers were carefully analyzed to make certain they fit in with the Christian doctrine. St. Augustine (354–430 A.D.) was one of the first religious men to blend classical philosophical teachings into a theological setting based on an all-powerful and all-knowing God (Cottingham, 1996). He divided intelligence into two parts: wisdom, or "sapientia," which is timeless and eternal, and "scientia," or knowledge of the material world. Wisdom was considered to be moral perfection and without sin. Because mankind is prey to sin and thus hindered from reaching the highest wisdom of God, wisdom seekers isolated themselves from worldly concerns to live in the spirit (Bates, 1993).

Thomas Aquinas (1225–1274) synthesized Western philosophy and Christian beliefs and maintained the distinction between philosophy and religion, or between reason and faith. He proposed three habits of the speculative intellect: wisdom, science, and understanding. He believed that science depended on understanding, a virtue of a higher degree, and that both depended on wisdom, which he considered the highest point. Wisdom judges all things and sets them in order. Wisdom is a type of science that judges not only conclusions but also first principles. Thus, it was a more perfect virtue than science. Wisdom, according to Aquinas, considered the highest causes (Aquinas, 1267/1952, pp. 36–37).

Eastern Wisdom

The Eastern traditions must not be overlooked as we explore the Western references to wisdom in history. It should be noted that while Europe was mired in the Dark Ages, some civilizations in Asia were

at the height of their development. Mohenjo-daro, on the banks of the
Indus River in India, is considered one of the oldest civilizations known
to man. Its reign has been placed between the fourth and third millennia
B.C. (Durant, 1935). The oldest known religion of India was animistic and
totemic worship of spirits found in animals, stones, and nature. Through
the "Vedas" we learn of ancient India. Veda means "knowledge" or
wisdom; thus, literally, Veda means the Book of Knowledge and refers
to all sacred early lore. Only four have survived: Rig-veda, knowledge
of hymns of praise; Sama-veda, knowledge of the melodies; Yajur-veda,
knowledge of sacrificial formulas; and Atharva-veda, knowledge of
magic formulas.

The Upanishads, 108 discourses composed by various saints and
sages representing the opinions and lessons of the many authors, were
originally transmitted orally and were not written until 800–500 B.C.
(Durant, 1935). The Upanishads sought to explain the unintelligible of
this world that is not accessible to the intellect. Thus, wisdom diverged
from the knowable, sensory world we live in to a vaster, more intuitive
understanding of the nature of life and death. The Upanishads remain
today a revered creed.

Prince Siddhartha Gautama (563–483 B.C.) was born in India. He
left his privileged life at age 29 to search for a higher truth (Dyer,
1998). After his enlightenment, he became known as the "Buddha" or
Awakened One. His teachings form the basis of Buddhism and he taught
through conversations, lectures, and stories. These were summarized
into "sutras" or threads to prompt memory (Durant, 1935). The sutra
of the Four Noble Truths is basic to Buddhism: (1) all life is suffering;
(2) suffering arises from desire; (3) wisdom lies in stilling all desire; and
(4) the eightfold path is the way to the cessation of suffering. The Buddha
focused on conduct rather than theology, ritual, or worship. He taught,
"Do not believe in authority or teachers or elders. But after careful observation and analysis, when it agrees with reason, it will benefit man
and all, then accept it and live by it" (Dyer, 1998, p. 5). Thus, wisdom
meant "knowing" something by personal observation and experience.

The exact age of Chinese civilization is unknown but it is estimated
to be 7,000 years old. China has never been one homogenous nation
but, rather, a "melting pot" of humanity from diverse origins, each with
their own distinctive language and culture (Durant, 1935). China is the
home of humanistic, nontheological philosophy. Lao-tzu was the greatest of pre-Confucian philosophers. The *Tao-Te-Ching*, or *Book of the Way
and Virtue*, is attributed to Lao-tzu, but authorship of ancient texts is

considered symbolic rather than historical (Cleary, 1991). The *Tao-Te-Ching* is one of the most important texts of Taoist philosophy. Literally translated, Tao means *the way* and teaches: "Sages minimize their affairs, which are thus orderly. They seek to have little, and thus are sufficed; they are benevolent without trying, trusted without speaking. They gain without seeking, succeed without striving" (Cleary, 1991, p. 26). Lao-tzu rejected reason and believed intuition and compassion were the path to wisdom (Bates, 1993). For him, the secret of wisdom was in obedience to nature and refusal to interfere in the natural course of things (Durant, 1935).

Confucius (551–479 B.C.) wrote five volumes known as the *Five Ching*, which along with four books written by his pupils makes up the collection known as the *Nine Classics* (Durant, 1935). The chaos in China when Confucius lived forced him to focus on morality and right living. Confucianism stood for rationalized social order based on personal cultivation (Yutang, 1938). The goal was for political order based on individual moral order. Therefore, wisdom began with the individual rectifying his own heart. From self-development followed social development. Confucius said, "To know what you know and know what you don't know is the characteristic of one who knows" (Yutang, 1938, p. 138). The Eastern traditions replaced the focus of wisdom from the physical world to an enlightened understanding of the relationship between the natural world and the Divine. It should be added that Asian concepts of wisdom, although well developed, did little to influence the emergence of empirical science in the West and psychology as a field of study.

The Renaissance

During the Renaissance, the concepts of wisdom and virtue became intertwined. Montaigne (1533–1592) felt that practical wisdom implied that life should be lived in accordance with nature, self-knowledge, knowledge of world, and self-management (Brugman, 2000). Wisdom included a critical attitude and the truly wise person was always aware of his ignorance. He believed that to assume knowledge from others without total understanding and to make it one's own was inadequate for wisdom; "... for though we could become learned by other men's learning, a man can never be wise but by his own wisdom" (Montaigne, 1580/1952, p. 58).

Francis Bacon (1561–1626), both a politician and a philosopher, was born in Elizabethan England. In *Essays* (1597), he wrote short treatises on major issues of life that became the precursor to social psychology

(Durant, 1926). Bacon is most often remembered for his book *Novum Organum*, or New Methods, which placed him on the cusp of the modern scientific age (Cottingham, 1996). He placed science as the point of highest order and introduced the concept of the scientific method. The very essence of science was written by Bacon in *The Advancement of Learning*, "... for we are not to imagine or suppose, but to *discover*, what nature does or may be made to do" (Eiseley, 1959, p. 179). Bacon proposed that man is subjected to four idols or obstacles to true knowledge: (1) "idols of the tribe," or human nature to mistake surface appearance for the true nature of things; (2) "idols of the cave," or personal preoccupations and obsessions; (3) "idols of the marketplace," or illusions stemming from language or the human tendency to rely on labels; and (4) "idols of the theater," or the fact that man gives power to the false system of traditional philosophy (Bacon, 1620/1996, p. 307). Thus, a wise man uses strict inductive reasoning along with systematic scientific inquiry to discover even the "underlying" forms or processes for all observed phenomena. For Bacon, "Knowledge is power" (Russell, 1945).

The Period of Enlightenment

Rene Descartes (1596–1650) was the first modern rationalist. He believed the sole basis of knowledge to be self-evident propositions deduced by reason, which arose from a doubting mind (Magee, 1998). According to Descartes, man should doubt everything until he reached the first principles that could not be doubted. The one thing he said he could not doubt was, "cognito ergo sum," "I think, therefore I am." Wisdom was attainable as cognitive knowing by using reflection, reason, and ethical deliberation. Religious wisdom, however, was based on faith and revelation from God (Bates, 1993).

The English philosopher John Locke (1632–1704) is best known for his book *An Essay Concerning Human Understanding*, and as the founder of the empirical school of philosophy. Locke believed that sensory experience is the source for all of our ideas and that knowledge arose from reflection on, and abstraction from, the original sensory input (Cottingham, 1996). The basis for this understanding rested on the doctrine of primary and secondary qualities. Primary qualities are those that are inseparable from the body and are classified as solidity, extension, figure, motion or rest, and number. Secondary qualities referred to everything else, for example, color, smell, sounds, and so on. Primary qualities reside in bodies, whereas secondary qualities are *only* in the perceiver (Russell, 1945). For Locke, reason consisted of two parts, an inquiry into what we know with certainty, and an investigation of propositions that we are wise to accept, even though they are only probable and not certain (Russell, 1945). When testing probability, we use our own experience or the assertion of another's experience. In Locke's writings, references to wise and wisdom are made in context with knowing God. In the *Essay*, he stated that the truest and best notions of God are acquired by thought and meditation. The wise and considerate man lives by a right and careful use of his thoughts and reason (Locke, 1690/1952).

Immanuel Kant (1724–1804), born in East Prussia, is often regarded as the one of the most outstanding philosophers since the Greeks. His propositions included the concept of two worlds: the phenomenal world, where knowledge is possible, and a noumenal world, which is transcendent and to which there is no access. For Kant, morality was founded on reason (Magee, 1998). Kant based his definition of philosophy on the ancient philo-sophia, or the desire for and love of the exercise of wisdom (Hadot, 1995). Kant believed philosophy to be the doctrine and exercise of wisdom. He wrote that men did not possess wisdom but only felt love for it. Wisdom remained the idea, the model, never to be attained but only to be sought after. Kant wrote: "The Idea of wisdom must be the foundation of philosophy, just as the Idea of sanctity is the foundation of Christianity" (Hadot, 1995, p. 267). Kant posited two ideas of philosophy, the scholastic concept and the worldly concept. The scholastic concept remained as pure theory, whereas the worldly concept was more cosmic. The cosmic philosophy of Kant referred to the search for wisdom, personified as the ideal philosopher or sage. The essential qualities of the sage were based on the laws of reason. For Kant, wisdom was in accordance with his categorical imperative, "Act only on that maxim whereby thou canst at the same time will that it should become a universal law" (Hadot, 1995, p. 269).

Arthur Schopenhauer (1788–1860) wrote the *World as Will and Idea* in 1818. He stated that in the noumenal world all beings are one, whereas in the phenomenal world we express ourselves as separate. He came into contact with Buddhist and Hindu texts that paralleled his beliefs (Magee, 1998). Schopenhauer felt that the empirical world was nothing and that one should not be taken in by it (Brugman, 2000). For Schopenhauer, genius was the highest form of will-less knowledge. The more a person knew his own desires, the less he was controlled by them. This allowed an objective view of the world without subjective bias (Durant, 1926).

Wisdom in the Psychological Sciences

The emergence of psychology as a research and scholarly subject in the 19th century was not accompanied by studies of wisdom. Although the 18th-century Period of Enlightenment in Germany appears to have freed scholars to be able to pursue rational thought on any subject, wisdom was not chosen for study. One explanation may be that since research in psychology began in Germany and influenced early American studies, it was modeled after the successes of physics and chemistry and the search for the principles of elemental processes and structures. Early studies in psychology were carried out in the tradition of psychophysics, which was a direct transfer of the model of physics. This was a "bottom-up" approach, whereas the study of wisdom implies a top-down approach, because the concept of wisdom refers to what appears to be the most complex function attributable to mankind.

Another factor that appears to have contributed to the neglect of wisdom by psychologists is that as a topic, wisdom was placed in the domain of philosophy and religion and not in the empirical sciences. There was a long standoff relationship between religion and empirical psychology that late in the 20th century began to erode. Books on religion and relationships to behavior and health began to appear and scientific meetings began to include this subject matter.

Although one of the fathers of American psychology in the 19th century, William James, explored many topics, he did not mention wisdom in his two-volume work *The Principles of Psychology* (1890). Furthermore, his next book on religious experience did not bring into discussion the role of religion and the emergence of wisdom. This neglects the long history of the role of religion in shaping experience and the emergence of wisdom (James, 1902). Although it must be said that his book focused on the emotional aspects of religious experience, emotion also can have an important role in the development and use of wisdom. Religion also was referred to in *Brett's History of Psychology* (Peters, 1962), which gives a long documented account of the intertwining of religious thought, philosophy, and the beginnings of psychology. However, the attention was given to the distinctions between the mind and the soul and not to the mind and its relationship to wisdom. The role of religion and spiritual quests in their many forms in strengthening wisdom appears to be a subject on the horizon for further research, as the topic of wisdom attracts additional empirical studies.

An American philosopher, John Dewey, influenced psychology in his attempts to bridge abstract thought and experience. One of his endeavors was to examine the nature of thought and its training. He held that the "origin of thinking is some perplexity, confusion or doubt" (Dewey, 1910, p. 12). In his view, an individual arriving at a solution goes beyond the data at hand. Furthermore, "Reflective thinking is always more or less troublesome because it involves overcoming the inertia that inclines one to accept suggestions at their face value; it involves willingness to endure a condition of mental unrest and disturbance. Reflective thinking, in short, means judgment suspended during further inquiry ..." (Dewey, 1910, p. 13). Here there was movement by a philosopher toward characterizing wisdom as deferring action based solely on knowledge.

The Swiss psychiatrist Carl Jung (1964) contributed psychological concepts of development in the early part of the 20th century. In his book *Man and His Symbols*, he discussed the self and included references to his view that dreams about the self involve the ideas about being a wise old woman or a wise old man. "In the dreams of a woman this center (the self) is usually personified as a superior female figure – a priestess, sorceress, earth mother, or goddess of nature or love. In the case of a man, it manifests itself as a masculine initiator and guardian (an Indian guru), a wise old man, a spirit of nature, and so forth" (Jung, 1964, p. 196). In Jung's view, the aspirations of men and women are to attain the state of being wise and this is expressed in their dreams and in the objects that artists create.

Further evidence of the absence of the topic of wisdom in contemporary psychology is that the *Handbook of General Psychology* (Wolman, 1973) does not include this topic, although it deals with "thinking and problem solving." The chapter by Dodd and Bourne on this aspect concluded with the view that "Finally, much of the new research may come to depend upon somewhat different notions of thinking. Such terms as strategy, rules, and principle seem to be replacing 'stimulus' and 'response.' The study of thinking seems more appropriately linked to such terms: current progress would suggest that they are less restrictive and no less 'scientific'" (1973, p. 565). This view would appear to invite access to the concepts of "wisdom" and "wise," although at present these terms remain relatively uncommon in the emergence of psychology and in contemporary research and publications in psychology.

Perhaps more pertinent is the contemporary book by Robinson (1995), *An Intellectual History of Psychology*, which has no indexed items to wisdom or wise. The book does, however, refer to knowledge, but in the ancient sense that eternal knowledge is the province of God and mankind can seek this knowledge by freeing itself from "sensory deceit" (Robinson, 1995, p. 77). It is also relevant that in another recent book, *Genius: The Natural History of Creativity*, Hans Eysenck did not include any reference to wisdom (Eysenck, 1995). Here, the question may be raised as to whether or not creativity is related to wisdom. In a sense, wisdom can give rise to new and creative solutions to old problems. Perhaps this is further evidence that the concept and the subject matter of wisdom has been avoided or neglected because of its past history in philosophy and religion. It appears to have been too far removed from the influential models of research of physics and chemistry to explore more elementary processes of psychology that were the roots of psychology in the 19th and early 20th centuries.

A book on cognitive psychology deals with the use of knowledge in problem solving and introduces the idea of thinking with the idea that problem solving is both productive and reproductive: ". . . we have the ability to change and mould our prior experience selectively, in purely conceptual ways, to make it applicable in new and unexpected situations" (Eysenck & Keane, 1990, p. 412). In reviewing the literature of reasoning and decision making, the authors further state that, "Reasoning and decision making are central intellectual abilities in our cognitive repertoire" (Eysenck & Keane, 1990, p. 417). To this might be added that the next step should include recognizing that wise thinking involves more than just cognitive processes, including the ability to defer action despite an impulse to hasty action, and insight and control over impinging emotions. In a broad view, psychology appears to be on the threshold of dealing with the subject of wisdom, which perhaps represents the highest order of human ability. Through further research, it is likely that we will identify the nature of wisdom and the circumstances leading to its development and expression, a quality that the ancients thought was solely found in gods and goddesses.

Definitions and Concepts of Wisdom

Looking back over time, we can see that the meaning and understanding of wisdom has changed throughout history. Brugman (2000) describes this transition succinctly: "Throughout history a gradual change took place in which wisdom coincided with rules for proper conduct as the Egyptian books of wisdom, and with virtue and faith as advocated by the churchfathers, to definitions with skeptical overtones in the writing of Nietzche and Schopenhauer" (p. 246).

The concept of wisdom as a human attribute has undergone changes as societies have evolved. During the last quarter of the 20th century, it has become a topic of research in the social and behavioral sciences. In contemporary empirical science, wisdom has come to be regarded as a trait that is ascribed to persons making wise decisions. Thus, the trait of wisdom is expressed in the process of making decisions, or having an effective decision-making style. In this sense, wisdom is a very broad trait of the highest level of mental functioning. Wisdom requires that an individual must have experience, seek information, and weigh alternative outcomes of a decision through complex or dialectical reasoning. Furthermore, the concept has evolved in psychological literature to include control over one's emotions and over any tendency toward hasty conclusions or actions. In this sense, the contemporary use of the term *wisdom* in psychology suggests that high intelligence and knowledge are not sufficient in and of themselves to lead to wise decisions. Having the intention to rise above one's tradition or self-interest is required in making wise decisions. Thus, broadly defined, wisdom is a difficult trait to evaluate in experimental designs that use prearranged decisions to be made in problem solving contexts.

The range of differences in approaches to the study of wisdom is apparent in the 1990 book edited by Sternberg, *Wisdom: Its Nature, Origins, and Development*. In the final chapter of this book, Birren and Fisher (1990) set forth an overview of the contents of all the chapters and the authors' views of the development of wisdom, traits of a wise person, products of wisdom, and research methodology. The diversity in approach is shown in the fact that 13 chapters yielded 13 quite different definitions of wisdom. Table 1.1 lists the definitions.

The definitions range from those reflecting early Greek and Christian views to contemporary views. Kramer (1990), in her organismic perspective, proposed the following definition, "Wisdom is the organismic integration of relativistic and dialectical modes of thinking, affect, and reflection; a *perspective on reality* developed within interrelationships" (p. 326). In their review, Birren and Fisher (1990) attempted to integrate the definition and offered theirs as: "Wisdom is the *integration of the affective, conative, and cognitive* aspects of human abilities in response to life's tasks and problems. Wisdom is a balance between the opposing valences of intense emotion and detachment, action and inaction, and knowledge and doubts. It tends to increase with experience and therefore age but is not exclusively found in old age" (Birren & Fisher, 1990, p. 326).

TABLE 1.1. *Definitions of Wisdom* (Birren & Fisher, 1990, pp. 325–326)

Author	Definition
Robinson	Three historical definitions: Greek: an intellectual, moral, practical life; a life lived in conformity with truth, beauty. Christian: a life lived in pursuit of divine, absolute truth. Contemporary: a scientific understanding of laws governing matter in motion.
Csikszentmihalyi and Rathunde	An evolutionary hermeneutical approach to the study of wisdom suggests that wisdom is a holistic cognitive process, a virtue or compelling guide for action, and a good, desirable state of being.
Labouvie-Vief	A smooth and balanced dialogue between two sets of attributes: outer, objective, logical forms of processing (logos) and inner, subjective, organismic forms (mythos).
Baltes and Smith	Wisdom is expertise in the domain of fundamental life pragmatics, such as life planning or life review. It requires a rich factual knowledge about life matters, rich procedural knowledge about life problems, knowledge of different life contexts and values or priorities, and knowledge about the unpredictability of life.
Chandler and Holliday	Contemporary philosophy of science limits conceptualization of wisdom to a technologic type of knowing. A more accurate description of wisdom may need well-defined, multidimensional, prototypically organized competence descriptors. It involves recovering age-old types of knowledge that have been forgotten.
Sternberg	Wisdom is a metacognitive style plus sagacity, knowing that one does not know everything, seeking the truth to the extent that it is knowable.
Orwoll and Perlmutter	A personologic study of wisdom suggests that wisdom is a mutltidimensional balance or integration of cognition with affect, affiliation, and social concerns. An advanced development of personality together with cognitive skills is the essence of wisdom.
Meacham	Wisdom is an awareness of the fallibility of knowing and is a striving for a balance between knowing and doubting. Age is explicitly not a component of wisdom; in fact, one may lose it with age. Age is associated with changes in wisdom, from simple to profound manifestations.

Author	Definition
Kitchener and Brenner	Wisdom is an intellectual ability to be aware of the limitations of knowing and how it impacts solving ill-defined problems and making judgments, characteristics of reflective judgment.
Arlin	Wisdom is closely associated with problem-finding ability, a fundamental cognitive process of reflection and judgment.
Pascual-Leone	Wisdom is a mode of symbolic processing by a highly developed will. It is a dialectical integration of all aspects of the personality, including affect, will, cognition, and life experiences.
Kramer	Wisdom is the organismic integration of relativistic and dialectical modes of thinking, affect, and reflection; a perspective on reality developed within interrelationships.
Birren and Fisher	Wisdom is the integration of the affective, conative, and cognitive aspects of human abilities in response to life's tasks and problems. Wisdom is a balance between the opposing valences of intense emotion and detachment, action and inaction, and knowledge and doubts. It tends to increase with experience and therefore age but is not exclusively found in old age.

Sternberg (1990) added an additional element to wisdom, "meta-cognitive." "Wisdom is a *metacognitive style* plus sagacity, knowing that one does not know everything, seeking the truth to the extent that it is knowable" (Birren & Fisher, 1990, p. 325). We might now wish to expand this definition to embrace the concept of metabehavioral, an overarching of control and management of behavior that includes intention, purpose, and will.

New researchers have added their views to the investigation of wisdom with more recent and varied definitions (see Table 1.2). The definitions range from the inclusion of wisdom as a state of enlightenment to ordinary and extraordinary concepts of wisdom.

The Development of Empirical Studies of Psychology of Wisdom

Theories of wisdom have been developed that attempt to understand and thus control the investigation of wisdom. Brugman (2000), in his comprehensive study *Wisdom: Source of Narrative Coherence and Eudaimonia*, not only reviewed the historical concepts of wisdom, but also the psychological theories of wisdom. He concluded that "The

TABLE 1.2. *Recent definitions of wisdom*

Christine A. Bates	It is no longer meaningful or sufficient to see wisdom as a singular phenomenon or as a kind of entity, or as a body of knowledge that would be prone to generate a particular content of responses. Now the notion of wisdom must incorporate a process of arriving at a truth, which fits the needs and context of individuals, a community, a nation, or a people. (Bates, 1993, p. 411)
Gerard Brugman	(Wisdom is) expertise in uncertainty. It encompasses a meta-cognitive, an affective, and a behavioral component. (Brugman, 2000, p. 263)
Howard M. Chandler	The Vedic Psychology of Maharishi Mahesh Yogi . . . proposes that the unified source of all knowledge and experience, including affect and cognition, is a transcendental field of pure consciousness (the Self) that can be known by direct experience (Self-knowledge). Wisdom is described as a state of enlightenment in which stabilized Self-knowledge results in a fully integrated personality. (Chandler, 1991, Dissertation Abstracts International, p. 5048B)
William Randall and Gary Kenyon	*Ordinary wisdom* is about finding meaning in life and suffering (spiritual–mystical dimension). It is about accepting, owning, and valuing our lives and our life stories, including both our unlived lives and our untold stories.
	Extraordinary wisdom includes six dimensions: (a) the cognitive dimension involves a degree of intellectual understanding, (b) the practical–experiential dimension has to do not only with abstract ideas or theories but with everyday life, (c) the interpersonal aspect to wisdom entails a perception of the larger story we live with, (d) the ethical–moral dimension is concerned with what the ancient Greeks referred to as "knowing and doing the good," (e) the idiosyncratic-expression, concerns the appearance of as many faces of wisdom as there are human beings, (f) the spiritual–mystical dimension of extraordinary wisdom, or the special experience of, and/or insight into, the nature of the cosmos and the human place within it. (Randall & Kenyon, 2001, p. 12)

history of the study of wisdom in psychology is a short one. Only at the end of the eighties (1980s), and the beginning of the nineties, wisdom research really started. Before that time there were only some theoretical endeavors" (Brugman, 2000, p. 95). The recency of the development of theories of wisdom is shown in his table that cites 19 studies (see Brugman, 2000, Table 3.7, p. 109, for complete data). The earliest year of publication of a cited reference was 1959, with a median year of 1987, a relatively recent date in the history of psychology.

Erik Erikson provided an example of an early reference to wisdom as a component of a lifespan theory of development. He proposed that wisdom is a result of the eighth stage of psychosocial development, or the mastery of "ego integrity versus despair" (Erikson, 1950). This does not preclude the possibility that wisdom could be achieved at other periods in life; just that it is a natural outcome of a successful mastery over ego despair that normally occurs in late life. Thus, for Erikson, wisdom was not studied alone but, rather, as the outcome of the successful completion of the final life development stage.

Only in recent decades has the study of wisdom in and of itself been addressed by the empirical social-psychological sciences. It is obvious from a historical perspective that the concept of wisdom is multidimensional and defies easy definition or operationalization that meets the scientific criteria for control, replication, and prediction. Furthermore, many complex topics were neglected in psychology's earlier history. Aging, creativity, and love were usually ignored as research topics. In other words, the psychology of wisdom was left unexplored. In the tradition of psychology, studies were built from the simple to the complex, rather than from the complex to the simple. This method emulated the success of physics in studying elemental particles and forces. In a sense, "wisdom" is the capstone of behavioral complexity. It leads to explanations of behavior from the top down, from purpose and intention to behavioral acts. Brugman (2000) reviewed six empirical studies of wisdom, reflecting the scarcity of research. The six studies largely concentrated on the question of whether or not wisdom increases with age. The findings suggest that there is not an increase in wisdom in later life. Brugman's conclusion is provocative, ". . . that one needs to be old and wise to see that wisdom does not come with age" (Brugman, 2000, p. 115).

It is significant that in one of the first empirical studies of wisdom, there were no references to prior publications of such work (Clayton, 1976). There were, however, references to components or contributors to wisdom, such as components of intellect, affect, and cognition. Additionally, there were references to such components that contributed to a working concept of wisdom. Wisdom "... was defined as a construct having underlying affective, cognitive, and cognitive style or problem solving components" (Clayton, 1976, p. 4).

Clayton and Birren (1980) encouraged the study of wisdom as a later life psychological competency of older persons. Their research examined the underlying structure of wisdom as perceived by differing age cohorts. They discovered that the concept of wisdom became more differentiated with an increase in age. There was an absence of a perceived relationship between the participant's own age and wisdom.

The Berlin research project (Max-Planck Institute for Human Development and Education) began in the late 1980s and developed a model that defined wisdom as "An expert knowledge system in the domain, fundamental life pragmatics (e.g., life planning, life management, life review)" (Baltes & Smith, 1990, p. 95). There are five components to the Berlin wisdom paradigm: rich factual knowledge, rich procedural knowledge, lifespan contextualism, relativism, and ability to understand and manage uncertainty. Wisdom, defined as synthesized intelligence, pertains to the pragmatics of life and adaptation. The five criteria allow the conceptualization and organization of expert knowledge in fundamental life pragmatics. They focus on wisdom as a body of knowledge and wise responses. The emphasis is on the pragmatic, on an expert knowledge system, and the goal is to acquire knowledge and become an expert. It is within the fundamental pragmatics of life that wisdom is manifest, and this includes matters of life, interpretation, and management (see Baltes & Smith, 1990, Table 5.2, p. 104).

Staudinger (1996) and her colleagues, working with the Berlin project, have defined the nature of wisdom as a social interactive product. In this approach, the genesis of wisdom is projected onto forces outside the individual in contrast to the "person centered paradigm." "On the basis of the extremely high demands that the elicitation of wisdom puts on knowledge and skill, one might even argue that wisdom by definition will hardly ever be found in an individual, but rather in cultural or social-interactive products" (Staudinger, 1996, p. 276). Wise individuals and wisdom in this point of view become the product of interactions with wise environments. Wisdom is apparent in decisions that are shaped by social contexts. Her research showed that wisdom increases with social interaction. Staudinger concluded that wisdom cannot develop without both distal and proximal social interaction. Wisdom is a balance between interactive and individual cognition. Excluded in this research is the contribution of evolution to the genesis of wisdom and individual traits or behavioral capacities that lead to the development of social institutions. However, Staudinger provided an excellent approach to defining and operationalizing wisdom in terms of culturally transmitted knowledge, what has been characterized as "social-interactive performance contexts" (1996, p. 294). Minimized in her approach are the noncognitive elements of wisdom such as affective and behavioral dispositions. Presumably an impetuous or action-prone person or someone disposed to anger will not usually display wisdom or benefit much from the knowledge available in his or her social-interactive contexts.

Research from Sternberg and Lubart (2001) suggested that intelligence and wisdom are correlated and that both use reasoning and problem-solving skills and the capacity to apply information and knowledge in useful ways. Six components for wisdom emerged from their work: reasoning ability, sagacity, learning from ideas and environment, judgment, expeditious use of information, and perspicacity (Sternberg & Lubart, 2001, p. 502). The Balance Theory is based on tacit knowledge, defined as action-oriented, acquired without help from others, that allows for achievement of personally valued goals (Sternberg & Lubart, 2001). Tacit knowledge refers to a "knowing how" rather than a "knowing that." This knowledge is relatively independent of academic and IQ levels. The definition of wisdom becomes "... the application of tacit knowledge toward the achievement of a common good through a balance among (a) intrapersonal, (b) interpersonal, and (c) extrapersonal interests to achieve a balance among (a) adaptation to existing environments, (b) shaping of existing environments, and (c) selection of new environments, over the long term as well as the short term" (Sternberg & Lubart, 2001, p. 507).

Taranto (1989) provided a thorough review of wisdom based on the psychological and philosophical literature to synthesize and cull a definition of wisdom. She concluded "... that wisdom involves a recognition of and response to human limitation" (Taranto, 1989, p. 15). Thus wisdom is concerned with both the limits of human nature and our understanding of human nature. The knowledge or understanding of human limitation extends to the recognition of the limits of human nature, as well as social interaction, physical abilities, one's own lifespan, and nature of knowledge. From this viewpoint, wisdom involves a recognition and response to our human limitations to solve interpersonal dilemmas and to find workable solutions.

Using an organismic framework, Kramer (1990) postulated that all knowledge evolves, leading to ever-increasing integration by means of the interplay of contradictions and resolutions. She stated, "The wise person may be seen as a lay theorist who maintains a certain set of assumptions about social reality and is able to effectively apply these to a variety of domains in order to resolve problems arising in his or her own experience, advise others in resolving their problems, shape social institutions, and seek meaning and continuity in experience. In this approach, cognition and affect are interdependent" (Kramer, 1990, p. 280). The central tenet of the organismic approach is "integration"; however, cognition and affect are interdependent and interact reciprocally to produce wisdom-related skills. The five functions of wisdom include: recognition of individuality, taking the context into account, encouraging cooperative strategies for interpersonal relations, recognition of possibilities for change and recognition of the necessity of integrating cognition and affect (Kramer, 1990, p. 300). This theory of wisdom stresses the importance of both cognitive and affective systems and their integration.

McKee and Barber (1999) believed that the core of wisdom is found in "seeing through illusion" (p. 151). In their definition of wisdom, they emphasize the distinction between "a priori," a definition not based on observation but intuitive insight, and "empirical," a definition based on observable phenomena. They suggested ". . . that wisdom does not lie in *what* one knows, but in *how* one knows" (McKee & Barber, 1999, p. 151). The essence of their definition of wisdom, or seeing through the illusion, was composed of three factors: clear insight that a belief is illusory; freedom from future vulnerability to the error or illusion; and empathy for those who remain subject to the illusion. Aristotle defined wisdom as knowledge of first principles, and "seeing through the illusion" is translated as knowledge of first principles. The knowledge of first principles suggests knowing the reality that is behind an unreal appearance. Thus, seeing through the illusion identifies wisdom as separate from knowledge.

According to Meacham (1990), wisdom required an understanding that knowledge is fallible and of maintaining a position between knowing and doubting. Since there is no limit to what can be known, one must understand what one does *not* know. Meacham developed the "knowledge context matrix" (1990, p. 184). One's position in the matrix is determined by one's perception of how much one knows, balanced with what one does not know, in relationship with all that can be known. Wisdom is not a set of beliefs or a fixed body of knowledge. Rather, the essence of wisdom is revealed in the way it is put to use. The core of wisdom is both knowing and doubting and the balance between the two. Dating back to ancient philosophers, the belief that one can see all that can be seen and know all that can be known is evidence of the *lack* of wisdom.

Kitchener and Brenner (1990) developed the "reflective judgment" model that described the development of epistemic cognition, the certainty for knowing, and the criteria for knowing. The model explained how individuals move from understanding when issues are certain through the process of reasoning when issues are uncertain. The reflective judgment model was based on the assumptions one holds regarding what can be "known" and what can't, "how" one can know, and how "certain" one can be in knowing. Research based on the reflective judgment model has shown that reasoning in the face of the uncertainty of knowing and making reasoned judgments is not associated with youth or the young adult. Rather, reasoning is observed only after the early 30s in well-educated groups. The basis for wise judgment is the ability for complex reasoning with abstractions.

From their research, Chandler and Holliday (1990) concluded that wisdom needs to be considered as "... a well-defined, multidimensional, prototypically organized competency descriptor" (Chandler & Holliday, 1990, pp. 137–138). Wisdom consists of the following five factors: (1) exceptional understanding, based on learning from experience and understanding "the big picture;" (2) judgment and communication skills, based on the ability to understand and judge correctly in daily life; (3) general competence, based on general intelligence and education; (4) interpersonal skills, based on capacity to be sensitive and social; and (5) social unobtrusiveness, which refers to being discrete and nonjudgmental.

Ardelt (2000) defined wisdom as containing three components: cognitive ability to see the truth or reality as it is; reflective, to become aware and transcend one's subjectivity and projection; and affective or empathy that refers to empathy and compassion for others. All components reinforce each other and wisdom is the result of the combination of all three. In a recent study, she tested the hypothesis that wisdom resulted from early psychosocial resources in childhood and that wisdom would have a positive effect on aging well. Her results showed that wisdom is not determined by one's childhood, but wise individuals aged more successfully than unwise individuals. This is an eclectic approach that stresses cognition, reflective, and affective components of wisdom. Her findings showed that wisdom had more impact on life satisfaction than did social relationships or objective life circumstances.

Brugman (2000) defined wisdom "...as expertise in uncertainty. It encompasses a (meta)cognitive, an affective, and a behavioural component" (p. 263). This clearly went beyond the ancient traditions of regarding wisdom as knowledge. In his research, he attempted to unravel the relationship between wisdom (eudaimonia), and the quality of one's narrative. He adapted the word "eudaimonia" from the Greek literature, because it was free from the implications of contemporary terms such as *life-satisfaction, happiness, well-being*, or *quality of life*. In his studies, the way individuals interpret their lives, or their narrative coherence, was related to wisdom and the good life, or eudaimonia. "Wisdom is the good demon" (Brugman, 2000, p. 247). Its measurement was determined by the "fraction of positive controllable (life) events of the total number of positive events reported and the fraction of negative controllable events of the total number of negative events" (Brugman, 2000, p. 242). In this train of thought, wisdom is accompanied by increasing doubt, with experience, with the graspability of reality. Wisdom is the product of a coherent self-account of life events. Wisdom also develops as a product of the integration and interpretation of life's experiences and also with the emergence and acceptance of uncertainty.

A 10-year longitudinal study of the effects of transcendental meditation on the development of wisdom was reported by Chandler (1990). In this doctoral dissertation study, "Wisdom is described as a state of enlightenment, in which stabilized Self-knowledge results in a fully integrated personality" (Chandler, 1991). Wisdom was operationalized by using Loevinger's measurement of ego or self-development, McAdams's intimacy motivation, and Rest's principled moral reasoning. Over a 10-year period, the participants who took part in transcendental meditation increased significantly on ego development and on principled moral reasoning. As a result of his findings, Chandler concluded that transcendental meditation is a practical pathway to reducing stress and "...allowing awareness to effortlessly transcend the limit of representational thought and language" (1990, p. 169). His data supported the view that a quiet internal psychophysiological state encouraged the expression of wisdom.

Bates (1993) made a comprehensive review of the background literature on wisdom in her thesis, *Wisdom: A Postmodern Exploration*. She reviewed the various dictionary definitions of wisdom and concluded that
"In most dictionary definitions there is the sense of wisdom consisting
of a special mastery of life, demonstrated in the domain of understanding people, and making decisions and judgment" (Bates, 1993, p. 416).
This does not preclude an illiterate person from being wise. She quoted
Csikszentmihalyi and Rathunde concerning wisdom, "If wisdom is a
type of knowledge that tries to understand the ultimate consequences
of events in a holistic, systemic way, then wisdom becomes the best
guide for what is the 'summum bonum', or 'supreme good'" (Bates,
1993, p. 127). But wisdom appears to be more than just knowledge and
includes an approach to the decision process and to action. Bates discussed extensively the underlying values of wisdom. That is, the values
placed on the outcomes of decisions determined whether the individual
displayed wisdom and whether the decision was a wise one. Her discussion extended into the process of adopting belief systems and their
content. That is, by our intent and assent we adopt belief systems that
provide a frame of reference for our decisions and actions. Furthermore,
Bates introduced the idea that retrospection contributed to wisdom. In
this context, she used a term from Jung, "enantiodromia," meaning to
flow backward (Bates, 1993, p. 182). Her thought is that a reworking of
the past contributes to wisdom. This view is compatible with the work
of Brugman (2000), who found that the quality of uncertainty emerges
from a review of life's experiences and contributes to wisdom.

Future Research Directions on Wisdom

After many years of neglect or avoidance, the subject of wisdom is now
attracting research interest. Many questions remain to be answered. Who
is wise and who is unwise? What environmental conditions facilitate
the development and expression of wisdom? What are the cognitive,
affective, motivational, and other behavior components that contribute
to the development and expression of wise behavior, and what is their
relative contribution?

Because of the complexity of wisdom, answering such questions
requires a wide range of research strategies and many different research designs. The long history of the development of research on
intelligence suggests that research on wisdom, being more complex
than intelligence, will take considerable time to evolve. However, significant improvements in research design, statistical procedures, and

data-gathering methods will facilitate the study of wisdom and provide insights into this multidimensional concept. Measurements of wisdom can be added to contemporary longitudinal studies so that the relative contributions to the development and expression of wisdom can be determined. Also, advances in neuropsychology and brain scanning methods suggest that it will be possible to determine the extent of involvement of different brain areas in wise and unwise persons.

There are potential questions to be answered based on the ancient attribution of wisdom as being feminine in character. This suggests the inclusion of gender in relationship to wisdom, not only the difference in structure between men and women, but also of its importance in making life decisions. The decision making of men and women has been described by Blenky, Clinchy, Goldberger, and Tarule (1986), and evokes the ancient views of feminine wisdom.

By listening to girls and women resolve serious moral dilemmas in their lives, Gilligan has traced the development of a morality organized around notions of responsibility and care. This conception of morality contrasts sharply with the morality of rights described by Piaget (1965) and Kohlberg (1981, 1984), which is based on the study of the evolution of moral reasoning in boys and men. People operating within a rights morality – more commonly men – evoke the metaphor of "blind justice" and rely on abstract laws and universal principles to adjudicate disputes and conflicts between conflicting claims impersonally, impartially, and fairly. Those operating within a morality of responsibility and care – primarily women – reject the strategy of blindness and impartiality. Instead, adherents argue for an understanding of the context for moral choice, claiming that the needs of individuals cannot always be deduced from general rules and principles and that moral choice must also be determined inductively from the particular experiences each participant brings to the situation. (p. 8)

These viewpoints should be extended in future studies of wisdom and wise behavior in men and women to investigate wise and moral judgments by gender. The extent to which research on wisdom can separate belief in moral systems and their values from the behavioral properties of wisdom remains to be demonstrated. However, it points to the need for research on wisdom to explore the process in individuals of wide cultural and religious backgrounds.

More detailed studies of diverse individuals within Western cultures can help to separate the underlying values from the processes of wisdom itself. In this approach, individuals judged to be wise and unwise can be studied across professional groups: lawyers, judges, physicians, administrators, professors in different specialties, and religious leaders, among others. The purpose of such studies is to determine the congruency in the concepts of wisdom and wise behavior across diverse groups of people with varied experience and different educational paths.

There remain many other areas for research on wisdom, including the possibility of the identification of wisdom in more primitive societies. Wisdom appears to be a trait more readily applied to the elders in traditional or preliterate societies. Whether it is primarily a social attribute or a behavioral capacity requires further research on the difference between seniority and wisdom. As a result of his research in sub-Saharan African culture, Rosenmayr (1988) concluded, "Most generally, seniority is a widely applicable principle of power distribution. Its formal scope is broader than the often quoted "experience" or "wisdom" of older individuals would legitimate" (p. 29).

Is wisdom that is attributed to older persons a product of age and experience or of the prestige and power derived from their seniority status? Rapid social change leads to the reduction of status of the elderly in highly technological societies and thus loss of power and prestige. Adaptation to change would appear to be a greater challenge to the elderly than to the young, who are in the process of acquiring their roles in a society. The process of lifelong maturation and self-management is an important aspect of wisdom and it should receive more attention in research on wisdom across cultures.

Many new areas of research on wisdom await exploration with the prospect of extending our knowledge and perhaps leading to avenues for the use of wisdom in the management of societies, groups, and individuals.

Summary and Conclusions

The history of wisdom is ancient and complex. Early religions and philosophies described wisdom in terms of the cultures of their times, based on available knowledge and expectations concerning the behavior of individuals. As cultures evolved, ideas about wisdom changed. A reading of past history leads to the conclusion that implicit or explicit values underlie the concepts of wisdom passed forward from ancient times. This legacy makes it difficult in the present context to define wisdom in such a way that it leads to operations or measurements not biased by culture. The values that underlie ideas about wisdom continue to evolve and determine the use of the term "wisdom" as a favorable trait. Decisions have different outcomes, some of which may touch on strong values in a society. A judge looked on as wise in one culture would be despised in another if he or she invoked the death penalty, a cultural value.

The Renaissance opened pathways to rational thought and the later Period of Enlightenment further encouraged empirical research and the founding of psychology as a science. However, early empirical research in psychology was patterned after the successes of physics and chemistry, and efforts were devoted to elemental processes. The background of the founding of psychology in America did not encourage the study of wisdom, a very complex, if not the most complex trait attributable to mankind. However, in the latter part of the 20th century, wisdom emerged as an area of scholarship and research.

The concept of wisdom that the present authors have developed during the course of their review of the literature led them to the view that wisdom is perhaps the most complex characteristic that can be attributed to individuals or to cultures. A wise culture is one that maximizes the pursuit, gathering, and passage of information to its members. Furthermore, a wise culture maximizes the prospects of developing a high proportion of wise persons. Encouraging the transmission of knowledge, learning, and discussion are assumed to be attributes of a wise culture. A wise person is one who maximizes the probability of wise decisions. In this sense, a wise person is one whose higher-level mental processes and knowledge are integrated and maximize the probability of productive decisions. In this view wisdom as a human trait has both "crystallized" and "fluid" components, or perhaps it may be defined as having both information and dynamic contributors. A wise person is likely to have relevant knowledge and experience (crystallized ability), seek information, discuss it with others, and use dialectical or complex reasoning in contrasting the outcomes of alternative decisions.

Psychology has been slow to initiate research on wisdom. As perhaps the most superordinating and complex form of human behavior, it has been neglected in favor of the study of traits that can be operationalized in terms of elemental functions, primarily those of cognition, which have been the main preoccupation of psychological research. Wisdom implies a high level of control and mastery of behavior in order that knowledge can be used or created to pursue valued goals.

Present-day studies of wisdom have a wide range of definitions and a wide range of measures that are used to operationalize it. Although at present wisdom appears to be in an early stage of sophistication in research and conceptualization, because of its importance, it is a topic that seems destined to attract increasing interest and research.

There are prospects for future research on wisdom that can have wide ranges of purposes and methods in exploring differences in ways wisdom has been defined by diverse cultures and religions. There also are many possibilities for studying individual differences in the expression of wise decision processes (e.g., by occupation, gender, education, and life experiences). However, the growth of the subject matter should be accompanied by increased rigor in both the definitions and the measurements used to assess both the independent and the dependent variables. Presently there is a wide range of posited outcomes of wisdom, from solving daily life problems to constructing a view of the self that promotes a productive and happy life. The history of wisdom leaves us with these questions: How much has the attributed wisdom of older persons been the product of their experience and reasoning, and how much has been derived from their power and seniority status?

References

Adler, M. J. (1952). *The great ideas: A syntopicon of great books of the western world.* (Vol. 2). Chicago: William Benton Publisher.

Aquinas, T. (1267/1952). Summa Theologica (Fathers of the English Dominican Province, Trans.). *Great books of the western world* (Vol. 20, pp. 36–37). Chicago: William Benton Publisher.

Ardelt, M. (2000). Antecedents and effects of wisdom in old age. *Research on Aging, 22*(4), 360–394.

Bacon, F. (1620/1996). Novum Organum. In J. Cottingham (Ed.), *Western philosophy: An anthology* (pp. 303–310). Oxford, UK: Blackwell Publishers.

Baltes, P., & Smith, J. (1990). Toward a psychology of wisdom and its ontogenesis. In R. Sternberg (Ed.). *Wisdom: Its nature, origins and development* (pp. 87–120). Cambridge: Cambridge University Press.

Bates, C. A. (1993). *Wisdom: A postmodern exploration.* Unpublished doctoral dissertation. University of Southern California. Los Angeles, California.

Birren, J. E., & Fisher, L. M. (1990). Conceptualizing wisdom: the primacy of affect-cognition relations. In R. J. Sternberg (Ed.), *Wisdom: Its nature, origins, and development* (pp. 317–332). New York: Cambridge University Press.

Blenky, M. F., Clinchy, B. M., Goldberger, N. R., & Tarule, J. M. (1986). *Women's ways of knowing: The development of self, voice, and mind.* New York: Basic Books.

Brugman, G. (2000). *Wisdom: Source of narrative coherence and eudaimonia.* Delft, The Netherlands: Uitgeverij Eberon.

Chandler, H. M. (1990). *Transcendental meditation and awakening wisdom: A 10-year longitudinal study of self development.* Unpublished doctoral dissertation, Maharishi International University, Fairfield, Iowa.

Chandler, H. M. (1991). Transcendental meditation and awakening wisdom: A 10-year longitudinal study of self development. *Dissertation Abstracts International, 51,* 5048B.

Chandler, M., & Holliday, S. (1990). Wisdom in a postapocalyptic age. In R. Sternberg (Ed.), *Wisdom: Its nature, origins, and development* (pp. 121–141). New York: Cambridge University Press.

Clayton, V. P. (1976). *A multidimensional scaling analysis of the concept of wisdom.* Unpublished doctoral dissertation, University of Southern California, Los Angeles, California.

Clayton, V. P., & Birren, J. E. (1980). The development of wisdom across the life-span: A reexamination of an ancient topic. In P. B. Baltes & O. G. Brim (Eds.), *Life-span*

Cottingham, J. (Ed.). (1996). *Western philosophy: An anthology.* Oxford, UK: Blackwell *development and behavior* (Vol. 3, pp. 101–135). New York: Academic Press.

Cleary, T. (1991). *Further teachings of Lao-tzu.* Boston: Shambhala.Publishers.

Csikszentmihalyi, M., & Rathunde, K. (1990). The psychology of wisdom: An evolutionary interpretation. In R. Sternberg (Ed.), *Wisdom: Its nature, origins, and development* (pp. 25–51). New York: Cambridge University Press.

Dewey, J. (1910). *How we think.*Boston: D. C. Heath & Co.

Dodd, D. H., & Bourne, L. E. (1973). Thinking and problem solving. In B. B. Wolman (Ed.), *Handbook of general psychology* (pp. 547–567). Englewood Cliffs, NJ: Prentice Hall.

Durant, W. (1926). *The story of philosophy.* New York: Simon & Schuster.

Durant, W. (1935). *Our oriental heritage.* New York: Simon & Schuster.

Dyer, W. (1998). *Wisdom of the ages.* New York: HarperCollins.

Eiseley, L. (1959). Francis Bacon. In J. Thorndike (Ed.), *The light of the past.* New York: American Heritage Publishing Co.

Erikson, E. (1950). *Childhood and society.* New York: W. W. Norton & Co.

Eysenck, H. (1995). *Genius, The natural history of creativity.* Cambridge: Cambridge University Press.

Eysenck, M., & Keane, M. (1990). *Cognitive psychology.* Manwah, NJ: Lawrence Erlbaum Associates Ltd.

Hadot, P. (1995). *What is ancient philosophy?* (M. Chase, Trans.). Cambridge, MA: Harvard University Press.

Holy Bible: *New Revised Standard Version.* 1989. New York: Oxford University Press.

James, W. (1890). *The principles of psychology.* New York: Holt.

James, W. (1902). *Varieties of religious experience.* New York: Longmans Green.

Jung, C. (1964). *Man and his symbols.* London: Aldus Books.

Kitchener, K., & Brenner, H. (1990). Wisdom and reflective judgment: Knowing in the face of uncertainty. In R. Sternberg (Ed.), *Wisdom: Its nature, origins, and development* (pp. 212–229). New York: Cambridge University Press.

Kramer, D. A. (1990). Conceptualizing wisdom: the primacy of affect-cognition relations. In R. J. Sternberg (Ed.), *Wisdom: Its nature, origins, and development* (pp. 279–313). New York: Cambridge University Press.

Kramer, S. N. (1959). O ye daughters of Sumer! In J. Thorndike (Ed.), *The light of the past* (pp. 48–49). New York: American Heritage Publishing Co.

Locke, J. (1690/1952). Concerning human understanding. In R. M. Hutchins (Ed.), *Great books of the western world* (Vol. 35, pp. 116–117). Chicago: William Benton Publishers.

Loevinger, J. (1979). Construct validity of the Sentence Completion Tests of Ego Development. *Applied Psychology Measurement, 3*, 281–311.

Magee, B. (1998). *The story of philosophy*. New York: DK Publishing.

McKee, P., & Barber, C. (1999). On defining wisdom. *International Journal of Aging and Human Development, 49*, 149–164.

McAdams, D. P. (1984). Scoring manual for the intimacy motive. *Psychological Documents, 14*, No. 2613.

Meacham, J. (1990). The loss of wisdom. In R. Sternberg (Ed.), *Wisdom: Its nature, origins, and development* (pp. 181–211). New York: Cambridge University Press.

Montaigne, M. (1580/1952). The Essays of Michel Eyquemde Montaigne (C. Cotton, Trans. and W. C. Hazlitt, Ed.). In R. M. Hutchins (Ed.), *Great books of the western world* (Vol. 25). Chicago: William. Benton Publisher.

Peters, R. S. (Ed.). (1962). *Brett's history of psychology: Abridged one volume edition*. New York: Macmillan Company.

Randall, W. L., & Kenyon, G. M. (2001). *Ordinary wisdom: Biographical aging and the journey of life*. Westport, CT: Praeger.

Readers Digest Association/London [RDA]. (1973). *The last two million years*. New York: Readers Digest Association.

Rest, J. R. (1986). *Moral development: Advances in research and theory*. New York: Praeger.

Robinson, D. N. (1995). *An intellectual history of psychology* (3rd ed.), London: Arnold.

Robinson, D. N. (1990). Wisdom through the ages. In R. J. Sternberg (Ed.), *Wisdom: Its nature, origins, and development* (pp. 13–24). New York: Cambridge University Press.

Rosenmayr, L. (1988). More than wisdom. *Journal of Cross-Cultural Gerontology, 3*, 21–40.

Russell, B. (1945). *A history of western philosophy*. New York: Simon & Schuster.

Staudinger, U. M. (1996). Wisdom and the social-interactive foundation of the mind. In P. B. Baltes & U. M. Staudinger (Eds.), *Interactive minds* (pp. 276–315). New York: Cambridge University Press.

Sternberg, R. J. (Ed.). (1990). *Wisdom: Its nature, origin, and development*. New York: Cambridge University Press.

Sternberg, R. J., & Lubart, T. (2001). Wisdom and creativity. In J. E. Birren & K. W. Schaie (Eds.), *Handbook of the psychology of aging* (pp. 500–522). New York: Academic Press.

Taranto, M. A. (1989). Facets of wisdom: A theoretical synthesis. *International Journal of Aging and Human Development, 29*, 1–21.

Wolman, B. B. (1973). *Handbook of general psychology*. Englewood Cliffs, NJ: Prentice Hall.

Yutang, L. (Ed. and Trans.). (1938). *The wisdom of Confucius*. New York: Random House.

2

Cultural Foundations of Wisdom

An Integrated Developmental Approach

Masami Takahashi and Willis F. Overton

We once asked an ethnically mixed group of college students to name "wise" persons. The responses varied from their personal acquaintances and family members to well-known historical figures from all over the world such as Socrates, Confucius, Mahatma Gandhi, and Nelson Mandela, to name just a few. These undergraduate students with diverse backgrounds clearly knew what was meant by "wise" and had concrete ideas of the concept in their own unique ways. Social scientists in the past few decades, on the other hand, have been debating over what exactly constitutes the concept of wisdom. Sternberg (1990), for example, stated in *Wisdom: Its Nature, Origins, and Development* that "Wisdom is about as elusive as psychological constructs get" (p. ix). Why are social scientists grappling with difficulty in defining the concept whose meanings seem already ingrained in our collective psyche?

The answer is probably multifaceted. For one, although wisdom is an ancient concept that has been adapted in different cultures, it remained mainly within the sphere of theology and religion throughout Western history (Robinson, 1990). As a result, it is a relatively new scientific construct that has been empirically investigated only for the past few decades. Second, because the concept has been around for so long in various parts of the world, it is extremely difficult to articulate and operationally define in a way that is cross-culturally acceptable. Third, in the climate of neopositivism that pervaded the behavioral sciences during the first half of the 20th century (Overton, 1998), coupled with a generally negative view toward aging in many societies, the concept of wisdom and its historical association with older age was viewed as paradoxical at best and until quite recently was vigorously excluded from serious scientific investigation (Baltes & Smith, 1990; Birren & Fisher, 1990; Holliday & Chandler, 1986).

Since the early 1980s, the concept of wisdom has been attracting growing attention among social scientists. This surging interest is probably because of the changing circumstances in the scientific community that now emphasize lifespan development (Labouvie-Vief, 1990; Lerner, 1984; Woodruff-Pak, 1989) and positive psychology (Baltes, 1993; Lerner, 2004; Sinnott & Cavanaugh, 1991). However, despite its origin and history, existing conceptualization and empirical research on wisdom have primarily been conducted in the Western hemisphere, and have neglected non-Western accounts of the concept.

In this chapter, both the Eastern and Western interpretations are reviewed to establish a culturally balanced definition of wisdom. In particular, we focus on examining cross-cultural studies of implicit theories (or folk conceptions) and historical accounts of wisdom from the Eastern and Western traditions because these analyses help decipher the important building blocks of its psychological definition (Sternberg, 1990). Furthermore, we also present a culturally inclusive model, partially drawn from a broadly defined Eriksonian developmental tradition, followed by an empirical analysis of this model. Although it is preliminary, this analysis should provide a foundation for further cross-cultural empirical research of wisdom.

Historical Accounts of Wisdom

One approach to exploring a construct that is as elusive and ancient as wisdom involves what Holliday and Chandler (1986) call "intellectual archeology" – excavating bodies of ancient literature to discover their traditional meanings. Although several such archeological projects have already been implemented, they often have limited their focus exclusively to the examination of ancient Western texts (e.g., Achenbaum & Orwoll, 1991; Robinson, 1990). To date, only a handful of studies have investigated the historical roots of wisdom both in the East and West (Assmann, 1994; Clayton & Birren, 1980; Takahashi, 2000). It is important, therefore, to further excavate the ancient literature, especially the neglected soil of the East, to discern how wisdom has been treated there.

In this section, we briefly examine the meanings and historical roots of wisdom both in the West and in the East. Western tradition includes the ancient Egyptian, biblical, and Greek literatures, which had a significant impact on many branches of Western thinking. However, it is the

Anglo-American tradition (e.g., logical positivism, neofunctionalism, etc.) that became the most influential and dominant heir in the Western scientific field (Kitchener, 1983; Overton, 1998). In the remainder of this section, therefore, "Western tradition" will refer only to the lineage between these ancient texts and Anglo-American tradition.

Following this section, we will describe Eastern interpretations of wisdom, paying particular attention to the ancient Vedic text and its later implications. Because the Eastern tradition is broad and consists of diverse microdoctrines, the present discussion limits its focus to the major teachings of the East, including Hinduism, Buddhism, Confucianism, and Taoism. It must be noted that although we claim that the differences between these Western and Eastern traditions are fundamental, we also acknowledge that these differences are not exhaustive by any means, and that they exclude other influential traditions such as that of Native American and African cultures. Nor do we claim that the Eastern and Western traditions are mutually exclusive. Some general features of the Eastern systems agree with some doctrines of the West (Sheldon, 1951). Thus, the following attempt is not to dichotomize our civilization into Western and Eastern cultures, but to describe normative characteristics of wisdom in the respective culture, which, in turn, lead to a fuller understanding of this concept.

Western Conceptualization of Wisdom

In the West, the concept of wisdom first appeared around 3000 B.C. in Egypt, and was expressed through song and parable as a sort of pragmatic tool to "make sense" or intellectualize human sufferings and the paradoxical nature of life (Bryce, 1979; Rylaarsdam et al., 1993). In this era, wisdom also referred to a set of socially accepted moral and religious codes. For example, the oldest Egyptian wisdom text, the *Instruction of Ptahhotep*, emphasized practical virtues like patience, honesty, and conformity while denouncing antisocial vice such as greed and selfishness (Bryce, 1979; Lichtheim, 1973–1980; Wood, 1967). Some investigators even claimed that the moral and religious codes portrayed in this ancient text were similar to those found in other ancient civilizations of different regions including Africa, Mesopotamia, and China (see Assmann, 1994, for review).

This ancient tradition was later incorporated into more organized documents known as the Hebraic wisdom literature (e.g., the books of Ben Sira, Solomon, Job, etc.) (Crenshaw, 1976). In addition to cultivating one's cognitive ability through formal education and parental guidance, the Hebraic tradition also emphasized a strict adherence to religious faith as an ultimate path to wisdom (Assmann, 1994). The Book of Job, a story about a man's struggle to find meaning amid a series of misfortunes, is illustrative of this point. In this story, wisdom entails one's recognition of his/her place in a Divine Order that is far beyond human cognitive capacity, and only the highest adherence to faith is believed to lead to this recognition (Rad, 1972).

In ancient Greek culture, another major contributor to the Western intellectual heritage, wisdom or σοφία ("sophia") was considered to be an ultimate form of virtue or knowledge about the true nature of things (Barrett, 1958; Robinson, 1990). As the Greek tradition generally emphasized the rational, analytical skills of being productive citizens while devaluing emotional and intuitive parts of human psyche as an obstruction of clear thinking (Katz, 1950), wisdom generally meant an extensive knowledge base and a high level of cognitive skill to utilize this knowledge base. For example, Socrates, who was proclaimed by Delphi as the wisest man in Athens, claimed that knowing one's cognitive limitation was an important wisdom quality that differentiated φιλόσοφος ("philosophers" or "wisdom loving person") from sophists (Reeve, 1989). Although it was believed that only the Greek gods could actually possess σοφία, the ancient Greek sages believed that it was important for humans to seek and strive for such wisdom through studying philosophy.

These ancient Western descriptions of wisdom were later reorganized in a systematic Christian framework. For example, St. Augustine, in his attempt to combine Platonism and Christian faith, claimed that cultivating the knowledge of the Christian God (*Sapientia*) is the ultimate path to attain wisdom. Note here that in the Western tradition God is viewed as the ultimate judge who holds the absolute truth, whereas humans are His creations who were to follow His truth. In other words, wisdom, even though ultimately unattainable by humans, was the means for narrowing the abyss between the knowledge of the Creator and His creation (Assmann, 1994). Although some Christians maintained an assumption of the essential unity of God and creation (e.g., Neoplatonists, Christian mystics) (McGinn, 1986), this assumption remained in the background and never became a prevailing principle in the mainstream Western tradition.

In the West, then, wisdom generally implied both the extent of one's relationship to God and various psychological skills. In particular, it was the cognitive features, such as possession of an extensive knowledge base and the ability to utilize such knowledge, that represented the dominant interpretation of wisdom. Although these accounts are not exhaustive by any means, it appears to be the case that, as suggested by Csikszentmihalyi and Rathunde (1990), in the West, wisdom "fails to be differentiated from knowledge; the two terms appear to be synonymous" (p. 42).

Eastern Conceptualization of Wisdom

In contrast to the Western intellectual tradition, which tends toward precise definitions of any given concept, the Eastern tradition often intentionally leaves the precise meaning of a concept open to enhance the potential flexibility of its interpretation (Rohlen, 1979). Accordingly, the Eastern interpretations of wisdom are often vague but tend to embrace a broader meaning by emphasizing noncognitive domains of wisdom. In particular, the transformative and integrative features of wisdom are often underscored. The transformational feature of wisdom is equated with transcendental experience associated with the Eastern spiritual practices (e.g., *yoga, zazen,* etc.) and concerns the progressive movement of human mind toward higher levels. This transformational sequence and the ultimate resulting state of mind are called, respectively, *darshana* and *goi* in Hinduism and *hachido* and *satori* in Buddhism (Moody, 1995; Ohta, 1983).

The integrative feature of wisdom emphasized in Eastern interpretations refers to the integration of various aspects of human consciousness (e.g., cognition, affect, intuition). Rooted in the ancient Vedic principle of "nonsplit" (Misra, Suvasini, & Strivastava, 2000; Northrop, 1947; Paranjpe, 1984), these aspects of consciousness are regarded as interdependent psychological processes necessary to the whole of wisdom and are meaningful only in their coaction in a given context (Sheldon, 1951). From this perspective, wisdom is a kind of understanding that is not mediated through reasoning by representational cognitive structure but as a more intuitive, personal experience. In other words, wisdom in the East refers to a process of direct understanding without overt intellectualization, and with a great deal of emotional involvement. Several Japanese expressions of "understanding" are illustrative of this point (Suzuki, 1959). When a situation requires an intense, emotion-laden understanding, instead of more formal and cognitive-oriented expressions such as *rikai,* Japanese tend to use expressions involving *hara* (or abdomen) to imply more direct, gut feeling understanding (Kawai, 1996). For example, "opening up each other's abdomen" (*hara wo waru*) refers to the cognitive as well as emotional experience of mutual understanding, and "accepting in the abdomen" (*hara ni osameru*) implies the generous understanding of emotion-laden issues.

This differentiation of representationally mediated and relatively unmediated understanding is important because Eastern teachings often deemphasize intellectual learning as a method of moving toward transformational and integrative wisdom. In the case of *Zen* Buddhism, for example, words – the primary vehicle of intellectual representation in the West – are neither necessary nor sufficient for wisdom but are thought of as an obstruction in the path to wisdom (Cragg, 1976; Nitobe, 1993). By the same token, the core of Confucius's teaching in *Analects* is not so much about truth finding through logic and knowledge, but about personal striving through a cultivation of one's moral, intellectual, emotional commitment to learning itself (Li, 2003). As a result, instead of instructing students "what" wisdom is through words, the Eastern disciplines instruct "how" to experience the transformation and integration through such media as yoga and meditation.

Finally, it is important to note that the Eastern tradition equally embraces – not unlike the Western conceptualization – the pragmatic and cognitive components of wisdom along with the transformational and integrative. For example, in Japan, an accumulated domestic knowledge is referred to as "a sack of grandma's wisdom" and is treasured by family members for its practical utility. Although this pragmatic component of wisdom is often considered as a desired knowledge, it also can carry a negative connotation if it is used for evil deed or for self-serving purposes (e.g., *waru-jie* or evil wisdom).

To summarize the historical accounts, the Western tradition offers a detailed description of the psychological nature of wisdom, yet its focus is relatively narrow in its limitation of wisdom to mainly cognitive features such as possession of an extensive knowledge database and an efficient information processing skill to utilize it. The Eastern tradition, by contrast, avoids articulating the parts but emphasizes the transformative and integrative process of the whole of wisdom. In this view, wisdom is viewed not only as a pragmatic knowledge but also as a progressively high level of experiential realization that integrates various psychological domains. Although this realization, traditionally referred to as transcendence or spiritual emancipation, may sound magical and elusive – and some early religious dogmas may have given rise to these connotations – the Eastern inclusive notion of wisdom essentially implies a reflective understanding that emerges through experience and gives equal weight to cognitive, affective, intuitive, and interpersonal domains of consciousness.

Given the different conceptualization of wisdom found in the historical literature of the East and West, it is of interest to know how these traditional meanings may have had an impact on the understanding of wisdom among contemporary culturally divergent populations. In the next section, we will describe the common-sense conceptualizations (implicit theories) of wisdom across cultures. Implicit theories are "pristine" theories that people maintain as a part of their day-to-day experience. The "discovery" of these theories occurs by simply asking people what the concept means to them (Sternberg, 1990). Because common-sense concepts reflect the dominant meanings of a culture, discovering these theories are useful in formulating a broad, inclusive definition of wisdom.

Implicit Theories of Wisdom

Several studies have been conducted with the aim of uncovering implicit theories of wisdom. These include studies that identify common factors underlying wisdom-related descriptors (Holliday & Chandler, 1986; Takayama, 2002; Yang, 2001) and their interrelationships (Clayton & Birren, 1980), make comparisons of wisdom with intelligence and creativity (Sternberg, 1986), and describe the characteristics of hypothetical wise people (Sowarka, 1987, 1989) or those of actual people who have been nominated as wise (Perlmutter, Adams, Nyquist, & Kaplan, 1988). Although, as one might expect, these studies failed to yield an identical set of implicit definitions, they all agree that (a) wisdom is not a unitary but a multidimensional construct and (b) is defined differently across various populations.

With regard to the research on the multidimensional nature of wisdom, several studies using different methodologies have so far identified a number of distinctive wisdom characteristics (e.g., Clayton & Birren, 1980; Holiday & Chandler, 1986; Sternberg, 1986). Although the number and nature of these dimensions are not identical across studies, these study findings suggest that wisdom is "a well-defined, multidimensional, prototypically organized competency descriptor" (Chandler & Holliday, 1990, pp. 137–138).

Another common finding among studies of implicit meaning is that wisdom is often understood differently among different populations. This effect has been observed for gender (Orwoll & Perlmutter, 1990), age (Clayton & Birren, 1980), and occupational groups (Sternberg, 1986). However, although implicit definitions of several wisdom-related concepts such as intelligence and spirituality have been cross-culturally investigated (e.g., Nisbett, 2003; Yang & Sternberg, 1997; Takahashi & Ide, (2003a), only a handful of studies to date have attempted to generalize the implicit theories of wisdom beyond the conventional European American population. Valdez (1994), for example, interviewed 15 Hispanic Americans who had been nominated as wise by their peers. She found that their definitions of wisdom stressed the spiritual and interpersonal dimensions while deemphasizing the cognitive aspect. Similarly, Levitt (1999) interviewed 13 Tibetan Buddhist monks living in the Himalayan region of India who defined wisdom as an understanding of Buddhist notions of void (a belief in the radical devaluation of phenomenal world) and of nonself (an assumption that the self is "coeval" with Buddha) (Takahashi, 2000). Each of these studies presents additional evidence to the common-sense variability of the meaning of wisdom, and demonstrates specific ways that wisdom has been conceptualized across cultures.

In a large-scale study, Takayama (2002) examined the implicit theories of wisdom among Japanese men and women who ranged in age from their 20s to their 90s. In this study, 2,000 subjects rated 22 behavioral attributes of wisdom on a 5-point Likert-type scale. The ratings were submitted to factor analysis, yielding four distinctive factors: *knowledge and education*, *understanding and judgment*, *sociability and interpersonal relationship*, and *introspective attitude*. Takayama concluded that Japanese are more likely to define wisdom as a "practical" and "experience-based" competence but less likely to associate wisdom with reasoning ability and general intelligence.

In a similar study involving 616 Taiwanese Chinese, Yang (2001) also found four comparable factors: *competencies and knowledge, benevolence and compassion, openness and profundity*, and *modesty and unobtrusiveness*. In contrast to the Hispanic Americans and Tibetan Buddhist Monks, these results suggested that the Taiwanese Chinese defined wisdom in a less spiritual and less religious fashion, but as a more pragmatic concept expressed in daily life that brings "harmony" to a society as a whole (e.g., "Is able to transform an adverse situation to one's and everyone's advantage."). Yang also emphasized that *modesty and unobtrusiveness* appears to be a wisdom characteristic that is relatively unique to Chinese-originated cultures. Based on the idea that nature works wonders unobtrusively, several Chinese classics that depict a code of conduct (e.g., *The Analects, Mencius, Chuang Tzu*) instruct the individual to keep a low profile regardless of his/her accomplishment. In fact, many Taiwanese Chinese strongly disagreed with statements that described wise people as "Is showy; draws excessive attention to self," "Conceited and stubborn, with a sense of superiority; is proud and arrogant;" "Is too clever for one's own good" (p. 670).

In our own project (Takahashi & Bordia, 2000), we made a direct comparison of implicit definitions of wisdom among young adult (mean age = 21.17) American, Australian, Indian, and Japanese participants. In this study, the participants rated the similarity of the adjective *wise* to other related descriptors (i.e., *aged, awakened, discreet, experienced, intuitive,* and *knowledgeable*) that had been generated in a pilot study. The study also explored the preference for these descriptors by asking participants to select adjectives that best described their ideal selves.

Multidimensional scaling analysis, in conjunction with a hierarchical cluster analysis, revealed an identical clustering pattern for both the American and Australian samples. For this group, *wise* was semantically most similar to *experienced* and *knowledgeable*, and least similar to *discreet*. This group also selected *knowledgeable* and *wise* as the two most preferred descriptors for an ideal self, whereas *aged* and *discreet* were ranked the lowest. These findings support the expectation that the "Western" understanding of wisdom stresses the analytical features such as a broad knowledge database and expertise accumulated through life experience.

In contrast, both the Indian and Japanese young adults understood *wise* as semantically most closely associated with *discreet* followed by *aged* and *experienced*, whereas *wise* and *knowledgeable* were among the least associated pairs. Furthermore, the Japanese selected *wise* and *discreet* as the most and second most preferred adjectives for an ideal self, whereas *knowledgeable* was selected on a relatively lower rank (sixth) on the preference dimension.

These findings strongly support the general hypothesis that the meaning of wisdom varies according to specific cultural contexts. More specifically, Indian and Japanese adults are less likely than their Western counterparts to relate *wise* with cognitive features such as an accumulation of knowledge. Instead, these "Eastern" cultures identify *wise* with the *discreet* characteristic, which requires not only having an extensive *knowledge* database but also prudence or the exercising of sound judgment in practical and emotional situations. In other words, *wise* is conceptualized among Indians and Japanese not solely as a cognitive ability but as a characteristic that encompasses a relatively direct understanding entailing some degree of emotional involvement, and a characteristic that facilitates the effective integration of multiple domains of psychological processing (e.g., cognition, emotion, intuition, etc.). The finding also supports several cross-cultural studies that report "intelligence" to be less likely understood in the East as analytical cognitive skills, and more likely conceptualized as a type of social competence (e.g., Nisbett, 2003; Yang & Sternberg, 1997).

It is also the case that, although *wise* and *aged* were closely associated in their meanings among both the Eastern and Western samples, they were found to be, respectively, the most and the least liked descriptors for an ideal self for all four cultural groups. Given the different cultural context of the East and West with respect to the societal perception of old age – ranging from the relatively gerontophilic attitude in the East to the gerontophobic attitude in the West (Covey, 1991; Palmore & Maeda, 1985), this consistent pattern (i.e., identifying *wise* and *aged* as similar concepts, yet liking the former while disliking the latter) across cultures is perplexing. One possible interpretation is that there is a double standard of aging experience regardless of historical and cultural tradition in contemporary societies. That is, young adults in any contemporary society tend to perceive old age as an undesirable characteristic to associate with the self for a variety of reasons (e.g., negative portrayal in the media, declined income and social status, etc.), yet they feel the need to attribute something positive to their inevitable old age. Although such a double standard was believed to be prevalent only in the West (Meacham, 1990), with rapid modernization the perception of old age may be changing in India and Japan as well. This speculation, however, requires further investigation, particularly on how people perceive the relation between wisdom and chronological age and what factors contribute to the changing perception of old age in other cultures.

From a different perspective, Takahashi and Ide (2003b) examined the applied use of implicit theories of wisdom among Japanese and Americans from three generations of family members (young, middle-aged, and old). Participants were instructed to rate the degree to which they agreed or disagreed with the characterization of eight internationally known individuals as wise. These well-known individuals were preselected as a part of a larger study on spirituality (Ide & Takahashi, 2002), and included Mahatma Gandhi, Nelson Mandela, John Paul II, Mother Teresa, Bill Clinton, Adolf Hitler, Saddam Hussein, and Shoukou Asahara. Nelson Mandela and Shoukou Asahara were excluded from subsequent analysis because more than a half of the participants in either the Japanese or American group claimed to "Know nothing about this person or what he/she has done."

The overall results demonstrated that, regardless of gender and age, across the three generations the Japanese rated Adolf Hitler and Saddam Hussein significantly "wiser" than did their American counterparts. Although the Japanese sample never perceived these two individuals as "wise" per se (the Japanese average was never higher than 3.0 in any of the groups and this score is "neutral" on the agree/disagree dimension), these results are interesting in the context of the role played by cultural meanings in the understanding of the concept. First, it is clear that distinct features of a universally "positive" concept such as wisdom do not entail the same degree of positive valence in all cultural settings. In the present case, the Japanese word *wise*, although generally regarded as positive, also can imply a negative characteristic (i.e., "evil wisdom") often used to describe a cunning strategist. Second, the finding may be accounted for by the cultural experience of the groups. Japanese participants quite possibly had significantly less emotional involvement than others with Hitler during World War II and Hussein during the Gulf War, while having had sufficient cognitive involvement to acknowledge their pragmatic skills for example, some of the American participants (and their relatives) were Holocaust survivors and understandably had an extremely strong feeling toward Hitler. By contrast, although the Japanese participants, including the older cohort (mean age = 76.92), knew "who *Hitler* was" or "what *Hitler* had done," their lack of direct involvement in the European fronts during World War II may have prevented them from fully understanding Hitler's deeds. At any rate, the research findings suggest that both the theoretical and applied definitions of a psychological concept such as wisdom can vary significantly between cultures. As a consequence, when exploring wisdom – a concept relevant to both East and West – it is essential that social scientists avoid cultural egocentrism and acknowledge the broadest and most inclusive meanings entailed by the concept.

To this point we have argued that culturally differentiated intellectual historical accounts of wisdom have formed the context for the development of culturally differentiated common-sense definitions of wisdom. Given that formal psychological theories derive largely from the implicit or common-sense theories of the scientists who formulate these formal theories (Sternberg, 1990), it is not surprising that contemporary psychological models have deep conceptual roots in specific cultural traditions, and in intellectual traditions that have been influenced by these cultural traditions (Overton, 1998). From cultural–intellectual root to stem and branch there grows finally the flowers of theoretical disagreements concerning the nature and criteria of wisdom. Any reconciliation of these disagreements must necessarily entail the recognition of cultures and intellectual traditions, not as dichotomies, but as complementary points of views on the universal human condition (Overton, 2003). This recognition establishes a base from which to search for an integration of the complements. With respect to wisdom, we have found accepting the various definitions as complements leads to the organization of wisdom around a broad culturally inclusive and developmental synthetic–analytic framework. In the next section, we will explore this framework and describe some of its implications in the context of an Eriksonian approach to personality development.

Culturally Inclusive Developmental Model of Wisdom

The synthetic–analytic framework considers wisdom as two moments or modes of the same psychological process. The analytical mode breaks down human experience into its simplest terms or elementary qualities, and examines the nature of their "part to part" relationship. This is a mode that focuses on the reduction or analysis of global systems into elementary qualities, and the exploration of the relations among these qualities. When exploring wisdom within the analytic mode, the "instrumental" or "adaptive" or "procedural" value of observed behavior and its variational changes become the focus of inquiry. As a consequence, inquiry within this mode examines specific knowledge content of individual differences in relation to several information processing functions and practical goals in life (e.g., solving problems, making judgments, etc.).

The synthetic mode focuses on experience as a holistic integrated "whole–part relationship," which is not derivable directly from an analysis of individual elements. Wisdom's synthetic mode entails the dialectic nature of the human mind (i.e., dialectic being defined as any system or structure that moves toward the states of increased integration) including the mind's momentary and developmental features (Basseches, 1984; Orwoll & Achenbaum, 1993; Sinnott, 1998). The dialectic principle assumes mind is a self-organizing system that, through experience, becomes transformed into more advanced, qualitatively new forms of integration across the life span (Overton, 1991). At any given point, the mind represents the integration of several domains of mental functioning (i.e., cognitive, emotional, motivational, intuitive processes); developmentally the mind transforms itself through the actions of the person operating in the world (i.e., experience), and moves toward increasingly adaptive levels of integration (e.g., actualization tendency, enlightenment). When exploring wisdom within the synthetic mode, observed behavior or action is understood as an "expression" of some fundamental underlying psychological organization or system, rather than as an "instrumental" means to attaining a practical goal (Overton, 1997, 1998).

To the extent that this synthetic–analytic framework is rejected and complements are treated as dichotomous *either/or* alternatives, theories are created that conceptualize the synthetic and the analytic not as moments, but as privileged realities. When the synthetic is treated as privileged reality, wisdom can be represented as if the expressive phenomenological pole of human experience – including self-actualization tendency, transformation of consciousness, and self-transcendence phenomena – constitutes the whole of wisdom. By contrast, when the analytic is treated as a privileged reality, wisdom is understood as an instrumental behavior of observed action that only serves the means to functional goals.

With respect to empirical investigations, a relatively exclusive focus on the synthetic (Vandenberg, 1991; Yalom, 1980) has primarily yielded existential–phenomenological case studies. Analytic approaches have yielded a wider variety of empirical investigations and these have been offered at times as the only legitimate account of wisdom in the West (Csikszentmihalyi & Rathunde, 1990). Contemporary research approaches that explore the analytic–based instrumental dimension of wisdom have included an "expert knowledge system" (Baltes, Lindenberger, & Staudinger, 1998), a balance theory of wisdom (Sternberg, 1998), a high level of "epistemic cognition" (Kitchener, 1983), a problem-solving ability (Arlin, 1990), and a balance between "knowing and doubting" (Meacham, 1990). Often these studies acknowledged the importance of a synthetic dimension of wisdom, but the research remains within a cognitive–behavioral analytic frame (Blanchard-Fields & Norris, 1995).

A common feature among contemporary analytical approaches to wisdom has been the differentiation of two analytical components: a knowledge database and a higher–level cognitive complexity that permits adequate utilization of the database. These two analytic components parallel those of the traditional Western definitions: possession of an extensive knowledge base (e.g., knowledge of religion, metaphysics, etc.) and an ability to utilize such knowledge (e.g., logical reasoning). From this perspective, Baltes and his colleagues, for example, identify two components of wisdom that they claim to be necessary for the understanding of life's central themes (i.e., lifespan contextualism, relativism, and uncertainty). These dimensions are: (a) factual/declarative knowledge and (b) procedural knowledge. The former represents a knowledge database about the fundamental pragmatics of life, whereas the latter is the strategic process involved in utilizing that database (Baltes & Staudinger, 2000). Although expressed differently, other analytical theories of wisdom also take this two-tier approach. Thus, for example, both Kitchener and Brenner (1990) and Meacham (1990) claim that wisdom is knowing about the limit of one's knowledge, the claim that mirrors Socrates' definition of wisdom (i.e., σοφία). In Meacham's words, wisdom is a balance between "knowing and doubting," implying the importance of access to the knowledge database (i.e., "knowing") and of the meta-level monitoring ability of that knowledge (i.e., "doubting"). Furthermore, Kitchener and Brenner emphasize the meta-level ability of differentiating and integrating abstract concepts, and analytically define wisdom as "the ability to reason complexly with abstraction" (1990, p. 225).

In contrast to relatively exclusive analytical approaches, in recent years an increasing number of investigators have begun exploring approaches that are more compatible with the synthetic–analytic complementary framework. Here wisdom has come to be understood as an inclusive relation of complementarities (Achenbaum & Orwoll, 1991; Ardelt, 1997; Blanchard-Fields & Norris, 1995; Csikszentmihalyi & Rathunde, 1990; Kramer, 1990; Labouvie-Vief, 1996; Sinnott, 1998; Wink & Helson, 1997). Following from a general relational metatheory that treats apparent antimonies as complements (Overton, 2003), this work incorporates the expressive and instrumental-functioning, along with transformational and variational changes into a broad unified matrix. This matrix, as differentiated complements, constitutes a stable platform from which science launches empirical inquiries, which may focus on the synthetic, the analytic, or the total system (Overton, 2003). This relational position resembles such traditional Eastern teachings as Buddhism and Taoism, and argues that although specific cognitive-processing skills for attaining practical goals are necessary, the integrated expressive functioning of multiple subsystems of human consciousness (i.e., cognition, emotion, motivation, intuition) and the transformations of the integrated unity are no less necessary (Takahashi, 2000).

Inclusive Eriksonian Model of Wisdom

Erikson's theory (1959) with its emphasis on the integrative and trans- formational features of wisdom – although simultaneously acknowl- edging the significance of specific analytical functions – is generally regarded as the paradigmatic model of a culturally inclusive comple- mentary approach to the development of wisdom. Framed by dialectical assumptions that generate images of an organic self-organizing system as a guiding metaphor of human development, inclusive approaches portray the developing person as an

inherently organized system of activity, constructing its affective and cognitive understanding and knowledge of the world, and growing in the direction of personhood, through a dialectical-relational process of regulation and transfor- mation. (Overton & Horowitz, 1991, p. 13)

Wisdom, within this context, develops from the person's coactions with the world and the transformation of the person's actions as they are directed toward the adaptive resolution of a series of psy- chosocial conflicts. Although specific individual conflicts vary, Erikson claims that the universal features of wisdom remain invariant across cultures (Erikson, 1963). Within this inclusive understanding of wis- dom, Erikson focuses on two features of experience: the synthetic/ transformational and the synthetic/integrative. Although both features are essential to a fuller understanding of wisdom, some contempo- rary inclusive investigators have emphasized the former (e.g., Chinen, 1984; Kegan, 1982, 1994; Kekes, 1983), whereas others emphasize the latter (e.g., Achenbaum & Orwoll, 1991; Cartensen, 1995; Happe, Winner, & Brownell, 1998; Kramer, 1990; Labouvie-Vief, 1996).

Synthetic/Transformational Moment of Wisdom
Enquiry into the synthetic/transformational is grounded and sus- tained by the Eriksonian view that wisdom entails "an informed and detached concern with life itself" (Erikson, 1982, p. 61) or "truly involved disinvolvement" (Erikson, 1982, p. 61). With this ground- ing, the synthetic/transformational feature of wisdom is broadly de- fined as "reflective understanding," a sense of detachment or a high

level of meta-awareness of the self and situational contexts (Erikson, Erikson, & Kivnick, 1986). Similar to the Eastern tradition that expands the meaning of "understanding" beyond an experience mediated only by representational cognitive structures, this feature of wisdom denotes a direct, intuitive, and emotional experience. It may be helpful to distinguish "reflective understanding" from "reflective thinking" to further elaborate the psychological meaning of the former, as the two are often conflated.

Chinen (1984) articulates this distinction in his discussion of logical modality, entailing the concepts of "object awareness" and "modal awareness." Object awareness implies what we usually refer to as "awareness" in everyday language. The focus of this modality is on the content of a particular object, and experience is largely mediated by representations of that content. In contrast, modal awareness, which is equivalent to the synthetic/transformational reflective understanding that emerges during late adulthood, entails an explicit awareness of the manner in which the object is attended to. This modality operates at a heightened level of consciousness. It is an appreciation of how persons experience their lives. This mode, often described as transcendental experience, is emphasized in many Eastern spiritual regimens including Zen Buddhism and Hinduism. To illustrate, imagine being in a museum, standing in front of a statue. From an object awareness perspective, we focus on the statue itself by attending to its texture, the use of negative space, and so on. Here our attention is on the content of the statue or the object itself, and our experience is primarily mediated by representational cognitive structures. Other features of reflective thinking in this situation might be our thoughts about whether we are standing too close or too far from the statue, whether we appreciate the statue to the same degree as an art critic who may be standing next to us, and so on. In these situations, our attention simply shifts from one object (i.e., the statue) to another (i.e., thinking self) and remains as object awareness.

In contrast, with modal awareness or reflective understanding, we attend not only to the statue itself but also relish the manner or "how" we experience the statue. Our attention expands beyond the content of the object and now includes the whole conscious experience of art appreciation. For example, a person may experience the statue by thinking how historically significant this statue is, feeling exuberant by its dynamic composition, and being impressed by its massive presence. In other words, our action is not only as an "instrument" to achieve goals (e.g., watching a statue) but also as an "expression" of subjective-functional meaning (e.g., appreciating a piece of art) that goes beyond its instrumental purpose (Boesch, 1991; Overton, 1997, 1998). Reflective understanding thus involves multiple psychological functions – cognitive, emotional, motivational, intuitive – which are essential components of this experience.

In late adulthood, as one reflects (i.e., reflective thinking) on a life of accomplishment and conflicts, modal awareness or reflective understanding facilitates an integrative experience that would not be possible if understanding were restricted to reflective thought. Modal awareness opens the possibility of appreciating a sense of completeness of life that is not available to reflective thought. In Hindi tradition, for example, this awareness is believed to develop during the last stage of wisdom passage, *Samayasa*, and enables a person to realize the ephemeral nature of the world (Paranjpe, 1984; Yogananda, 1946). This realization would, in turn, free the self from bondage to earthly desires. Thus, with the development of reflective understanding the person acquires the capacity to secure contentment with the way he/she arranged each experience to create his/her own life. Action and a history of action can, with the acquisition of reflective understanding, be appreciated both as "instrumental" and as an "expression" of the subjective-functional meaning of life. It is an ability to accept and appreciate the mergence between one's psychological identity and his/her personal instrumental history. Erikson defines this mergence as the syntonic potential of wisdom or "ego integrity":

> It is the acceptance of one's own and only life cycle and of the people who have become significant to it as something had to be and that by necessity, permitted of no substitution. (Erikson, 1959, p. 98)

It must be remembered that it is the outcome of the dialectical tension of ego integrity and despair, not an overdevelopment of this syntonic potential, that identifies the attainment of wisdom. Thus, it is important not to confuse ego integrity and presumptuousness or dogmatism. In the latter case, a person may assume that his/her personal experiences have had an objective correctness to them. This stance reflects an "object awareness" because the individual attends solely to the content of the life experiences. With modal awareness, by contrast, the individual comes to appreciate not merely what was done in life, but how he/she now experiences life. Here the modal emphasis shifts from the objective significance of life's content (e.g., social status, possession of material wealth, etc.) to subjective evaluation of one's whole past (e.g., (dis)contentment, sense of fulfillment or regret, etc.). Chinen (1984) states,

> The experience of ego-integrity is explicitly acknowledged to be independent of particular past actions and beliefs. Logically speaking, the sense of absoluteness is recognized to be a modal quality, not an objective feature of the content. (p. 52)

This conceptualization of the synthetic/transformational moment of wisdom is also shared by Kekes (1983), who claims that wisdom must involve two types of knowledge: descriptive and interpretative knowledge. Descriptive knowledge is the factual content of personal experience or instrumental knowledge, whereas interpretative knowledge resembles Chinen's modal awareness or reflective understanding. Interpretive knowledge involves reflectively understanding the significance or value of descriptively known facts. Kekes argues that the inclusive understanding of one's limitations and possibilities both cognitively and affectively are important wisdom qualities that keep an individual from becoming egocentric or dogmatic.

The distinction between interpretive knowledge/modal awareness/ reflective understanding, on the one hand, and descriptive knowledge/ object awareness/reflective thinking, on the other, is implicated in empirical studies that have examined the recall style of narrative stories (e.g., Adams, Labouvie-Vief, Hobart, & Dorosz, 1990; Labouvie-Vief, Schell, & Weaverdyck, 1982). In these studies, older adults who presumably had a capacity for modal awareness demonstrated a recall style that emphasized evaluation of the story by transforming the descriptive meanings into "moral, metaphoric, or social normative meaning" (Adams et al., 1990, p. 20). Younger adults, in contrast, who presumably lacked modal awareness and therefore out of necessity relied on object awareness, tended to exhibit a more text-based, literal recall style. In other words, individuals with a capacity for modal awareness or interpretive knowledge seem to be better able to address the psychological and symbolic meanings of a story as well as its logical and descriptive features.

Synthetic/Integrative Moment of Wisdom

Erikson's theory is not limited to an exploration of the synthetic/ transformational mode of wisdom. A second equally important synthetic mode of wisdom discussed by Erikson is the synthetic/ integrative mode. This mode entails the coordination of the various modes of human consciousness. It corresponds to the ancient Vedic principle of "nonsplit" in which the various modes of consciousness are integrated and are meaningful only in their coaction to the whole of wisdom. Specifically, Erikson emphasizes emotional integration as an important key to successful aging (Erikson, 1963). This is illustrated in Erikson's definition of successful late adulthood – representing the final psychosocial virtue of wisdom – as an equilibrium that manifests "an increased sense of inner unity" (Erikson, 1959, p. 51) or "a sense of coherence and wholeness" (Erikson et al., 1986, p. 65).

Focusing on this point from a neo-Piagetian perspective, Labouvie-Vief and her colleagues describe wisdom as an integration of two irreducible, complementary modes: *mythos* and *logos*. The *mythos* mode refers to holistic, affective, and experiential knowing, whereas *logos* implies cognitive faculties such as reasoning, counting, and explaining (Labouvie-Vief, 1990, 1994, 1996). The logos mode develops to suppress the mythos mode until adolescence, and thus a person becomes more logical, objective, or "decentered" during this period. However, once the person reaches the highest form of logos (i.e., formal operation), the developmental aim shifts its focus to "recentration" or the integration of the two modes, resulting in superior understanding and control of the emotional experience (Labouvie-Vief, 1990; Riegel, 1973; Sinnott, 1998). With this understanding, similar to that of the abdomen-oriented experience of the East, a person is now willing and able to take appropriate, responsible action by integrating his/her knowledge about the situation and the emotional responses that arise from it (Kramer, 1990; Kramer, Kahlbaugh, & Goldston, 1992).

Labouvie-Vief and her colleagues have examined the developmental model of mythos/logos integration empirically with a particular focus on emotional control and emotional understanding. In one study (Labouvie-Vief et al., 1989), for example, the participants from young, middle-aged, and older cohorts were asked to recall their recent emotional experiences of sadness, anger, fear, and happiness. Following the recall session, they were asked to describe their own interpretation of each emotional state and regulatory strategies of the emotion. The results suggested that the middle-aged and older adults were more likely than the younger group to express their emotional states with more sophisticated language of self-regulation that was dynamic, possessed less conventional and more unique standards of judgment about their emotional life, and displayed better understanding of their inner locus of emotion. These findings corroborate the results of other studies in which older adults are more likely than younger adults to invest effort in regulating their emotions and thus experience less emotional conflict (Cartensen, 1995), are better able to deal with emotional issues (Blanchard-Fields, 1986; Cornelius & Caspi, 1987; Staudinger, 1989) and infer others' feelings (Happe et al., 1998), and perform well on recall tests if the material involved others' internal state, such as emotion (Hashtroudi, Johnson, & Chrosniak, 1990).

In addition, compatible with the traditional Eastern views of wisdom as an "expansive" mental process, the theoretical claim is also made by Csikszentmihalyi and Rathunde (1990) that with the synthesis that ultimately arises out of the several transformations of consciousness, the intrinsic reward of being comes to be experienced through a sense of appreciation and a sense of purpose in one's existence and life. It is a form of experience that humans most strive for and a form that is lived through by those individuals who have been described as "Junzi" (Li, 2003), "One Minded" (Suzuki, 1959), "Ubermensch" (Nietzsche, 1968), "self-actualized" (Maslow, 1971), and "fully functioning" (Rogers, 1959). Ardelt (1997) provides empirical evidence to support this claim by demonstrating a significant relationship between a high level of synthetic wisdom and subjective well-being among older adults regardless of contextual variables such as physical health, physical environment, and socioeconomic status.

From this inclusive perspective, then, wisdom is defined developmentally as a relatively late-emerging form of cognitive/affective understanding that grows dialectically from earlier analytic and synthetic skills and integrates these into a broader fabric of reflectivity. Furthermore, from a broadly defined Eriksonian perspective, this type of understanding brings about an internal sense of reward by appreciating the subjective functional meaning of life.

Culturally Inclusive Developmental Model of Wisdom: An Empirical Study

As an attempt to empirically investigate this inclusive model, we have conducted cross-cultural research examining five fundamental wisdom components in two modes: (a) the analytical mode (knowledge database and abstract reasoning) and (b) the synthetic mode (reflective understanding, emotional empathy, and emotional regulation) (Takahashi & Overton, 2002). In the absence of any previous cross-cultural study directly investigating wisdom qualities, our exploratory study used relatively simple protocols that were readily available and readily translatable.

For the analytical mode, knowledge database and abstract reasoning ability were measured by using, respectively, the Vocabulary subset and Similarity subset of the Wechsler Adult Intelligence Scale–Revised (WAIS-R). For the synthetic mode, reflective understanding, emotional empathy, and emotional regulation were assessed through the Short Index of Self-Actualization (Jones & Crandall, 1986), the Empathetic subscale of the Interpersonality Reactivity Index (Davis, 1980), and the Negative Mood Regulation scale (Catanzaro & Mearns, 1990), respectively. Although these measures do not yield as comprehensive a picture of wisdom as do other complex procedures (e.g., Baltes et al., 1998), this aggregated instrument provided us for the first time a convenient avenue to explore wisdom cross-culturally.

A total of 136 American and Japanese community-dwelling adults, with an equal number of men and women from two cohort groups (middle-aged: mean age = 45.3; and older: mean age = 70.1) participated in the study. Although they were all primarily upper-middle to upper class according to the Hollingshead's Social Position Index (1975), their cultural orientations measured by Individualism–Collectivism Scale (Hui & Yee, 1994) differed significantly, with the Americans being more individualistic than the Japanese.

Several noteworthy findings were revealed in this study. First, older adults generally performed better on these wisdom measures regardless of gender or their cultural background. Although the development of wisdom may be more influenced by the content of life events and social changes than chronological age per se, they often are intertwined because having lived longer generally implies that he/she had more opportunities for psychological maturity through a variety of life experience (Erikson, 1982). Furthermore, this finding supports previous study results involving only Western populations that have found that older adults outperformed younger cohorts (Kramer et al., 1992) and that more older adults are "top performers" on various wisdom tasks (Baltes & Smith, 1990).

Second, contrary to conventional Western conceptualization that wisdom can be solely understood within an analytic cognitive framework, this study showed that both the analytic and synthetic dimensions are equally important in understanding the functioning of wisdom in late adulthood.

Third, these wisdom components and life satisfaction were found to be positively correlated, supporting the assumption that wisdom functions, especially those of the synthetic features, were believed to be self-discovering, self-expanding processes that often accompany an intrinsically rewarding and satisfying experience (Chinen, 1984). This result was further corroborated by the fact that several older participants stated that as they experienced losses (e.g., loss of loved ones, physical impairment, income decline, etc.) through the years, they gradually gained an insight into the value of what they still had. This, in turn, intensified a sense of appreciation and satisfaction about self and life in general. Although some participants complained about their losses, those who had gone through this insightful, self-expanding process claimed that it was worthwhile for the peace of mind they had gained, despite painful experience.

Conclusion

In this chapter, we have presented an inclusive developmental model of wisdom based on cross-cultural studies of implicit theories (or folk conceptions) and historical accounts of wisdom from the Eastern and Western traditions. The model, conceptually drawn from a broadly defined Eriksonian framework, integrates two moments or modes of wisdom: the analytical mode and the synthetic mode. The analytic mode concerns the reduction of global systems of wisdom into elementary qualities, and inquiry into this mode primarily entails the exploration of specific knowledge content or information-processing functions. This mode shares its essential qualities with the traditional Western interpretation of wisdom underscoring possession of an extensive knowledge database and a high level of cognitive complexity to utilize such knowledge.

By contrast, the synthetic mode is compatible with the traditional Eastern interpretation and concerns the integration of psychological systems and transformational changes that characterize this integration. In particular, this wisdom mode pertains to cognition/affect integration and a reflective level of conscious experience. This mode has been explored from several perspectives including neo-Piagetian, ego development, modal logic, and interpretive knowledge. Although rudimentary in its methodology and operationalization, we have demonstrated the usefulness of this inclusive framework in our empirical work and in the finding that these two moments remain essential in understanding wisdom throughout adulthood.

The application of this inclusive framework should not be confused as an attempt to ontologically dichotomize the concept of wisdom. On the contrary, our assumption is that the unity of wisdom subsystems (e.g., synthetic–analytical, the East–West, expressive–instrumental) is fundamental and that these subsystems are equally valued and implicated during the inquiry. In other words, our intention is to retain wisdom as a holistic concept through the use of this synthetic–analytic framework as a sort of ad hoc explanatory category. Only by doing so are we able to examine inclusively, both culturally and developmentally, this relatively new empirical concept with a long tail of ancient history.

References

Achenbaum, W. A., & Orwoll, L. (1991). Becoming wise: A psycho-gerontological interpretation of the Book of Job. *International Journal of Aging and Human Development, 32,* 21–39.

Adams, C., Labouvie-Vief, G., Hobart, C. J., & Dorosz, M. (1990). Adult age group differences in story recall style. *Journal of Gerontology, 45*(1), 17–27.

Ardelt, M. (1997). Wisdom and life satisfaction in old age. *Journal of Gerontology, 52,* 15–27.

Arlin, P. K. (1990). Wisdom: The art of problem finding. In R. J. Sternberg (Ed.), *Wisdom: Its nature, origins, and development* (pp. 230–243). New York: Cambridge University Press.

Assmann, A. (1994). Wholesome knowledge: Concepts of wisdom in a historical and cross-cultural perspective. In D. L. Featherman, R. M. Learner, & M. Perlmutter (Eds.), *Life-span development and behavior* (Vol. 12, pp. 187–224). Hillsdale, NJ: Lawrence Erlbaum.

Baltes, P. B. (1993). The aging mind: Potentials and limits. *Gerontologists, 33,* 580–594.

Baltes, P. B., Lindenberger, U., & Staudinger, U. M. (1998). Life-span theory in developmental psychology. In W. Damon (Series Ed.) & R. M. Lerner (Vol. Ed.), *Handbook of child psychology: Vol. I. Theoretical model of human development* (5th ed., pp. 1029–1144). New York: Wiley.

Baltes, P. B., & Smith, J. (1990). Toward a psychology of wisdom and its ontogenesis. In R. J. Sternberg (Ed.), *Wisdom: Its nature, origins, and development* (pp. 87–120). New York: Cambridge University Press.

Baltes, P. B., & Staudinger, U. M. (2000). Wisdom: A metaheuristic (pragmatic) to orchestrate mind and virtue toward excellence. *American Psychologist, 55,* 122–136.

Barrett, W. (1958). *Irrational man: A study in existential philosophy.* Garden City, NY: Doubleday.

Basseches, M. A. (1984). Dialectic thinking as a metasystematic form of cognitive orientation. In M. L. Commons, F. A. Richards, & C. Armon (Eds.), *Beyond formal operations* (pp. 216–328). New York: Praeger.

Birren, J. E., & Fisher, L. M. (1990). The elements of wisdom: Overview and integration. In R. J. Sternberg (Ed.), *Wisdom: Its nature, origins, and development* (pp. 317–332). New York: Cambridge University Press.

Blanchard-Fields, F. C. (1986). Reasoning on social dilemmas varying emotional saliency: An adult development perspective. *Psychology and Aging, 1,* 325–332.

Blanchard-Fields, F. C., & Norris, L. (1995). The development of wisdom. In M. A. Kimble, S. H. McFadden, J. W. Ellor, & J. J. Seeber (Eds.), *Aging, spirituality, and religion* (pp. 102–118). Minneapolis, MN: Fortress Press.

Boesch, E. E. (1991). *Symbolic action theory and cultural psychology.* Berlin, Germany: Springer-Verlag.

Bryce, G. E. (1979). *A legacy of wisdom: The Egyptian contribution to the wisdom of Israel.* Lewisburg, PA: Bucknell University Press.

Cartensen, L. L. (1995). Evidence for a life span theory of socioemotional selectivity. *Current Direction in Psychological Research, 4,* 151–156.

Catanzaro, S. J., & Mearns, J. (1990). Measuring generalized expectancies for negative mood regulation: Initial scale development and implications. *Journal of Personality Assessment, 54,* 546–563.

Chandler, M. J., & Holliday, S. (1990). Wisdom in a postapocalyptic age. In R. J. Sternberg (Ed.), *Wisdom: Its nature, origins, and development* (pp. 121–141). New York: Cambridge University Press.

Chinen, A. B. (1984). Modal logic: A new paradigm of development and late-life potential. *Human Development, 27,* 42–56.

Clayton, V., & Birren, J. E. (1980). The development of wisdom across the life span: A reexamination of an ancient topic. In P. B. Baltes & O. G. Brim (Eds.), *Life-span development and behavior* (Vol. 3, pp. 103–135). New York: Academic Press.

Cornelius, S. W., & Caspi, A. (1987). Everyday problem solving in adulthood and old age. *Psychology and Aging, 2,* 144–153.

Covey, H. C. (1991). Old age and historical examples of miser. *Gerontologist, 31*(5), 673–678.

Cragg, K. (1976). *The wisdom of the Sufis.* New York: New Directions.

Crenshaw, J. (1976). *Studies in ancient Israeli wisdom.* New York: Klave Publishing House.

Csikszentmihalyi, M., & Rathunde, K. (1990). The psychology of wisdom: An Evolutionary interpretation. In R. J. Sternberg (Ed.), *Wisdom: Its nature, origins, and development* (pp. 25–51). New York: Cambridge University Press.

Damasio, A. (1994). *Descarte's error: Emotion, reason, and the human brain.* New York: Avon Books.

Damasio, A. (1999). *The feeling of what happens: Body and emotion in the making of consciousness.* New York: Harcourt Brace & Company.

Davis, M. (1980). A multidimensional approach to individual differences in empathy. *JSAS Catalog of Selected Documents in Psychology, 10,* 1–17.

Erikson, E. H. (1959). Identity and the life cycle. *Psychological Issues, 1,* 1–173.

Erikson, E. H. (1963). *Childhood and society.* New York: W. W. Norton.

Erikson, E. H. (1982). *The life cycle completed.* New York: W. W. Norton.

Erikson, E. H., Erikson, J. M., & Kivnick, H. Q. (1986). *Vital involvement in old age: The experience of old age in our time.* New York: W. W. Norton.

Happe, F. G. H., Winner, E., & Brownell, H. (1998). The getting of wisdom: Theory of mind in old age. *Developmental Psychology, 34*(2), 358–362.

Hashtroudi, S., Johnson, M. K., & Chrosniak, L. D. (1990). Aging and qualitative characteristics of memories for perceived and imagined complex events. *Psychology and Aging, 5*, 119–126.

Holliday, S. G., & Chandler, M. J. (1986). *Wisdom: Explorations in adult competence.* Basel, Switzerland: Karger.

Hollingshead, A. B. (1975). *Four factor index of social issues.* Unpublished manuscript, Yale University, Sociology Department, New Haven, CT.

Hui, H. C., & Yee, C. (1994). The shortened individualism and collectivism scale: Its relationship to demographic and work related variables. *Journal of Research in Personality, 28*, 409–424.

Ide, S., & Takahashi, M. (2002). Everyday meanings of spirituality and religiosity in the U.S. and Japan: A cross-generational comparison. *The Bulletin of Health Science University of Hokkaido, School of Nursing and Social Services*, 107–113.

Jones, A., & Crandall, R. (1986). Validation of a Short Index of Self-Actualization. *Personality and Social Psychology Bulletin, 12*, 63–73.

Katz, J. (1950). *Philosophy of Plotinus.* New York: Appleton Century Crofts.

Kawai, H. (1996). Creativity of living. In K. Oe, H. Kawai, & S. Tanikawa (Eds.), *Nihongoto nihonjinno kokoro* [Japanese language and Japanese mind]. Tokyo: Iwanami.

Kegan, R. (1982). *The evolving self.* Cambridge, MA: Harvard University Press.

Kegan, R. (1994). *In over our heads.* Cambridge, MA: Harvard University Press

Kekes, (1983). Wisdom. *American Philosophical Quarterly, 20*(3), 277–286.

Kitchener, R. F. (1983). Changing conceptions of the philosophy of science and the foundations of developmental psychology. *Human Development, 8*, 1–30.

Kitchener, R. F., & Brenner, H. G. (1990). Wisdom and reflective judgment: Knowing in the face of uncertainty. In R. J. Sternberg (Ed.), *Wisdom: Its nature, origins, and development* (pp. 212–229). New York: Cambridge University Press.

Kramer, D. A. (1990). Conceptualizing wisdom: The primacy of affect–cognition relations. In R. J. Sternberg (Ed.), *Wisdom: Its nature, origins, and development* (pp. 279–316). New York: Cambridge University Press.

Kramer, D. A., Kahlbaugh, P. E., & Goldston, R. B. (1992). A measure of paradigm beliefs about the social world. *Journal of Gerontology, 47*(3), 180–189.

Kwon, Y. (1995). *Wisdom in Korean families: Its development, correlates, and consequences for life adaptation.* Unpublished doctoral dissertation, Cornell University, Ithaca, New York.

Labouvie-Vief, G. (1990). Wisdom as integrated thought: Historical and developmental perspectives. In R. J. Sternberg (Ed.), *Wisdom: Its nature, origins, and development* (pp. 52–86). New York: Cambridge University Press.

Labouvie-Vief, G. (1994). *Psyche and Eros: Mind and gender in the life course.* New York: Cambridge University Press.

Labouvie-Vief, G. (1996) *Knowledge across generations: Wisdom and integration of knowing.* Paper presented at the meeting of the centennial of Jean Piaget's birth, Geneva, Switzerland.

Labouvie-Vief, G., Hakim-Larson, J., DeVoe, M., & Schoeberlein, S. (1989). Emotions and self-regulation: A life-span view. *Human Development, 32*, 279–299.

Labouvie-Vief, G., Schell, D., & Weaverdyck, S. (1982). *Recall deficit in the aged: A fable recalled.* Unpublished manuscript, Wayne State University, Detroit, MI.

Lahey, L., Souvaine, E., Kegan, R., Goodman, R., & Felix, S. (1988). *A guide to the subject-object interview: Its administration and interpretation.* Cambridge, MA: Subject-Object Research Group.

Lerner, R. M. (1984). *On the nature of human plasticity.* Cambridge: Cambridge University Press.

Lerner, R. M. (2004). Liberty: Thriving and civic engagement among America's youth. Thousand Oaks, CA: Sage.

Levitt, H. M. (1999). The development of wisdom: An analysis of Tibetan Buddhist experience. *The Humanistic Psychology, 39*(2), 86–105.

Li, J. (2003). The core of Confucian learning. *American Psychologist, 58*(2), 146–149.

Lichtheim, M. (1973–1980). *Ancient Egyptian literature* (Vols. 1–3). Berkeley: University of California Press.

Maslow, A. H. (1971). *The farther reaches of human nature.* New York: Penguin.

McGinn, B. (Ed.). (1986). *Meister Eckhart: Teacher and preacher.* Mahwah, NJ: Paulist.

Meacham, J. A. (1990). The loss of wisdom. In R. J. Sternberg (Ed.), *Wisdom: Its nature, origins, and development* (pp. 181–211). New York: Cambridge University Press.

Misra, G., Suvasini, C., & Strivastava, A. K. (2000). Psychology of wisdom: Western and Eastern perspectives. *Journal of Indian Psychology, 18*(1–2), 1–32.

Moody, H. R. (1995). Mysticism. In J. W. Ellor, M. A. Kimble, S. H. McFadden, & J. J. Seeber (Eds.), *Handbook on religion, spirituality, and aging* (pp. 87–101). Minneapolis, MN: Fortress Press.

Muller, U., & Overton, W. F. (1998). Action theory of mind and representational theory of mind. Is dialogue possible? *Human Development, 41*, 127–133.

Nietzsche, F. (1968). *The portable Nietzsche* (W. Kaufman, Trans.). New York: Viking.

Nitobe, I. (1993). *Bushi-do.* Tokyo: Mikasa Shobo.

Nisbett, R. (2003). *The geography of thought.* New York: Free Press.

Northrop, F. S. C. (1947). *The meeting of East and West.* New York: Macmillan.

Ohta, K. (1983). *Bukkyouno shinsoushinri* [Depth psychology of Buddhism]. Tokyo: Yuubikaku.

Orwoll, L., & Achenbaum, W. A. (1993). Gender and the development of wisdom. *Human Development, 36*, 276–296.

Orwoll, L., & Perlmutter, M. (1990). The study of wise persons: Integrating a personality perspective. In R. J. Sternberg (Ed.), *Wisdom: Its nature, origins, and development* (pp. 160–180). New York: Cambridge University Press.

Overton, W. F. (1991). Historical and contemporary perspectives on developmental theory and research strategies. In R. Downs, L. Liben, & D. Palermo (Eds.), *Visions of aesthetics, the environment, and development: The legacy of Joachim Wohlwil* (pp. 263–331). Hillsdale, NJ: Erlbaum.

Overton, W. F. (1997). Beyond dichotomy: An embedded active agent for cultural psychology. *Culture and Psychology, 3*, 315–334.

Overton, W. F. (1998). Developmental psychology. Philosophy, concepts and methods. In W. Damon (Series Ed.) & R. M. Lerner (Vol. Ed.), *Handbook of child* *psychology:*Vol. 1. *Theoretical model of human development* (5th ed., pp. 107–188). New York: Wiley.

Overton, W. F. (2002). Understanding, explanation, and reductionism: Finding a cure for Cartesian anxiety. In L. Smith & T. Brown (Eds.), *Reductionism* (pp. 29–51). Mahwah, NJ: Lawrence Erlbaum Associates.

Overton, W. F. (2003). Embodied development: Ending the nativism–empiricism debate. In C. Garcia Coll, R. E. Bearer, & R. Lerner (Eds.), *Nature and nurture: The complex interplay of genetic and environmental influences on human behavior and development* (pp. 203–223). Mahwah, NJ: Lawrence Erlbaum Associates.

Overton, W. F., & Horowitz, H. (1991). Developmental psychology: Differentiations and integrations. In D. Cicchetti & S. Toth (Eds.), *Rochester symposium on developmental psychopathology* (Vol. 3, pp. 1–41). Rochester, NY: University of Rochester Press.

Palmore, E., & Maeda, D. (1985). *The honorable elders revisited.* Durham, NC: Duke University Press.

Paranjpe, A. C. (1984). *Theoretical psychology: The meeting of East and West.* New York: Plenum.

Perlmutter, M., Adams, C., Nyquist, L., & Kaplan, C. (1988). *Beliefs about wisdom.* Unpublished data.

Rad, G. (1972). *Wisdom in Israel.* New York: Abington Press.

Rylaarsdam, J. C., Frederickesen, L., Faherty, R. L., Sarna, N. M., Davis, H. G., Flusser, D., Stendahl, K., Sander, E. T., & Grant, R. M. (Eds.). (1993). Biblical literature. In *The New Encyclopedia Britannica* (Vol. 14, pp. 903–1006). Chicago: Encyclopedia Britannica.

Reeve, C. D. C. (1989). *Socrates in the Apology: An essay on Plato's Apology of Socrates.* Indianapolis, IN: Hackett.

Riegel, K. F. (1973). Dialectic operation: The final period of cognitive development. *Human development, 16,* 346–370.

Robinson, D. N. (1990). Wisdom through the ages. In R. J. Sternberg (Ed.), *Wisdom: Its nature, origins, and development* (pp. 3–12). New York: Cambridge University Press.

Rogers, C. (1959). A theory of therapy, personality, and interpersonal relationships as developed in the client-centered framework. In S. Koch (Ed.), *Psychology: A study of a science: Vol. 3. Formations of the persons and the social context.* New York: McGraw-Hill.

Rohlen, T. P. (1979). The promise of adulthood in Japanese spiritualism. In E. H. Erikson (Ed.), *Adulthood* (pp. 129–147). New York: W. W. Norton.

Sheldon, W. H. (1951). Main contrasts between Eastern and Western philosophy. In C. A. Moore (Ed.), *Essays in East–West philosophy.* Honolulu, Hawaii: University of Hawaii.

Sinnott, J. D. (1998). *The development of logic in adulthood: Postformal thoughts and its applications.* New York: Plenum.

Sinnott, J. D., & Cavanaugh, J. C. (Eds.). (1991). *Bridging paradigms: Positive development in adulthood and cognitive aging.* New York: Praeger.

Smith, J., Dixon, R. A., & Baltes, P. B. (1989). Expertise in life planning: A new research approach to investigating aspects of wisdom. In M. L. Commons,

J. Sinnott, F. A. Richards, & C. Armons (Eds.), *Beyond formal operations II: Comparisons and applications of adolescents and adult development models* (pp. 307–331). New York: Praeger.

Staudinger, U. M. (1989). *The study of life review: An approach to the investigation of intellectual development across the life span* (Vol. 47). Berlin, Germany: Sigma.

Sowarka, D. (1987). *Wisdom in the context of persons, situations, and actions: Commonsense view of elderly women and men.* Unpublished manuscript, Max Planck Institute for Human Development and Education, Federal Republic of Germany.

Sowarka, D. (1989). Weisheit und weise personen: Common-sense-Konzepte alterer menschen. *Zeitschrift fur Entwicklungspsychologie und Padagogische Psychologie, 21,* 87–109.

Sternberg, R. J. (1986). Implicit theories of intelligence, creativity, and wisdom. *Journal of Personality and Social Psychology, 49,* 607–627.

Sternberg, R. J. (1990). Wisdom and its relations to intelligence and creativity. In R. J. Sternberg (Ed.), *Wisdom: Its nature, origins, and development* (pp. 142–159). New York: Cambridge University Press.

Sternberg, R. J. (1998). A balance theory of wisdom. *A Review of General Psychology, 2,* 347–365.

Suzuki, D. T. (1959). *Zen and Japanese culture.* Princeton, NJ: Princeton University Press.

Takahashi, M. (2000). Toward a culturally inclusive understanding of wisdom: Historical roots in the East and West. *International Journal of Aging and Human Development, 51*(3), 217–230.

Takahashi, M., & Bordia, P. (2000). The concept of wisdom: A cross-cultural comparison. *International Journal of Psychology, 35*(1), 1–9.

Takahashi, M., & Ide, S. (2003a). Implicit theories of spirituality across three generations: A cross-cultural comparison in the U.S. and Japan. *Journal of Religious Gerontology, 15*(4),15–38.

Takahashi, M. & Ide, S. (2003b). *Wisdom of famous people.* Unpublished manuscript, Northeastern Illinois University, Chicago, IL.

Takahashi, M., & Overton, W. F. (2002). Wisdom: A culturally inclusive developmental perspective. *International Journal of Behavioral Development, 26,* 267–277.

Takayama, M. (2002). *The concept of wisdom and wise people in Japan.* Unpublished doctoral dissertation, Tokyo University, Japan.

Valdez, J. M. (1994). *Wisdom: A Hispanic perspective.* Unpublished doctoral dissertation, Fort Collins, Colorado State University.

Vandenberg, B. (1991). Is epistemology enough?: An existential consideration of development. *American Psychologists, 46*(12), 1278–1286.

Wink, P., & Helson, R. (1997). Practical and transcendent wisdom: Their nature and some longitudinal findings. *Journal of Adult Development, 4,* 1–16.

Wood, J. (1967). *Wisdom literature: An introduction.* London: Duckworth.

Woodruff-Pak, D. S. (1989). Aging and intelligence: Changing perspectives in the twentieth century. *Journal of Aging Studies, 3*(2), 91–118.

Yalom, I. D. (1980). *Existential Psychotherapy.* New York: Basic Books.

Yang, S. (2001). Conceptions of wisdom among Taiwanese Chinese. *The Journal of Cross-Cultural Psychology, 32*(6), 662–680.

Yang, S., & Sternberg, R. J. (1997). Taiwanese Chinese people's conceptions of intelligence. *Intelligence, 25*(1), 21–36.

Yogananda, P. (1946). *The autobiography of a yogi.* Los Angeles: Self Realization Fellowship.

Zelazo, P. D. (1999). Language, levels of consciousness, and the development of intentional action. In P. D. Zelazo, J. W. Astington, & D. R. Olson (Eds.), *Development theories of intention: Social understanding and self-control* (pp. 95–115). Mahwah, NJ: Lawrence Erlbaum Associates.

3

Philosophical Theories of Wisdom

Lisa M. Osbeck and Daniel N. Robinson

A Cautionary Preface

To take up the topic of wisdom in any philosophical sense we are obliged, first, to consider what has become of it. In the Routledge *Encyclopedia of Philosophy's* entry for "wisdom," Nicolas Smith notes that "It is interesting to ask how the concept of wisdom has come to vanish entirely from the philosophical map" (1998). Few concepts have greater seeming density and significance; nonetheless, there are few concepts toward which contemporary philosophers show greater reticence. Unless within the rather removed context of the history of ideas, wisdom generally is not in the set of principal or even legitimate philosophical concerns. The recent practices and objectives of most academic philosophers, that is, rarely include reflective analysis on concepts of wisdom and their implications, much less the goal of pursuing wisdom, however this is understood.

It was not always so, of course. Well known to any introductory philosophy student is the etymological root of philosophy as the love (*philia*) of wisdom (*sophia* – the highest form of wisdom). Conway (2000), uncommon in his explicit interest in the concept of wisdom as a philosophical problem, acknowledges the discrepancy between the original and contemporary concerns of philosophy as follows:

> Few present day philosophers, however, seem to have much idea of, or to be concerned with that which philosophers supposedly loved and were seeking to acquire by engaging in the subject ... what wisdom is and what its supposed attractions were for the original lovers. (2000, p. 16)

Of course, many interwoven explanations might be offered for the turn away from wisdom as the end and aim of philosophy, which would be akin to explaining the changes in philosophy itself and the world(s) in which philosophy is practiced. This is not the purpose here. We might only note, rather obviously, that questions explicitly tied to what is ultimately real or true have fallen out of favor in the circles of serious academic inquiry, and it is just these sorts of questions that are inevitably bound to conceptions of wisdom. The controlling maxim might be, "No accessible reality, no wisdom!" Put another way, ascriptions of wisdom presuppose the bearers to enjoy an epistemologically or morally privileged position. Such a position itself presupposes a settled, noncontextual body of truths and imperatives. Once this comes to be regarded as mistaken, even chimerical, wisdom itself can rise no higher than a local achievement on par with any other.

There are recent and interesting attempts to ground epistemology in "the real world" of perception of natural kinds (e.g. Prinz, 2002). However, the discussion here is focused on the neural mechanisms grounding and sustaining our conceptual structures. The putative existence of such kinds and, particularly, how our access to them might bear on the moral and psychological realms remains to be explained. Indeed, the thesis of real-world access itself remains controversial.

Beyond the laboratory and the seminar room, wisdom remains a compelling notion. So, too, do questions concerning the nature of reality and the meaning and purpose of human existence, those questions that originally launched and powered philosophical dialogue. Moreover, concepts and beliefs related to wisdom are tied historically to vital pragmatic ends, to the pursuit of a reliable basis for judgment. The early dialogues of Plato, for example, are rooted in an understanding that denying human access to knowledge of "the real" and enduring would lead to a merely conventional grounding for law and conduct. The search for epistemic access to what is invariable and noncontingent reflects awareness that any attempt to establish and justify a state of ordered liberty on grounds firmer than those of habit presupposes the reality of invariable precepts and the possibility, at least, of rational beings discovering them.

Ancient debates between foundationalists and their skeptical critics are echoed in contemporary disagreements over the extent to which our knowledge is constructed through cultural and discursive conventions or is reflective of invariant realities in the natural world of which we are a part. Bound up with this are questions as to just what constitutes the realm of the "natural."

At issue here are matters of critical concern, for two radically different worlds are envisaged by participants in this long debate. Just in case there is an *essential* human nature, able to be corrupted or refined by the larger cultural and civic dimensions of life, the task and very sign of "wisdom" is the identification of those foundational principles on which the right sort of life is to be based. On the contrary, just in case "wisdom" is but a code word for local, situated, contextually bounded agreements and conventions needed to preserve the physical and social integrity of a given community, the entire project of philosophy as originally conceived would be jejune.

As there is little in contemporary philosophy to guide a systematic inquiry into the nature of wisdom, the task is daunting. It is all the more daunting in that it invites an unwitting begging of the central question. The very concept of "wisdom" is a foundational concept akin to "rationality" or "physicality" or "the good." As such, it is easier to illustrate than define, but each candidate illustration can be challenged as question-begging. Of course, criticism here cuts both ways. To challenge a foundationalist argument for "wisdom" by citing cultural variations also begs the question by assuming that conventionalism is self-validating.

What, then, of the total skeptic in such matters? Consider the principles of normal physiology. The foundationalist argues that these cannot be refuted by evidence of pathological processes, for absent such principles, there can be no means of identifying pathology. To the total skeptic who insists that this is question-begging and who then argues that, indeed, there *isn't* real pathology – only processes so judged within a given culture and context – there can be no serious reply. At the outset, then, we must be clear as to the plan and purpose of this chapter. We have no reply to the total skeptic regarding wisdom. If, in taking counsel with the wise, we beg the question itself, our defense must itself be foundational; to wit: All inquiry requires a starting point. The ancient mathematicians referred to those *common notions* on which any and every mathematical system must depend. So, too, with "wisdom." Human history, as well as biography, brought into sharper focus by the tools of philosophical analysis, must be the evidentiary grounding of the concept of "wisdom." We take it further that questions calling for wisdom arise in different contexts – personal, interpersonal, broadly social, cultural, civic, aesthetic, moral – in a way that questions calling for mathematics or for observation or for consensus arise in different contexts. Notwithstanding the many types and limitless tokens, however, there are (we shall argue) wise and less wise and unwise approaches and answers to the questions that continue to haunt and inspire across millennia.

In the interest of economy we must limit our inquiry to two distinct but related sets of questions. First, in keeping with the tradition of "mapping" conceptual territory before exploring it, we consider the ways in which wisdom was originally understood and its relation to emerging schools of philosophy. Included here are reflections on the forms of wisdom recognized by ancient philosophers, how they come to be possessed, how they are recognized, and how they relate to such goods as truth, virtue, morality, knowledge, intelligence, success, and achievement.

The second set of questions focuses sharply on concepts of intuition, for it is within the school of intuitionism that distinctions are most sharply drawn between wisdom and intelligence, knowledge, rationality, experience, and so on. "Intuitively" is a frequent answer to the question of how one becomes wise. To refer to something as possessed "intuitively" is, however, not to provide an explanation but to set the stage for one. It is necessary then to examine the conditions, and the cognitive faculties favoring the appearance of wisdom, as well as the range or class of problems over which it is then effectively applied. Specifically omitted in this chapter are considerations of wisdom as "revealed"; that is, wisdom as construed in some religious traditions.

Wisdom from Homer to Aristotle: The Greek Way

It is commonplace to contrast philosophy before and after Socrates in terms of a cosmocentric (oriented toward an understanding of the origin and nature of the universe) and anthropocentric (directed at man himself) focus. But the deeper expressions of thought in the ancient Greek world were always directed toward the human condition, as much in the Homeric epics and in Hesiod's *Works and Days* as later in the tragic works of Aeschylus, Euripedes, and Sophocles.

The themes that came to dominate reflection in the philosophic age of Greece were firmly established in the *Iliad* and the *Odyssey*. It is within these works that the contours of character are drawn, thereupon leading the reader to comprehend and even predict how the actor is likely to behave under a wide range of conditions. Indeed, the first lines of the *Iliad* announce the motive that impels the action and threatens the outcome: *anger*. It is in the triumph of emotion over reason, of passion over prudence, that destruction is wrought and once flourishing communities are reduced to ruin. As Homer's songs continue, one meets a truly "representative" array of human types, their defining strengths and foibles instructively revealed. Consider the radiantly beautiful Helen whose every utterance is self-referential. Consider prideful Achilles, at first eager to visit defeat on his own countrymen owing to his peevish indignation, and then this same anger driving him to deeds of legendary heroism as he sets out to avenge the death of his dearest friend.

Old Nestor is presented by Homer as the wise counselor, but the presentation is nearly a parody of wisdom. In Book I of the *Iliad*, his sagacity takes the form of a peevish backlash against disrespect: "In my time I have dealt with better men than you are, and never once did they disregard me ... these listened to the counsels I gave and heeded my bidding ... " (Bk. I, ll. 560–573). The authentic form is personified in the Olympians, chiefly Athena, who in her various manifestations guides her chosen heroes toward the right course of action. It is useful to recall that the Greek word for justice, δικη, initially referred to a bifurcating path, the right path being that which the gods ordained. Common across this literature is the understanding that wisdom is more a gift than an achievement, and often one recognized too late.

The language of the ancient Greeks clearly distinguishes wisdom from knowledge, σοπηια from επιστημη. No degree of scientific comprehension or detailed factual accounts will, in and of themselves, rise to the level of wisdom. Rather, it is the person who has that practical intelligence (φρονησις) needed for prudence and proper conduct who is able to rise to the level of comprehension that warrants the term "wisdom." What the word σοπηια is intended to reach is the combination of virtue and the most refined intelligence, neither of which refers to bookish knowledge or mere intellectual agility. As Socrates notes, one will often see "the narrow intelligence flashing from the keen eye of a clever rogue" (*Republic*, 519). This must never be mistaken for wisdom. Indeed, Socrates is so grudging in this regard as to reserve the term "wise" for the gods, saying of the greatest of men only that they are "lovers of wisdom or philosophers" (*Phaedrus*, 278). And, although habits of virtue can be acquired, wisdom itself is innate. It "contains a divine element" stable across time and circumstance (*Republic*, 519).

In the works of Aristotle wisdom becomes more precisely aligned with rationality itself and with those virtuous habits that finally ground all significant actions in the rule of reason. Among other considerations, the wise person is one in whom the rational principle (λογον εχων) rules, and the irrational (αλογος) obeys (*Eudemian Ethics*, 1219b). The ultimate goal of action is happiness in the sense of flourishing (ενδαιμονια). Plato had taught that only the wise are truly happy in this sense. Aristotle, here faithful to his teacher, analyzes this more closely, concluding that such happiness is in the form of "activity in accordance with . . . the highest virtue," this being the rule of reason itself (*Ethics*, 1177a). In this same place, he speculates that this very element is either divine or is at least the most divine feature of humanity.

Against the background of Aristotle's theory of the basic virtues, this elevated standing of the rule of reason becomes vivid. Aristotle is not merely echoing the well-known claim of the *Academy* to the effect that there is a divine element within human beings. He is also endorsing the conclusion reached by Plato regarding the transcendental nature of wisdom itself, thus understood. A closer review of his position is useful, for no one before Aristotle, and arguably not many after him, offered so systematic and broadly inclusive an account of the factors that enter into an understanding of what constitutes the wise person.

Aristotle on Wisdom

Dante's "Master of those who know" has had such an authoritative position in both historical and current discussions of politics, ethics, and moral philosophy that he earns a central place in any consideration of "wisdom." Accordingly, this longest section of the chapter is reserved for a review of "Aristotelian" conceptions of the good life, the grounding of knowledge, the standards of truth and proof, and similar notions.

In several places, but centrally in Book VI of his *Nichomachean Ethics*, Aristotle classifies those intellectual powers that would be the grounding of "wisdom" in its various manifestations. The most general distinction of the powers or faculties of the soul is that between the rational and the irrational. The rational powers require still further analysis and Aristotle argues that two distinct operations or powers can be subsumed under rationality, the *scientific* (επιστημονικον) and the calculative (λογιστικον). Note that "scientific" (as given in the translation of επιστημονικον) refers to those necessary truths arising from what are taken to be the fixed laws of nature. Thus, to have a "scientific" comprehension of anything is, among other considerations, to know the invariant relationships of which the event in question is exemplary.

The means by which the truth or the "reality" (αλητηειας) of a situation is apprehended are sensation, intellect, and desire. The first of these does not initiate that class of actions marked by deliberated choice (προαιρηεσις). Rather, such actions are the product at once of intellect and desire, where the right choice depends on the right desire. This leads directly to Aristotle's conclusion that choice reflects character (ηθος) in the sense of character as a settled disposition. Considering further that for Aristotle character itself is the result of both innate and acquired dispositions, shaped over the course of a lifetime and, to a considerable degree, dependent on the manner in which one actually chooses to live one's life, it becomes clear that a very organic and complicated theory of "wisdom" is advanced here.

In this same context, Aristotle distinguishes five conditions ("states") by which truth is obtained: art, scientific knowledge, practical wisdom (*phronesis*), philosophic wisdom (*sophia*), intuitive reason. As a set these are distinguished from mere judgment and opinion by the possibility of error and mistake that pervade the latter. Although treated separately for the sake of analysis, the rational aspect of mind ("the rational soul") is common to all states through which truth might be obtained. This aspect in turn is the basis of the possibility of wisdom.

A primary distinction between forms of wisdom stems from parts or functions distinguished within the rational soul itself, as noted earlier. Aristotle calls practical wisdom "a reasoned and true state of capacity to act with regard to human goods" (*Ethics* VI, 5). He notes that society bestows the attribution of practical wisdom on those who display momentous accomplishments in civic leadership (e.g., Pericles) as well as those who are particularly adept in the management of smaller social units such as households. Both entail judgments about actions: "what is to be done" (*Ethics* VI, 5). Political savvy is not to be equated with practical wisdom, however.

Although Aristotle occasionally refers to political art *or* practical wisdom (e.g., *Ethics* VI, 7), as though these were interchangeable, practical wisdom is said to be different from political wisdom "in essence," and this must be borne in mind (*Ethics* VI, 8). The attribution of practical wisdom is particularly reserved for application of knowledge toward the engendering of moral virtue, toward ends that encourage human flourishing (whether in relation to one's own life or to human life more generally), in accordance with a rational understanding of human nature. However, because Aristotle elsewhere equates practical wisdom with political wisdom "in state of mind," it is important to consider the ways in which these are alike to distinguish them from forms of wisdom that differ in terms of the rational faculty employed in the attainment and execution of wisdom. One interpretation might be that political wisdom is a subtype of practical wisdom, or that political wisdom becomes practical wisdom only when employed correctly, that is, toward virtuous ends.

Importantly, then, whether in relation to state leadership (e.g., Pericles), household management, conducting one's own life in accordance with moral virtue, or promoting the general betterment of humankind, wise discrimination of appropriate action is accomplished through deliberation or calculation, one part of the more general category of rational power or rational soul with which we are naturally endowed (although to different degrees).

Deliberation is a particular mode of rational thought that seems to be equated with judgment or inference. Through deliberation some persons are led to an understanding of what will facilitate desirable consequences in their own lives. From such understanding they are led to reflect on and understand the kinds of activity facilitative of the good life for humankind. Powers of deliberation, then, are themselves marks of practical wisdom when employed in the service of sound judgment. Importantly, however, Aristotle acknowledges that deliberation is an activity associated only with what is *variable*. Thus, if one is schooled in geometry and informed of its universal principles, one will not "deliberate" over, for example, the Pythagorean Theorem. Deliberation is engaged by alternatives, the choice depending on desire and on those intellectual powers that ground inferences and deductions. The need to choose arises in those variable circumstances for which "practical reason" is required. Thus, the contemplation of variable things is the function of practical wisdom, distinguishing it from other intellectual operations.

What might variable things include? Variable, we suggest, may be understood in three distinct but overlapping ways. First, the relation of practical wisdom to political action and civic governance suggests that the contingent states of human affairs, occurrences associated with particular circumstances and groups of people, are the objects of contemplation here. The wisdom of Pericles is demonstrated in relation to the conditions of a specific time and place, conditions that are capable of being otherwise. It is for this reason that the young, though expert in mathematics and kindred branches of knowledge, are not known for prudence (φρονιμος), which is what is required in adjusting to new and particular circumstances.

The specific actions that facilitate harmony, subsistence, security, and cultural flourishing in Athens will differ from the specific requirements for Rome, and these from New York. Similarly, sound action relating to the management of a household depends upon the specific composition and circumstances (e.g., age, health, disposition, financial circumstances) of the household's occupants. Practical wisdom is concerned with what is the best course of action in each case, in each situation, in accordance with this nature. In contemporary parlance, practical wisdom is inherently relational in this sense.

Importantly, however, underlying the variation in what is good for Athens and New York are consistent rational principles from which the particularities of action are worked out in relation to the group and set of circumstances at hand. Therefore, variable (as in contemplation of variant objects) should not be read as "arbitrary." Constraints are imposed by the world's real natures, including the nature of humankind. Abiding principles facilitate the good life on which sound decisions are based; these are determined by the essential and unchanging nature of man. However, what is conducive to good and healthful living is dependent on the sort of thing one is – "what is good or healthy is different for men and fishes" (*Ethics* VI, 7). This, then, represents a second sense of variable in relation to practical wisdom. This variation in what is good across kind or species renders ethical matters different in kind than, for example, the invariant relationships of mathematical axioms. Thus, for this reason, also practical wisdom is differentiated from wisdom that has *in*variants as its objects of contemplation.

A third sense in which practical wisdom concerns what is variable is in its relation to human will, choice, or agency. Although Aristotle gives even animals credit for a manner of practical wisdom in that they demonstrate action facilitative of their own and their offsprings' survival (i.e., what is "good" for their form of life) (*Ethics* VI, 7, 1141a), animals do not engage in action that is subject to judgments concerning its moral or ethical status. To qualify as moral or ethical every action must involve some degree of *choice* on the part of the actor. If actions are automatic and invariant, governed solely by natural forces and not the desire and intent of an actor, there are no grounds on which to consider the actions worthy of praise or blame. (For detailed discussion of this matter see Robinson, 2002.) The element of choice also, then, makes human action inherently variable in the sense of being the sort of thing not governed by necessity.

If wisdom is understood as deliberation over what is variable, or as the application of knowledge through sound judgment to the contingencies of human affairs, one may then ask just who it is who has such practical wisdom and under what conditions is it reached?

There appear to be two requirements for practical wisdom. First, this form of wisdom, fostered as it is by familiarity with the consequences of particular actions in relation to an array of circumstances, is a state achieved through actual experience in the world of human affairs. This is consistent, of course, with what we might take as common sense. Unseasoned persons rarely make sound judges or effective or reliable leaders. Experience teaches us the consequences of actions, and modifies actions undertaken in relation to novel or changing events. Eventually, strongly ingrained habits conducive to the good life arise from courses of action repeatedly undertaken. From this state wise choices appear to emerge more automatically or with less deliberative effort. One is not born wise!

However, neither does experience alone give knowledge or understanding. In fact, Aristotle considers knowledge and understanding reflective of "art" more than experience. Because art consists in "knowledge of how to make things" (*Ethics* VI), the "making" here implies the making of human life, implying purposeful effort in directing choices toward the development of character in accordance with knowledge of what is good. "A man should have practical wisdom," Aristotle notes, "for the sake of becoming good" (*Ethics* VI, 12). Experience may influence and shape, but purposeful self-direction toward the good life is not implied or required by experience alone. Many are experienced but unwise.

What is required for *phronesis* is the ability to reflect deliberately and carefully about choices in relation to knowledge of human nature. The powers of judgment or rational deliberation on which this requirement hinges do appear to be more naturally developed in certain persons. Thus, the propensity for practical wisdom is at least in part a matter of native endowment, just as is any talent or particular ability. For Aristotle, such rational powers incline one more readily to reach right conclusions concerning the nature of man and the courses of action engendering of human health and happiness. This native endowment, however, does not undermine the potential for rational powers to increase in strength with sustained execution or practice.

Scientific Knowledge

Because a primary division is drawn between the aspect of rationality involved in practical wisdom and that involved in scientific knowledge, this would seem to imply that scientific knowledge is philosophical wisdom, as, unlike practical wisdom, both concern what is *in*variant. However, Aristotle distinguishes scientific knowledge itself (*episteme*) from philosophic wisdom (*sophia*). Although puzzling in this context, such a distinction is also consistent with common sense or lay views (and with many religious texts, e.g., Ecclesiastes), for few would consider the accumulation of scientific knowledge identical to wisdom. A distinction between scientific knowledge and scientific wisdom is, in fact, the subject of an interesting essay by the molecular biologist Robert Pollack (1999), wherein he argues that wisdom inheres in the sound application, not the discovery or collection of scientific fact, and that sound application is that which facilitates the betterment of human kind. Yet, in stressing application of science in the service of human good, the form of wisdom implied by Pollack's distinction is, as we have seen, that of practical wisdom only.

What, then, is the distinction between scientific knowledge and theoretical wisdom? This is clarified by examining Aristotle's conception of science itself. The immediate focus of scientific knowledge is the observation of existing things in the sensible world, but the end and purpose of this observation is knowledge of what is invariant – what is impervious to changes over time or in a particular "situated" human standpoint, namely, universals and lawful relationships (first principles) governing their functioning. Induction based on observation (sensory experience) paves the way to the discovery of relationships through identification of similarities between observations, but the necessity of any relationship between observed particulars is ascertained through demonstration. By demonstration Aristotle refers to "a scientific deduction . . . one in virtue of which, by having it, we understand something" (*Post. Anal.*, 70b16–19).

Demonstration leading to understanding is accomplished through the syllogism, the point of which is to make clear that some conclusion follows by necessity from something assumed previously. Understanding carries an assumption that "it is not possible for this to be otherwise" (*Post. Anal.*, 70b10–12). The minor premise contains some observed fact, the major premise a statement concerning a universal truth, in the form: "If all men are rational (major premise), and Smith is a man (minor premise), then Smith is rational" (conclusion). The relationship between the premises from which the conclusion (understanding) is drawn *must* hold because the relationship accords with the inherent rules or logical structure of mind itself. The conclusion is necessary for the very reason that we are unable to make sense of (unable to "process" we might say today) any other. Through this means of demonstration, observed facts are transformed to scientific knowledge, on the assumption that knowledge entails necessity.

What, however, establishes the truth of the major premise? It is well known that the formal (logical) necessity of the syllogism makes possible the attainment of false conclusions if the major premise is itself false. The truth of the major premise in a syllogism, from which the conclusion is forced by logical necessity, is itself not the product of logical but of *natural* necessity. The truth of the major premise is a function of the *existence* and *essence* of what is signified by its terms. We are told that understanding (through demonstration) depends on "things which are true and primitive and immediate and more familiar than and prior to and explanatory of the conclusion" (*Post. Anal.*, 70a28–30). Existing things, to Aristotle, are clearly prior to our knowledge of them, where "prior" has to do with "that which is in some way the cause of the other's existence." Things precede concepts, then, and cause them. Aristotle notes: "Whereas the true statement is in no way the cause of the actual thing's existence, the actual thing does seem in some way the cause of the statement's being true: it is because the actual thing exists or does not that the statement is called true or false" (*Categories*, 14b20–23). The fact that our thinking is structured by the law of contradiction, for example, must reflect that "contradictories cannot belong to the same *thing* at the same time" (*Metaphysics*, 1011b16).

But how could the formal arrangement, the logical structure of our thought, be in harmony with the things of the world if the things themselves are ephemeral, transitory, variable? Flowers, oceans, clouds, and every animal (including ourselves) undergo continuous changes, such that the enduring nature of any thing is impossible to ascertain from its appearance alone. Here it is important to remember that essence is more than and different from mere appearances. Essence is tied to the particular end or purpose of an existing thing and for all things of its kind: its identifying *function*. Certain necessities pertain such that, given what *kind* something is, its function and relation to other sorts of things could not be otherwise without its then being a different kind of thing altogether. Because to lose what is essential is to cease to exist, essence by *necessity* does not alter. Essence is "necessary in nature" (*Physics*, 200a32).

For demonstration that yields knowledge, true conclusion, or genuine understanding, the truth of the major premise is self-evident because it is reflective of real kinds, of essences, and of real relationships between existing things. Self-evident principles prevent demonstration from falling into an infinite regress since they cannot be proved by reference to any prior principle or principles. They cannot, that is, be demonstrated, and thus they are not the objects of scientific knowledge. The nature of the self-evident, that which does not require demonstration to be taken as true, is tied to the notion of first principles for Aristotle. Aristotle clarifies that "the first principle from which what is scientifically known follows cannot be an object of scientific knowledge, of art, or of practical wisdom" (*Ethics* VI, 6). Aristotle calls first principles "immediate propositions," in which "an immediate proposition is one to which there is no other prior" (*Post. Anal.*, 72a7–9).

Theoretical Wisdom (Sophia)

Aristotle's distinction between *episteme* and *sophia* reflects the peculiar nature of first principles that renders demonstration and hence scientific knowledge possible. These principles are the originative source of scientific knowledge and the only kind of knowledge that is "more precise" than it (*Post. Anal.*, 100b9). Because of the dependence of scientific knowledge on first principles, Aristotle tells us that all science starts from what is already known (*Ethics* VI, 6).

Despite their formative role in all demonstration (and hence all scientific knowledge), first principles do not belong to a particular science but are common to all sciences. Thus, they constitute a science unto themselves, a science on which all the sciences are dependent (including those applicable to man) but that itself depends on no other sciences. This independent science has been termed "metaphysics" (coined by early translators who noted that this was the work to which Aristotle referred as coming after his examination of natural science. Thus, "after natural science" becomes μετα τα φνσικα).

Knowledge of first principles, then, understood as knowledge of the causal structure of the world, is the object of *sophia* and by extension, the original concern of philosophy. That knowledge of metaphysics or first principles, which is, effectively, *sophia* itself, is considered not only more general but also higher or greater than knowledge belonging to any particular science is evident in Aristotle's identification of philosophic wisdom as the "most finished" form of knowledge (*Ethics* VI, 6), "the superior part of us" (*Ethics* VI, 13), concerned with what is "highest by nature" (*Ethics* VI, 7). Notwithstanding the role of first principles in scientific demonstration, the goal of *sophia* itself is knowledge for its own sake: reflection on what is ultimately real is the activity or accomplishment or end equated with the wisdom in its highest form. In just the sense that what is ultimately real, prior, and causative may be considered in some way "divine," *sophia* bears resemblance to the wisdom of the Judeo-Christian tradition (e.g., Ecclesiastes) wherein wisdom is equated with knowledge of the creator. Moreover, although *sophia* fosters practical wisdom (through understanding of human nature and its ends), *sophia* itself requires no concern for application to human action. The value of *sophia* is inherent.

Points of correspondence adhere between Platonism and what one finds in the Hebrew prophets, not the least being the conviction that ultimate reality transcends the level of the sensible. Hebrew and Greek texts display remarkable similarities on the point of wisdom as the highest, deepest, and most worthy of pursuits. It is not a coincidence that in both the Platonic and biblical traditions "wisdom" and "justice" are equated, both proceeding from a pious devotion to all that is good. The same rationale had much to do with the tendency of the Christian fathers (notably Tertullian) to find in Plato something of a bridge that the Christian might use to journey back to an otherwise irrelevant pagan past. Tertullian's famous "What has Jerusalem to say to Athens" recorded the general view that the Christian now possessed in valid form the very "wisdom" that pagan philosophers pursued with such futility. Thus did Aristotelian thought, with the exception of the valiant scholarship of Boethius in the sixth century, recede from the Western centers of philosophical activity until the thirteenth century.

Stoicism

Despite the unparalleled influence of Plato and Aristotle on later thought, challenges to the idea that we can have certain knowledge through intellectual access to the world's real nature have rarely been far removed from epistemological debate. The first written expressions of such challenges are given by Skeptics, who attempted to discredit the foundational status of any claims and the notion of self-evident truth itself, on which a notion of wisdom ultimately is incumbent. Although there is some indication that Skeptics accepted the logical necessity of certain propositions, they rejected the notion that this necessity is in any way informative about the world itself or a suitable foundation for knowledge (Long, 1986).

In their rebuttals of skeptical assertions, Stoic philosophers reify the solid grounding of knowledge and secure a framework for wisdom. Their infusion of the universe itself with a rational principle (*logos*) dynamically flowing between man and world allows Zeno of Cittium and his followers to oppose spirit–matter dualisms they regard as problematic in Plato and to a lesser extent, Aristotle. This universal rationality and its resonance in the structure of psyche enables, too, Stoic commitment to a view of mind at birth as *tabula rasa*, the world itself giving rise to concepts which then find expression in language (*Stoicorum Veterum Fragmenta* = *SVF* II 83). Through these commitments Stoics made considerable contributions to logic, building on and complementing Aristotle's accomplishments therein.

The Stoic emphasis on the global rational order leads them to interpretations of virtue and wisdom that differ subtly and interestingly from those of Aristotle. Since the standard by which one is to live is a universal or cosmic standard, there is no local citizenship or polis to which one is beholden (e.g., see MacIntyre, 1984). Moreover, the rational is valued to such an extent that emotions and emotional investment come to be regarded as an infective, dangerous nuisance to be suppressed. The idea of suppression the Stoics envisioned differs meaningfully from Aristotle's more moderate view of prudent governance by the rational faculty toward the middle of emotional extremes. Aristotle, far from disparaging emotions out of hand, understands them as entirely natural and capable of direction toward appropriate and virtuous ends.

Intuition and Wisdom

We have thus far outlined various forms of wisdom and indicated, where possible, conditions through which it is sought or acquired. We turn now to a closer examination of the rational faculties themselves that enable the apprehension of first principles that encompasses *sophia* and enables *phronesis* and *episteme*.

Aristotle tells us that the principles underlying scientific knowledge are known not by demonstration and not by induction; it is also plain that these principles are not gained through deliberation. The question, then, is just how knowledge of first principles is acquired, the cognitive faculties that enable it and the conditions under which *sophia* (and by extension *episteme* and *phronesis*) is made possible. In other words, what establishes our access to what is real and invariant?

Insight into this matter is facilitated by considering that Aristotle identifies philosophic wisdom as "the union" of science with what is translated as "intuitive reason" (e.g., Aristotle, 1998, as translated by Ross). This is exceedingly important and worthy of considerable explication. The word "intuitive" is currently bandied about so cavalierly and in relation to so many disparate phenomena that it is easy to lose sight of the original epistemic heft and specificity of this concept (and those analogous).

The founding systems of Western philosophy (Plato, Aristotle, Stoic epistemology) and what are arguably the most influential systems to build on or revise these (e.g., Descartes, Locke, Kant) all distinguish a special form or mode of apprehension that is *direct* or *immediate* from forms or modes that are indirect, that follow from and are grounded in what is known directly. St. Anselm first uses the term *intuitus* to designate knowledge not arising or following from any previous knowledge or speculation (e.g., Peirce, 1868). Notions in the work of earlier scholars conveying a similar sense of directness are thus frequently translated as "intuition" or "intuitive" (see, for example, O'Connor, 1964; Irwin, 1988).

If the meaning of direct apprehension or knowledge is not immediately obvious, clarification is added by considering how the term "direct" is employed in nonphilosophical contexts. To claim that a package will be delivered directly is to indicate that it will not be detained or delayed, perhaps that there will be no intermediate stops or deliveries. A message directly communicated is one not clouded by hints or tangential asides. Similarly, direct knowledge is traditionally understood as that which is "given" to consciousness or understanding without any mediating steps, without any intervening idea or representation (hence *im*mediately). It is thus the most evident (i.e., "self-evident") form of apprehension; the least obscured.

Because Descartes' *Rules for the Direction of the Mind* (1628) is the first comprehensive analysis of the special faculty of direct knowing termed intuition, particular reference will be made to this work before returning to the analogous notion in Aristotle and earlier accounts.

Descartes equates intuition with "clear and distinct perception," a very particular act and function of the mind, occurring when we direct attention toward thought objects that are *simple*, *clear*, and *distinct*. Although the nuances of each of these terms is debated by Cartesean scholars, a prominent interpretation is that "simple" here implies that these are ideas discovered wholly and completely, and thus incapable of further analysis or definition. "Clear" means ideas experienced vividly and convincingly, so convincingly that one cannot or does not doubt them. When clear, no aspect is "hidden" from understanding; thus, a clear idea is one that the intellect recognizes as something that is the case necessarily. Distinct ideas are those not contaminated or clouded with other ideas. The objects of mathematics are exemplary here because of their purity, meaning that they are not obscured by the perspective of any perceiver. They presuppose nothing dependent on experience and require no confirmation or elaboration. (See, for example, Joachim, 1998, for commentary on this work.)

Despite the stipulation of separate laws governing physical and mental realms, for which reason Descartes is too often and too facilely dismissed as a naive dualist, the contents of mind (its objects or ideas) are furnished in part by the intuitive grasp of material natures. Clear ideas that are "purely intellectual" (*Regulae* XII, 419) would be propositions of which the logical necessity is grasped (e.g., the meaning of the terms contained in the premises), but clear ideas of the "purely material" (*Regulae* XII, 419) grasp the necessity arising from the definitive nature of the object. Full appreciation of this text and of the role of intuition outlined here requires a careful treatment of what was understood by "idea," which is beyond the scope of this chapter. However, it bears stressing that by means of this kind of intuition we are able to navigate through our worlds by understanding that natural objects endure despite changes in condition and appearance (e.g., wax held by fire). Thus intuition is a capacity at once so ordinary that it grounds our action and adaptation, and is the basis of our most developed and "highest levels" of knowledge.

For Descartes, the clarity associated with intuition is enabled by the mind's "natural light," the intrinsic power of intellect in terms of which the possibility of knowledge is grounded. In later work, for example, intuition is the basis of the *cogito*, it grounds the certainty of deductive conclusions, and it is the cornerstone of Descartes' critical "method" for evaluating the possibilities and limitations of scientific knowledge (See Descartes, *Discourse on Method*; *Meditations*). Importantly, Descartes considers intuition the under girding of a wise and ethical life; he implores man to "increase the natural light of his reason . . . in order that the intellect should show his will what decision it ought to make in each of life's contingencies" (*Regulae* I, 361). The legacy of this stipulation of clear, distinct, and simple ideas is evident in later intuitionist theories of ethics, in which "the good" is portrayed as a "simple" notion recognized immediately when perceived (e.g., Moore, 1903/1968).

The simple, clear, and distinct objects of intuition are portrayed as passively recognized by the intellect in a manner analogous to the eye's reception of objects in the visual field. Descartes' use of the Latin verb "*intueri*," translates "to look into," or simply, "to look to," and connects his notion of intuition to a similar metaphor employed by earlier scholars, notably Plato, Aristotle, and Augustine in relation, as noted, to direct apprehension of this kind.

Returning to the ancient sources of Descartes' vision metaphor, for Plato as for Pythagoras, the special power of reason itself by which the world's invariant generalities can be discovered is grounded in an irreducible insight that is at once wholly natural and profoundly "spiritual"; this is the base and essence of reason itself. Reichenbach (1973), commenting on Pythagoras and the role of this power in the search for certainty, identifies the epistemic grounding of this tradition as "acts of supersensuous vision" (p. 33). The power of intuition is such that, as with vision, there is an effortless recognition of such a convincing nature that intuitions (the products of intuitive knowledge) impose themselves immediately on the intellect; they are understood and accepted as true without justification as soon as encountered (reflected on, recognized). For Pythagoras, as for Descartes, this is the hallmark of the mathematical axiom, but the very possibility of such clear apprehension convinces Plato of its application to other (e.g., ethical) truths. He depicts Socrates linking this special power to "the eye of my soul," which "might be blinded altogether if I looked at things with my eyes or tried to apprehend them by the help of the senses" (*Phaedo*, 99). This soul eye is responsible for seeing the truth of first principles and for Plato is also the means by which we apprehend the common qualities that make possible our understanding of particulars. This intellectual vision enables us to "see" in the light of truth and constitutes knowledge itself.

The notion of "seeing" essential natures and first principles with the intellect is adopted and extended by a number of later scholars such as Augustine and, as noted, Descartes (and even in his way, Locke). The grounding, irreducible nature of this power renders it incapable of more precise description or explanation than that of the vision metaphor, but it is for this reason no less meaningful than similar grounding metaphors in more recent philosophy, such as the discursive "scaffolding" of thought in Wittgenstein (OC, 210) or the "grasp" of concepts in analytic philosophy (e.g., Frege, 1984). The metaphor, in fact, might be seen as a recognition that epistemic foundations must be entirely different in nature from that which they support in order to save knowledge from infinite epistemological regress (see Stroll, 1994, on the principle of inhomogeneity). Intuition, then, and the first principles that are intuited, must be entirely different in nature from all inferences that follow from them. This end point (and beginning) is signaled by metaphor.

Note that this view of intuition as the cornerstone of rational apprehension and knowledge of the invariant is at some odds with more recent conceptions of intuition as a process contrasting with, even opposing logical analysis and related rational processes. As one recent example, David Myer's (2002) interesting and comprehensive text on intuition reviews far-ranging findings from cognitive and social psychology. The introductory chapter of this book equates intuition with "right brain premonitions," perceptual errors, face recognition, "feeling," "unbidden hunches," "subjective truth," "gut reactions," "the unconscious mind." Notions contrasted with intuition in this same chapter include "objective truth," "reality," the deliberate and analytic.

In recent studies intuition is frequently linked with the automatic processing system, considered to represent a form of rapid, spreading activation, interwoven with associative memory, in keeping with the interest in preattentive or implicit processes that has increased for several decades across experimental psychology and cognitive science. Within this context, references to intuition are most frequently in the context of studies in which research participants display inferior judgment when relying on unsystematic inferences or "hunches" in a variety of problem solving tasks (as summarized by Dorfman, Shames, & Kihlstrom, 1996; Kleinmuntz, 1990; Myers, 2002).

More positive views of intuition emphasize its relation to innovation, creativity, and "expertise" (e.g., Dreyfus & Dreyfus, 1986; Hammond, 1996). The special and seemingly effortless insights of a person with substantial experience in a given domain of knowledge or performance of a particular kind of task is not unlike the enhancement in practical wisdom because of the attainment of experience. Although the range of tasks with which intuition has been associated in this context (including, for example, expertise in "chicken sexing") is broader than we might envision Aristotle including among the habits conducive of *eudaimonia*, there is an important point to be extracted here. Namely, the fluent, dexterous apprehension characteristic of expertise in any capacity bears conceptual similarity to the unbridled intellectual vision on which the discernment of invariant realities and necessary connections depends. The vision metaphor, is, of course obvious in the term "insight." In the case of necessary connections, however, the nature of intellectual vision is such that things cannot be seen otherwise. This is a crucial distinction.

An implication from the metaphor of intellectual vision would seem to be that intuition is a passive process, with the intellect acted on by the objects of knowledge within its "view." Yet, Socrates stresses that it is only with proper activity (careful reflection, efforts to free the mind from sensory distortion and prejudices) that recollection (seeing) can occur. For Aristotle, first principles are not seen automatically or without preliminary preparation. The "right" cognitive capacity or frame of mind for Aristotle, that which prepares one to grasp foundational premises, is acquired by familiarity with the particular case, that is, through experience, through induction. Particular cases, pave the way to understanding the general rule: "Thus it is clear that it is necessary for us to become familiar with the primitives by induction" (*Post. Anal.*, 100b1–5). Intuitive knowledge of universals requires repeated sense experience of some similarity, which leaves a trace of experience in the mind through the work of memory. Experience alone, or more accurately, sense experience alone, is not sufficient to gain understanding of invariant realities or principles. The very understanding of some relationships as necessary is not the work of the senses but of the rational faculty through the special power of intuition. Rational intuition makes knowledge, and by extension wisdom, possible. Thus, the rational potential with which children are endowed is strengthened through life by means of contact with the objects of experience. Accordingly, one might be expected to "intuit" more frequently and thoroughly throughout the life span as experience mounts and rational powers increase in magnitude.

It is here that a link back to earlier points made about the conditions for practical wisdom (*phronesis*) might be made, for it was noted that persons endowed with particular rational powers could be expected to gain in practical wisdom as they gain life experience. The grasping of generalities relating to human essence from which decisions and habits of thought and conduct conducive of *eudaemonia* proceed is furthered by experience in the world of human affairs.

What of the role of intuition in the pursuit (love) of *sophia*, the highest form of wisdom? Quite simply, there is no *sophia* in the absence of intuition; it is only by means of intuition that access to first principles is accomplished. The conditions that maximize intuition, then, are the conditions that maximize *sophia*. Important to Descartes' analysis of intuition is an element of responsibility on the part of the knower despite the implication that we receive ideas as the eye receives images. We must be in the right frame of mind, must demonstrate a particular reflective attentiveness, an active turning toward some particular objects of thought in order to "see." For Plato, the effort and preparedness facilitative of *sophia* emerge only through dialogue and protracted discussion: "For this knowledge is not something that can be put into words like other sciences, but after long-continued intercourse between teacher and pupil, in joint pursuit of the subject, suddenly, like light flashing forth when a fire is kindled, it is born in the soul and straightway nourishes itself" (*Letters*, VII, 341).

A Cautionary Conclusion

To those who reject foundationalism out of hand, this appeal to intuition as the conduit and content of wisdom will inspire little. We believe, however, that applications can indeed be drawn. Implications engendered by the depiction of wisdom in the sources briefly outlined here are less obviously about the specifics of particular ethical judgments than about the status of wisdom as a birthright, but one that is perhaps insufficiently acknowledged or claimed. The historical tie of wisdom to reason grounds it in the most enduring of human attributes, yet the embedding of reason itself in intuitive powers secures its special status and direct access to realities that precede and survive the particularities of custom and culture.

Equally evident, however, is that wisdom requires effort. Plato speaks of philosophy as a "daily discipline" on which one must enter "with all earnestness," "without ceasing" (*Letters*, VII, 340). The vision metaphor itself reminds us that one must "look" to see, must engage in deliberate activities that enable intuition and thus reason. Impairments of vision are endemic to this age as to any other. Nevertheless, we have an ongoing potential to "see" more clearly, to gain in wisdom and understanding with habits inducing of these ends. Philosophical accounts of intuition suggest that this phenomenon occurs on the condition of a mind deliberately made attentive, willfully and actively turned toward an aspect of thought and opened to it through reflective presence. Specifically implied is that wisdom cannot be developed to potential without habits that encourage this reflective state, or, as for Plato, zealous joint pursuit of enduring truths. Thus prepared, we are in a state to "receive" the insights or intuitions facilitative of any form of wisdom. Intuition is to be followed, then, by a honing and refinement through sustained and careful analysis. Important is the view of these aspects or phases of reasoning as complementary and co-constitutive, not in any sort of competition.

What habits, then, might be seen as obstacles to wisdom? Candidates include uncritical acceptance of ideas in vogue, blind following of popular trends of practice without reflection on their merits and implications, the conflation of technological advance with considered understanding of human progress, overuse of technology intended to deflect attention in ever-increasing speed from anything *but* the content of one's own ideas, pedagogical goals directed at performance to a common standard over encouragement of good reasoning and pertinent interchange.

Wisdom's current academic status as a quaint relic of outmoded philosophical systems does not undermine substantively the enduring importance of *sophia* and *phronesis*. We have not outgrown or out-"scienced" a need for wisdom; we have grown restless and distracted and impatient with what wisdom requires. Chief among these requirements are a revaluing of reflection for its own sake, concomitant with a deep understanding that such reflection is a necessary condition of "the good life" and a more just and worthy society.

References

Aristotle. (1995). *Complete works* (J. Barnes, Trans.). Princeton, NJ: Princeton University Press.

Aristotle. (1998). *The Nicomachean ethics* (D. Ross, Trans.). Oxford: Oxford University Press.

Conway, D. (2000). *The rediscovery of wisdom. From here to antiquity in quest of sophia*. London: Macmillan Press.

Descartes, R. (1980). *Discourse on method* and *Meditations on first philosophy*. (D. Cross, Trans.). Indianapolis, IN: Hackett.

Descartes, R. (1994). *Rules for the direction of the mind (Regulae ad Directionem Ingenii)*. (J. Cottingham, R. Soothoff, & D. Murdoch, Trans.). Cambridge: University Press. (Original work published 1684; assumed written 1628)

Dorfman, J., Shames, V., & Kihlstrom, J. (1996). Intuition, incubation, and insight: Implicit cognition in problem solving. In G. Underwood (Ed.), *Implicit cognition*. Oxford: Oxford University Press.

Dreyfus, H., & Dreyfus, S. (1986). *Mind over machine: The power of human intuition and expertise in the era of the computer*. New York: Free Press.

Frege, G. (1984). *Collected papers on mathematics, logic, and philosophy* (B. McGuinness, Ed., M. Black, Trans.). Oxford: Blackwell.

Hammond, K. (1996). *Human judgment and social policy*. New York: Oxford University Press.

Homer. (1951). *Iliad* (Richmond Lattimore, Trans.). Chicago: Chicago University Press.

Irwin, T. (1988). *Aristotle's first principles*. Oxford, UK: Clarendon Press.

Joachim, H. (1998). *Descartes' rules for the direction of the mind* (E. Harris, Ed.). London: Thoemmes Press.

Kleinmuntz, B. (1990). Why we still use our heads instead of formulas: Toward an integrative approach. *Psychological Bulletin, 107*(3), 296–310.

Long, A. (1986). *Hellenistic philosophy: Stoics, Epicureans, Skeptics* (2nd ed.). London: Gerald Duckworth & Co. Ltd.

MacIntyre, A. (1984). *After virtue*. Notre Dame, IN. University of Notre Dame Press.

Moore, G. E. (1903). *Principia ethica*. Cambridge: Cambridge University Press.

Myers, D. (2002). *Intuition: Its powers and its perils*. New Haven, CT: Yale University Press.

O'Connor, D. J. (1964). Aristotle. In D. O'Connor (Ed.), *A critical history of western philosophy*. New York: The Free Press.

Peirce, C. (1868). *Collected papers of Charles Sanders Peirce* (C. Hartshorne and P. Weiss, Eds.). Cambridge, MA: Belknap Press.

Plato. (1997). *Complete works* (J. M. Cooper & D. S. Hutchinson, Eds.). Indianapolis, IN: Hackett Publishing Co.

Prinz, J. (2002). *Furnishing the mind. Concepts and their perceptual basis.* Cambridge, MA: MIT Press.

Pollack, R. (1999). *The missing moment. How the unconscious shapes modern science.* New York: Houghton Mifflin.

Reichenbach, H. (1973). *The rise of scientific philosophy*. Berkeley, CA: University of California Press. Originally published 1951.

Robinson, D. N. (2002). *Praise and blame: Moral realism and its implications.* Princeton, NJ: Princeton University Press.

Smith, N. (1998). Wisdom. In E. Craig & L. Floridi (Eds.), *The Routledge encyclopedia of philosophy*. New York: Routledge.

Stroll, A. (1994). *Wittgenstein and Moore on certainty.* New York: Oxford University Press.

Von Arnim, H. (1902–1905). *Stoicorum Veterum Fragmenta.* 4 vols. Leipzig: Tenbuer.

Wittgenstein, L. (1969). *On certainty* (G. E. M. Anscombe & G. H. von Wright (Eds., G. E. M. Anscombe & D. Paul, Trans.). Oxford: Blackwell.

4

From the Inside Out

People's Implicit Theories of Wisdom

Susan Bluck and Judith Glück

Wisdom is a virtue. Wisdom is a plague. Although wisdom historically has been considered a virtue, it also has a legacy of being avoided as a research topic by social scientists. A search of the wisdom literature in psychology provides interesting but not copious reading. It seems odd that researchers would avoid this epitome of human virtue like a plague. Or does it? Because wisdom is highly valued as a virtue but does not have a universally accepted objective definition, it appears (to some) as a questionable topic for scientific psychology (Baltes, Glück, & Kunzmann, 2002). That is, psychologists must enter the world of defining values and virtues to study wisdom. They must be concerned not only with rational thought processes but with reflective and experiential ways of thinking (Labouvie-Vief, 1990). This has been somewhat frowned on in a discipline that only relatively recently emerged from behaviorism and still highly values objectivity. Psychologists who ask "How wise is this person compared to that one?" must be able to defend that they have a reliable as well as internally and, most open to criticism, an externally valid way of defining and measuring levels of wisdom (for a review of *philosophical* definitions, see Brugman, 2000). Several prominent psychologists (e.g., Paul Baltes, Robert Sternberg) have successfully done just that.

Other researchers have, for various reasons, side-stepped the task of explicitly, or objectively, measuring wisdom by asking a different question. That is, "what do people *think* wisdom is?" This latter approach does not use an a priori definition to determine how wise people are, but instead examines individuals' mental representations of what constitutes wisdom, that is, people's implicit theories of wisdom (Sternberg,

1985). This empirical approach to defining wisdom, and the research it has produced, are the focus of our chapter.

In taking the implicit theory approach, social scientists are on more "acceptable ground;" measuring not virtues and values but mental representations and beliefs. Regardless of this greater congruence with traditional disciplinary boundaries, implicit theory research is still relatively scarce, though a resurgence over the last decade is evident (Webster, 2003). The publication of this handbook, the gerontological focus on successful aging (Ardelt, 2000; Baltes, Staudinger, & Sowarka, 1990), and the growth of the positive psychology movement (Seligman & Csikszentmihalyi, 2000), provide encouragement for future work on wisdom.

Scope and Objectives

This chapter focuses squarely on implicit theories of wisdom. Note that cultural differences in views of wisdom could be seen as within this scope. Because another chapter is devoted solely to culture, however (see Takahashi & Overton, this volume), we do not review that literature here. We begin by defining wisdom, and implicit theories of wisdom, followed by a brief discussion of how implicit theories are mentally represented, and how they are important in everyday life. Next, further understanding of implicit theories is gained through explicating the implicit–explicit wisdom dichotomy: how it arose and why it is useful. We also examine how implicit theories inform explicit theories.

After discussion of these definitional and conceptual issues, a review of the empirical literature on implicit theories of wisdom is presented, focusing on both findings and methods. Where data is available, this section includes the extent to which age is part of individuals' implicit theories of wisdom. Finally, age is considered in a different manner: We examine the literature on whether implicit theories of wisdom differ at different points in the lifespan. The chapter ends with a summary including future directions for research.

Definitions: Wisdom, and Implicit Theories of Wisdom

To establish a clear understanding of implicit theories we first define wisdom in general. We then move to a discussion of how implicit theories of wisdom have been defined.

Wisdom

How can one begin to define wisdom? One place to start is with its denotative linguistic meaning. The *Oxford Dictionary* defines wisdom as "experience, knowledge, and the power of applying them; prudence, common sense..." (p. 762). The *American Heritage Dictionary* provides a similar definition: "understanding of what is true, right, or lasting; common sense, sagacity, good judgment" (p. 1469). Note that although there are some differences in these definitions, there is also overlap. The word *wisdom* has existed across centuries in (at least) Old English, Greek, and German, and is based on the Indo-European word *wede*, meaning "to see" or "to know" (Holliday & Chandler, 1986). Thus, although there are some variations in how the term is denotatively defined, there is also an essential core to the definition that exists across cultures and history. Already, however, we begin to see that defining wisdom is not a straightforward matter. If even denotative dictionary definitions differ, we can expect that people's implicit theories of wisdom may also vary around an essential core meaning.

Psychological researchers have not relied solely on a dictionary definition of wisdom but have provided conceptual psychological definitions that are congruent with, but go beyond, what is found in the dictionary (see, for example, Baltes & Smith, 1990; Sternberg, 1998, 2000). As one example, Baltes and Smith (1990) provide a multidimensional definition of wisdom as a type of expertise: being an expert in knowledge involving good judgment and advice in the domain of the fundamental pragmatics of life. In general, there is convergence in these dictionary and psychological definitions, but different dictionaries and different scholars have defined wisdom slightly differently (for a discussion of defining wisdom, see McKee & Barber, 1999). What is meant, however, by an "implicit theory of wisdom?"

Implicit Theories of Wisdom

Implicit theory approaches to wisdom assess how people define wisdom. This relies on the notion that individuals carry a concept in their head of what wisdom entails. This concept of who and what is wise has been formed not through directed study of what philosophers, psychologists, or dictionaries have to say. Instead, it is formed simply through living in society and learning its language and meanings so that one can express the self and understand others.

The goal of research on implicit theories is to map out the common features of wisdom as held in the minds of groups of individuals. Various methods for collecting people's implicit theories of wisdom are detailed below. Regardless of the method, "the data of interest in the discovery of people's implicit theories are people's communications, in whatever form, regarding their notions as to the nature of the psychological construct [in this case, wisdom] under investigation" (Sternberg, 1985, p. 608, text in brackets added). Implicit theories have been variously referred to as lay perceptions (Hershey & Farrell, 1997), folk conceptions (Sternberg, 2000), folk ideas (Montgomery, Barber, & McKee, 2002), or the underlying structure of perceptions (Clayton & Birren, 1980). Despite these varying terms, the definition of an implicit theory of wisdom has been made clear.

We suggest, however, that what is most interesting about implicit theories of wisdom is that they deserve definition at all! That is, for a moment imagine that this is not a chapter about wisdom but about the study of memory, or, to be fanciful, of roses. Do memory researchers ask people what memory is? Would a researcher interested in studying roses have a separate subarea that focused on people's implicit theories of roses? Of course, that sounds ridiculous. Experts and philosophers, psychologists, botanists, and all individuals are assumed to carry the same (or a roughly similar) representation of the rose construct in their mind. There is no question about implicit theories of roses because there is an assumption of agreement and continuity across people's conceptions. A rose is a rose is a rose (Stein, 1972). If this is so, then why and how is wisdom different?

We argue that basically it is not all that different. What makes implicit theories of wisdom more interesting than implicit theories of roses is that wisdom is an abstract, highly valued, multidimensional human virtue. Thus, although psychologists, philosophers, linguists, and laypeople all have a rather similar core conception of wisdom, its meaning may also vary in important ways among different subgroups and across individuals. We discuss some of that systematic variation later in our literature review of implicit theories and age. Given that complex mental representations of wisdom do occur, we turn now to what basic form such representations may take.

Mental Representation of Implicit Theories

The focus of most implicit wisdom research has been to document the *content* of people's implicit theories, but psychologists also may want to ask what *form* such mental representations take. Original work by

Holliday and Chandler (1986) suggested that past studies of implicit wisdom often involve an informal category analysis. The assumption in studies that ask participants to name the characteristics of a wise person, for example, is that one's representation of wisdom is a mental category that contains defining features that can be named. Holliday and Chandler provide a more formal category analysis based on categorization theory (Rosch, 1975). The theory suggests that wisdom, like other constructs (including roses), is a category that is both horizontally and vertically (hierarchically) organized to aid information processing (e.g., recognition, recall, organization). Superordinate aspects of the category are more encompassing and less detailed, and subordinate aspects are more specific and detail-rich. Similar categories (e.g., intelligence) may overlap partially, but every category also has unique features that distinguish it.

Roschian theory also introduced the idea of prototypes: Categories are organized around prototypes that are completely unambiguous and clear instances of the category. This prototype-feature approach has been the largely unspoken underpinning for most work on implicit theories. Neisser (1979) utilized it to analyze implicit theories of intelligence, and Sternberg (1985) specifically follows this conceptualization in his early work on implicit theories of wisdom. Thus, although the content of implicit theories has received much more attention than their form, most research assumes a category-based view of implicit theories of wisdom that relies on prototypes and features.

Understanding of the form of implicit theories has recently been enriched by illumination of the role that exemplars play (Paulhus, Wehr, Harms, & Strausser, 2002). Although their work focuses largely on implicit theories of intelligence, these authors argue that exemplars (e.g., specific people who exemplify wisdom) are often important in implicit theory representations. That is, people's conceptions of intelligence, or wisdom, revolve around exemplars that are based on memories of interactions with particular, distinctive, others. These may include famous others whom one "interacts with" through news and television media, or nonfamous individuals such as family and friends with whom one interacts more closely. Paulhus et al.'s research shows that individuals within a culture hold common exemplars of wisdom (e.g., Gandhi, the Dali Lama, Mother Teresa) that are largely distinct from those held for intelligence (e.g., Einstein, Newton, Edison). They conclude, and we would agree, that the study of the form of implicit theories is best seen in terms of the interaction, and perhaps iteration, between abstract schemata (e.g., prototypes with distinguishing features), and real-world exemplars.

Implicit Theories in Everyday Life

Discussing the mental representations of wisdom in terms of features and prototypes takes us into the dark hallways of the mind. But the importance of these representations, or implicit theories, lies in their use in the light of everyday life. Implicit theories are important because they are the lens through which we perceive others' and our own wisdom (Sternberg, 1985) as we move through life. As such, implicit theories held by cultures, and by individuals, may affect such things as who is revered as a cultural icon, who is successful in school and job applications, and how voting preferences are formed (Paulhus et al., 2002).

We propose that in considering the use of implicit theories in everyday life, a three-level analysis is appropriate. This includes the way in which cultures and societies employ wisdom (societal level), the way that people judge other individuals' relative wisdom (interpersonal level), and the way that people view their own behavior, feelings, and thoughts as wise or unwise (intrapersonal level). Thus, a fully developed understanding of implicit theories might involve analysis of differences and similarities in (i) how cultures collectively form and employ views of the abstract concept of wisdom and of "the great wise people of history or of our time" (societal level); (ii) how individuals identify others in their own lives who can be relied on to see things wisely or give wise advice (interpersonal level); and (iii) how one views one's own self-development of wisdom (intrapersonal level).

The Implicit–Explicit Dichotomy

History of the Dichotomy

Implicit theories were defined earlier. Explicit theories of wisdom, in contrast, "are constructions of (supposedly) expert theorists and researchers rather than of laypeople" (Sternberg, 2000, p. 633). Explicit theories are based on philosophical definitions and psychological constructs of human development. Such definitions are aimed at developing measures with which to test people's level of wisdom (Sternberg, 1985).

The implicit–explicit dichotomy was first used in relation to intelligence, another psychological construct for which there is some divergence between what is measured by psychologists and how individuals define and employ the term in everyday life (Sternberg, Conway, Ketron, & Bernstein, 1981). In the wisdom literature, the dichotomy has been a useful one for organizing research findings, and promoting two interesting and distinct lines of research. Thus, the growth of the field has surely benefited from researchers specializing in either an implicit or an explicit approach.

For those new to the field of wisdom the dichotomy labels may be misleading, however, so we present a short clarification. Cognitive psychologists often refer to implicit versus explicit learning or memory. The use of these same terms in reference to subareas of the study of wisdom implies no similarity to their usage in the study of learning and memory. That is, for example, implicit wisdom does not infer being wise without realizing that one was wise and explicit theories of wisdom do not refer to wisdom that one can "produce on demand." Instead, as already discussed, implicit theories of wisdom are the conceptions of wisdom that laypersons hold, and explicit theories of wisdom are those that are constructed and tested by psychologists and other experts.

The Role of Implicit Theories in Informing Explicit Theories

Although implicit and explicit theories of wisdom have been labeled dichotomously, some authors have argued for greater cross-pollination between approaches. For example, Sternberg (1985) suggests that since explicit definitions of wisdom often differ across researchers, and are themselves partly derived from scientists' implicit theories of the construct, implicit theoretical research can help to refine explicit definitions. Both approaches seek to provide a universal definition (Hershey & Farrell, 1997): They simply go about it from different angles. Psychologists working within the implicit theory tradition believe that wisdom can best be defined, for example, by querying laypersons for the characteristics of a wise individual (Holliday & Chandler, 1986). By identifying an empirically based definition of wisdom, such psychologists hope to contribute a useful foundation for the development of explicit wisdom theory and to produce methods for examining the values of a given culture (Hershey & Farrell, 1997). Those working within the explicit wisdom approach believe that a universal definition is better constructed from expert knowledge and theory.

Both approaches have merits. There is a tendency to view explicit theories of wisdom as "the real thing" and implicit theories simply as perceptions that could easily be laypersons' mistaken ideas about what wisdom really is. The notion that an entire culture would carry around an organized construct of wisdom that is wrong, or incorrect, is a slightly bizarre one. It suggests that human language and thought do not reflect reality. Especially with a construct that in itself is defined by culture, rather than by a biological substrate, it seems odd to argue that what people in that culture think wisdom is could be entirely wrong. One can certainly argue that there may be limitations to any single person's concept of wisdom, or perhaps that it is difficult to truly know what wisdom is without being wise (although this would apply equally to explicit theories). Still, an explicit theory of wisdom that was totally inconsistent with laypeople's understanding of the term would be hard to defend. There is an additional reason for accepting that implicit theories of wisdom reflect real wisdom: implicit and explicit, lay and expert definitions of wisdom converge in a basic sense on the same set of features as central in defining wisdom. Thus, at least in terms of lay and expert definitions of wisdom, no strong dichotomy exists. Instead, implicit theories research captures how wisdom is perceived, and explicit theories of wisdom, based on philosophical and psychological constructs, give more formal accounts of how wisdom manifests, and who has how much.

Empirical Review of Implicit Theories: Methodologies and Findings

In this section, we review the empirical work on implicit theories of wisdom, distinguishing three lines of research. In the first and oldest tradition, participants generate descriptors of wisdom, or they rate descriptors in terms of their typicality for wisdom. In the second line of research, participants are asked about personal experiences of wisdom. In the third, participants are presented with experimentally manipulated information (e.g., texts, videos) and asked to judge them for wisdom.

Descriptor-Rating Studies: What Characteristics Are Perceived as Wise?

These studies focus on characteristics that laypeople judge as typically wise. Researchers collect and analyze relationships among these characteristics to identify subcomponents of wisdom. Different subcomponents have been identified across studies, although this is sometimes largely a matter of labeling. In Table 4.1, we conceptually categorize differently labeled subcomponents found across studies. At the end of this section, we further describe the conceptual categories presented in the table.

TABLE 4.1. *Subcomponents of Wisdom Identified in Descriptor-Rating Studies*

	Cognitive Ability	Insight	Reflective Attitude	Concern for Others	Real-world Skills
Clayton & Birren	*Cognitive:* knowledgeable, experienced, pragmatic, observant, intelligent		*Reflective:* introspective, intuitive	*Affective:* peaceful, understanding, gentle	
Holliday & Chandler	*General competencies:* intellectual, open, thoughtful, knowledgeable, educated	*Exceptional understanding:* experienced/skilled in everyday affairs, can see essentials, understands self/others	*Social unobtrusiveness:* "wisdom is expressed in subtle rather than dramatic ways"	*Interpersonal skills:* positive, respecting, and accepting manner toward others	*Judgment and communication skills:* vigilant of the world, balanced, tolerant, problem-solving skills, gives good advice
Sternberg	*Reasoning ability:* has problem-solving ability, logical mind, has knowledge and is able to apply it	*Perspicacity:* has intuition, insight, offers solutions on the side of right and truth; *Expeditious use of information:* learns from experience, seeks information	*Learning from ideas and environment:* receptive, attaches importance to ideas, learns from mistakes	*Sagacity:* concern for others, understanding, fair, open to learn from others	*Judgment:* acts within limits, sensible, thinks before acting or speaking
Hershey & Farrell			*Basic Temperament:* withdrawn, quiet, reflective	*Non-Egotism:* not extravagant, commanding, or arrogant	
Jason et al.	*Intelligence:* has genius, problem-solving ability, intelligence			*Warmth:* has humor, kindness, compassion, animation	

Note: Labels in italics are those produced by the original authors. Descriptors are short summaries of original factors.

Studies using this method generally consist of at least two parts. In the first part, lists of assumedly wisdom-related characteristics are generated. In the second part, these lists of characteristics are rated by participants with respect to their relation to wisdom. Of course, the results of the second part depend on the quality of the lists generated in the first part.

Generating characteristics. Holliday and Chandler (1986) provided the most careful method of compiling a list. They had a large sample generate wisdom-related characteristics and then asked four judges to replace synonyms and redundancies. The final list was compiled of characteristics mentioned at least twice across participants. They also added theoretical characteristics from the wisdom literature and some characteristics unrelated to wisdom. Clayton and Birren (1980) had a relatively small number of pilot study participants list relevant adjectives; in their final study they used only 12 wisdom-related adjectives plus the words "aged," "wise," and "myself." Sternberg (1985) had pilot study participants (laypersons and professors from four different fields) generate lists of behaviors of wise persons. He then created field-specific lists of wise behaviors using characteristics that had been listed at least twice. Hershey and Farrell (1997) used lists of personality characteristics and lists of occupations; they generated the lists themselves trying to select a heterogeneous sample of descriptors including some which would not be perceived as wisdom-related. Jason, Reichler, King, Madsen, Camacho, and Marchese (2001) used qualitative pilot interviews as sources of characteristics and then added theoretical characteristics from the literature. Thus, researchers have used a variety of methods to generate lists of wisdom characteristics.

Ratings. There is also quite some methodological variation in the second part of the studies, where participants rate the characteristics with respect to their typicality for wisdom. Holliday and Chandler (1986) had participants rate their list of 123 characteristics on a scale from "almost never true of wise people" to "almost always true of wise people." Clayton and Birren (1980) presented participants with all possible pairs of the 15 characteristics in their list and had participants rate the similarity of each pair, assuming that all adjectives were related to wisdom because of the way they had been generated. Sternberg (1985) first had other people (laypersons or professors) rate the behaviors collected in the pilot study with respect to their typicality for wisdom. Then, in a third study, using the 40 characteristics rated as most wisdom-typical, he asked students to card-sort them into piles representing which would be likely to be found together in a person. Hershey and Farrell (1997) asked participants to rate 96 personality characteristics and 96 occupations on a scale from "extremely unwise" to "extremely wise." Jason et al. (2001), using a questionnaire, asked participants to rate 38 items on a scale from "not at all" to "definitely" in terms of the extent to which they describe a wise person.

Analyses. The methods of data analysis also differ across studies, with two main techniques (dimensions identified through both analytic techniques are shown in Table 4.1). Clayton and Birren (1980) and Sternberg (1985) used multidimensional scaling (MDS), allowing a graphical representation of the structural similarity of data. Descriptors rated as highly similar or related appear close to one another in the graphic structure. Clayton and Birren interpreted their results in terms of clusters of adjectives, whereas Sternberg identified three dimensions underlying the structure, and described each dimension by the behaviors closest to its two poles.

The other authors used factor analysis, a method that analyzes intercorrelations among characteristics to derive factors, or dimensions, underlying their relationships. Holliday and Chandler (1986), Hershey and Farrell (1997), and Jason et al. (2001) used such analyses to identify dimensions of implicit wisdom. Factor analyses, although technically easy, can be quite misleading. In particular, the number of factors needed to describe a structure is dependent on the intercorrelations among items. If intercorrelations are high, few factors will explain most of the variance, whereas if intercorrelations are low, a larger number of relatively unreliable factors will result. The problem is that if all characteristics that participants rate are highly wisdom-salient, they will all receive high ratings. In such a case, correlations among ratings are low and factor structures become spurious. By contrast, if items negatively related to wisdom are included in a list, item intercorrelations will be high, but the resulting factors may be very broad, as is the case in Hershey and Farrell's (1997) study. To avoid both extremes, it may be a good idea for lists of characteristics to include other positively valued characteristics such as intelligence, creativity, or friendliness, but to exclude aspects negatively related to wisdom.

Another frequent misunderstanding with factor-analytic results is that a high factor loading does not imply high wisdom-relatedness. As mentioned earlier, if all participants judge a particular descriptor to be highly wisdom-salient, this descriptor will not correlate highly with others descriptors and will not have a strong factor loading (this is, for example, the case with "experienced," the highest-rated characteristic in Hershey and Farrell's 1997 study). Therefore, it is important to report means in addition to factor loadings in such studies. MDS may generally be preferable to factor analysis for analyzing such data. The disadvantage of MDS is that it requires similarity data, which may be more difficult to obtain than simple ratings.

Many Subcomponents: Few Conceptual Categories

Obtained subcomponents of implicit theories of wisdom have most often been labeled differently by different authors across various studies. This makes it appear as if there are many diverse subcomponents. The conceptual contents of these components, however, often overlap. For example, the intelligence-related component of wisdom has been labelled "cognitive" (Clayton & Birren, 1980), "general competencies" (Holliday & Chandler, 1986), and "reasoning ability" (Sternberg, 1985). To integrate these similar subcomponents, we have conceptually grouped all subcomponents found in more than one study into five essential, empirically grounded aspects of wisdom (see Table 4.1). These overarching aspects can be criticized as interrelated or overlapping; we believe, however, that they allow for summarizing the key aspects of implicit wisdom findings across studies. Note that although we developed these five aspects of wisdom from a conceptual review of the literature, they are similar to, although more comprehensive than, those identified empirically by Holliday and Chandler (1986).

All studies have identified a strong *cognitive basis* of wisdom, which comprises a number of aspects. Aspects of intelligence, a precondition for good problem-solving, was seen across all studies. Here, both fluid intelligence (such as logical thinking, good reasoning ability) and crystallized intelligence (knowledge and experience) were consistently mentioned across studies.

The second component is *insight*, that is, the motivation and ability to clearly understand a problem by seeing through the obvious and grasping the essence. This includes intuition and a deep understanding of others' perspectives as well as of one's own ideas and motives. It also may include collecting additional information when needed to gain a deeper understanding.

The third component refers to a *reflective attitude*, that is, a basic motivation to think deeply about things, people, and oneself, and to think before acting or speaking. It is often described in combination with an unobtrusive, quiet way of presenting oneself.

The fourth component is *concern for others*. It contains a general attitude of kindness and interest in others, the ability to see others' perspective and understand their feelings, as well as fairness and respect for others.

The fifth component refers to *real-world problem-solving skills*, and really refers to the application of all the other components to real-life situations. It contains good judgment in understanding problems, sensibility, knowledge of one's limitations, and the social skills required to give good, practical, advice.

The structure we have arrived at also includes the aspects contained in Hershey and Farrell's *perceptive judgment* factor; however, this broad factor has aspects that occur across all of our components. For example, it includes the items *rational, logical, enlightened, reflective, thoughtful, sympathetic, friendly, flexible,* and *honest.*

The only work not well represented in Table 4.1 is that of Jason et al. (2001). Three of their five factors (spirituality, connecting to nature, harmony) are not included in the table. As the authors do not report item means, it is not clear to what degree each of these factors was endorsed as related to wisdom. In terms of the *spirituality*-related factor, their pilot study suggested that some, but not all, participants associate wisdom with a spiritual union with God. This is congruent with Hershey and Farrell's (1997) factor analysis of wisdom-related occupations: they found a factor containing only "minister" and "priest." Obviously, some people view spirituality as highly related to wisdom, whereas others do not. Jason et al.'s *connecting to nature* factor may represent an alternative nature-based form of spirituality. Their *harmony* factor contained aspects of our insight and real-world skills factors but also aspects of self-esteem and self-love that did not appear in any other studies.

Do People Think Older Is Wiser?

From descriptor-rating studies, it appears that age plays a part in people's implicit theories of wisdom. In Clayton and Birren's (1980) study, "aged" was placed quite close to wisdom. In the other studies, the perceived relationship of age to wisdom was not analysed. The fact that life experience played a large role in the results of all studies suggests, however, that chronological age (as a rough proxy for experience) might at least be viewed as a facilitating variable for wisdom. Additional evidence is provided by Heckhausen, Dixon, and Baltes (1989), who focused directly on beliefs about development in adulthood. The authors presented participants with a list of person characteristics, including "wise," and asked them to rate whether they believed each characteristic to increase in adulthood. In a second session, they used only those 148 adjectives that had been expected to increase with age, and asked participants to rate the desirability of increases and to specify the onset and ending age for each characteristic. With increasing age, more undesirable changes were expected – with two exceptions: "dignified" and "wise" were rated as highly desirable and expected to begin to increase around 55 years of age and to decrease, if at all, only at the very end of life.

Studies of Wisdom as Perceived in People's Own Lives

The second line of research is on wisdom as perceived in people's own lives. A number of researchers have asked participants to nominate people who they consider wise in their own life (people they have known personally or public figures), and then analyzed characteristics of these persons. Alternatively, our own research has focused on autobiographical narratives concerning times when people feel that they displayed wisdom in their own lives.

Wisdom Nominees: Who Is Considered Wise?

Paulhus, Wehr, Harms, and Strausser (2002) asked undergraduates to list the wisest, most intelligent, and most famous people they could think of. The 15 most-listed wise persons were (in descending order) Gandhi, Confucius, Jesus Christ, Martin Luther King Jr., Socrates, Mother Teresa, Solomon, Buddha, the Pope, Oprah Winfrey, Winston Churchill, the Dalai Lama, Ann Landers, Nelson Mandela, and Queen Elizabeth. Oprah Winfrey also was listed in the intelligence top 15, and Jesus Christ and Nelson Mandela also were listed in the top 15 for sheer fame. As it is not clear how much knowledge the study participants really had about the people they named, the names in the list reflect a stereotypic view of wisdom (although such stereotypes probably play a role in implicit theories). It is interesting to note that many persons in the wisdom list are spiritual or religious leaders, or individuals who changed the world through peaceful or compassionate means.

Most studies on wisdom nominees focus on characteristics of people considered as wise, rather than on simply obtaining their identities. Among such studies, some focus on basic characteristics such as age or gender, and others focus on qualitative characteristics of people nominated as wise.

Age and gender of wisdom nominees. The most general finding from studies on basic characteristics is that most wisdom nominees are relatively old, at least older than the person nominating them. Perlmutter, Adams, Nyquist, and Kaplan (1988) found that 78% of their participants related wisdom to age; persons nominated as wise were mostly aged 50 or above, and nominee age increased with participant age. Denney, Dew, and Kroupa (1995) also found that nominee age was relatively high and increased with participant age. Jason et al. (2001) reported an average nominee age of 60; a similar age mean was reported by Baltes, Staudinger, Maercker, and Smith (1995) for their group of wisdom nominees.

Although only 16% in Perlmutter et al.'s (1988) study thought that wisdom was related to gender, the majority of persons they nominated were male. In Jason et al.'s (2001) sample (81% women), 66% of those nominated as wise were men. The same pattern was reported by Denney et al. (1995) and by Sowarka (1989). In addition, Denney et al. (1995) found that older people were more likely to nominate men as wise, and that more women were nominated when participants were asked about interpersonal wisdom, as opposed to wisdom in general. Sowarka (1989) found that women mostly nominated family members, whereas men often nominated individuals from professional contexts.

What is wise about wisdom nominees? Jason et al. (2001) asked participants what characteristics of the nominee made them wise. Most participants talked about the nominees' drive, leadership, or insight/ spirituality. Being smart and loving were also often mentioned. Asked about effects of wise nominees on their own lives, most participants said that they had helped them either to define their directions and goals, or to develop their values and beliefs. Montgomery, Barber, and McKee (2002) interviewed six older people about wisdom in their own lives. Using phenomenological analysis, the authors derived six general principles of implicit wisdom. *Guidance* was mentioned most often: Participants talked about how a wise person had helped them to see something in a new way, see a broader perspective, or find a focus in a complex situation. The other four principles were specific aspects of guidance. *Knowledge* referred to using both one's own and externally available knowledge to solve problems. *Experience* was distinguished from knowledge in that it concerned using abstract knowledge in one's own life, thereby linking wisdom and age. *Moral principles* were mentioned as an aspect that guides wise decisions; wise people were seen as having personal values and striving to adhere to them. The last aspect, *compassionate relationships*, often came up in descriptions of wisdom-related situations. The people described as wise in the interviews had been mentors to the participants, and had encouraged them to have their own insights through showing them empathy. Sowarka (1989) analyzed interviews about wise persons and how they had shown their wisdom. Most narratives were about highly difficult situations the wise persons were able to resolve by suggesting novel and successful ways of dealing with the problem.

Who seems wise? In sum, the results of nominee studies show that the relation of wisdom to age is strongly represented in people's implicit theories. Chronological age itself, however, is viewed as a necessary, but not sufficient condition for wisdom. What other characteristics are reflected in wisdom nominees?

Interestingly, most of them are male. As this effect is related to participant age, it is possibly in part a cohort effect. In the current generation of older adults, relatively few women were professionally active and in positions where they could be visible as wise. Thus, exemplars are not easy to name. One also might speculate, based on Denney et al.'s (1995) findings, that people may have a different idea of "female" than of "male" wisdom (cf. Orwoll & Achenbaum, 1993). Women may be seen as more interpersonally wise and men more intellectually wise. Regardless, when generic wisdom is asked for, it is men who are nominated. This fits well with Jung's (1956) archetype of wisdom as an old man.

With respect to the characteristics that make a person wise in the eyes of others, the aspect of guidance came out quite clearly. That is, people are perceived as wise when they have helped others to solve a problem in a way that went beyond what they had been able to see and do before. Interestingly, the guidance aspect did not explicitly come out in the descriptor-rating studies, although it is somewhat implicit in the combination of concern for others and real-world problem-solving skills. This aspect, which is contextual in nature, is obviously more salient when people are asked about their own experiences with wisdom than when they think about the abstract concept of wisdom.

Autobiographical Narratives: Can I Be Wise?
A different method from the wisdom nominee procedure also exists for studying wisdom in people's own lives. Using our "experienced wisdom" procedure, we investigated people's perceptions of themselves as wise. Bluck and Glück (2004) interviewed participants about events in their own lives when they believed they had said, thought, or done

something wise. Most of our participants talked about life decisions, reactions to negative events, or life management strategies. The reported events usually started out as difficult, negative situations that were transformed to positive outcomes through the use of wisdom. The autobiographical narratives participants provided were of important life events that had effects on their later lives, their personality development, or their life philosophy or perspective.

Glück, Bluck, Baron, and McAdams (2003) studied the forms that people describe wisdom as taking in their lives. We identified three different forms of wisdom from autobiographical narratives: *Empathy and support* refers to seeing others' perspectives and feelings, and helping them resolve difficult situations. *Self-determination and assertion* refers to taking control of a situation and standing by one's values, goals, or priorities. *Knowledge and flexibility* consists of relying on one's own experience as well as having the ability to compromise, and showing tolerance for uncertainty. In a second study, we found that both the types of situations requiring wisdom and the forms wisdom takes are indeed specific to wisdom situations: They are less often found in "peak" events of people's lives or in situations where people thought they were foolish.

As the types of situations in which people perceive wisdom as required have not been measured previously, our findings contribute to implicit theories of wisdom by detailing when people perceive that wisdom is usually employed (e.g., when making life decisions). The forms that wisdom takes fit loosely with the components of wisdom we identified in Table 4.1. *Empathy and support* and *knowledge and flexibility* map neatly onto that structure. *Self-determination and assertion* is a new aspect of people's implicit theories that may be recognized largely when people are asked about their own life (as we do in this procedure) but not particularly in judging others or in rating lists of descriptors. Our research also suggests cross-cultural differences in implicit views of wisdom as related to one's self. Although the above forms were found in a German sample, a later American sample showed almost exclusively *empathy and support* (Glück et al., 2003).

Experimental Studies of Implicit Wisdom

In this third line of research, participants are provided with information on a target person and then asked to judge that person's wisdom. The experimental manipulation involves different groups of participants receiving different information, allowing researchers to study the independent and interactive effect of certain characteristics on the perception of wisdom. The most commonly manipulated characteristics are chronological age and gender of the target.

Knight and Parr (1999) presented participants with 12 vignettes, each giving the age of the target person (young, middle-aged, or old) and two wisdom-salient or creativity-salient characteristics (borrowed from Sternberg's [1985] dimensions of wisdom). Older target persons were generally judged as wiser than middle-aged and younger targets, independent of whether they were described as wise or creative in the vignette.

This effect was not replicated, however, by Hira and Faulkender (1997), who manipulated both age and gender. They videotaped four actors – one young male, one young female, one old male, and one old female – reading texts that consisted of actual people's responses to wisdom-related life problems. Participants rated the targets with respect to nine questions about aspects of wisdom (derived from Smith & Baltes, 1990), and with respect to their own understanding of wisdom. Results showed a surprising interaction: The old man and the young woman were judged as significantly wiser than the young man and the old woman. As the authors stated, this result was most likely because of nonverbal cues such as facial expressivity in the actors' behavior. Thus, neither the content of what was said nor chronological age was a sufficient criterion for predicting who was judged as wise.

Stange, Kunzmann, and Baltes (2003) studied these nonverbal aspects in more detail. Participants viewed silent videos of either young or old target persons listening to a young person obviously talking about a difficult problem. The targets' listening behavior was either empathetic or disinterested and negative. Afterward, participants were presented with a letter that the advice-giver had allegedly written to the young advice-seeker. The content of the letter was either high or low in wisdom (as defined in the Berlin Wisdom Paradigm). Participants then rated the targets' wisdom. The three manipulated aspects had independent effects on the wisdom ratings: age, listening behavior, and content of the advice, were all related to wisdom ratings. There were no interactions.

As this experimental method has only recently been applied to the study of wisdom, it is not surprising that findings are somewhat inconsistent. In agreement with the other types of studies, however, chronological age of the target seems to be a significant predictor of wisdom ratings. These may be moderated, however, by other criteria such as facial expressivity, listening behavior, or quality of advice given. This again suggests that age in itself is not a sufficient cue for the perception of someone as wise. Clearly, in judging persons as wise in everyday life, behavioral cues also are of great importance. It is somewhat surprising to note that such cues may overrule actual content of wise advice (Stange, Kunzmann, & Baltes, 2003). Thus, in planning future studies it may be important to assess the extent to which participants rely on obvious cues such as age, in comparison with more subtle cues, as well as the extent to which the message itself plays a role in what is judged as wise.

Summary of Findings: Methodological Differences and Their Effect on Results

We have reported findings from three different lines of research: descriptor-rating studies, studies of wisdom as perceived in real life, and experimental studies. Results show some convergence and also some differences across study types. It appears that differences can largely be explained by variations in method, and the convergence across studies has led to some solid findings. We suggest that all three lines of research will continue to be useful in forming a complete picture of implicit theories of wisdom.

Descriptor-rating studies are aimed at describing the abstract concept of wisdom as viewed by laypeople. As our review has shown (see Table 4.1), these studies have contributed to our understanding that implicit theories of wisdom are multidimensional (though dimensions vary somewhat across studies). What is missing in such studies, however, is the contextualization of wisdom in everyday life: what characterizes wise people in real-life, concrete situations. For example, guidance, which came out quite clearly in nominee studies, was not found in descriptor-rating studies. Descriptor studies contribute by offering a glimpse at the abstract and linguistic representation of implicit theories of wisdom.

Studies of wisdom as perceived in people's own lives have added valuable knowledge while putting wisdom in the context of the life lived. For example, studies of wisdom nominees have shown fairly consistent age and gender effects. In addition, more qualitative aspects of what wise people do in real life have been gained. The autobiographical approach to wisdom allows us to study wisdom as it is perceived spontaneously in people's lives. It suggests that implicit theories of wisdom that one applies to others may not be exactly the same as what is applied to self.

The experimental studies have a different strength: They offer the potential for analyzing precisely what causes a person's perception of someone as wise. There is one aspect one may be critical of in these studies, that is, the potential difference between spontaneous ascriptions of wisdom and laboratory wisdom ratings. If a researcher asks a participant to rate how wise a person is, this process is very different from a situation in which a person spontaneously thinks "Wow, that was really wise advice!" Even if a participant rates a target as relatively wise (when asked to by the experimenter), this does not mean she would have thought of this person as wise had she run across them in everyday life.

Using these three methods, and others yet to be discovered, researchers will continue to examine how implicit theories are formed and applied both inside and outside the laboratory.

Individual Differences in Implicit Theories: Age from a Different Angle

We have already shown that age is perceived as a critical variable with respect to wisdom. Now, we look at age from a different angle. Do implicit theories of wisdom differ systematically with age? That is, are the conceptions of wisdom of young adults, middle-aged adults, and older adults the same?

Clayton and Birren (1980) found a number of interesting age differences. First of all, in the MDS solution (described above) for the older participants, the stimuli "aged" and "experienced" were located at a significantly larger distance from "wise" than in the middle-aged and young participants. Thus, older participants were more critical of the idea that wisdom comes with old age. Consistent with this, there were no age differences in the distance between the stimuli "myself" and "wise," showing that the older participants did not view themselves as wiser than the two younger groups. Perlmutter et al. (1988) did not find an increase across age groups in self-ratings of wisdom either, and nor did we when we asked for self-ratings in our "experienced wisdom" study. Thus, one age difference seems to be that older adults' implicit theories reveal skepticism that wisdom comes with age.

Clayton and Birren (1980) also found structural differences between the age groups, suggesting older adults have a more differentiated understanding of wisdom. Older adults' cognitive component of wisdom was divided into two clusters that loosely can be described as crystallized (knowledgeable, experienced) and fluid (pragmatic, observant, aged, intelligent). In the middle-aged group, there were some indications of a differentiation of these two components, whereas in the young adults, the cognitive component was undifferentiated. In Knight and Parr's (1999) vignette study, older adults rated wise behaviors as wiser than middle-aged and young adults did and creative behaviors as less wise than young adults did. These results also suggest a more differentiated, sensitive conception of wisdom in older adults.

Apart from judging age as less related to wisdom and having a more differentiated conception of wisdom, older adults may also weight different components of wisdom differently. In Clayton and Birren's study (1980), "understanding" and "empathetic" were located closer to "wise" in the oldest group than in the other groups. In Knight and Parr's study (1999), older adults rated wise targets described in terms of sagacity (see Table 4.1) as wiser than the other age groups did, whereas young adults rated wise targets described in terms of reasoning ability as wiser than the other age groups did.

Glück et al. (2003) also found age differences in implicit theories as related to people's view of wisdom in their own life. In their Study 1, conducted in Germany, they found that adolescents most often reported situations in which they had provided empathy and support, young adults most often talked about showing self-determination and assertion, and older adults most often talked about using knowledge and flexibility. Thus, each age group seemed to show a preference for the form of wisdom that fit with their predominant developmental tasks. This result was not found in an American sample, however (Study 2), suggesting that age and culture may interact in shaping people's implicit theories.

In summary, it appears that older adults' implicit theories of wisdom do differ from those endorsed by younger people. One thing older adults seem to fully embrace is that age does not necessarily bring wisdom! In addition, they appear to have a more differentiated view of wisdom, and they are familiar with instances of wisdom among people they know (Sowarka, 1989). In addition, older adults may emphasize different components of wisdom than do individuals in other life phases. How individuals weight different aspects of wisdom within their implicit theories, and whether that weighting is relative to one's age, is an area for future research.

Before ending this section on age differences we must stress that all of these studies are cross-sectional. Based on the current evidence we have no means to distinguish whether identified age differences are the result of individual development, or whether they are cohort effects.

People's Implicit Theories of Wisdom: Summary and Future Directions

Implicit theories are important in everyday life because they are the filter through which people view and judge cultures, individuals, and themselves. People carry views of wisdom in their heads that they have learned or constructed through their interactions in the world. Researchers have gained significant ground in delineating those views, despite definitional, conceptual, and methodological challenges. Implicit theories of wisdom represent individuals', and sometimes cultures', view of the nature of wisdom. Alternatively, explicit theories of wisdom rely on definitions of wisdom drawn from experts, scholars, and philosophers. Of course, there is much overlap between explicit and implicit theories: If there were not, something would be terribly wrong!

Research on implicit theories of wisdom is based on the assumption that individuals have a construct of wisdom that is mentally represented similarly to other mental constructs, that is, through schematic representations linked to prototypes and exemplars. The majority of research, however, has not focused on structure, but rather content of people's implicit theories. Studies have employed a variety of methodologies (descriptor ratings, wisdom nominees, autobiographical narratives, experimental manipulation of person characteristics related to wisdom) and analytical techniques (factor analysis, MDS, qualitative analysis) to creatively tap and measure implicit theories of wisdom.

Although each study makes a unique contribution, looking across studies shows us some general patterns. Implicit theories of wisdom are composed of an interactive combination of factors that come into play in certain individuals in given contexts. These include having high-level cognitive abilities, being particularly insightful or intuitive, being willing to reflect carefully on issues, and having genuine compassionate concern for other's welfare. Thus, wisdom involves not only competencies but also motivations, in particular, the motivation to help others. A final hallmark of wisdom (as reflected in implicit theories) is the ability to put skills and capabilities together with complexity and moderation in the face of real-world problems and issues. As seen in the nominee studies, wise individuals are those who have shown an ability to lead, guide, teach, and give good advice to others in the context of real-world problems, and based on their own rich life experience.

Wisdom has long been proverbially associated with age. Across studies we see empirical support for chronological age being associated with wisdom in people's implicit theories. This finding is clear in the nominee studies, but more complex when experimental studies are reviewed. In general, however, people associate advanced age (often through life experience) with wisdom. Age seems to be viewed as a necessary, rather than as a sufficient, condition for wisdom. Experimental studies have directed our attention to the relative roles of person characteristics (e.g., age, gender) and quality of the actual message or advice given.

Aside from age showing an association with wisdom in people's implicit theories, research also has addressed age differences in the contents of implicit theories of wisdom. Little research exists in this area but what does exist suggests that older people are less likely to think that older is necessarily wiser, and that they have a more complex, differentiated view of wisdom than do younger individuals. In addition, there is some emergent evidence that in different life phases people may have implicit theories of wisdom that are geared toward the developmental tasks of their current life phase.

This chapter provides an overview of what we now know, and what we don't know, about people's implicit theories of wisdom. In closing, we would like to briefly point out two directions for future research that could fill important gaps in the literature. In these two areas, and across the field more generally, close attention will need to be paid to balancing qualitative and contextual features of how wisdom is perceived and experienced in everyday life, with the power of rigor and control often found only in the laboratory.

First, further research is necessary on how gender is related to implicit theories of wisdom – both with respect to gender differences in implicit theories and with respect to the role of gender in people's implicit theories of wisdom. The cultural mythos linking wisdom to men is less obvious than that linking wisdom and age. It seems, however, that implicit theories often do relate wisdom to men more than to women. The few studies that have addressed this directly suggest that women's wisdom may be viewed as qualitatively different than men's, with the weight on social–compassionate features more than on intellect–insight features. Wisdom, however, purportedly requires the combination of these stereotypically feminine and masculine traits. The way in which these aspects of wisdom are weighted could have important implications for the range of individuals that people view as wise (young, old, men, women) and even the likelihood of seeing one's own self as wise. There is also no work on whether men and women differ in what they see as wise, except that women are somewhat less likely to nominate men as wise.

A second area of research involves how implicit theories of wisdom develop in childhood (potentially influenced by characters in popular stories, fairy tales, or movies) and adolescence, and to what extent implicit theories are consistent or changing as individuals move across the life span. In some ways, wisdom is a culturally defined value that all of us must uniformly learn and adopt to share our culture's general connotative sense of wisdom. This suggests relatively early learning of the construct, and consistency over time. Regardless of this common culturally shared meaning, however, individuals will fine-tune and hone their definition as they move through life: this may occur through observations and experiences of self and others facing life challenges and decisions that require wisdom. What major factors affect how implicit theories of wisdom are idiosyncratically shaped across the life span? What role does life phase play?

Of course, these are just two among the many interesting questions left to answer. We began this chapter by talking about the relative paucity of research on implicit theories of wisdom and also by noting that the climate is currently right for further exploration of this compelling topic. Our review has pointed to many interesting and creative methods for research, and has shown not only how much has already been learned about the views of wisdom that people "carry in their heads" but also how much there is still left to know and understand about this psychologically complex human virtue. Research on implicit theories will continue to be useful in understanding wisdom from the inside out.

References

Ardelt, M. (2000). Intellectual versus wisdom-related knowledge: The case for a different kind of learning in the later years of life. *Educational Gerontology, 26,* 771–789.

Baltes, P. B., Glück, J., & Kunzmann, U. (2002). Wisdom: Its structure and function in regulating successful lifespan development. In C. R. Snyder & S. J. Lopez (Eds.), *The handbook of positive psychology* (pp. 327–347). London: Oxford University Press.

Baltes, P. B., & Smith, J. E. (1990). Toward a psychology of wisdom and its ontogenesis. In R. J. Sternberg (Ed.), *Wisdom: Its nature, origins, and development* (pp. 87–120). New York: Cambridge University Press.

Baltes, P. B., Staudinger, U. M., & Sowarka, D. (1990). Wisdom: one facet of successful aging? In M. Perlmutter (Ed.), *Late life potential* (pp. 63–81). Washington, DC: Gerontological Society of America.

Baltes, P. B., Staudinger, U. M., Maercker, A., & Smith, J. (1995). People nominated as wise: A comparison study of wisdom-related knowledge. *Psychology and Aging, 10,* 155–166.

Bluck, S., & Glück, J. (2004). Making things better and learning a lesson: "Wisdom of experience" narratives across the lifespan. *Journal of Personality, 72,* 543–573.

Bronfenbrenner, U., & Ceci, S. J. (1994). Nature–nurture reconceptualized in developmental perspective: A bioecological model. *Psychological Review, 101,* 568–586.

Brugman, G. (2000). *Wisdom: Source of narrative coherence and eudaimonia.* Delft: Netherlands: Eburon.

Clayton, V. P., & Birren, J. E. (1980). The development of wisdom across the lifespan: A reexamination of an ancient topic. In P. B. Baltes & O. G. Brim (Eds.), *Life-span development and behavior* (Vol. 3, pp. 103–135). San Diego, CA: Academic Press.

Denney, N., Dew, J., & Kroupa, S. (1995). Perceptions of wisdom: What is wisdom and who has it? *Journal of Adult Development, 2,* 37–47.

Glück, J., Bluck, S., Baron, & McAdams, D. P. (2003). *The wisdom of experience: autobiographical narratives across adulthood.* Manuscript under review.

Heckhausen J., Dixon, R., & Baltes, P. (1989). Gains and losses in development throughout adulthood as perceived by different adult age groups. *Developmental Psychology, 25,* 109–121.

Hershey, D. A., & Farrell, A. H. (1997). Perceptions of wisdom associated with selected occupations and personality characteristics. *Current Psychology: Developmental, Learning, Personality, Social, 16,* 115–130.

Hira, F., & Faulkender, P. (1997). Perceiving wisdom: Do age and gender play a part? *International Journal of Aging and Human Development, 44,* 85–101.

Holliday, S. G., & Chandler, M. J. (1986). *Wisdom: Explorations in adult competence.* New York: Karger.

Jason, L. A., Reichler, A., King, C., Madsen, D., Camacho, J., & Marchese, W. (2001). The measurement of wisdom: A preliminary effort. *Journal Of Community Psychology, 29,* 585–598.

Jung, C. G. (1956). *Collected works: Vol. 5. Symbols of transformation.* Princeton, NJ: Princeton University Press.

Knight, A., & Parr, W. (1999). Age as a factor in judgements of wisdom and creativity. *New Zealand Journal of Psychology, 28*(1), 37–47.

Kunzmann, U., & Baltes, P. (2003). Wisdom-related knowledge: Affective, motivational, and interpersonal correlates. *Personality and Social Psychology Bulletin, 29,* 1104–1119.

Labouvie-Vief, G. (1990). Wisdom as integrated thought: Historical and developmental perspectives. In R. J. Sternberg (Ed.), *Wisdom: Its nature, origins, and development* (pp. 52–86). New York: Cambridge University Press.

McKee, P., & Barber, C. (1999). On defining wisdom. *International Journal of Human Development, 49*, 149–164.

Montgomery, A., Barber, C., & McKee, P. (2002). A phenomenological study of wisdom in later life. *International Journal of Aging and Human Development, 52*, 139–157.

Neisser, U. (1979). The concept of intelligence. In R. J. Sternberg & D. K. Detterman (Eds.), *Human intelligence: Perspectives on its theory and measurement*, (pp. 179–189). Norwood, NJ: Ablex.

Orwoll, L., & Achenbaum, W. A. (1993). Gender and the development of wisdom. *Human Development, 36*, 274–296.

Paulhus, D. L., Wehr, P., Harms, P. D., & Strausser, D. I. (2002). Use of exemplar surveys to reveal implicit types of intelligence. *Personality and Social Psychology Bulletin, 28*, 1051–1062.

Perlmutter, M., Adams, C., Nyquist, L., & Kaplan, C. (1988). [Beliefs about wisdom]. Unpublished data. (Cited in Orwoll & Perlmuter, 1990).

Rosch, E. (1975). Cognitive representations of semantic categories. *Journal of Experimental Psychology: General, 104*, 192–233.

Seligman, M. E. P., & Csikszentmihalyi, M. (2000). Positive psychology: An introduction. *American Psychologist, 55*, 5–14.

Smith, J., & Baltes, P. B. (1990). Wisdom-related knowledge: Age/Cohort differences in response to life-planning problems. *Developmental Psychology, 26*, 494–505.

Sowarka, D. (1989). Weisheit und weise Personen: Common-Sense-Konzepte älterer Menschen. [Wisdom and wise persons: Common-sense conceptions of older people.] *Zeitschrift für Entwicklungspsychologie und Paedagogische Psychologie, 21*, 87–109.

Stange, A., Kunzmann, U., & Baltes, P. B. (August, 2003). *Perceived wisdom: The interplay of age, wisdom-related knowledge, and social behavior*. Poster presented at the Annual Convention of the American Psychological Association, Toronto, Canada.

Stein, G. (1972). *Selected writings of Gertrude Stein* (C. Van Vechten, Ed.). New York: Vintage Books, Random House.

Sternberg, R. J., Conway, B. E., Ketron, J. L., & Bernstein, M. (1981). People's conceptions of intelligence. *Journal of Personality and Social Psychology, 41*, 37–55.

Sternberg, R. J. (1985). Implicit theories of intelligence, creativity, and wisdom. *Journal of Personality and Social Psychology, 49*, 607–627.

Sternberg, R. J. (1998). A balance theory of wisdom. *Review of General Psychology, 2*(4), 347–365.

Sternberg, R. J. (2000). Intelligence and wisdom. In R. J. Sternberg (Ed.), *Handbook of intelligence* (pp. 631–649). New York: Cambridge University Press.

Takahashi, M., & Bordia, P. (2000). The concept of wisdom: A cross-cultural comparison. *International Journal of Psychology, 35*, 1–9.

Webster, J. D. (2003). An exploratory analysis of a self-assessed wisdom scale. *Journal of Adult Development, 10*, 13–22.

Yang, S. (2001). Conceptions of wisdom among Taiwanese Chinese. *Journal of Cross-Cultural Psychology, 32*, 662–680.

5

The Psychology of Wisdom

Theoretical and Empirical Challenges

Ute Kunzmann and Paul B. Baltes

The search for human strengths has a long history in philosophical and religious writings. Since antiquity, one guide in this search has been the concept of wisdom (e.g., Assmann, 1994; Hall, 1922; Kekes, 1996; Oelmüller, 1989). At the core of this concept is the notion of a perfect, perhaps utopian, integration of knowledge and character, mind and virtue (e.g., Baltes & Staudinger, 2000; Baltes & Kunzmann, 2003).

Because wisdom can be considered an ideal end point of human development, lifespan psychologists and researchers interested in aging were among the first to consider this concept from a psychological point of view (e.g., Baltes, Dittmann-Kohli, & Dixon, 1984; Baltes & Smith, 1990; Clayton & Birren, 1980; Hall, 1922; Staudinger, 2001; Sternberg, 1990). In the meantime, wisdom has been studied in other fields of psychology as well, including social and personality research (e.g., Staudinger & Baltes, 1996; Wink & Helson, 1997), intelligence research (e.g., Li & Kunzmann, 2004; Sternberg, 1998), language pragmatics (Pennebaker & Stone, 2003; Sowarka, 1989), and motivational psychology (e.g., Baltes & Freund, 2003; Kunzmann & Baltes, 2003a).

Proponents of these different research fields agree on the notion that wisdom is a human resource that as a correlate and consequence is intrinsically involved in many facets of successful development. Furthermore, wisdom applies not only to our lives as individuals but also to societal functioning. In this sense, wisdom has been said to refer to time-tested, universal knowledge that guides our behavior in ways that optimize productivity and well-being on the level of individuals *and* on the level of society at large (e.g., Assmann, 1994; Baltes & Staudinger, 2000; Kramer, 2000; Sternberg, 1990, 1998). Especially during times of personal or societal transition (e.g., fundamental economic, cultural, and social change), becoming aware of wisdom, its nature and functions, is appealing to many (see also Baltes, forthcoming).

The objective of this chapter is to present psychological work on wisdom, with a focus on the Berlin Wisdom Paradigm developed by the second author and his collaborators (e.g., Baltes & Smith, 1990; Baltes & Staudinger, 2000; Baltes, Glück, & Kunzmann, 2002; Dittmann-Kohli & Baltes, 1990). In doing so, we will discuss some of the arguably major theoretical and empirical challenges that a psychology of wisdom has to deal with. On a theoretical level, one challenge lies in defining those core elements of wisdom that set wisdom apart from other human strengths (e.g., Aspinwall & Staudinger, 2003; Snyder & Lopez, 2002). As we have argued in the past, it is not necessarily the ingredients (specific elements or competencies) that distinguish wisdom from other competencies such as social intelligence, creativity, or practical intelligence (e.g., Gardner, 1999; Sternberg, 1999); rather, it is the way in which these elements interact in wisdom that is unique. The result of this interaction is an integrative and holistic approach toward life's challenges and problems – an approach to the meaning and conduct of life that embraces past, present, and future dimensions of phenomena, considers contextual variation, emphasizes value tolerance, and acknowledges the uncertainties inherent in any sense-making of the past, present, or future (e.g., Baltes et al., 2002; Baltes & Staudinger, 2000; Kunzmann & Baltes, 2003b).

On an empirical level, the challenge lies in formulating a definition of wisdom that can be used for empirical assessment and, in addition, permits experimental analyses to understand the causal factors associated with the acquisition of wisdom. We believe that the unique qualities of wisdom can be captured neither by standard personality questionnaires nor by traditional psychometric intelligence tests (see also Baltes & Smith, 1990; Baltes & Staudinger, 2000). This also has been demonstrated in empirical work on construct validation and differentiation (e.g., Staudinger, Lopez, & Baltes, 1997). In our approach, assessing wisdom involves the development of performance-based tasks that deal with fundamental (i.e., serious, complex, and ill-defined) problems as they potentially occur in real life. It is those problems that require wisdom and its associated orchestration of mind (knowledge) and virtue (character).

We hope to convince the reader that it is worth the effort to face the theoretical and empirical challenges involved in developing a psychology of wisdom. Perhaps most important, a psychology of wisdom helps reveal the strongest "general" if not universal qualities of humans as they have evolved through the experience of successive generations. Certainly only few do achieve wisdom in its higher form. Yet, in our view, it is the utopian mental representation of wisdom and the existence of wisdom-near persons who hold the key to what humans could be at their best.

Psychological Definitions of Wisdom

Approaches to a Psychological Definition of Wisdom
Although the concept of wisdom has had a long history in philosophy and religion, the psychology of wisdom is a relatively new field. Given that wisdom is an enormously rich and broad concept with varied meanings, developing a comprehensive psychological definition and operationalization of wisdom is difficult, if not impossible. Figure 5.1 presents seven general characteristics of wisdom as identified by the second author in his cultural–historical analysis. These seven characteristics have been repeatedly discussed in philosophical treatments of

---

Facets of Wisdom:
Based on Cultural–Historical Analysis

Wisdom...

- addresses difficult problems regarding the meaning and conduct of life

- represents truly outstanding knowledge, judgment, and advice

- is a perfect integration of knowledge and character, mind and virtue

- coordinates and promotes individual and societal growth

- involves balance and moderation

- includes an awareness of the limits of knowledge and uncertainties of the world

- is difficult to achieve but easily recognized.

FIGURE 5.1. General Facets of Wisdom. Based on the analysis of cultural–historical work on wisdom, these six characteristics were identified as core facets of wisdom. All facets have been discussed repeatedly in philosophical and religious writings about wisdom (for details, see Baltes, 2003).

wisdom (for more details see Baltes, 1993, 2003). Together, the seven properties constitute a general conceptualization of wisdom that can be used as a guide in psychological work. One can consider this general conceptualization as a working model that represents agreed-on properties of wisdom. Definitions of this concept that have been introduced in the psychological literature more recently can be evaluated on the basis of this working model, especially in terms of their comprehensiveness.

A second starting point for the development of psychological wisdom models is evidence from implicit theories on wisdom. This line of research has investigated the beliefs and mental representations people have about wisdom and wise persons. Put differently, the central question in this research has been if, and if so how, wisdom is represented in everyday language (Clayton & Birren, 1980; Holliday & Chandler, 1986; Orwoll & Perlmutter, 1990; Sowarka, 1989; Sternberg, 1985). To investigate this question empirically, people of different ages and with different social backgrounds typically are instructed to rate a large set of attributes (e.g., smart, cheerful, helpful, loving, foolish, relaxed) according to the degree to which each is typical of wisdom or wise persons. To establish conceptual differentiation, participants also rate how typical the same attributes are for other concepts such as creativity or intelligence.

What are the results from these studies? First, laypeople can clearly distinguish wisdom from other human capacities such as intelligence or creativity. Second, in laypeople's conceptions of wisdom, it represents human excellence at its very best. Third, lay conceptions of wisdom emphasize the multidimensional conception of wisdom. Given that past studies differ in the attributes rated by the participants as being more or less typical of wisdom, it is not surprising that the nature and number of the extracted dimensions differ somewhat across studies. It is, however, striking that all of the past studies have shown that lay conceptions of wisdom and wise persons entail a coalition of cognitive (e.g., outstanding knowledge about the self and the world), social (e.g., empathic concern, the ability to give good advice), emotional (e.g., the ability to regulate one's own feelings), and motivational (e.g., orientation toward personal growth) capacities.

There is much overlap between implicit theories of wisdom and conceptualizations of wisdom in cultural–historical and philosophical work; however, these two approaches to defining the nature of wisdom have different strengths. Philosophical and cultural–historical work offers an abstract, comprehensive, and systematic description of the wisdom concept. Implicit theories on wisdom are less comprehensive and more specific and concrete in terms of the human strengths that might be subsumed under this concept. This is understandable because laypeople have not articulated an abstract framework of wisdom as a theoretical construct; rather their representations are likely to be linked to specific exemplars and wisdom-related experiences. When considered together, philosophical and implicit approaches to wisdom provide an excellent starting point for explicit psychological work on wisdom.

Explicit Psychological Definitions of Wisdom

To psychologists, implicit theories and cultural-historical work on wisdom are important because the two lines of research can inform explicit definitions of wisdom. Put differently, in our view, there should be sufficient agreement between explicit psychological wisdom models and conceptualizations of wisdom held by laypeople and philosophers. By contrast, however, psychological researchers are interested in testing whether implicit and philosophical theories on wisdom and wise persons are "right" or "wrong" in an empirical sense. In doing so, psychologists have begun to develop definitions of wisdom that allow the operationalization and measurement of wisdom-related performance, at least in an approximate sense (e.g., Baltes & Smith, 1990; Baltes & Staudinger, 2000; Sternberg, 1998).

Three types of explicit conceptualizations of wisdom have been identified in the literature, namely, conceptualizations of wisdom as an aspect of personality development in adulthood (Erikson, 1959; Wink & Helson, 1997), conceptualizations of wisdom as postformal dialectic thinking (Kramer, 2000; Labouvie-Vief, 1990), and definitions of wisdom as an expanded form of intelligence and cognitive–emotional expertise (e.g., Baltes & Smith, 1990; Baltes & Staudinger, 2000; Sternberg, 1998).

Erikson's work is an example of a definition that views wisdom as part of personality. For Erikson, personality development requires the attainment and resolution of a sequence of psychosocial crises, each emerging at a particular stage in the life cycle (Erikson, 1959). Wisdom is thought to result from resolving the final crises occurring in old age when a person faces his or her own death and dying. Erikson proposed that dealing with death and dying can result in either despair or integrity (i.e., wisdom). Resolution with integrity means that a person can accept that his or her own life is coming to a conclusion. This insight allows one to have a detached concern with life and to evaluate problems from a holistic and abstract perspective. Another consequence of the acceptance that one's life comes to an end is the feeling that one is responsible for passing one's knowledge on to future generations. Thus, according to Erikson, wisdom involves a detached view on the world of human affairs and transcendence beyond self-centered interests.

Theorists of cognitive development in the Piagetian tradition, or those influenced by it, treat wisdom as a late stage of cognitive development characterized by the emergence of dialectical thought (e.g., Riegel, 1973). Dialectical thinking derives from the insight that knowledge about self, others, and the world evolves in an everlasting process of theses, antitheses, and syntheses. From this perspective, wisdom has been described as the integration of different modes of knowing (Labouvie-Vief, 1990); of opposing points of view (Kitchener & Brenner, 1990); or of different intrapsychic systems such as cognition, emotion, and motivation (Birren & Fisher, 1990; Kramer, 2000; Orwoll & Perlmutter, 1990).

Finally, wisdom has been conceptualized in the context of psychometric models of intelligence. Although these definitions draw on models of intelligence, they also make explicit the ways in which wisdom is different from this concept (e.g., Baltes & Smith, 1990; Baltes & Staudinger, 2000; Sternberg, 1998). Our own approach to wisdom, which we will describe in greater detail later, is grounded in this third tradition. It defines wisdom as a special "expertise-like" case of the pragmatics of intelligence (intellect) that includes knowledge about cognitive, motivational, and emotional aspects of adaptive functioning in a specific domain, that is, the meaning and conduct of life (e.g., Dixon & Baltes, 1986). Sternberg's wisdom model represents another prominent approach. Proceeding from his triarchic theory of intelligence, Sternberg (1998) viewed tacit knowledge – a component of practical intelligence – as the core feature of wisdom. Tacit knowledge is action oriented, it helps individuals to achieve goals they personally value, and it can be acquired only through learning from one's own experiences, not "vicariously" through reading books or through others' instructions. Importantly, wisdom is not tacit knowledge per se. Rather, wisdom is involved when practical intelligence (tacit knowledge) is applied to maximizing not just one's own or someone else's self-interests but a balance of various self-interests (intrapersonal) with the interests of others (interpersonal) and other aspects of the context in which one lives (extrapersonal), such as one's city, country, environment, or even God (Sternberg, 1998). From this view, what sets wisdom apart from (practical) intelligence is its orientation toward the maximization of a common good, rather than individual well-being.

In our assessment, explicit wisdom models are by and large in agreement with cultural–historical and implicit wisdom theories. Despite their different origins, they share at least three assumptions about the nature of wisdom; namely, wisdom is integrative and holistic, it refers to outstanding performance, and it guides a person's behavior in ways that simultaneously optimize this person's own potential and that of fellow mortals.

The Berlin Wisdom Paradigm

Historical Background
In our approach, wisdom is embedded in a theoretical framework for the study of intellectual development that highlights two distinct but interacting categories of intellectual functioning: the mechanics and the pragmatics of intelligence (Baltes, 1987; Baltes, Staudinger, & Lindenberger, 1999). This framework draws on earlier theories of intelligence, such as the theory of fluid and crystallized intelligence by Cattell and Horn (e.g., Cattell, 1971; Horn & Hofer, 1992). The cognitive mechanics, on the one hand, refer to the neurophysiological architecture of the brain as it has evolved during biological evolution. Speed, accuracy, and the coordination of basic information processing operations are examples of the cognitive mechanics. Given their biological basis, the cognitive mechanics are assumed to decline relatively early in the life span. The cognitive pragmatics, on the other hand, are indicated by culturally transmitted bodies of knowledge. Typical examples are reading and writing skills, educational qualifications, or skills related to practical problems of everyday life. Because of the importance of experience in acquiring knowledge-based skills, the cognitive pragmatics are thought to show stability or even selected growth into old age.

In our view, wisdom represents one prototypical example of the cognitive pragmatics. The bodies of knowledge that are typical of wisdom, however, go beyond those subsumed under other more limited forms of pragmatic intelligence. In fact, our definition of wisdom as expert knowledge about fundamental life problems is meant to expand the traditional dual-process model of intellectual functioning and its close link to the psychometric method. Studying wisdom as a component of the cognitive pragmatics requires a return to the original conception of intelligence as general adaptation to the changing biological and environmental conditions inevitably taking place throughout the lifespan (e.g., Baltes, 1987; Baltes, Staudinger, & Lindenberger, 1999; Dixon & Baltes, 1986). The notion that intelligence and intelligent behavior need to serve a broader purpose than academic achievement has been an important motivating factor for our decision to begin to develop a research program on wisdom (e.g., Dixon & Baltes, 1986; Dittmann-Kohli & Baltes, 1990; Smith & Baltes, 1990). More recently, Krampe and Baltes (2003) have proposed a general theoretical framework that delineates a wide range of everyday contexts to which people of different ages can allocate their intellectual resources. This framework points to the limits of conventional models of intelligence as well.

Definition: Wisdom as Expertise in the Fundamental Pragmatics of Life

In the Berlin paradigm, wisdom has been defined as a highly valued and outstanding expertise in dealing with fundamental, that is, existential, problems related to the meaning and conduct of life (e.g., Baltes & Smith, 1990; Baltes & Staudinger, 1993, 2000). These problems are typically complex and poorly defined, and have multiple, yet unknown, solutions. Deciding on a particular career path, accepting the death of a loved one, dealing with personal mortality, or solving long-lasting conflicts among family members exemplify the type of problem that calls for wisdom-related expertise. In contrast, more circumscribed everyday problems can be effectively handled by using more limited abilities. To solve a math problem, for example, wisdom-related expertise usually is not particularly helpful.

To assess wisdom-related products, we developed five criteria. Expert knowledge about the meaning and conduct of life is thought to approach wisdom if it meets *all* five criteria. Two criteria are labeled basic because they are characteristic of all types of expertise; these are: (a) rich factual knowledge about human nature and the life course and (b) rich procedural knowledge about ways of dealing with life problems. The three other criteria are labeled meta-criteria because they are thought to be unique to wisdom and, in addition, carry the notion of being universal: (c) lifespan contextualism, that is, an awareness and understanding of the many contexts of life, how they relate to each other and change over the lifespan; (d) value relativism and tolerance, that is, an acknowledgment of individual, social, and cultural differences in values and life priorities; and (e) knowledge about handling uncertainty, including the limits of one's own knowledge (for details, see Baltes & Staudinger, 2000).

These five wisdom criteria were designed to reflect a balance between two wisdom faculties – intellect and character. Put differently, these criteria do not favor technical or exclusively intellectual knowledge such as fluid–mechanical intelligence. On the contrary, according to our criteria, expertise in the fundamental pragmatics of life reflects pragmatic knowledge about all relevant conditions of behavioral expression, including emotional and motivational ones. Knowledge about life's uncertainties and about ways of dealing with them, for example, requires knowledge about the emotions intertwined with uncertainty, feelings of insecurity, fear, or anxiety, as well as knowledge about the dynamics between the personal and other-oriented good.

Our definition of wisdom suggests that wisdom is different from academic intelligence and it implies that a wise person differs in important respects from an academically intelligent person. The notion of a successful integration of mind and character in wisdom results in a different prototypical person – a person who uses his or her intellectual abilities for the "right" purposes, for example, to strengthen his or her character and to help others develop their strengths and potential (see also Sternberg, 1998).

The Development, Structure, and Functions of Wisdom: A Theoretical Model

Conceptualizing wisdom as expertise and linking it to lifespan psychology (Baltes, 1987, 1997) suggest a number of conditions under which wisdom is likely to develop. First, as is typical for the development of any expertise, we assume that wisdom is acquired through an extended and intensive process of learning and practice. This process clearly requires a high degree of motivation to strive for excellence as well as supportive environmental conditions.

Second, because wisdom is different from other more circumscribed positive characteristics in that it involves an integration of intellect and character, its development and refinement require multiple factors and processes, including certain intellectual abilities, the availability of mentors, mastery of critical life experiences, openness to new experiences, and values referring to personal growth, benevolence, and tolerance.

Third, there are most likely several paths leading to wisdom, rather than only one. Put differently, similar levels of wisdom may result from different combinations of facilitative factors and processes. If a certain coalition of facilitative factors is present, some individuals continue a developmental trajectory toward higher levels of wisdom-related

knowledge. Potentially facilitating factors such as a certain family background, the occurrence and mastery of critical life events, professional
practice, or societal transitions, such as the separation and reunion of
Germany, may interact in complex additive, compensatory, or time-
lagged ways.

These general theoretical perspectives are summarized in our theoretical model of wisdom depicted in Figure 5.2. This model states
that three types of factors are influential for the development of
wisdom-related knowledge, namely, *facilitative contexts*, as determined
for example by a person's gender, social context, or culture; *expertise-
specific factors* such as life experience, professional practice, or receiving
and providing mentorship; and finally, *person-related factors* such as certain intellectual capacities, personality traits, or emotional dispositions.
These three types of factors are thought to have an influence on the development of wisdom-related knowledge because they determine the
ways in which people experience the world and plan, manage, or make
sense out of their lives (i.e., the context of developmental regulation). All
relations among the three components of our model – facilitative factors,
context of developmental regulation, and wisdom-related knowledge –
are meant to be bi-directional and accumulative over the life course.

Assessment: The Method of Thinking Aloud about Fundamental Questions of Life

Until the present, psychological work on wisdom has been primarily
theoretical. This lack of empirical investigation is probably because of
the difficulties involved in developing methods to assess wisdom – an
immensely broad concept with many distinct facets. Our own assessment method is based on a modified version of the method of "thinking aloud," which was originally developed in cognitive psychology
(Ericsson & Simon, 1984).

To test for wisdom, we instruct our study participants to think aloud
about hypothetical life problems. One might be: "Imagine that someone
gets a call from a good friend who says that he or she cannot go on
anymore and wants to commit suicide." Another problem reads: "A
15-year-old girl wants to get married right away. What could one
consider and do?" Before we present a hypothetical problem we let our
participants know (a) that they should talk about what they think without pausing, (b) that there is no right or wrong solution to the problem,
(c) that we are interested in specific and general aspects of the problem, and (d) that they themselves should decide when they would like to

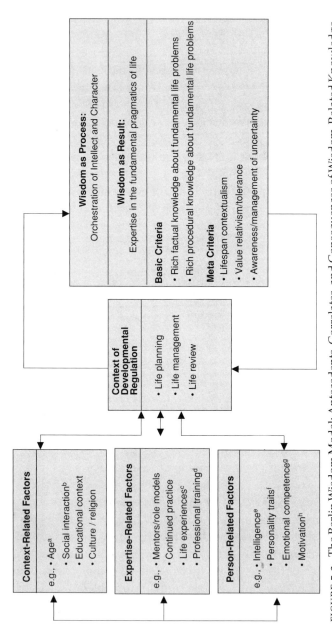

FIGURE 5.2. The Berlin Wisdom Model: Antecedents, Correlates, and Consequences of Wisdom-Related Knowledge. The development and expression of wisdom, as defined in the model, requires an expertise-facilitating coalition of internal and external factors. At the same time, wisdom represents a resource that potentially has beneficial short- and long-term consequences for the development of individuals, groups, and the society at large.

[a] Pasupathi, Staudinger, and Baltes (2001); Smith and Baltes (1990); Staudinger (1999a); [b] Staudinger & Baltes (1996); [c] Baltes, Staudinger, Maerker, & Smith (1995); [d] Smith and Baltes (1994); Staudinger, Smith, & Baltes (1992); [e,f] Staudinger, Lopez, & Baltes (1997); [g,h] Kunzmann & Baltes (2003a)

finish. Participants then think aloud about a given problem without further intervention. An excerpt of a participants' response to the 15-year-old girl problem might be: "Well, on the surface, this seems like an easy problem. On average, marriage for 15-year-old girls is not a good thing. On the other hand, thinking about getting married is not the same as actually doing it. I guess many girls think about it without getting married in the end. . . . There are situations where the average case doesn't fit. Perhaps special life circumstances are involved. The girl may have a terminal illness. She may not be from this country or perhaps she lives in another culture."

Trained raters evaluate responses such as this one by using the five criteria that we specified as defining wisdom-related knowledge. The assessment of wisdom-related knowledge on the basis of these criteria exhibits satisfactory reliability and validity. For example, middle-aged and older public figures from Berlin nominated as life experienced or wise by a panel of journalists – independently of our definition of wisdom – were among the top performers in our wisdom tasks and outperformed same-aged adults that were not nominated (Baltes, Staudinger, Maerker, & Smith, 1995).

Past Empirical Evidence

Past and ongoing research in our project has been based on our theoretical model of the development, structure, and functions of wisdom (see also Figure 5.2). In other words, we have studied factors and processes that can be considered as antecedents, correlates, and consequences of the development of wisdom-related knowledge during ontogenesis. We also investigated ways of optimizing the expression of wisdom-related performance by using intervention strategies. What were our major findings?

First, and consistent with the idea that wisdom is an ideal, rather than a state of being, high levels of wisdom-related knowledge were rare. Many adults are on the way toward wisdom, but very few people approach a high level of wisdom-related knowledge as we measure it. This finding is consistent with the cultural–historical position that wisdom as manifested in a person does not exist in pure form.

Second, the period of late adolescence and early adulthood is the primary age window for a first foundation of wisdom-related knowledge to emerge. On our 7-point wisdom scale, the average score achieved in the sample studied was $M = 2.97$ ($SD = .83$). In the older-than-young-adulthood samples, we observed no further changes in the average level of wisdom beyond the level achieved in early adulthood (Pasupathi, Staudinger, & Baltes, 2001; Smith & Baltes, 1990; Staudinger, 1999a). In addition, and as expected, during adolescence and young adulthood, individual differences in psychometric intelligence were significant predictors of wisdom-related knowledge. During middle- and older adulthood, however, the contribution of intelligence to wisdom-related knowledge is nonsignificant.

Third, for wisdom-related knowledge and judgment to develop further, either beyond the level achieved in early adulthood or in one's own course of lifespan development, other factors than age become critical (Staudinger et al., 1997; Staudinger, Maciel, Smith, & Baltes, 1998). Consistent with our theoretical model, findings suggest that it takes a complex coalition of expertise-enhancing factors from different domains, ranging from a person's social–cognitive style (e.g., social intelligence, openness to experience) over this person's immediate social context (e.g., presence of role models) to societal and cultural conditions (e.g., exposure to societal transitions). Our prediction studies of wisdom suggest that neither academic intelligence nor basic personality traits play a major role in the development of wisdom-related knowledge during adulthood. General life experiences, professional training and practice, and certain motivational preferences such as an interest in understanding others seem to be more important (e.g., Staudinger et al., 1997; Smith & Baltes, 1994; Staudinger, Smith, & Baltes, 1992). If such a coalition of facilitating factors is present, some individuals may continue a developmental trajectory toward higher levels of wisdom-related knowledge. Therefore, simply getting older is not a sufficient condition for the development of higher levels of wisdom-related knowledge, and yet, older adults are among the top performers in wisdom-related tasks.

Fourth, the expression of wisdom-related performance, as we have measured it, can be enhanced by relatively simple social interventions. Boehmig-Krumhaar, Staudinger, and Baltes (2002), demonstrated how a memory strategy, namely, a version of the method of loci, in which participants were instructed to travel on a cloud around the world can be used to focus people's attention on cultural relativism and tolerance. As predicted, following this intervention, participants expressed higher levels of wisdom-related knowledge, especially value relativism and tolerance. Furthermore, Staudinger and Baltes (1996) conducted an experiment in which study participants were asked to think aloud about a wisdom problem under several experimental conditions involving imagined and actual social interactions. Specifically, before responding individually, some participants had the opportunity to discuss the problem with a person they brought into the laboratory and with whom they usually discuss difficult life problems; others were asked to engage in an inner dialogue about the problem with a person of their choice, or to simply think about the problem on their own. Actual social dialogue and the inner-voice dialogue increased performance levels by almost one standard deviation. One important implication of these two studies is that many adults have the latent potential to perform better on wisdom tasks than they actually often do.

Ongoing Research Program

In our ongoing research we have expanded our earlier work on non-cognitive correlates of wisdom. As reviewed earlier, in the past we have demonstrated that wisdom-related knowledge is different from academic intelligence in that it requires a complex coalition of social-cognitive dispositions (e.g., openness to experience, interest in understanding others) as well as accumulated experience with critical life events (e.g., Staudinger et al., 1997). In our current research, we have begun to study the emotional-motivational side to wisdom more explicitly than we did in the past. In this work, we consider emotional and motivational traits, habits, and preferences as antecedents, constituents, and consequences of wisdom-related knowledge (e.g., Baltes et al., 2002; Kunzmann & Baltes, 2003a).

Wisdom and emotion: Theoretical considerations and empirical evidence. As mentioned earlier, certain emotional experiences and dispositions are fundamental to the acquisition of wisdom, defined as an expertise in the meaning and conduct of life. Emotional dispositions can facilitate or hinder the development of wisdom in multiple ways. For example, stimulating social environments, exposure to good educational systems, or a supportive family all contribute to the development of wisdom-related knowledge. The effectiveness of these environmental factors, however, is moderated by a person's affective dispositions and experiences, for example, by his or her emotional stability, impulsivity, or level of neuroticism. It is also likely that the expression of wisdom-related knowledge in a particular situation is moderated by certain emotional dispositions, habits, or behaviors. An advice-giver who is not able or willing to imagine how a needy person feels, for example, is unlikely to make the effort to engage in wisdom-related thinking, which would involve an effortful and time-consuming analysis of the advice-seeker's problem. Similarly, during a mutual conflict with another person, being able to imagine how this person feels or how one would feel in the other's place may be one stepping-stone to value tolerance and a cooperative approach typical of wisdom.

At the same time, however, one can easily think of emotional reactions that are likely to hinder a wisdom-like approach to difficult and potentially stressful situations. Candidates are self-centered negative feelings, especially if they are intense and long lasting. For example, strong and chronic feelings of anxiety most likely inhibit wisdom-related thinking, which requires distance to the immediate situation, balance, and elaboration. It is in this sense that "cold" cognition and "hot" emotion have been described as two forces that antagonize one another (cf. Keltner & Gross, 1999).

Therefore, the links between other- and self-centered emotions, on the one hand, and wisdom-related knowledge, on the other, can take many directions. The idea that certain emotions hinder or facilitate the activation of wisdom-related knowledge and behavior may be less popular in the literature than the notion that it is wisdom that regulates a person's emotional experiences and reactions. Our conception of wisdom, for example, suggests that wisdom refers to integrative and holistic knowledge that represents phenomena on various levels of abstraction and in different time frames. Therefore, it should help people to regard phenomena from a broader viewpoint, to relativize the emotional implications, and to adopt a detached and less emotional attitude. This is not to say that people with high levels of wisdom-related knowledge do not experience emotions at all or that their emotional life is reduced and flat. On the contrary, people high on wisdom-related knowledge have a deep understanding of the complexity of life and the dynamics of gains and losses during development. Given their awareness and understanding of life, including its low points, wiser people are likely to occasionally experience some level of what Baltes (1997) has called "constructive melancholy." Put differently, people with high levels of wisdom-related knowledge may spontaneously react strongly to certain fundamental life events because of their deep understanding of the significance of these events. Seen over time, however, wisdom-related knowledge should facilitate the down-regulation of negative emotions so that they do not become dysfunctional.

To begin to test these predictions, we recently conducted an experiment in which we exposed people with different levels of wisdom-related knowledge to three life problems, each presented in a short film clip of about 10 minutes' duration. The problems dealt with an older woman who learns that she has Alzheimer's disease (Alzheimer's film), a woman who mourns for her husband and young daughter, who were killed in a car accident (family loss film), and a middle-aged woman who escapes her frustrating family life to travel and find herself (personal growth film). We know from previous studies that these films evoke strong emotional reactions, especially sympathy with the main protagonists, feelings of sadness in response to the family loss and Alzheimer's films, and feelings of happiness in response to the personal growth film (Kunzmann & Grühn, 2003).

We had the following more specific predictions for people with high levels of wisdom-related knowledge: (a) Because they are likely to recognize the significance and deeper meaning of events and phenomena, people with high levels of wisdom-related knowledge should first show a salient emotional response when confronted with another person's serious life problem (empathy hypothesis); (b) after further processing of the information, however, people with high levels of wisdom-related knowledge will exhibit effective down-regulation of their emotional responses to distance themselves and to bring their wisdom-related knowledge into foreground (regulation hypothesis).

Our initial findings are consistent with the empathy prediction. As predicted, people with higher levels of wisdom-related knowledge showed greater emotional reactions to two fundamental life scenarios. They reported to experience greater pleasure in response to the personal growth film, and they experienced greater sadness in response to the film dealing with Alzheimer's. In the near future, we will test our second prediction that people with higher levels of wisdom-related knowledge will distance themselves and down-regulate their first emotional response after further processing of the information about the emotion-arousing life scenario.

Wisdom and motivation: Theoretical considerations and empirical evidence. Another focus of our more recent work on explicating the structure and function of wisdom-related knowledge involves the consideration of values and behavioral preferences as they may become relevant when people grapple with fundamental questions regarding the meaning and conduct of life. This line of research is relevant to the work of several modern philosophers influenced by the tradition of early Greek philosophy who have argued that wisdom is knowledge about ways of developing oneself, not only without violating others' rights but also with coproducing resources for others to develop (e.g., Kekes, 1996). From this view, wisdom involves certain motivational dispositions, values, and behavioral preferences that facilitate a good life on the individual, group, and societal levels (see also Baltes & Staudinger, 2000; Kramer, 2000; Sternberg, 1998).

This idea that wisdom involves a joint consideration of self- and other-related interests, however, has rarely been tested empirically. A questionnaire study from our laboratory can be considered a first step in demonstrating that wisdom is inherently of an intra- and interpersonal nature (Kunzmann & Baltes, 2003a). In this study we assessed wisdom-related knowledge by our standard procedure and, in addition, measured several motivational and emotional dispositions such as value orientations (i.e., preference for a pleasurable life, personal growth, insight, well-being of friends, environmental protection, societal engagement), preferred modes of conflict management (i.e., dominance, submission, avoidance, cooperation) and affective experiences (pleasantness, positive involvement, and negative affect).

As mentioned earlier, our specific predictions were based on the notion that wisdom-related knowledge requires and reflects a joint concern for developing one's own and others' potential (see also Sternberg, 1998). In contrast, a predominant search for self-centered pleasure and comfort should not be associated with wisdom. Accordingly, people high on wisdom-related knowledge should report (a) a profile of values that is oriented toward personal growth, insight, and the well-being of others, rather than a pleasurable and comfortable life, (b) a cooperative approach to managing interpersonal conflicts rather than a dominant, submissive, or avoidant style, and (c) an affective structure that is process- and environment-oriented rather than evaluative and self-centered.

The findings reported in Kunzmann and Baltes (2003a) were consistent with our theory-guided predictions. People with higher levels of wisdom-related knowledge reported less preference for values revolving around a pleasurable and comfortable life. Instead, they reported preferring self-oriented values such as personal growth and insight, as well as a preference for other-oriented values related to environmental protection, societal engagement, and the well-being of friends. People with high levels of wisdom-related knowledge also showed less preference for conflict management strategies that reflect either a one-sided concern with one's own interests (i.e., dominance), a one-sided concern with others' interests (i.e., submission), or no concern at all (i.e., avoidance). As predicted, they preferred a cooperative approach reflecting a joint concern for one's own and the opponent's interests. Finally, people with high levels of wisdom-related knowledge reported that they less frequently experience self-centered pleasant feelings (e.g., happiness, amusement) but more frequently felt process-oriented and environment-centered positive emotions (e.g., interest, inspiration).

More recently, we also have added to this work on wisdom another line of inquiry that links wisdom-related knowledge to general processes of successful development as conceptualized in the model of successful development "Selective Optimization with Compensation" (SOC; Baltes & Baltes, 1990; Baltes, 1997; Freund & Baltes, 2003). The SOC model posits that the orchestration of three regulatory processes produce successful development: selection of goals, optimization of goal-relevant means, and compensation of lost means by substitute means (Baltes & Baltes, 1990; Freund & Baltes, 2002).

How do wisdom and SOC interact and produce a successful development? In our conception, they cooperate. A successful development requires the pursuit of selection, optimization, and compensation. Past empirical work has supported the view that people who engage in these processes attain high levels of functioning in the realms selected, for example, professional expertise or physical fitness (e.g., Freund & Riediger, 2003; Wiese, Freund, & Baltes, 2002).

Selection, optimization, and compensation, however, can be applied to any outcomes, including socially undesirable ones. From this point of view, a corrupt but powerful politician can be as successful as Mother Theresa because both are thought to be successful at selecting and pursuing their goals. In our view, it is here that wisdom comes into play. Wisdom as an expert system in the fundamental pragmatics of life can define the most general range of what goals and what means are socially acceptable and desirable in human development. For example, a person high on wisdom-related knowledge is likely to select and pursue goals that do not violate the rights of others and co-produce collective resources. The life management strategy of selective optimization with compensation, on the one hand, is value-neutral and specifies the conditions by which progress in any domain of human efficacy and performance is possible. Wisdom, on the other hand, helps evaluating the moral–ethical dimension of the goals and means involved. Therefore, for positive development on the individual and societal levels to evolve, wisdom needs to intervene and give direction to the behavioral processes related to selection, optimization, and compensation.

Conclusions and Directions for Future Research

Defining Wisdom: Theoretical Challenges

As we reviewed earlier, several promising psychological definitions of wisdom have recently been proposed in the literature (for reviews see Baltes & Staudinger, 2000; Kramer, 2000; Sternberg, 1998). By and large, these models are consistent with cultural–historical work and implicit theories of wisdom. Furthermore, psychological models share important ideas about the nature of wisdom, for example, that wisdom is different from other human strengths in that it is integrative and inherently an inter- and intrapersonal concept (e.g., Baltes & Staudinger, 2000; Kramer, 2000; Sternberg, 1998).

In our own approach, we have pursued a line of inquiry that reflects transdisciplinary theoretical analysis, on the one hand, and empirical experimental work, on the other. The focus of our theoretical work has been to define wisdom as an expert system in human thought and behavior that coordinates knowledge and virtue, mind and character. Depending on the preferred level of analysis and research questions pursued, both wisdom components, the more cognitively driven intellect and the more emotionally driven character, can be studied in interaction or broken down into specific units. Put differently, the conceptualization of wisdom as an orchestration of intellect and personality is hierarchical and ranges from broad dispositions and abilities to more specific performances and preferences on the behavioral level.

Certainly, the field of psychological wisdom research, including our own research program, is an evolving one. On a more theoretical level of analysis, at least two major questions deserve further study. The first question refers to the number and nature of the more specific intellectual and personality-related facets that are critical to the expression and development of wisdom. A comprehensive psychological theory of wisdom needs to also explicate the ways in which these facets interact in a given context and over time.

In this chapter, for example, we reported work from our laboratory that could provide some guidance for the investigation of emotional–motivational strengths that are associated with wisdom. Our findings oppose the view that wisdom generally involves emotional distance and detachment (e.g., Erikson, 1959). Rather, in our view, it is the ability to dynamically adjust to given contextual demands that is important. Therefore, wise people are able to sympathize with their fellow mortals when functional, regardless of whether they are experiencing life transitions that potentially lead to personal growth or are going through existential problems dealing with their own death and dying. If cognitive processing and evaluation is in the foreground, however, they would be able to exhibit distancing. Other research from our laboratory suggests that people high in wisdom-related knowledge are likely to frequently experience process- and environment-oriented feelings such as high levels of inspiration and interest. As to be expected, however, a constantly higher level of pleasant feelings, which are primarily self-centered and evaluative (e.g., pride, happiness, or joy), appear not to be characteristic of wise persons. In terms of motivational dispositions, our theory is consistent with Sternberg's notion that a central aspect of wisdom is a joint concern for developing one's own potential *and* that of others (Sternberg, 1998). We were able to demonstrate this link on the level of general value orientations as well as on the level of specific conflict management strategies (Kunzmann & Baltes, 2003a).

A major second theme of future work on wisdom should be the standing of wisdom in the context of other psychological concepts. Past work on the prediction of wisdom suggests that our measure of wisdom has a high degree of uniqueness (e.g., Staudinger et al., 1997). We demonstrated discriminant validity with traditional measures of academic intelligence and basic personality traits.

It also will be interesting to see the relationships between wisdom and other expanded forms of pragmatic intelligence (e.g., Snyder & Lopez, 2002; Sternberg, Lautry, & Lubart, 2003; Aspinwall & Staudinger, 2003). There are a number of human capacities that people can bring to bear when dealing with life's challenges and problems, including practical, emotional, or interpersonal abilities (e.g., Gardner, 1999; Mayer & Salovey, 1993; Sternberg, 1999). Similar to wisdom, these human strengths help us deal with challenges and problems as they occur in our everyday lives. In our view, however, an important difference is that they are tailored to relatively specific problems. For example, creativity can help a person in dealing with a problem that requires a particular invention or social intelligence can help in a conflict with others, but how can a person coordinate his or her behavior to find solutions that are acceptable from a broader viewpoint extending over time and space? It is here that wisdom-related knowledge comes into play. Because of its holistic and integrative nature, wisdom can be seen as the most general framework that directs and optimizes individual development. For example, the presence of wisdom-related knowledge can issue warnings when we apply our emotional intelligence to harm others rather than to support them, when we do not use our intellectual capacities to develop ourselves, or when we focus too much on the present and do not consider the triangulation of past, present, and future conditions. These and similar considerations should be addressed more systematically in future research both on theoretical and empirical levels.

Assessing Wisdom: Empirical Challenges

With few exceptions, past research on wisdom has been theoretical rather than empirical. What is still missing, in our view, is work that exemplifies the core of psychology as a discipline, that is, the development of a theory that is based on and consistent with empirical evidence. Whereas most philosophers have used human reason as the defining and guiding principle, psychologists can add the method of experimental investigation. With this empirical experimental method, it may not be possible to consider all facets of wisdom. In fact, some wisdom facets most likely are not testable in the strict sense. We do believe, however, that developing empirically testable definitions of wisdom identifies the special contributions that psychologists can make to an interdisciplinary theory of wisdom, eventually resulting in a more comprehensive and deeper understanding of wisdom-related phenomena (see also Baltes, 2003).

In this chapter, we presented our own research program on wisdom, which is one of the few exceptions to the lack of empirical research in this field. We would like to emphasize that we consider our empirical wisdom paradigm as one way of operationalizing wisdom; it has advantages as well as disadvantages. A disadvantage of our method is that it is resource- and time-consuming because it involves the processing of qualitative data; however, there is also an important advantage of our method. Specifically, our measure focuses on one important outcome of a successful orchestration of intellect and character, namely, an expertise in fundamental questions regarding the meaning and conduct of life. Put differently, wisdom, as we have defined and measured it, reflects both components of wisdom: intellect and character. Other measures primarily capture only one of these two components. For example, some researchers have proposed to develop wisdom measures by modifying existing personality questionnaires (e.g., Ardelt, 2003; Wink & Helson, 1997). It is impossible to assess intellectual functioning through personality questionnaires. Maybe even more problematic, there is research suggesting that people's subjective reports about who they are and what they can do are often inconsistent with their objective competencies and traits (e.g., Salovey et al., 2002; Taylor & Brown, 1988); and the discrepancy between subjective self-evaluations and objective competencies seems to become larger with advancing age (e.g., Kunzmann, Little, & Smith, 2002; Smith & Baltes, 1997).

Given that wisdom may not be adequately assessed by standard personality questionnaires, we suggest that future research on the assessment of wisdom should explore new methods and tests. Our own approach is only one way to do this. Other approaches may focus on tasks that explicitly require knowledge and expertise about the self and one's own development, rather than general knowledge about the world and lifespan development (e.g., Staudinger, 1999b). Developing tasks that provide more information about the people confronted with a given fundamental problem than the tasks that we used in the past also might be valuable. It is important, we believe, that people demonstrate their wisdom-related knowledge and competence in dealing with existential and complex human problems. Filling out personality tests does not require wisdom but rather other, more limited and less integrative, holistic abilities and traits.

We hope that we were able to convince the reader that wisdom is a unique concept that deserves a central place in contemporary psychological research. Wisdom differs from other human strengths in that it involves an orchestration of mind and virtue, intellect and character. This orchestration results in an integrative and holistic perspective on life that we have conceptualized as an expertise in the fundamental pragmatics of life.

References

Aspinwall, L. G., & Staudinger, U. M. (Eds.) (2003). *A psychology of human strengths: Fundamental questions and future directions for a positive psychology.* Washington, DC: American Psychological Association.

Ardelt, M. (2003). Empirical assessment of a three-dimensional wisdom scale. *Research on Aging, 25,* 275–324.

Assmann, A. (1994). Wholesome knowledge: Concepts of wisdom in a historical and cross-cultural perspective. In D. L. Featherman, R. M. Lerner, & M. Perlmutter (Eds.), *Life-span development and behavior* (Vol. 12, pp. 187–224). Hillsdale, NJ: Erlbaum.

Baltes, P. B. (1987). Theoretical propositions of life-span developmental psychology: On the dynamics between growth and decline. *Developmental Psychology, 23,* 611–626.

Baltes, P. B. (1993). The aging mind: Potential and limits. *Gerontologist, 33,* 580–594.

Baltes, P. B. (1997). Wolfgang Edelstein: Über ein Wissenschaftlerleben in konstruktivistischer Melancholie [Wolfgang Edelstein: A scientific life in constructive melancholy]. *Reden zur Emeritierung von Wolfgang Edelstein.* Berlin, Germany: Max Planck Institute for Human Development.

Baltes, P. B. (1997). On the incomplete architecture of human ontogeny: Selection, optimization, and compensation as foundation of developmental theory. *American Psychologist, 52,* 366–380.

Baltes, P. B. (2004). *Wisdom: The orchestration of mind and virtue.* Book in preparation. http//www.mpib-berlin.mpg.de/dok/full/baltes/orchestr/index.htm.

Baltes, P. B., & Baltes, M. M. (1990). Psychological perspectives on successful aging: The model of selective optimization with compensation. In P. B. Baltes & M. M. Baltes (Eds.), *Successful aging: Perspectives from the behavioral sciences* (pp. 27–34). Cambridge: Cambridge University Press.

Baltes, P. B., Dittmann-Kohli, F., & Dixon, R. A. (1984). New perspectives on the development of intelligence in adulthood: Toward a dual-process conception and a model of selective optimization with compensation. In P. B. Baltes & O. G. Brim Jr. (Eds.), *Life-span development and behavior* (Vol. 6, pp. 33–76). New York: Academic Press.

Baltes, P. B., & Freund, A. M. (2003). Human strength as the orchestration of wisdom and SOC. In U. M. Staudinger & L. Aspinwall (Eds.), *A psychology of human strengths: Perspectives on an emerging field* (pp. 23–35). Washington, DC: APA Books.

Baltes, P. B., Glück, J., & Kunzmann, U. (2002). Wisdom: Its structure and function in successful lifespan development. In C. R. Snyder & S. J. Lopez (Eds.), *Handbook of positive psychology* (pp. 327–350). New York: Oxford University Press.

Baltes, P. B., & Kunzmann, U. (2003). Wisdom: The peak of human excellence in the orchestration of mind and virtue. *The Psychologist, 16,* 131–133.

Baltes, P. B., & Smith, J. (1990). The psychology of wisdom and its ontogenesis. In R. J. Sternberg (Ed.), *Wisdom: Its nature, origins, and development* (pp. 87–120). New York: Cambridge University Press.

Baltes, P. B., & Staudinger, U. M. (1993). The search for a psychology of wisdom. *Current Directions in Psychological Science, 2,* 75–80.

Baltes, P. B., & Staudinger, U. M. (2000). Wisdom: A metaheuristic (pragmatic) to orchestrate mind and virtue toward excellence. *American Psychologist, 55,* 122–136.

Baltes, P. B, Staudinger, U. M., & Lindenberger, U. (1999). Lifespan psychology: Theory and application to intellectual functioning. *Annual Review of Psychology, 50,* 471–507.

Baltes, P. B., Staudinger, U. M., Maerker, A., & Smith, J. (1995). People nominated as wise: A comparative study of wisdom-related knowledge. *Psychology and Aging, 10,* 155–166.

Birren, J. E., & Fisher, L. M. (1990). The elements of wisdom: Overview and integration. In R. J. Sternberg (Ed.), *Wisdom: Its nature, origins, and development* (pp. 317–323). New York: Cambridge University Press.

Boehmig-Krumhaar, S. A., Staudinger, U. M., & Baltes, P. B. (2002). In search of more tolerance: Testing the facilitative effect of a knowledge-activating mnemonic strategy on value relativism. *Journal of Developmental Psychology and Educational Psychology, 34*, 30–43.

Cattell, R. (1971). *Abilities: Their structure, growth, and action.* New York: Houghton Mifflin.

Clayton, V. P., & Birren, J. E. (1980). The development of wisdom across the life span: A reexamination of an ancient topic. In P. B. Baltes & O. G. Brim Jr. (Eds.), *Life-span development and behavior* (Vol. 3, pp. 103–135). New York: Academic Press.

Dittmann-Kohli, F., & Baltes, P. B. (1990). Toward a neofunctionalist conception of adult intellectual development: wisdom as a prototypical case of intellectual growth. In: *Higher stages of human development* (pp. 54–78). New York: Oxford University.

Dixon, R. A., & Baltes, P. B. (1986). Toward life-span research on the functions and pragmatics of intelligence. In R. J. Sternberg & R. K. Wagner (Eds.), *Practical intelligence: Nature and origins of competence in the everyday world* (pp. 203–235). Cambridge, England: Cambridge University Press.

Ericsson, K. A., & Simon, H. A. (1984). *Protocol analysis: verbal reports as data.* Cambridge, MA: MIT Press.

Erikson, E. H. (1959). *Identity and the life cycle.* New York: International University Press.

Freund, A. M., & Baltes, P. B. (2002). Life-management strategies of selection, optimization, and compensation: Measurement by self-report and construct validity. *Journal of Personality and Social Psychology, 82*, 642–662.

Freund, A. M., & Riediger, M. (2003). Successful aging. In: R. M. Lerner, M. A. Easterbrooks, & J. Mistry (Eds.), *Handbook of psychology. Volume 6: Developmental Psychology* (pp. 601–628). Hoboken, NJ: Wiley.

Gardner, H. (1999). *Intelligence reframed: Multiple intelligences for the 21st century.* New York: Basic Books.

Hall, G. S. (1922). *Senescence: The last half of life.* New York: Appleton.

Helson, R., & Srivastava, S. (2002). Creative and wise people: Similarities, differences, and how they develop. *Personality and Social Psychology Bulletin, 28*, 1430–1440.

Holliday, S. G., & Chandler, M. J. (1986). Wisdom: Explorations in adult competence. In J. A. Meacham (Ed.), *Contributions to human development* (Vol. 17, pp. 1–96). Basel, Switzerland: Karger.

Horn, J. L., & Hofer, S. M. (1992). Major abilities and development in the adult period. In R. J. Sternberg & C. A. Berg (Eds.), *Intellectual development* (pp. 44–49). Cambridge, England: Cambridge University Press.

Kekes, J. (1996). *Moral wisdom and good lives.* Ithaca, NY: Cornell University Press.

Keltner, D., & Gross, J. J. (1999). Functional accounts of emotions. *Cognition and Emotion, 13*, 467–480.

Kitchener, K. S., & Brenner, H. G. (1990). Wisdom and reflective judgment: Knowing in the face of uncertainty. In R. J. Sternberg (Ed.), *Wisdom: Its nature, origins, and development* (pp. 212–229). New York: Cambridge University Press.

Kramer, D. A. (2000). Wisdom as a classical source of human strength: Conceptualizing and empirical inquiry. *Journal of Social and Clinical Psychology, 19*, 83–101.

Krampe, R. Th., & Baltes, P. B. (2003). Intelligence as adaptive resource development and resource allocation: A new look through the lenses of SOC and expertise. In: R. J. Sternberg, & E. L. Grigorenko (Eds.), *The psychology of abilities, competencies, and expertise* (pp. 31–69). Cambridge: Cambridge University Press.

Kunzmann, U. (2004). Approaches to a good life: The emotional-motivational side to wisdom. In P. A. Linley & S. Joseph (Eds.), *Positive psychology in practice* (pp. 504–517). Hoboken, NJ: John Wiley and Sons.

Kunzmann, U., & Baltes, P. B. (2003a). Wisdom-related knowledge: Affective, motivational, and interpersonal correlates. *Personality and Social Psychology Bulletin*, 1104–1119.

Kunzmann, U., & Baltes, P. B. (2003b). Beyond the traditional scope of intelligence: Wisdom in action. In R. J. Sternberg, J. Lautry, & T. I. Lubart (Eds.), *Models of intelligence for the next millennium* (pp. 329–343). Washington, DC: American Psychological Association.

Kunzmann, U., & Grühn, D. (2003). [Age differences in emotional reactions to sad films: Evidence for greater reactivity in old age]. Manuscript under revision.

Kunzmann U., Little, T. D., & Smith, J. (2002). Perceiving control: A double-edged sword in old age. *Journals of Gerontology: Psychological Sciences, 57*, 484–491.

Labouvie-Vief, G. (1990). Wisdom as integrated thought: historical and developmental perspectives. In R. J. Sternberg (Ed.), *Wisdom: Its nature, origins, and development* (pp. 52–83). Cambridge, MA: Cambridge University Press.

Li, S.-C., & Kunzmann, U. (2004). Research of Intelligence in German-speaking Nations. In R. J. Sternberg (Ed.), *International handbook of the psychology of human intelligence* (pp. 135–169). New York: Cambridge University Press.

Mayer, J. D., & Salovey, P. (1993). The intelligence of emotional intelligence. *Intelligence, 17*, 433–442.

Oelmüller, W. (Ed.) (1989). *Philosophie und Weisheit* [Philosophy and wisdom]. Paderborn, Germany: Ferdinand Schöningh.

Orwoll, L., & Perlmutter, M. (1990). The study of wise persons: Integrating a personality perspective. In R. J. Sternberg (Ed.), *Wisdom: Its nature, origins, and development* (pp. 160–177). Cambridge, MA: Cambridge University Press.

Pasupathi, M., Staudinger, U. M., & Baltes, P. B. (2001). Seeds of wisdom: adolescents' knowledge and judgment about difficult life problems. *Developmental Psychology, 37*, 351–361.

Pennebaker, J. W., & Stone, L. D. (2003). Words of wisdom: Language use over the life span. *Journal of Personality & Social Psychology, 85*, 291–301.

Riegel, K. F. (1973). Dialectical operations: The final period of cognitive development. *Human Development, 16*, 346–370.

Salovey, P., Mayer, J. D., & Caruso, D. (2002). The positive psychology of emotional intelligence. In C. R. Snyder & S. J. Lopez (Eds.), *Handbook of positive psychology* (pp. 159–171). New York: Oxford University Press.

Smith, J., & Baltes, P. B. (1990). Wisdom-related knowledge: Age/cohort differences in response to life-planning problems. *Developmental Psychology, 26*, 494–505.

Smith, J., and Baltes, P. B. (1997). Profiles of psychological functioning in the old and oldest old. *Psychology and Aging, 12*, 458–472.

Snyder, C. R., & Lopez, S. J. (Eds). (2002). *Handbook of positive psychology*. New York: Oxford University Press.

Sowarka, D. (1989). Weisheit und weise Personen: Common-Sense-Konzepte älterer Menschen [Wisdom and wise persons: Common-sense concepts of older people]. *Zeitschrift für Entwicklungspsychologie und Pädagogische Psychologie, 21*, 87–109.

Staudinger U. M. (1999a). Older and wiser? Integrating results on the relationship between age and wisdom-related performance. *International Journal of Behavioral Development, 23*, 641–664.

Staudinger, U. M. (1999b). Social cognition and a psychological approach to the art of life. In T. H. Hess & F. Blanchard-Fields (Eds.), *Social cognition and aging* (pp. 343–375). San Diego, CA: Academic Press.

Staudinger, U. M. (2001). The theory of lifespan development. In N. J. Smelser & P. B. Baltes (Eds.), *International encyclopedia of the social & behavioral sciences*, Vol. adulthood and adult development (pp. 8844–8848). Elsevier.

Staudinger, U. M., & Baltes, P. B. (1996). Interactive minds: A facilitative setting for wisdom-related performance? *Journal of Personality and Social Psychology, 71*, 746–762.

Staudinger, U. M., Lopez, D. F., & Baltes, P. B. (1997). The psychometric location of wisdom-related performance: Intelligence, personality, and more? *Personality and Social Psychology Bulletin, 23*, 1200–1214.

Staudinger, U. M., Maciel, A. G., Smith, J., & Baltes, P. B. (1998). What predicts wisdom-related performance? A first look at personality, intelligence, and facilitative experiential contexts. *European Journal of Personality, 12*, 1–17.

Staudinger, U. M., Smith, J., & Baltes, P. B. (1992). Wisdom-related knowledge in a life review task: Age differences and the role of professional specialization. *Psychology and Aging, 7*, 271–281.

Sternberg, R. J., Lautry, J., & Lubart, T. I. (Eds.) (2003). *Models of intelligence for the next millennium*. Washington, DC: American Psychological Association.

Sternberg, R. J. (1985). Implicit theories of intelligence, creativity, and wisdom. *Journal of Personality and Social Psychology, 49*, 607–627.

Sternberg, R. J. (Ed.). (1990). *Wisdom: Its nature, origins, and development*. New York: Cambridge University Press.

Sternberg, R. J. (1998). A balance theory of wisdom. *Review of General Psychology, 2*, –365.

Sternberg, R. J. (1999). The theory of successful intelligence. *Review of General Psychology, 3*, 292–316.

Taylor, S. E., & Brown, J. D. (1988). Illusion and well-being: A social psychological perspective on mental health. *Psychological Bulletin, 105*, 193–210.

Wiese, B. S., Freund, A. M., & Baltes, P. B. (2002). Subjective career success and emotional well-being: longitudinal predictive power of selection, optimization, and compensation. *Journal of Vocational Behavior, 60*, 321–335.

Wink, P., & Helson, R. (1997). Practical and transcendent wisdom: Their nature and some longitudinal findings. *Journal of Adult Development, 4*, 1–15.

PART II

THE DEVELOPMENT OF WISDOM ACROSS
THE LIFESPAN

6

Young and Growing Wiser

Wisdom during Adolescence and Young Adulthood

M. J. Richardson and M. Pasupathi

Wisdom is commonly viewed as a development in the latter part of the life span (Clayton & Birren, 1980; Sternberg, 1986; Sowarka, 1989; Orwoll & Perlmutter, 1990), although at least one theorist has argued that wisdom is lost over time, not gained (Meacham, 1990). In contrast, empirical work supports the idea that many crucial "building blocks" for wisdom are emerging during adolescence and young adulthood (Pasupathi, Staudinger, & Baltes, 2001; Staudinger & Pasupathi, 2003). The limited direct evidence on wisdom among adolescents supports the idea that adolescence is a key period for the development of wisdom. First, however, we must say something about what we mean by wisdom.

Theoretical Perspectives on Wisdom
Several proposed wisdom-related characteristics appear to overlap across theories, allowing for a consideration of common definitions of wisdom. One example of shared or overlapping characteristics is the notion that wise persons have developed an expert level of knowledge. For example, laypersons have described wisdom as including the ability to learn from ideas and environments, and the expeditious use of information (Sternberg, 1986). Such a view is consistent with other views of wisdom, which include the idea that wisdom requires some expert knowledge or expert use of knowledge. The types of knowledge associated with wisdom have been described as competence and exceptional understanding (Holliday & Chandler, 1986), rich factual and procedural knowledge (Baltes, Smith, & Staudinger, 1992), knowledge about the limits of knowing, and reflective judgment (Kitchener & Brenner, 1990).

Another commonly theorized characteristic of wisdom includes some recognition of the unknown or unknowable, and the ability to act in the face of such uncertainty (see, e.g., Kitchener & Brenner, 1990; Smith & Baltes, 1990), or use of uncertainty as a basis for action that is hoped to result in greater knowledge. Meacham (1990) retells the story of Solomon and the baby, suggesting that Solomon was uncertain who was the mother, but acted in a way that such knowledge would most likely be forthcoming. Similarly, Arlin (1990) draws parallels between the actions of problem finders, who are inspired by uncertainty, and the actions of wise persons. In addition, Sternberg's (1998) view of creativity as pushing beyond the boundaries of what is known seems to overlap with previously mentioned descriptions of action in the face of uncertainty, or action resulting from uncertainty.

A third commonly mentioned wisdom-related characteristic, similar to the recognition of uncertainty, involves the recognition that different points of view exist, such as considerations of value relativism and lifespan contextualism (Baltes & Staudinger, 1993; Smith & Baltes, 1990). Other views that have articulated such a recognition as being relevant to wisdom include the view that wise persons first recognize a diversity of viewpoints and then develop a holistic or systemic and ecological awareness (Csikszentmihalyi & Rathunde, 1990), or otherwise integrate multiple viewpoints in searching for solutions (Kitchener & Brenner, 1990; Labouvie-Vief, 1990). This component of wisdom is also reflected in Sternberg's (1998) theory, which calls for a balance among intrapersonal, interpersonal, and extrapersonal interests.

So there is consensus that wisdom is characterized by a high level of knowledge, an awareness of uncertainty, or the limitations of knowledge, and a consideration of multiple points of view. Of course, these characteristics may apply to wisdom as knowledge, action, or even motivation. Wisdom-related knowledge involves the expertise needed for understanding a situation in a deep, insightful, or wise manner. Wisdom-related action is the capacity to act on those insights. This distinction allows for a consideration of characteristics that may open the door for wisdom-related knowledge, but not necessarily lead to wise action, and also permits us to identify those whose astute insight is not necessarily evident in their own behavior. A motivation to become wise or to act in wise ways may also be suggested in these characteristics, particularly in action that pushes beyond the boundaries of knowledge to expand those boundaries. Although theorists in the field have acknowledged these distinctions (e.g., Baltes & Staudinger, 2000;

Kunzmann & Baltes, 2003), the majority of work on wisdom relates primarily to knowledge. As has been noted in research on moral reasoning, higher-level reasoning ability does not necessarily lead to moral action or imply a striving toward morality (Bandura, 1991; Turiel, 1998); the same is likely true for wisdom. Distinctions among knowledge, action, and motivation may especially enhance our understanding of wisdom during adolescence, when emerging personality characteristics such as sensation-seeking may undermine wise action, whereas a developing capacity for considering multiple outcomes may enhance wise knowledge, and, more speculatively, a motivation to acquire wisdom may determine which adolescents become wise adults. These distinctions also provide a useful framework for considering how developing wisdom-related characteristics may be manifested in wisdom-related knowledge, wise action, and motivations to become wise or to act in wise ways.

Wisdom is stereotypically considered the province of later life. However, previous research on adulthood has demonstrated that wisdom is not an inevitable associate of age (Staudinger, 1999). Adolescence and young adulthood may represent exceptions to this rule (Pasupathi, Staudinger, & Baltes, 2001; Glück & Baltes, under review). Interestingly, there is both indirect and direct evidence that this is a period of normative growth in wisdom-related characteristics. Indirect evidence includes the substantial growth during adolescence and young adulthood in capacities that are either theoretically or empirically linked to wisdom. Although direct evidence is much sparser, there have been a few studies directly assessing wisdom in adolescent and young adult populations, and these also indicate substantial growth potential during this period of life. In what follows we first review indirect evidence for the development of wisdom in adolescence through developing intellectual capacities, personality characteristics, capacities at the interface of intellectual and personality development, and the encoding of experiences during adolescence. We then review the limited direct evidence for the development of wisdom in adolescence. Finally, we consider some of the implications of what we found.

Adolescents Are Growing Wiser: Indirect Evidence

Wisdom as an individual quality is typically seen as emerging from an integrative relationship among various characteristics (see, e.g., Baltes et al., 1992; Holliday & Chandler, 1986; Labouvie-Vief, 1990; Sternberg, 1998), rather than residing in any single attribute. Such characteristics include intellectual capacities, personality characteristics, and capacities at the interface of personality and cognition (see, e.g., Staudinger, Lopez, & Baltes, 1997; Staudinger, Maciel, Smith, & Baltes, 1998; Staudinger & Pasupathi, 2003). Developing intellectual capacities may facilitate the development of wisdom by allowing for the integration of different facets or types of knowledge (Baltes et al., 1992; Sternberg, 1998; Labouvie-Vief, 1990), and also by allowing for the development of exceptional understanding and judgment (Holliday & Chandler, 1986). Personality characteristics such as open-mindedness (Staudinger & Pasupathi, 2003) and social unobtrusiveness (Holliday & Chandler, 1986) also may contribute to the development of wisdom. Wisdom-related capacities at the interface of intelligence and personality have been hypothesized to include social intelligence, moral reasoning, and creativity (Staudinger & Pasupathi, 2003). All of these capacities have been linked to higher levels of wisdom-related knowledge in research with adult samples (Pasupathi & Staudinger, 1999; Staudinger et al., 1997; Staudinger et al., 1998; Staudinger & Pasupathi, 2003). Another aspect of adolescence that will be considered in relation to wisdom is the privileged encoding of experiences during adolescence (Rubin & Schulkind, 1997), which may facilitate the development of a basic knowledge base during this time period. To explore the notion of emerging wisdom in adolescence, we review examples of such underlying characteristics as they are developing during the same period, and discuss how they may facilitate wisdom-related knowledge and/or action.

Intellectual development. Cognitive abilities are increasing during adolescence along with an increase in knowledge. These increases may be prerequisites for the higher-level thinking associated with wisdom. Abilities such as a general ability to think abstractly, an ability to consider the hypothetical, and sophistication of information processing strategies, as well as the abilities to think about multiple aspects of a situation at once, including self-reflective thinking, are increasing during adolescence (Case, 1992; Piaget & Inhelder, 1973). In addition, speed, automaticity, and cognitive capacity are thought to increase. Breadth of knowledge increases in diverse domains during adolescence (Keating, 1990). Strategy changes in solving analogies are also associated with adolescence (Sternberg & Nigro, 1980). Increases in breadth of knowledge and cognitive capacities may eventually facilitate the development of expert levels of knowledge associated with wisdom. In addition, strategy changes associated with solving analogies may point to an application of a broadening knowledge base, which requires the integration of such knowledge.

Deductive reasoning has been defined as the ability to combine premises to arrive at logical conclusions (Ward & Overton, 1990). Again, the integration of knowledge associated with wisdom is brought to mind with the integration of premises associated with deductive reasoning. An increasing breadth of knowledge may be of limited use in specific contexts or situations unless such integration occurs. Deductive reasoning is an expectation for adolescents in educational settings, and the ability to reach appropriate conclusions and explain the associated reasoning process does increase during adolescence (see, e.g., Klaczynski, 1993; Klaczynski & Narasimham, 1998; Markovits & Vachon, 1990; Moshman & Franks, 1986; Ward & Overton, 1990).

The ability to come to appropriate conclusions and decide on a course of action is a necessary first step in learning to apply wisdom-related knowledge and beginning to act wisely. The ability to effectively allocate attention in situations involving two tasks has been found to increase markedly during adolescence and then to level off somewhat in adulthood (Manis, Keating, & Morrison, 1980). Such ability seems to be a possible prerequisite for navigating intrapersonal, interpersonal, and extrapersonal balance issues (Sternberg, 1998), as well as for weighing complex and divergent information that may be necessary for effective decision making. Increases in decision-making competence have been found during adolescence (Lewis, 1981), which include increases in the mention of potential risks and consequences, cautious treatment of vested interests, and advice to seek professional opinions. Such consideration of potential risk may provide a potential counterbalance to what otherwise may be a time of increasing risk-taking behavior (see, e.g., DiClemente, Hansen, & Ponton, 1995). Similarly, other research suggests that adolescents may perceive themselves as more vulnerable than adults (Quadrel, Fischhoff, & Davis, 1993), and may tend to estimate greater risk associated with natural hazards and behavior-linked risks than young adults (Millstein & Halpern-Felsher, 2002). Although adolescents may be less likely than young adults to see themselves as invulnerable, both adolescents and young adults overestimated the actual risks associated with the situations described in a study by Millstein and Halpern-Felsher (2002). Still, such overestimation of risk suggests an awareness of uncertainty and may potentially lead to caution in dealing with such uncertainty.

Intellectual capacities have been primarily associated with the acquisition of knowledge, including wisdom-related knowledge. Less clear is the relationship between intellectual capacities and wisdom-related action or motivations to become wise. Increasing decision-making capacity may implicitly suggest action if a decision is followed through with, but reasoning about decisions may not inevitably lead to action. Thus, one area with potential for future research includes a look at how increasing intellectual capacities may facilitate wise action as well as wise knowledge.

Basic Personality and Self-Development during Adolescence

According to many models of wisdom, personality traits and self-conceptions should be related to people's wisdom-related knowledge (Baltes & Staudinger, 2000; Staudinger & Pasupathi, 2003), and potentially also to their ability to act wisely (Kunzmann & Baltes, 2003). Theoretically, adolescence is the time of life in which basic personality traits and self-conceptions that are often retained throughout adulthood emerge (Erikson & Erikson, 1997; Harter, 1988; Roberts & Caspi, 2003). Below, we outline briefly how personality and self-development during adolescence and early adulthood are likely to facilitate the motivation to be wise and the acquisition of knowledge related to wisdom. At the same time, personality and self-development during this period are likely to hinder the application of knowledge and motivation to action.

Self-/Identity development. Self- and/or identity development, defined as the individual's conception of himself or herself and the individual's central commitments to particular ideologies (Erikson & Erikson, 1997), is theorized as the primary developmental task for adolescents. Recent work suggests that this process continues into early adulthood (J. J. Arnett, 2000; Pals, 1999). One aspect of identity that may be achieved during this phase is a general commitment to, or motivation to strive for, wisdom. Although virtually no work examines such a construct, there are aspects of identity development that may be conceptually related.

Harter (1988) outlined self-development during childhood and adolescence as a process involving increasing capacities for abstraction, generalizing, and addressing inconsistency. She also highlighted the connection between self-conceptions and motivational processes that facilitate children's further growth in other domains. One specific aspect of self-development may be the integration of moral purposes into the self – or, in more Eriksonian terms, a commitment to moral purposes (Damon, 2000). Such a purpose would presumably orient adolescents toward the idea of balancing their own and others' interests, a central feature of wisdom as conceptualized by Sternberg (1998).

Personality development. Being open to new experiences (e.g., Costa & McCrae, 1994) is related to both lay conceptions of wise people (e.g., Clayton & Birren, 1980; Holliday & Chandler, 1986) and to wisdom-related knowledge and judgment (Staudinger et al., 1997; Staudinger et al., 1998). More open-minded individuals are viewed as more like "wise" people, and they demonstrate higher levels of wisdom-related knowledge when asked to reason about hypothetical life dilemmas. Adolescents increase in their level of open-mindedness until around age 30, at which point individual levels of open-mindedness stabilize (e.g., Caspi, 1998; Costa & McCrae, 1994; Roberts & Caspi, 2003; van Lieshout & Haselager, 1992), again, consistent with the idea that adolescence is a time of strong potential for wisdom-related knowledge.

Related to the idea of openness to experience is the quality of uncertainty orientation (e.g., Sorrentino, Raynor, Zubek, & Short, 1990), defined as the capacity to confront and engage with uncertainty. Individuals that are low in this quality actively avoid uncertainty. Thus, this capacity relates directly to the issue of recognizing and managing uncertainty that is central to existing conceptions of wise knowledge. Sorrentino and colleagues have documented age-related increases in uncertainty orientation across adolescence (Sorrentino et al., 1990), and decreases with age in adulthood (Sorrentino, Holmes, Hanna, & Sharp, 1995). Education is also positively associated with uncertainty orientation in adults (Sorrentino et al., 1995). There are no direct investigations of uncertainty orientation and its relationships with wisdom or wise knowledge. However, Sorrentino and colleagues view uncertainty orientation as a key capacity for attaining higher levels of cognitive development, moral reasoning ability, and ego development (Sorrentino et al., 1990), which, as we review next, also may be connected to wise knowledge.

Another facet of self/personality development is the construct of ego development (Loevinger, 1966). Ego development can be understood as the emergence, over time, of characteristic ways individuals address differences between the aspects of themselves that are controllable, and those aspects of the self that influence the person. Loevinger's original work defined the endpoint, or highest level of ego development, as one in which people are able to integrate various aspects of the self into a coherent identity, and to cherish individuality in self and others. Development moves people increasingly away from egocentric, dependent, and self-centered modes of being toward the capacity to take perspectives on the self and others, and to experience positive, helpful, responsible, and mutual interactions with others. So described, ego development has substantial conceptual overlap with some of the dimensions of wisdom outlined earlier. And, a recent review (Cohn, 1998) shows that large gains in ego development are attained in adolescence and early adulthood, with stability thereafter. There is no direct work linking measures of ego development to measures of wisdom, but this is clearly an area with potential for future work.

Wise action also may be linked to personality and, in particular, to a balance between action and reflection. Kunzmann and Baltes (2003) have theorized about a variety of factors, especially those associated with emotion, that may moderate the expression of wisdom in action. Although there is no research directly examining wise action among adolescents, there is a considerable body of work examining risky or foolish behavior in adolescents, and personality/self contributors to those behaviors. Across adolescence and young adulthood, personal characteristics such as negative emotionality or neuroticism, sensation-seeking, low self-esteem, poor coping and emotion regulation, and impulsivity are at their lifespan peak (J. Arnett, 1992; J. J. Arnett, 2000; Cooper, Wood, Orcutt, & Albino, 2003; Jessor, Turbin, & Costa, 1998; Jessor, 1992). Thus, although adolescence may be a time of burgeoning wisdom-related knowledge, it is unlikely to be a peak period for wise action. Essentially, the data available suggest a kind of "lag" hypothesis about the developmental connections between wisdom-related knowledge and motivations, and wisdom-related action that is amenable to empirical testing. Specifically, a jump in wisdom-related knowledge in adolescence and early adulthood may be followed by a subsequent increase in wisdom-related action in early adulthood and middle age.

The "Interface" of Cognition and Personality

Drawing from integrative approaches to wisdom, Staudinger et al. (1997) suggested that capacities that integrate cognitive or intellectual functioning and personality functioning may be closely related to what has been described as wisdom-related performance (or performance that draws on the same capacities as wise performance, but that may not yet reach expert levels). Representative integrative or "interface" capacities were hypothesized to include social intelligence such as perspective-taking ability, creativity, and moral reasoning. Sternberg (1998) also considered creativity, as well as the recognition of interpersonal interests (associated with the construct of social intelligence), to be aspects of wisdom, and Damon (2000) indicated that personal concerns must be integrated with moral concerns for wisdom to emerge.

Perspective taking. As has been noted, a common element in conceptions of wisdom is the ability to recognize multiple perspectives and to seek solutions that take those perspectives into account. The initial recognition of multiple perspectives may represent one facet of wisdom-related knowledge. Seeking solutions that take multiple perspectives into account may represent a facet of wisdom-related action.

Theory of mind research suggests that the ability to understand what others are thinking and feeling increases during adolescence, along with the ability to differentiate mental states (e.g., Fabricius, Schwanenflugel, Kyllonen, Barclay, & Denton, 1989). Research examining social reasoning also shows advances from childhood through adolescence and into adulthood in handling areas of interpersonal conflict, friendship, and distributive justice problems (e.g., Blanchard-Fields, 1986; Keller & Wood, 1989; Turiel, 1998; Wainryb, 1995). These advances suggest an increased ability to see situations from the perspective of others rather than simply from one's own perspective.

Lapsley and Murphy (1985) associated the imaginary audience phenomenon that is prevalent during adolescence with the ability to step outside of oneself and anticipate the reactions of others, or in other words, to see things from their perspective. Similarly, Selman (1980) suggested that perspective-taking ability increases during adolescence, and Barenboim (1981) found that adolescents are more likely than children to consider contextual and situational variability in understanding others, as well as considering both previously acquired and current information about the person. This implies an ability not only to imagine what another person might perceive, but also to take into consideration other factors that may influence what they perceive.

Moral reasoning. Colby, Kohlberg, Gibbs, and Lieberman (1983) examined adolescent reasoning abilities in relation to Kohlberg's stages of moral reasoning, and found that most adolescents function at stage three reasoning. During this stage adolescents are not only acknowledging multiple viewpoints but also seek to integrate or transcend differences through focusing on fostering relationships. This level of reasoning, based on such ideas as loyalty and care, is not uncommon among adults, and is thought to form the foundation for moral reasoning that transcends individual differences and even conventional rules and laws. Piaget's (1932) autonomous morality, which considers multiple viewpoints and emphasizes consensual, or integrated, rules of right and wrong, is also expected to increase during adolescence because of the increasing salience of peer interactions during that time. Such reasoning may open the doors for a balance of intrapersonal and interpersonal needs necessary for wisdom (Sternberg, 1998) as well as allow youth to begin to push beyond formerly unexamined social norms and look for unique or creative solutions to resolve wider interpersonal concerns. Pasupathi and Staudinger (2001) found a significant, though moderate, relationship between moral reasoning and wisdom-related knowledge as measured by the Berlin Wisdom Paradigm in a sample of adults, and moral reasoning was also related to wisdom-related knowledge in a sample of adolescents (Staudinger & Pasupathi, 2003).

However, it has been noted that moral reasoning is not the same as moral action (Bandura, 1991). Thus, although the capacity for wisdom-related action may be dependent on developing moral reasoning ability, the propensity to act wisely may not automatically increase. This distinction also may help account for a possible discrepancy between wisdom-related knowledge and wisdom-related action in adolescence. For example, Damon (2000) interviewed adolescents and found that they were capable of considering and integrating moral and personal concerns. Damon suggests that such integration of moral and personal concerns is relevant to the development of wisdom. A contrasting narrative, from an adolescent who seemed to show a general lack of wise action, demonstrated that this youth mentioned the same personal and moral dimensions as other youths, but indicated that they were lacking in his life. Although this youth did not demonstrate wise action, he was capable of expressing relatively wise thinking about his own folly.

Creativity. Creativity is also considered relevant to the concept of wisdom (Staudinger et al., 1997; Sternberg, 1998). Indeed, when dealing with uncertainty, a certain amount of pushing beyond the limits of what is known (Sternberg, 1998) would seem to be necessary to find wise solutions to such unfamiliar problems. As we mentioned previously, a recognition of the limits of knowledge may be an aspect of wisdom-related knowledge, whereas action in the face of such uncertainty (sometimes characterized as "creative") may potentially be considered wisdom-related action if it leads to greater knowledge and/or is considered beneficial to self and others.

Unfortunately, little empirical evidence is available on the development of creativity in adolescence. Components of creativity such as ideational flexibility, uniqueness, and fluency have been reported to increase in adolescence (e.g., Kogan & Pankove, 1972). Creativity in adolescence also has been associated with academic achievement (Kogan, 1983).

Conversely, Albert (1996) notes a break in creativity corresponding with late childhood and early adolescence, and suggests that diminishing creativity in adolescence may be associated with increasing family and social pressure to engage in conventional behaviors. This explanation would still indicate that adolescence is an important period for creativity, such that creativity may be continuously pursued throughout adolescence only when conventional pressures on adolescents are either diminished or resisted.

Autobiographical Experiences: Privileged Encoding During Adolescence and Young Adulthood

Thus far, we have focused primarily on the development of individual capacities that are theorized to facilitate one or another aspect of wisdom. A different line of work suggests that adolescence and young adulthood are periods of privileged encoding of autobiographical and other types of experiences. Thus, the foundational knowledge base from which individuals can think and act when wisdom is required may be laid down during this age period as well.

The primary evidence for this assertion lies in the so-called reminiscence bump (Rubin & Schulkind, 1997). The reminiscence bump is a phenomenon in which middle-aged people asked to recall autobiographical memories from their entire lifespan and then to date the memories will typically overrepresent memories from adolescence and early adulthood. The "bump" seems related to identity transformations, in the sense that geographical moves and significant political happenings are associated with bumps at other points in the lifespan (e.g., Schrauf & Rubin, 1998, 2000). That is, periods in which people's identities are developed (adolescence and early adulthood) or undergo transformations (experiencing emigration) are associated with heightened memory for the associated experiences. The same phenomenon is also evident in general knowledge of news and cultural events (Holmes & Conway, 1999), suggesting that adolescence and young adulthood are enormously important periods for the acquisition of foundational knowledge about the self and the world. Because such knowledge is the bedrock for wise thinking and action, adolescence and young adulthood again should be key periods for wisdom-related development.

In sum, the key building blocks for wisdom-related motivation and knowledge are emerging during adolescence and young adulthood. These include basic intellectual and personality capacities, capabilities at the interface of intelligence and personality, such as creativity and social intelligence, and foundational knowledge about oneself and the world. At the same time, some of the personality development occurring during this period may have negative effects on the capacity to translate wise thought into wise action; such "translation" may need to await the improved self-regulatory capabilities of adulthood and old age. Next, we review the very limited direct evidence on wisdom during adolescence and young adulthood.

Direct Empirical Evidence of Wisdom-Related Knowledge in Adolescence

Empirical work that directly addresses wisdom in adolescence is sparse. Current research on wisdom-related performance during adolescence comes primarily from an approach to wisdom as expert knowledge and judgment in the fundamental pragmatics of life (e.g. Baltes et al., 1992). Based on this definition, "wisdom" is the term reserved for expert-level performance, whereas performance below expert levels on similar criteria is labeled "wisdom-related" (Staudinger & Pasupathi, 2003). In a study by Pasupathi, Staudinger, and Baltes (2001), adolescents and young adults were compared based on responses to hypothetical, broad, and ill-defined life dilemmas. Ages of the participants ranged from 14 to 37. Participants were asked to consider what a person might do or might consider in the situation and were rated based on five wisdom criteria: rich factual and rich procedural knowledge about life, lifespan contextualism, value relativism, and recognition and management of uncertainty (see Baltes et al., 1992; Smith & Baltes, 1990). Although adolescents performed at lower levels than young adults (demonstrating "wisdom-related" rather than wise performance), adolescents demonstrated age-related increases in performance. However, in adulthood (after about age 24), age was no longer associated with performance on these wisdom criteria.

A similar study also found a general increase in performance on the same wisdom criteria from adolescence to young adulthood (Anderson, 1998). Participants in this study (Anderson, 1998) ranged in age from 15 to 27, and increases in performance spanned the age groups considered in the study. Perhaps because the upper age limit for this study was close to the age at which performance increases began to level off in the Berlin study (Pasupathi et al., 2001), such a shift was not reported in this study.

However, it is noted that increases in performance were most notable in the areas of relativistic thinking and thinking about uncertainty. It is noteworthy that increases in wisdom-related performance documented in the previously mentioned Berlin study (Pasupathi et al., 2001) were replicated in this study, which was conducted in Toronto and which employed somewhat different measurement strategies.

Earlier, when we discussed indirect evidence for adolescence as an important growth period for wisdom, we implied that adolescent increases in wisdom-related knowledge are likely associated with growth in other capacities during this period. That, in itself, is an empirically testable proposal. Staudinger and Pasupathi (2003) linked wisdom-related performance (see Baltes et al., 1992; Smith & Baltes, 1990) to the developing personality and cognitive capacities of adolescents as well as capacities at the interface of personality and cognition. They found significant relationships between wisdom-related performance and other developmental capacities in adolescence. In addition, the pattern of relationships between wisdom-related performance and other capacities changed for adults, with basic cognitive and personality factors playing a smaller role in predicting wisdom-related knowledge, and interface characteristics playing a larger role. This may suggest that trait-like and crystallized functions are less salient for the development of wisdom as time goes on. Importantly, this study involved the same participants as those reported on in Pasupathi et al. (2001). A recent replication of both age differences in wisdom-related knowledge and of age differences in predictors of wisdom (Glück & Baltes, under review) again found nearly identical results.

One other study has addressed wisdom in adolescence and adulthood, but this time from the perspective of experienced wisdom. Allowing participants to subjectively define their own wise actions, Bluck and Glück (2004), also made comparisons between adolescent wisdom and adult wisdom, as well as comparisons between these subjective implicit accounts of wisdom and theoretical views of wisdom. Based on the idea that anyone can be wise, under certain circumstances, and that situational wisdom may be more common than a global wisdom, the authors asked adolescent, young adult, and older adult participants to list situations in which they acted wisely. Subsequently the participant was instructed to choose a situation in which he or she acted most wise and to elaborate in a narrative/interview. It was found that the participants' experiences of wisdom largely reflected what might theoretically be expected in wisdom-related experiences such as most often dealing with fundamental pragmatics of life (e.g., Baltes & Staudinger, 2000).

Similarly, Bluck and Glück hypothesized that individuals' wisdom-related experiences would involve a general shift from a negative or challenging precipitating event to a more positive outcome, and that some lessons would be learned and generalized from the experience. Adolescent narratives were similar to adult narratives in both number of events recalled and in the relation of those events to fundamental life experiences. In addition, the groups were comparable in that the majority of the narratives reflected a general shift from negative or challenging to more positive outcomes as a result of the wise action.

Adolescents and adults differed, however, in both the tendency to generalize the lessons learned to other specific contexts, and in connecting the experience to the larger life context. Adults were more likely than adolescents to generalize experiences, and to present a coherent picture of the role of the experience in a greater life context. The authors suggest that possible reasons for these differences may be that adolescents have not yet developed a coherent view of their life, or that they simply have not had enough experiences yet to generalize and connect their experiences as widely as adults. Another implication of this view is that adolescents may have the ability to truly act wisely in certain situations but may not yet fully benefit from an accumulation of experience broad enough for wider generalization.

Summary and Implications

Adolescence and early adulthood are periods of strong growth in wisdom-related knowledge. The growth of such knowledge is likely related to cognitive and intellectual development, personality development, and development of capacities at the interface of intellectual and personality development such as creativity, moral reasoning, and perspective taking ability. In addition, the privileged encoding of experiences during adolescence may provide the basic knowledge of self and environment that can be called upon when wise thought is needed. Such developing capacities and characteristics provide indirect evidence for the growth of wisdom-related knowledge in adolescence. Some of these developing capacities (e.g. intellectual capacities) have been well documented during adolescence. Others (e.g. creativity) have received less attention. Direct evidence for the growth of wisdom-related knowledge, though somewhat sparse, has also been found during adolescence.

Less information is available on the development of wisdom-related action or a motivation to become wise during adolescence, leaving several questions unanswered. The motivation to become wise is virtually unexamined, but may be crucial for the development of wise thought and action. Does a general motivation to become wise during adolescence predict subsequent levels of adult wisdom, whether assessed in knowledge or in action? Is such motivation equally predictive of wisdom-related knowledge and wisdom-related action?

Wisdom-related action may be a critical aspect for our society to understand, and it is also poorly understood. Is there a similar development of wisdom-related action during adolescence, including a leveling off of such growth during adulthood? Is the development of wisdom-related knowledge during adolescence predictive of growth in wisdom-related action during adolescence? Or is such growth in wisdom-related action delayed until young or later adulthood? If such a delay exists, what aspects of adolescent experience may account for the delay? One possibility may be that a growing awareness of contextual variation and a relativistic perspective, coupled with an underdeveloped sense of how to balance such perspectives, may lead to a temporary abandonment of specific values, and subsequently result in what is perceived as greater risk-taking behavior. Another possibility may be that a growing adolescent awareness of diverse perspectives may lead to both increased caution and a desire to explore an ever-widening horizon. Again, without some higher sense of balance, an increasing awareness of risk coupled with a drive to increase knowledge though experiencing the world may account for the fluctuating and sometimes unpredictable adolescent evaluations of self and environment. Perhaps wise action is a more difficult domain in which to achieve balance than wisdom-related knowledge or motivation, and such balance only comes with experience.

Other questions include whether adolescents' implicit conceptualizations of wisdom change over time, and whether such conceptualizations are related to growth in explicit measurements of wisdom. What is the relationship between the experience of "being wise" and external measures of wisdom such as the Berlin Wisdom Paradigm? Future research also may address whether wisdom-related characteristics during adolescence facilitate other aspects of adolescent development. For example, do adolescents who demonstrate higher levels of wisdom-related knowledge demonstrate a commitment to the greater good, and is such a commitment related to a greater ability to delay personal gratification? Or do adolescents with higher levels of wisdom-related knowledge attract a wider social network? Finally, can adolescents learn from foolishness? How do adolescents (or adults) finally come to balance an awareness of risk with the need for seeking experiential knowledge that often entails risk?

If the answers to such questions suggest that developing higher levels of wisdom-related knowledge, motivation, or action during adolescence is beneficial both to the adolescent and to a wider environment, then adolescence may be a key period for interventions aimed at enhancing wisdom. At least for wisdom-related knowledge, adolescence has been shown to be a time of normative growth. The same is not true of adulthood. It also has been noted that wisdom is not necessarily a common characteristic, and even people who are considered wise, may not be wise in all situations. If wisdom is something we could use more of, then adolescence, as a time when wisdom-related characteristics may be naturally developing, may provide a unique opportunity to increase both individual and societal levels of this important resource.

What might interventions look like? Baltes, Staudinger, and their colleagues have developed some interventions for improving wisdom-related knowledge over the short term in adult samples. One such intervention involved allowing participants to consult with important others, either "virtually" or in actuality (Staudinger & Baltes, 1996); such consultation improved participants subsequent performance in thinking about fundamental life problems. Another such intervention involved asking participants to imagine a trip around the world in thinking about the dilemma; this intervention improved participants' ability to incorporate differing value systems into their responses (Boehmig-Krumhaar, Staudinger, & Baltes, 2002). Thus, interventions focusing on wisdom-related knowledge and judgment already exist, although their utility is demonstrated only for short-term effects and adult populations. Because wise action and the motive to attain wisdom are so underexamined, it is not clear what might promote either of those qualities. If wisdom in all its facets is, as all seem to agree (Baltes & Staudinger, 2000), a desirable and ideal endpoint for human development, then it is well worth our time to find ways to increase wisdom.

References

Albert, R. A. (1996). Some reasons why childhood creativity often fails to make it past puberty into the real world. In W. Damon (Series Ed.) & M. A. Runco (Vol. Ed.), *New Directions for Child Development:*Vol. 72. *Creativity from childhood through adulthood: The developmental issues* (pp. 43–56). San Francisco, CA: Jossey-Bass.

Anderson, B. J. (1998). *Development of wisdom-related knowledge in adolescence and young adulthood*. Unpublished doctoral dissertation, University of Toronto.

Arlin, P. K. (1990). Wisdom: The art of problem finding In R. J. Sternberg (Ed.), *Wisdom: Its nature, origins, and development* (pp. 230–243). New York: Cambridge University Press.

Arnett, J. (1992). Reckless behavior in adolescence: A developmental perspective. *Developmental Review, 12*, 339–373.

Arnett, J. J. (2000). Emerging adulthood: A theory of development from the late teens through the twenties. *American Psychologist, 55*, 469–480.

Baltes, P. B., Smith, J., & Staudinger, U. M. (1992). Wisdom as successful aging. In T. B. Sonderegger (Ed.), *Nebraska Symposium on Motivation* (Vol. 39, pp. 123–167). Lincoln: University of Nebraska Press.

Baltes, P. B., & Staudinger, U. M. (1993).The search for psychology of wisdom. *Current Directions in Psychological Science, 2*, 75–80.

Baltes, P. B., & Staudinger, U. M. (2000). Wisdom: A meta-heuristic (pragmatic) to orchestrate mind and virtue toward excellence. *American Psychologist, 55*, 122–136.

Bandura, A. (1991). Social cognitive theory of moral thought and action. In W. M. Kurtines & J. L. Gewirtz (Eds.), *Handbook of Moral Behavior and Development* (pp. 45–103). Hillsdale, NJ: Lawrence Erlbaum Associates.

Barenboim, C. (1981). The development of person perception in childhood and adolescence: From behavioral comparisons to psychological constructs to psychological comparisons. *Child Development, 52*, 129–144.

Blanchard-Fields, F. (1986). Reasoning in adolescents and adults on social dilemmas varying in emotional saliency: An adult developmental perspective. *Psychology and Aging, 1*, 325–333.

Bluck, S., & Glück, J. (2004). Making things better and learning a lesson: Experiencing wisdom across the lifespan. *Journal of Personality.*

Boehmig-Krumhaar, S. A., Staudinger, U. M., & Baltes, P. B. (2002). In search of more tolerance: Testing the facilitative effect of a knowledge-activating mnemonic strategy on value relativism. *Zeitschrift für Entwicklungspsychologie und Paedagogische Psychologie, 34*, 30–43.

Case, R. (Ed.). (1992). *The Mind's Staircase: Exploring the Conceptual Underpinnings of Children's Thought and Knowledge*. New York. Erlbaum.

Caspi, A. (1998). Personality development across the life course. In N. Eisenberg (Ed.), *Handbook of child psychology: Social, emotional, and personality development* (5th ed., Vol. 3, pp. 311–387). New York: Wiley.

Clayton, V. P., & Birren, J. E. (1980). The development of wisdom across the life span: a re-examination of an ancient topic. In P. B. Baltes & O. G. Brim (Eds.), *Life-Span Development and Behavior* (Vol. 3, pp. 103–135). New York: Academic Press.

Colby, A., Kohlberg, L., Gibbs, J., & Lieberman, M. (1983). A longitudinal study of moral development. *Monographs of the Society for Research in Child Development, 48*, 1–96.

Cohn, L. D. (1998). Age trends in personality development: A quantitative review. In P. M. Westenberg, A. Blasi, & L. D. Cohn, (Eds). *Personality development:*

Theoretical, empirical, and clinical investigations of Loevinger's conception of ego development (pp. 133–143). Mahwah, NJ: Lawrence Erlbaum Associates.

Cooper, M. L., Wood, P. K., Orcutt, H. K., & Albino, A. (2003). Personality and the predisposition to engage in risky or problem behaviors during adolescence. *Journal of Personality and Social Psychology, 84*, 390–410.

Costa, P. T., & McCrae, R. R. (1994). Set like plaster? Evidence for the stability of adult personality. In T. F. Heatherton & J. L. Weinberger (Eds.), *Can personality change?* (pp. 21–40). Washington, DC: American Psychological Association.

Csikszentmihalyi, M. & Rathunde, K. (1990). The psychology of wisdom: an evolutionary interpretation. In R. J. Sternberg (Ed.), *Wisdom: Its nature, origins, and development* (pp. 25–51). New York: Cambridge University Press.

Damon, W. (2000). Setting the stage for the development of wisdom: Self understanding and moral identity during adolescence. In W. S. Brown (Ed.), *Understanding Wisdom: Sources, Science, & Society* (pp. 339–360). Radnor, PA: Templeton Foundation Press.

DiClemente, R. J., Hansen, W. B., & Ponton, L. E. (1995). *Handbook of adolescent health risk behavior.* New York: Plenum Press.

Dittmann-Kohli, F., & Baltes, P. B. (1990). Toward a neo-functionalist conception of adult development: Wisdom as a prototypical case of intellectual growth. In C. Alexander & E. Langer (Eds.), *Higher stages of human development* (pp. 53–78). New York: Oxford University Press.

Dixon, R. A., & Baltes, P. B. (1986). Toward life-span research on the functions and pragmatics of intelligence. In R. J. Sternberg & R. K. Wagner (Eds.), *Practical intelligence: Nature and origins of competence in the everyday world* (pp. 203–234). Cambridge: Cambridge University Press.

Ericsson, K. A., & Smith, J. (Eds.). (1991). *Toward a general theory of expertise: Prospects and limits.* Cambridge: Cambridge University Press.

Erikson, E. H., & Erikson, J. M. (1997). *The life cycle completed: Extended version.* New York, NY: W. W. Norton & Company.

Fabricius, W. V., Schwanenflugel, P. J., Kyllonen, P. C., Barclay, C. R., & Denton, S. M. (1989). Developing theories of the mind: Children's and adults' concepts of mental activities. *Child Development, 60*, 1278–1290.

Glück, J. & Baltes, P. B. (under review). Enhancing the expression of wisdom-related knowledge in adolescents, adults and older adults: Does activating the concept of wisdom help and whom? Max Planck Institute for Human Development, Berlin.

Harter, S. (1988). Developmental processes in the construction of the self. In T. D. Yawkey & J. E. Johnson (Eds.), *Integrative processes and socialization: Early to middle childhood.* Hillsdale, NJ: Lawrence Erlbaum.

Holliday, S. G., & Chandler, M. J. (1986). *Wisdom: explorations in adult competence.* Basil, Switzerland: Karger.

Holmes, A., & Conway, M. A. (1999). Generation identity and the reminiscence bump: Memory for public and private events. *Journal of Adult Development, 6*, 21–34.

Jessor, Turbin, M. S., & Costa, F. M. (1998). Protective factors in adolescent health behavior. *Journal of Personality and Social Psychology, 75*, 788–800.

Jessor, R. (1992). Risk behavior in adolescence: A psychosocial framework for understanding and action. *Developmental Review, 12*, 374–390.

Kagan, J., Snidman, N., & Arcus, D. (1998). Childhood derivatives of high and low reactivity in infancy. *Child Development, 69*, 1483–1493.

Keating, D. P. (1990). Adolescent thinking. In S. S. Feldman & G. R. Elliott (Eds.), *At the threshold: The developing adolescent* (pp. 54–89). Cambridge, MA: Harvard University Press.

Keller, M., & Wood, P. (1989). Development of friendship reasoning: A study of interindividual differences in intraindividual change. *Developmental Psychology, 25*, 820–826.

Kitchener, K. S., & Brenner, H. G. (1990). Wisdom and reflective judgment: knowing in the face of uncertainty. In R. J. Sternberg (Ed.), *Wisdom: Its nature, origins, and development* (pp. 212–229). New York, NY: Cambridge University Press.

Klaczynski, P. A. (1993). Reasoning schema effects on adolescent rule acquisition and transfer. *Journal of Educational Psychology, 85*, 679–692.

Klaczynski, P. A., & Narasimham, G. (1998). Representations as mediators of adolescent deductive reasoning. *Developmental Psychology, 34*, 865–881.

Kogan, N. (1983). Stylistic variation in childhood and adolescence: Creativity, metaphor, and cognitive styles. In P. H. Mussen (Ed.), *Handbook of child psychology* (Vol. 3, pp. 630–706). New York: Wiley.

Kogan, N., & Pankove, E. (1972). Creative ability over a five-year span. *Child Development, 43*, 427–442.

Kunzmann U., & Baltes, P. B. (2003). Beyond the scope of traditional intelligence: Wisdom in action. In R. J. Sternberg, J. Lautry, & T. I. Lubart (Eds.), *Models of Intelligence: International Perspectives* (pp. 329–343). Washington, DC: American Psychological Association.

Labouvie-Vief, G. (1990). Wisdom as integrated thought: historical and developmental perspectives. In R. J. Sternberg (Ed.), *Wisdom: Its nature, origins, and development* (pp. 52–83). New York: Cambridge University Press.

Lapsley, D. K., & Murphy, M. N. (1985). Another look at the theoretical assumptions of adolescent egocentrism. *Developmental Review, 5*, 201–217.

Lewis, C. G. (1981). How adolescents approach decisions: Changes over grades seven to twelve and policy implications. *Child Development, 52*, 538–554.

Loevinger, J. (1966). The meaning and measurement of ego development. *American Psychologist, 21*, 195–206.

Manis, F. R., Keating, D. P., & Morrison, F. J. (1980). Developmental differences in the allocation of processing capacity. *Journal of Experimental Child Psychology, 29*, 156–169.

Markovits, H., & Vachon, R. (1990). Conditional reasoning, representation, and abstraction. *Developmental Psychology, 26*, 942–951.

Meacham, J. A. (1990). The loss of wisdom. In R. J. Sternberg (Ed.), *Wisdom: Its nature, origins, and development* (pp. 181–211). New York: Cambridge University Press.

Millstein, S. G., & Halpern-Felsher, B. L. (2002). Judgments about risk and perceived invulnerability in adolescents and young adults. *Journal of Research on Adolescence, 12*, 399–422.

Moshman, D., & Franks, B. A. (1986). Development of the concept of inferential validity. *Child Development, 57*, 153–165.

Orwoll, L., & Perlmutter, M. (1990). The study of wise persons: integrating a personality perspective. In R. J. Sternberg (Ed.), *Wisdom: Its nature, origins, and development* (pp. 160–177). New York: Cambridge University Press.

Pals, J. L. (1999). Identity consolidation in early adulthood: Relations with ego-resiliency, the context of marriage, and personality change. *Journal of Personality, 67*, 295–329.

Pasupathi, M., & Staudinger, U. M. (2001). Do advanced moral reasoners also show wisdom? Linking moral reasoning and wisdom-related knowledge and judgment. *International Journal of Behavioral Development, 25*, 401–415.

Pasupathi, M., Staudinger, U. M., & Baltes, P. B. (2001). Seeds of Wisdom: Adolescents' knowledge and judgment about difficult life problems. *Developmental Psychology, 37*, 351–361.

Piaget, J. (1932). *The Moral Judgment of the Child.* New York: Harcourt Brace Jovanovich.

Piaget, J., & Inhelder, B. (1973). *Memory and Intelligence.* London: Routledge and Kegan Paul.

Quadrel, M. J., Fischhoff, B., & Davis, W. (1993). Adolescent (in)vulnerability. *American Psychologist, 48*(2), 102–116.

Roberts, B. W., & Caspi, A. (2003). The cumulative continuity model of personality development: Striking a balance between continuity and change in personality traits across the life course. In U. M. Staudinger and U. Lindenberger (Eds.), *Understanding human development: Lifespan psychology in exchange with other disciplines.* Dordrecht: Kluwer Academic Publishers.

Rubin, D. C., & Schulkind, M. D. (1997). Distribution of important and word-cued autobiographical memories in 20-, 35-, and 70-year-old adults. *Psychology and Aging, 12*, 524–535.

Schrauf, R. W., & Rubin, D. C. (1998). Bilingual autobiographical memory in older adult immigrants: A test of cognitive explanations of the reminiscence bump and the linguistic encoding of memories. *Journal of Memory and Language, 39*, 437–457.

Schrauf, R. W., & Rubin, D. C. (2000). Internal languages of retrieval: The bilingual encoding of memories for the personal past. *Memory and Cognition, 28*, 616–623.

Selman, R. L. (1980). *The growth of interpersonal understanding.* New York: Academic Press.

Smith, J., & Baltes, P. B. (1990). Wisdom-related knowledge: Age/cohort differences in response to life-planning problems. *Developmental Psychology, 26*, 494–505.

Sorrentino, R. M., Raynor, J. O., Zubek, J. M., & Short, J. C. (1990). A theory of personality functioning and change: Reinterpretation of cognitive-development theories in terms of information and affective value. In E. T. Higgins and R. M. Sorrentino (Eds.), *The Handbook of Motivation and Cognition: Foundations of Social Behavior* (Vol. 2, pp. 193–228). New York: Guilford Press.

Sorrentino, R. M., Holmes, J. G., Hanna, S. E., & Sharp, A. (1995) Uncertainty orientation and trust: Individual differences in close relationships. *Journal of Personality and Social Psychology, 68*, 314–327.

Sowarka, D. (1989). Weisheit und weise Personen: Common-Sense Konzepte älterer Menschen. *Zeitschrift für Entwicklungspsychologie und Pädagogischer Psychologie, 21*, 87–109.

Staudinger, U. M. (1999). Older and wiser? Integrating results on the relationship between age and wisdom-related performance. *International Journal of Behavioral Development, 23*, 641–664.

Staudinger, U. M., & Baltes, P. B. (1996). Interactive minds: A facilitative setting for wisdom-related performance? *Journal of Personality and Social Psychology, 71*, 746–762.

Staudinger, U. M., Lopez, D. F., & Baltes, P. B. (1997). The psychometric location of wisdom-related performance. *Personality and Social Psychology Bulletin, 23*, 1200–1214.

Staudinger, U. M., Maciel, A. G., Smith, J., & Baltes, P. B. (1998). What predicts wisdom-related performance? A first look at personality, intelligence, and facilitative experiential contexts. *European Journal of Personality, 12*, 1–17.

Staudinger, U. M., & Pasupathi, M. (2000). Lifespan perspectives on self, personality, and social cognition. In T. Salthouse & F. Craik (Eds.), *Handbook of cognition and aging* (pp. 633–688). Mahwah, NJ: Erlbaum.

Staudinger, U. M., & Pasupathi, M. (2003). Correlates of wisdom-related performance in adolescence and adulthood: Age-graded differences in "paths" towards desirable development. *Journal of Research on Adolescence, 13*, 239–268.

Sternberg, R. J. (1986). Implicit theories of intelligence, creativity, and wisdom. *Journal of Personality and Social Psychology, 49*, 607–627.

Sternberg, R. J. (1998). A balance theory of wisdom. *Review of General Psychology, 2*, 347–365.

Sternberg, R. J., & Nigro, C. (1980). Developmental patterns in the solution of verbal analogies. *Child Development, 51*, 27–38.

Turiel, E. (1998). The development of morality. In W. Damon & N. Eisenberg (Eds.), *Handbook of child psychology* (Vol. 3, pp. 863–932). New York: Wiley.

van Lieshout, C. F. M., & Haselager, G. J. T. (1992). Persoonlijkheidsfactoren in Q-sort persoonsbeschrijvingen van kinderen: Relatie tot het vijf-factorenmodel [Personality factors in Q-sort descriptions of children: Relationships to the five-factor model]. *Pedagogishe Studien, 69*, 23–39.

Wainryb, C. (1995). Reasoning about social conflicts in different cultures: Druze and Jewish children in Israel. *Child Development, 66*, 390–401.

Ward, S. L., & Overton, W. F. (1990). Semantic familiarity, relevance, and the development of deductive reasoning. *Developmental Psychology, 26*, 488–493.

7

The Quest for Wisdom in Adulthood

A Psychological Perspective

Jennifer Jordan

In 1513, the Spanish explorer Ponce de Leon set sail from Puerto Rico on a quest to find the fabled "Fountain of Youth." De Leon dedicated two more explorations to this goal, but died in 1521, having never discovered the elusive fountain. This obsession with eternal youth did not follow de Leon to his grave. Oscar Wilde's late-19th-century classic novel, *The Picture of Dorian Gray*, tells the story of a man willing to sell his soul to the devil in exchange for the ability to stay young forever. And the 20th-century film *Cocoon* recounts the story of a group of retirees who discover the Fountain of Youth, only to have to deal with the realities of aging once this fountain is no longer accessible to them.

Countless examples of how society continues to tirelessly pursue youthfulness, albeit by more realistic and seemingly obtainable means, abound. One need to look no further than television commercials, magazines, and newspapers to find advertisements for myriad antiaging potions, diets, nutritional supplements, and surgeries meant to postpone this inevitable stage of the lifespan.

Perhaps the search (and desire) to find wisdom in old age is another quixotic quest for the Fountain of Youth: "There is no such thing as the old age of the wise." (Sophocles, 497–406/5 B.C.) and "The wise man does not grow old, but ripens" (Victor Hugo, 1802–1885). As these quotes express, wisdom may be (or at least may be perceived as) this elusive fountain that retains one's youth, irrespective of the aging physical vessel. It may be the one positive aspect of an otherwise development-free life trajectory.

Like the elusive Fountain of Youth, wisdom in old age (and young adulthood) is considered, both by scientists and the lay population, as a rare treasure. It is not something that is automatically bestowed on the elderly, nor is it something that is more likely to exist in elderly individuals (Clayton & Birren, 1980; Hira & Faulkender, 1997). Given the results from research on wisdom and aging during adulthood, there is likely no systematic relationship between the two variables (Staudinger, 1999).

This chapter examines the relationship between wisdom and adult age, meaning those years of the lifespan above the age of 18. (For a review of wisdom in adolescence, see Chapter 6 in this volume by Monisha Pasupathi and Michael Richardson.) One could choose to examine this topic from a philosophical, scientific–theoretical, or religious perspective – for each has something significant to contribute to the topic (see Sternberg, 1990); however, this chapter is primarily devoted to examining the empirical findings on the relationship between wisdom and adult age that exist in the psychological literature. In the process, lay conceptions of wisdom and age, unanswered questions in the literature, and possible future directions for research also will be addressed.

Three Models of Wisdom and Aging

There are conceivably three models for the relationship between wisdom and aging in the years following adolescence. The first, and perhaps most optimistic, is that wisdom continues to increase across the life span. This model, which I term the Positive Model, predicts a direct positive relationship between wisdom and age, meaning that adding years to one's life also means adding wisdom. Unfortunately, there is no empirical evidence to support this model.

The second model, which I term the Decline Model, is more pessimistic in its prediction for wisdom and aging. It proposes that beginning in young adulthood, the amount of wisdom one possesses decreases as one increases in adult age. This model also posits that those few elderly individuals who do possess wisdom are those who were able to maintain the wisdom that they began with in young adulthood (Meacham, 1990). This model also has no empirical support.

The third and final model proposes that wisdom (or to use Baltes and Smith's [1990] term *wisdom-related knowledge)* behaves like crystallized intelligence, maintaining itself from early adulthood into old age

(Schaie, 1996). This model, which I term the Crystallized Model, predicts that older adults are equally as likely as young adults to be among the greatest possessors of wisdom, but that wisdom does not systematically increase over the lifespan (Baltes & Staudinger, 2000; Baltes, Staudinger, Maercker, & Smith, 1995; Smith & Baltes, 1990). Other than a possible decline during the very late years of the lifespan (Baltes et al., 1995), the Crystallized Model predicts no correlation between wisdom and adult age. It predicts that old age does not bring wisdom, nor does it rob one of wisdom.

From the empirical evidence available, it appears that the Crystallized Model of wisdom is the most accurate depiction of wisdom's development across the adult lifespan. Thus, if it is asked if old age automatically bestows wisdom, the answer is that it most likely does not. In addition, if it is asked if old age leads to a decline in wisdom, the answer is likely the same. Research examining the relationship between age and wisdom has shown very few age-related trends (Baltes & Staudinger, 2000; Staudinger, 1999). Even studies asking laypeople for their implicit conceptions of wisdom have not found that there is a widely held conception that wisdom and age are directly related; in fact, most studies find no perceived relationship between the two variables.

Has this belief always been the case? The following quotes, representing a span of more than two thousand years, each express the same conclusion – that wisdom and old age are not directly related: "It is not white hair that engenders wisdom" (Menander, 342–292 B.C.); "The older I grow the more I distrust the familiar doctrine that age brings wisdom" (H. L. Mencken, 1880–1956); and "Wisdom doesn't automatically come with old age. Nothing does – except wrinkles. It's true, some wines improve with age. But only if the grapes were good in the first place" (Abigail Van Buren, 1918–).

In examining the relationship between wisdom and age, the more appropriate question may be that if age does not bring or take away wisdom,[1] what relationship does exist between the two variables? This chapter seeks to answer this question.

---

[1] Throughout this chapter, it is important to remember that two variables are described as related, this is referring to "relatedness" in the statistical sense of the word. Very few variables show absolutely no relationship with one another; however, to be considered related in empirical psychology, two variables must demonstrate a relationship to each other beyond that predicted by chance (i.e., at a higher probability than the .05 criterion level).

Important Considerations in the Relationship
Between Wisdom and Aging

Wisdom Is Rare

Wisdom is an uncommon ability. Throughout biblical, philosophical, and historical writings, wisdom is expressed as a rare gift – something bestowed on only a select few – and in some cases, only available to philosophers and deities (Clayton & Birren, 1980). Thus, no matter what age group is examined, one is unlikely to find a high prevalence of wise individuals. This appears also to be true in empirical research. Results from a study by Smith and Baltes (1990) demonstrated that among 240 responses, only 11 resembled the prototype of a wise response.

This perception of wisdom as a rare quality can also be found within popular culture. Modern-day film and book characters, such as *The Karate Kid*'s Mr. Miyagi and *Tuesdays with Morrie*'s Morrie Schwartz, portray wisdom as a rare gem. These portrayals propagate the notion of the wise, sage-like elder who serves as a guide to the younger generation. This individual typically disseminates knowledge from his life experience in a way that constructively guides and nurtures a younger, and often troubled, individual. But even societal portrayals do not always depict all elderly individuals as possessing wisdom. In both of the examples presented earlier, the elderly character's depth and life-insight are portrayed as the exception rather than the rule. Old rarely equals wise.

Studying Wisdom and Aging Is Currently Relevant

By the year 2020, it is estimated that 23% of the North American population will be more than 65 years of age, making this the largest percentage of older adults in history (*World populations prospects population database: 2000–2020, North America*, 2001). Thus, examining factors that affect this population may be more important than ever before. In contrast to the change in conventional intellectual abilities, the development or decay of practical cognitive abilities, including wisdom, during the latter part of the lifespan is still a topic of debate within the psychological community (Berg, 2000). Most studies have not found wisdom to increase with age; however, they also have not found it to decline (Smith & Baltes, 1990; Smith, Staudinger, & Baltes, 1994; Staudinger, Smith, & Baltes, 1992). In fact, older adults are equally as likely as younger adults to be among the top scorers on wisdom-related knowledge (Smith & Baltes, 1990). And

in some instances, older adults even outperform their younger counterparts (Baltes et al., 1995; Pasupathi & Staudinger, 2001; Staudinger &
Baltes, 1996).

The possibility that wisdom is a positive aspect of the aging process
positions it as a topic worthy of inquiry. Demonstrating that under the
right conditions older adults can perform at and above the level of
younger adults makes wisdom-related knowledge something that deserves focus within science. The majority of research on cognitive and
physical aging focuses on decline. This focus can and may contribute to
society's stereotyping of older people as a less useful and productive cohort. It has been found that these stereotypes can have negative effects
on the health and well-being of older people (Levy, Slade, Kunkel, &
Kasl, 2002). Focusing on aspects of the aging process that do not show
declines may bring greater respect and reverence to this population.

Can Wisdom Be Measured?

The most critical, and perhaps the most heavily debated, topic within
research on wisdom is the fundamental question of whether wisdom is
capable of being measured and quantified. As with any construct, the
question of how to define wisdom is of primary concern. When it comes
to a construct as mysterious, complex, and extraordinary as wisdom,
the question takes on an even greater significance. The layperson's conception of wisdom has been found to be dependent on the cultural background and personal qualities of who is asked (Clayton & Birren, 1980;
Takahashi & Bordia, 2000). Thus, it is doubtful that a single definition
can claim to fully capture all that wisdom encompasses. This fact considered, discovering an ability that does correspond to lay conceptions
of wisdom and distinguishes itself from other related constructs, does
(at least in psychological terms) contain discriminant validity, meaning that it is identified as a distinct construct. Research on wisdom has
shown that it is distinct from, albeit related to, personality traits such as
openness to experience and extraversion, and to crystallized and fluid
intelligence (Staudinger, Maciel, Smith, & Baltes, 1998).

The second step to validating a construct is to demonstrate its predictive validity. Establishing a construct's predictive validity means
that possessing a large or small amount of it predicts similar or dissimilar scores on other related abilities or states to which it should
show a relationship. Research on wisdom has demonstrated its predictive validity. For example, those who possess wisdom, in the sense of

wisdom-related knowledge (Staudinger, Smith, & Baltes, 1994), also experience more feelings of positive involvement and use a cooperative strategy when managing conflicts (Kunzmann & Baltes, 2003). In addition, those nominated by others (based on implicit notions of wisdom) as wise also tend to score higher than those not nominated, on measures of wisdom-related knowledge (Baltes et al., 1995).

Studying Wisdom Is Difficult

Explicit theories of wisdom have flourished since the early 1990s. Less than two decades ago, scholars were describing wisdom research as being "truly in its infancy" (Baltes & Smith, 1990, p. 88). Today, there are numerous books and articles on the operationalization of wisdom (Brown, 2000; Sternberg, 1990) and its relationship with other related constructs, such as intelligence (Staudinger et al., 1998), personality, and morality (Pasupathi & Staudinger, 2001).

Despite these recent advances, it is understandable why wisdom has received little empirical investigation throughout science's past. Even with a considerable amount of wisdom research already completed, it continues to be viewed as something impossible to fully understand within the confines of laboratory investigation (Baltes, 1993).

It is unlikely that the scientific method will ever lead to a complete understanding of the components and limitations of wisdom, or to a full understanding of wisdom's relationship to other domains of knowledge and character. Psychology's goal cannot be to claim a complete understanding of wisdom. Rather, its goal must be to discover more about what comprises the wise individual, to confirm through empirical investigation that explicit theories represent valid conceptions of the construct, and to identify other facets of social and cognitive functioning are related to wisdom.

There are two methods for investigating wisdom. One method is to study implicit, or lay, conceptions. The other is to study explicit, or expert-defined, theories. Explicit theories are often influenced by or based on implicit theories and thus the two may demonstrate considerable overlap. One benefit of studying explicit theories is that they are developed by experts. Often created by combining the implicit theories of both laypeople and scientists, explicit theories are an integration of a scientist's concept and research on a topic (Sternberg, 1985).

The Berlin Wisdom Paradigm. One explicit theory, and the only one yet to be empirically tested, is the Berlin Wisdom Paradigm (Baltes &

Smith, 1990; Staudinger et al., 1994). The development of the Berlin Wisdom Paradigm was prompted by three motivations: to study high levels of human performance, to identify strengths that emerge in the aging process, and to study facets of intelligence that reflect strengths in the pragmatics of human functioning (Baltes & Smith, 1990). The paradigm defines wisdom as an expert knowledge system, and like all such systems, it requires a quantitative and qualitative dimension of knowledge. The quantitative dimension of wisdom includes the volume of knowledge amassed by an individual, whereas the qualitative dimension involves how the individual is able to use and apply this knowledge.

The Berlin Wisdom Paradigm defines wisdom as expert knowledge in the fundamental pragmatics of life, which is important knowledge about everyday routines. Because developing expertise in a domain is expected to take a considerable amount of time and practice, it is hypothesized that older adults hold the possibility of having such a level of expertise. This considered, it also is possible that the development of wisdom in older adulthood may be stymied because of its dependence on the cognitive mechanics of the mind and physical health. Because neither increase in old age (Berg, 2000), wisdom may not either. The Berlin Wisdom Paradigm proposes that wisdom's growth may be hindered by age-related limits that are unrelated to fundamental life knowledge (Smith & Baltes, 1990) and more related to the cognitive and physical declines that accompany the aging process. If individuals were capable of transcending these limitations, they might be able to develop their wisdom-related knowledge to a level of expertise.

The paradigm bases wisdom-related knowledge on five criteria, each having its origins in developmental theories of expertise. The first two criteria, rich factual and procedural knowledge, are relevant to all domains of expert knowledge (Anderson, 1982). They can be conceived as the "what is" and "how to" dimensions of an ability. The three metacriteria are lifespan contextualism, relativism, and uncertainty, and are criteria applicable to the specific domain of "fundamental pragmatics of life."

The Berlin Wisdom Paradigm proposes that the development of wisdom is dependent on the influence of general, specific, and modifying factors. General factors include one's level of cognitive, personal, and social efficacy. Specific factors include practice with difficult life dilemmas, mentorship interactions, and motivational dispositions, like generativity. Finally, modifying factors are qualities and characteristics of the individual, such as age, education level, and professional status. It has been shown that some modifying factors, such as professional training (Smith et al., 1994; Staudinger et al., 1992), are related to one's wisdom-related knowledge, whereas others, such as adult age (Smith & Baltes, 1990), are not.

The Berlin Wisdom Paradigm does not predict that older adults will have greater wisdom-related knowledge than will young adults; however, it does predict that under ideal cognitive and physical health conditions, older adults will demonstrate an advantage due to greater life experience (i.e., practice). It also proposes that older adults will hold the "world records" in wisdom, meaning that the highest scorers on the measure will disproportionately be older adults, even though there will not be a systematic increase in wisdom with age (Baltes et al., 1995; Baltes & Staudinger, 2000).

Implicit Theories of Wisdom in Adulthood

As stated earlier, there are two methods that can be used to study wisdom and age. One method is to use explicit, expert-defined theories of wisdom. Another method is to ask laypeople what they believe defines wisdom and the wise individual. This is considered an implicit approach to defining wisdom. Implicit theories often provide the framework for the development of explicit theories (Sternberg, 1985). Implicit theories of wisdom can be derived from laboratory investigations (Clayton & Birren, 1980; Hira & Faulkender, 1997; Orwell & Perlmutter, 1990; Sternberg, 1985; Takahashi & Bordia, 2000), as well as from examinations of historical literature on the topic (Robinson, 1990). Below is a sampling of investigations of modern implicit theories of wisdom and adult age.

Describing the wise person. In one of the first laboratory investigations of implicit theories of wisdom, Clayton and Birren (1980) examined conceptions of wisdom in individuals of varying ages. Young, middle-aged, and older persons were asked to judge the similarity between adjectives related to the wise person (*experienced, intuitive, introspective, pragmatic, understanding, gentle, empathetic, intelligent, peaceful, knowledgeable, sense of humor,* and *observant* [from Clayton, 1975]) with the adjectives, *wise* and *aged* and the pronoun *myself*. These pairings revealed that across age groups, people perceived wisdom to include affective, reflective, and cognitive components. All age groups agreed on what adjectives comprised the affective (*understanding, empathy*) and reflective (*introspection, intuition*) components of wisdom but showed a differentiation on the cognitive component. Older adults identified two distinct cognitive components of wisdom, one that was time-dependent (*knowledge, experience*) and one that was cognitive-specific (*intelligent, pragmatic–observant*), whereas young and middle-aged adults grouped these adjectives into one general cognitive construct.

There also were age-group differences in perceptions of the adjectives most related to wisdom. Young and middle-aged adults rated *wise* as more similar to the adjectives *aged* and *experienced*, whereas older adults rated *wise* as most similar to *understanding* and *empathetic*. Finally, older participants judged the pronoun *myself* to be no more similar to *wise* than did younger participants.

This study demonstrates that one's concept of wisdom becomes more differentiated (i.e., multidimensional) with age. It also demonstrates that young people may perceive a stronger relationship between wisdom and age than do older people, indicating that there is not a universal conception that wisdom and age are closely related. And, finally, it may indicate that individuals do not perceive themselves as increasing in wisdom with increases in age.

Another method used to investigate implicit theories of wisdom is to have people view a wisdom-related response and then rate how much wisdom-related knowledge they believe to be incorporated in that response. This type of methodology allows one to determine characteristics independent from the content of the response that may influence it to be viewed as wise or unwise.

Wisdom and respondent characteristics. Hira and Faulkender (1997) examined perceptions of wisdom-related knowledge as a function of the respondents' age and gender. This study addressed the question of whether perceptions of wise-responding are a function of the actual advice being given or of the visible attributes of the individual giving the advice. It required participants to rate their perceptions of an adult on videotape who was responding to a dilemma dealing with a fundamental life issue (Smith & Baltes, 1990). The response previously had been rated as incorporating an average amount of wisdom-related knowledge (Staudinger et al., 1994).

Results showed that the young female and older male respondents were rated as responding to the problem with a higher level of wisdom-related knowledge than did the young male and older female. Participants also judged the latter two respondents as considerably younger in chronological age than they actually were. This error in judgment may demonstrate that perceptions of age are related to implicit perceptions of wisdom-related knowledge. In other words, having a lower level of wisdom-related knowledge might cause one to be perceived as younger than one actually is, indicating that people may perceive that having higher levels of wisdom indicate that the person is chronologically older (Clayton & Birren, 1980; Takahashi & Bordia, 2000). But because both the older male and female were not rated has having the highest level of wisdom-related knowledge, it also demonstrates that old age is not considered a sole criterion for wisdom-related knowledge.

There is another alternative explanation for this result. The tendency for the older male to be rated as giving a wiser response than the older female may be a result of perceiving older males as having greater life experience than older females. The older female may be perceived as having less life experience because of the social norms of individuals in her cohort and gender group. Life experience is seen as a predictor of wisdom in religious (Rudolph, 1987), philosophical (Clayton & Birren, 1980), and modern implicit theories. Thus, perceptions that one may have limited life experience may lead to the belief that one also has a limited amount of wisdom-related knowledge.

In summary, these results support the notion that age is not a sufficient condition for the possession of wisdom. They also allow for the possibility that one's age may be judged according to one's perceived level of wisdom-related knowledge and that perceptions of wisdom may be related not only to what is said, but to the characteristics of who said it.

Perceptions of wisdom and age across cultures. A study examining cross-cultural definitions of wisdom demonstrated that conceptions of wisdom vary based on the norms and values of the society in which they are embedded (Takahashi & Bordia, 2000). When young adults from the United States, Australia, India, and Japan were asked to rate the similarity of character adjectives (*aged, awakened, discreet, experienced, intuitive,* and *knowledgeable*) and the adjective *wise,* Americans and Australians rated *wise* to be most similar to the adjectives *experienced* and *knowledgeable,* whereas Indians and Japanese rated *wise* to be most similar to *discreet* (India only), *aged,* and *experienced* (Japan only).

This study also had participants rank, on a scale from 1 to 8, adjectives that were descriptors of the ideal self. Although participants from all cultures rated *wise* as a descriptor of the ideal self, they also considered *aged* to be the least desirable descriptor, indicating perhaps that none of the participants considered *aged* to be a requirement for the possession of wisdom.

One limitation of this study is that only young adults, namely, undergraduate students, were sampled. Consequently, these reported differences between cultures may be conservative estimates of the actual differences that exist within a broader sample. Because of their greater exposure to multiple cultures, young adults, particularly university students, may be more likely to have less culturally sensitive conceptions of culturally influenced constructs. The results of this study might have shown more differentiated ratings across the cultures had middle-aged and older adults been sampled.

Perceptions of the growth and decline of cognitive mechanics with age. When asked, laypeople consider certain domains of practical intelligence to be capable of both increasing and decreasing across the life span. In a study by Berg and Sternberg (1992), participants were asked to rate how likely young, middle-aged, and older adults of average and exceptional intelligence were to engage in a variety of cognitive behaviors. They also were asked to provide a list of intellectual abilities that they perceived to increase and decrease across the life span.

Results showed that participants perceived that the domain of *everyday competence*, which included such abilities as dealing effectively with problems and displaying wisdom, as more likely to be found in older adults than in young adults. It was also found that the majority of participants rated intellectual abilities as being capable of both increasing and decreasing with age, with *using past experience advantageously* and *understanding others* as abilities that are likely to increase with age, and those such as memory as likely to decrease.

Similarly, a study by Heckhausen, Dixon, and Baltes (1989) showed that young, middle-aged, and older adults perceive intellectual development across the lifespan to be multidirectional, capable of both increasing and decreasing with age. Participants' amount of perceived gains outnumbered those of perceived losses. A finding from this study that may be even more pertinent to the question of the relationship between wisdom and age is that when asked to rate on a 9-point scale to what extent an intellectually related adjective was perceived to increase over the lifespan, participants gave *wise* a mean rating of 6.71, the seventh highest on a list of 148. *Wise* was also rated as having its onset in middle age (i.e., 55 years old) and not decreasing until the very late years of the life span (i.e., 86 years old).

Summarizing Implicit Investigations

Few laboratory investigations of implicit theories have found *wise* and *aged* to be adjectives closely related in participants' mental schemas. In addition, the absence of a relationship is even more pronounced when examining these conceptions in older adults (Clayton & Birren, 1980). In comparison to older persons young adults consider the two to be more closely related. If wisdom is knowing what one does not know (Meacham, 1983), this may be evidence that older people do possess greater levels of wisdom than do their younger counterparts. Or it could be evidence that older adults do not possess greater levels of wisdom – for those without wisdom may be the best judges of its absence. But even when wisdom and age are considered to be closely related constructs, *aged* is not considered a desired characteristic for young adults (Takahashi & Bordia, 2000).

Just because these investigations do not consistently show a link between wisdom and old age does not mean that people believe that wisdom cannot increase with age and that older people are incapable of possessing wisdom. Investigations of implicit theories of cognitive development indicate that cognitive abilities are perceived to both increase and decrease over the lifespan, with wisdom being one facet of cognitive functioning more likely to increase (Berg & Sternberg, 1992). The latter portion of the lifespan is not solely perceived as a time of cognitive loss or of cognitive gain. In addition, the cognitive pragmatics of the mind, those more involved with practical abilities (Baltes, 1993), are perceived to increase. Finally, wisdom is perceived as one ability most likely to increase during adulthood, having its onset in middle age (Heckhausen et al., 1989).

These implicit investigations are directive within the question of the relationship between wisdom and age; however, the interpretation of their results must be accompanied by some qualifications. First, implicit theories of wisdom are not able to claim any internal or external validity in their operationalization of the construct. Even though large numbers of people may perceive wisdom and age to be related or unrelated, this does not make it so. In addition, these results are biased by the characteristics (Clayton & Birren, 1980) and cultural environment (Takahashi & Bordia, 2000) of the respondent and thus must be interpreted within this framework. Results from implicit theories can help shape explicit theories (Sternberg, 1985), but until those explicit theories withstand external validation they can only be considered theoretically directive.

Empirical Evidence for the Null Relationship Between Wisdom and Adult Age

Like implicit studies of wisdom, empirical studies on wisdom's development across the lifespan have shown that wisdom and age are not directly related. Over and over again, laboratory investigations of wisdom have shown that wisdom is equally likely to be possessed by young and older adults (Baltes et al., 1995; Smith & Baltes, 1990; Smith et al., 1994; Staudinger et al., 1992).

Smith and Baltes (1990) conducted one of the first laboratory measurements of wisdom. Using the Berlin Wisdom Paradigm, they examined wisdom-related knowledge in young, middle-aged, and older adult individuals in response to a life-planning task. The task included four problems related to work and family and varied the age of the target in the task (young vs. older) and the life decision being made (normative vs. nonnormative[2]). To define the type of decision needing to be made and to cue alternative views of the problem, each task specified two options that the principal character could choose to resolve the dilemma. The participants were then asked to formulate a plan for what the character should do in the next 3 to 5 years.[3] Each of the four combinations of young/older and normative/nonnormative dilemmas was presented to participants.

Across all four task responses, results showed only age-related trends; no overall age differences were statistically significant. Young adult subjects were rated higher on wisdom-related knowledge than were older adult subjects, with middle-aged subjects falling in between. In examining responses to the four dilemmas individually across age groups, young and middle-aged participants were rated significantly higher on both the young target dilemmas and the old/normative dilemma, but no between group differences were found in response to the old/nonnormative dilemma. Comparing participants within age

---

[2] Normative versus nonnormative life decisions are categorized according to the frequency at which they occur during a life stage. Normative events are those that have a high correlation with age, meaning that a majority of people in the same life stage would be expected to experience these events in relatively similar time period. Both terms refer to statistical orientation and not value orientation (Baltes & Nesselroade, 1984).

[3] Below are two examples of dilemmas used to test participants' wisdom-related knowledge. There were a total of four dilemmas administered to participants (Smith & Baltes, 1990):

Elizabeth, 33 years old and a successful professional for 8 years, was recently offered a major promotion. Her new responsibilities would require an increased time commitment. She and her husband also would like to have children before it is too late. Elizabeth is considering the following options: She could plan to accept the promotion, or she could plan to start a family. **(Young target/Normative life decision)**

Joyce, a 60-year-old widow, recently completed a degree in business management and opened her own business. She has been looking forward to this new challenge. She has just heard that her son has been left with two small children to care for. Joyce is considering the following options: She could plan to give up her business and live with her son, or she could plan to arrange for financial assistance for her son to cover child-care costs. **(Older target/Nonnormative life decision)**

groups revealed that young participants were rated significantly lower on the old/nonnormative problem and the older participants were rated significantly higher on the old/nonnormative problem in comparison with their scores on the other three dilemmas.

What should be noted from these results is that few participants from any cohort performed in a way that would be considered wise. Of the 240 responses produced (4 dilemmas x 60 subjects), only 11 were considered to contain expert levels of wisdom-related knowledge. These responses were evenly distributed across all three cohorts, meaning that older adults were as likely as young adults to be among the top scorers. All high-level responses from older (60–81 years old) adults were produced in response to the older/nonnormative problem.

It is unknown why the older adults performed best and the young and middle-aged adults performed the poorest on the older/nonnormative life-planning problem, but both young and older adults performed better (although in the case of young adults, not significantly better) when responding to the nonnormative dilemma that contained a target in their own cohort. One hypothesis is that participants gave the most wisdom-related responses when faced with dilemmas that they found unusual, and thus most difficult. Those dilemmas that were nonnormative may have been seen as the most unique and challenging and, as a result, provoked more thought from the participants. In addition, if wisdom is an expertise, it may be enhanced through deliberate practice (Ericsson & Smith, 1991). It is likely that an individual would have greater practice in dealing with problems related to his or her own age cohort.

Following this seminal study by Smith and Baltes (1990), a number of investigations using the Berlin Wisdom Paradigm followed and each demonstrated null findings in the relationship between wisdom and adult age. A study by Staudinger, Smith, and Baltes (1992) examined wisdom within a population of clinical psychologists. This population was chosen because of their training and experience in dealing with and giving advice on problems related to the fundamental pragmatics of life. Therefore, they were expected to have above-average levels of wisdom-related knowledge. Although few clinical psychologists were expected to generate responses that could be considered to contain expert levels of wisdom-related knowledge – just as few people trained in any profession are expected to become experts in that field – the group of clinical psychologists was expected to contain a greater number of wise respondents in comparison to professionals from non-human-service-related fields.

The participants (i.e., clinical psychologists and control professionals) were administered a think-aloud task similar to the one presented in the study described earlier (Smith & Baltes, 1990); however, in this study the dilemma dealt with life review rather than life planning. Related to knowledge about the fundamental pragmatics of life, life review is defined as the construction, interpretation, and evaluation of an individual's life course (Staudinger et al., 1992). This type of life task was used because the investigators wanted to access participant's knowledge of events within the life structure and course, which was thought to be a component of wisdom-related knowledge. The life-review task asked participants to construct the life review of either a young or older woman after she comes in contact with a longtime friend who took a different life path from her own.

Across area of professional specialization, no age differences on wisdom-related knowledge were found. Older clinical psychologists did provide higher-level responses than did young nonclinical professionals; however, their responses were no better than those of young clinical psychologists.

Across cohort, participants gave significantly better responses to dilemmas involving a target within their same age group. And within cohort, there were no differences on responses to young and old target dilemmas. This result differs from that found in response to life-planning dilemmas (Smith & Baltes, 1990).

Investigating this between-profession effect on wisdom-related knowledge, a similar study was conducted, this time comparing clinical psychologists with control professionals in response to two tasks related to life planning (Smith et al., 1994). These life-planning tasks were the same nonnormative dilemmas used in a previous study involving work- and family-related life-planning dilemmas (Smith & Baltes, 1990). As was found before, there were no age group differences. Young adults did perform better than older adults on the young-target problem; however, there were no age group differences on the older-target problem. Within-age-group comparisons revealed that young adults provided higher-level responses on the young-target dilemma and older adults provided higher-level responses on the older-target dilemma. And similar to the results found in the study on life review (Staudinger et al., 1992), older clinical psychologists did not show overall advantages on the life-planning dilemmas in comparison with young clinical psychologists.

Out of concern that clinical psychologists may have performed better than control professionals on the Berlin Wisdom Paradigm protocol because of their shared training with the measure's developers, a study was conducted to compare the wisdom-related knowledge of persons nominated as wise with that of clinical psychologists and control professionals (Baltes et al., 1995). This research design was undertaken to be able to conclude that if nominees performed at levels greater than or equal to that of clinical psychologists, then one could have greater confidence that clinical psychologists demonstrated an advantage because of their knowledge about fundamental life matters, rather than because of their shared professional background with the measure's developers. In addition, demonstrating that persons nominated as wise, in an implicit sense, also score higher than a control population on the Berlin Wisdom Paradigm would provide external validity to the measure.

This was the first study to use a question about life management to measure wisdom-related knowledge. Namely, participants were asked about how they would respond if they received a phone call from a close friend who was planning to commit suicide. They also were given a life-planning problem used in previous studies (Smith & Baltes, 1990; Smith et al., 1994).

Results demonstrated that within the control group (i.e., those not clinical psychologists nor wisdom nominees), there was no main effect of participant age. In addition, although the clinical psychologists (mean age ≈ 66 years) and wisdom nominees (mean age ≈ 64 years) performed better than the young and old control groups on both tasks, when compared against each other, clinical psychologists and wisdom nominees performed equally well. Finally, although the older control subjects (mean age ≈ 68 years) did not contribute their expected share to the range of top scorers, the clinical psychologists and wisdom nominees contributed almost more than double their expected share to this group.

Conclusions on Empirical Investigations of Wisdom and Age

First and foremost, what can be concluded from these four studies is that wisdom and adult age are not directly related. It also can be concluded that, contrary to findings on fluid intelligence (Schaie, 1996), older adults are equally likely as young adults (except for results from Baltes et al. [1995]) to be among the top scorers on wisdom-related knowledge.

These results also show that for life-planning tasks, but not life-review tasks (Staudinger et al., 1992), dealing with a problem relevant to one's own age group provides no overall advantage (Baltes et al., 1995; Smith & Baltes, 1990; Smith et al., 1994). It is hypothesized that this cohort advantage on the age-similar life-review tasks and not on the life-planning tasks comes from a difference in prior experience with the task and the subject matter of the dilemma. Young adults are not expected to participate in hypothetical life reviews in old age but are expected to hypothetically plan for life in old age, whereas older adults may regularly participate in life reviews related to old age, giving them a performance advantage on this task (Staudinger, 1999).

Factors that May Lead to an Increase in Wisdom over the Life Span
From the research that has been done, it is evident that wisdom and adult age are not directly related. This, however, does not mean that wisdom cannot and does not increase across the lifespan. It also does not mean that older people do not possess wisdom. As described above, older adults are as likely as their younger counterparts to be among the top scores in wisdom-related knowledge (Smith & Baltes, 1990; Smith et al., 1994; Staudinger et al., 1992).

Certain factors have been found to facilitate the expression of wisdom in older people. Thus, even if old age may not bring wisdom, it is possible that the presence of other, related factors in young, middle-aged, and older adulthood may facilitate its maintenance and development across the life span. The following section will explore some factors that have been found to be facilitative of wisdom-related knowledge in older adulthood.

Moral Reasoning

Wisdom-related knowledge and morality share many attributes, making it conceivable that the possession of one may lead to development of the other. Investigations examining implicit theories of wisdom have shown that laypeople perceive wisdom to be correlated with morality-related characteristics like reasoning ability and judgment (Sternberg, 1985). Explicit theories have also drawn parallels between wisdom and morality, relating wisdom to such abilities as being able to take into account the greater interest of the common good in decision-making situations (Sternberg, 1998) and understanding that wise decision making incorporates the relativity of values (Smith & Baltes, 1990). At the same time, experts (and laypeople) have explicitly distinguished the two constructs (Clayton & Birren, 1980; Smith & Baltes, 1990; Sternberg,

1985), suggesting that wisdom-related knowledge and decision making are broader in focus than is morality, and whereas wisdom is situation-based, morality is situation-independent. Wisdom is the ability to know what to do and how to do it when faced with a difficult life dilemma (Baltes & Smith, 1990; Sternberg, 1998), whereas morality is the universal application of abstract principles like fairness and justice to all dilemmas that one may encounter (Kohlberg, 1973). Lastly, in contrast to highly moral decisions, highly wise decisions are not required to transcend the conventional value system within a society (Pasupathi & Staudinger, 2001). One can make a wise decision by applying conventional societal values, if these are appropriate for the dilemma at hand. Thus, although wisdom and morality are similar, there is not a direct overlap between the two constructs and ability in one is not expected to highly predict ability in the other.

A study by Pasupathi and Staudinger (2001) found that for adults who performed above the median level on moral reasoning, age was positively associated with wisdom-related knowledge ($r = .16$), but for those that scored below the median, age was unrelated to wisdom-related knowledge ($r = .03$). It is important to consider that in this study, moral reasoning was found to completely share predictive variance with person characteristics (i.e., creativity and a thinking style that prefers to reach goals by setting priorities), thus, it is impossible to know how much this relationship between age and wisdom was because of levels of moral reasoning and not to other characteristics related to moral reasoning. This considered, the relationship between these two constructs is pertinent to the relationship (or lack thereof) between wisdom and age. One reason is that moral reasoning has not been found to decrease over the lifespan (Pratt, Diessner, Pratt, Hunsberger, & Pancer, 1996), thus, if wisdom increases with age in those with higher levels of moral reasoning, decreases in moral reasoning because of age is not a likely threat to wisdom.

Does superior moral reasoning develop wisdom or vice versa? Because of the correlational design of this study, it is impossible to tell; however, moral reasoning is hypothesized to be a facilitative factor in the amassing of wisdom, for it creates a more reflective and evaluative way to perceive and integrate life experiences into one's own knowledge base (Pasupathi & Staudinger, 2001). Because it has been shown that wisdom is related to positive measures of subjective well-being (Ardelt, 2000; Kunzmann & Baltes, 2003), it would be advantageous to implement programs designed to increase levels of moral reasoning during adulthood and to examine if this is facilitative to the development of wisdom-related knowledge.

Professional Training and Practice

According to the Berlin Wisdom Paradigm, wisdom is an expertise in the meaning and conduct of life (Baltes & Smith, 1990). In all domains of expertise, increased training and practice should facilitate the ability's development – but, just as not all those who receive training and practice in a domain are expected to become experts, the same is true for the domain of wisdom.

Training and practice in a domain related to fundamental life issues have been found to enhance wisdom-related knowledge (Baltes et al., 1995; Smith et al., 1994; Staudinger et al., 1992). Examining this phenomenon within the context of training and practice in clinical psychology, it was found that clinical psychologists showed performance advantages in comparison to professionals without training in human service-related fields. Although it was not found that wisdom-related knowledge improved with age within the population of clinical psychologists, the benefits provided by this training lasted throughout the professional's lifespan, with older clinical psychologists continuing to show greater levels than young nonclinical psychologists. It also has been hypothesized that training and practice in other human service professions, including theology, family medicine, and education policy, would provide similar benefits (Smith et al., 1994).

Contact and Discussion with a Valued Other

The idea that other individuals facilitate the development of wisdom is not novel. Ancient conceptions of wisdom include the notion that mentors are responsible for developing a young person into a wise community member (Clayton & Birren, 1980), and modern investigations of wisdom find that people nominated as wise mention mentors as formative factors in their development of wisdom (Staudinger & Baltes, 1996). Among other facilitative effects, mentors are able to help individuals synthesize their life experiences in a way that allows for the experience to become a catalyst for the development of wisdom-related knowledge. They also can guide individuals to choose the best course of action when faced with a difficult life dilemma (Staudinger, 1999).

Research has shown that consultation with others, termed interactive minds, is facilitative of wisdom-related knowledge (Staudinger & Baltes, 1996). The concept of interactive minds is defined as the influence of one person's cognitions by the cognitions of others. This influence can shape and guide the individual's thoughts, as well as help him or her to generate new thoughts. Because wisdom is a socially developed construct (one cannot be wise in situations void of other people), it is understandable that wise decision-making or wisdom-related knowledge would be enhanced by the presence of and/or consultation with another individual. In addition, a decision is considered to be wise or unwise by those who are affected by or observe a resolution in action; thus, the subjective nature of this judgment makes it a construct that could be enhanced by consultation with other individuals – that is, those who would potentially be evaluating the decisions after they are implemented.

Another reason why wisdom-related knowledge could be increased by the assistance of interactive minds comes from research on reflective judgment. This research has shown that simply having people read other good responses increases the developmental level of their own responses to a problem (Kitchener, Lynch, Fischer, & Wood, 1993). Thus, it may only take knowing or thinking about what someone else would do to experience the benefit of interactive minds.

People are aware of the benefits of having another person available to consult about difficult and uncertain life dilemmas. When asked how they resolve life dilemmas, people report considering what others would do and consulting with others as two actions that they would be equally likely to take (Staudinger & Baltes, 1996). A study by Staudinger and Baltes (1996) examined how consulting with another familiar individual about a problem related to the fundamental pragmatics of life affected the content of one's response. It was not expected that interactive minds would be a substitute for the individual mind; however, it was expected that interactive minds would facilitate an individual's judgment ability.

In this study, participants brought a familiar partner, either a spouse, romantic partner, relative, or friend, into the lab and were presented with the Berlin Wisdom Paradigm (Staudinger et al., 1994). The interview consisted of asking participants to respond to three problems on life planning, review, and management. The participants were randomly assigned to one of five experimental groups. Two of the groups (Groups 1 & 2) consisted of participants and their partners partaking in the training and the interview together. The partners were separated when it came time to respond to the three scenarios. In one of these two conditions, participants were also allowed additional time to think about the problem on their own before being asked to respond (Group 2).

In the other three conditions (individual conditions), participants were interviewed and provided their responses without a partner present. In these conditions, participants were either asked to engage in an internal dialogue about the dilemma with a valued other (Group 3), think about the problem without any instruction (Group 4), or were given no time to think about the scenario between its presentation and the prompting for a response (Group 5).

Focusing on results related to wisdom and aging, the researchers demonstrated that the highest scoring group was older adults from the external-dialogue plus internal-thought condition (*Group 2*). Older adults in this condition performed significantly better than did their younger counterparts. It was hypothesized that older adults were better able to use the interaction with the other individual as a stimulus for their own knowledge and judgment. This is the first time that an intervention condition was found to increase older individuals' performance to a level higher than that of young adults.

These findings are particularly interesting in regard to the implications they have for the older population in modern society. The older population is often one that has limited social interactions because of life factors such as failing health, the death of a spouse, and less time spent with grown children. It is possible that these negative factors related to the aging process significantly affect the development of wisdom. This negative effect may be even more pronounced in Western societies, where the elderly are less likely to stay in their children's homes as they age (Silver, 1998). All research related to the Berlin Wisdom Paradigm has been conducted in Western Europe; thus, it is almost impossible to know if the paucity of positive age-related results can be attributed to the cultural environment in which measurement is taking place. In addition, as the East becomes more globalized and loses the tradition of keeping elderly family members within the home, the facilitative benefits of a collectivist culture (presuming that any exist) may also be diminished.

To examine this question in more detail, research needs to be conducted to examine the different life factors that may affect the development of wisdom into the latter years of the lifespan. These factors could include amount of in-depth social interactions a person has, the health of one's spouse, the amount of interaction one has with other generations and younger family members, and one's cultural environment.

Factors that May Limit Wisdom's Development

Several factors that may lead to increases in wisdom-related knowledge with increasing age were identified above. There is also the possibility that certain factors may limit the growth of wisdom over the lifespan. The finding that wisdom is able to maintain itself across the lifespan is very interesting. It leads one to question what wisdom's trajectory would look like if certain environmental factors and challenges were absent or abated. The following section will briefly examine this possibility.

Isolation of Older People

One factor that has been identified as facilitative of wisdom-related knowledge is interaction with another, familiar human mind when trying to resolve a difficult life dilemma (Staudinger & Baltes, 1996). Modern societies, especially those in the West, continue to isolate the older population at increasing rates (Hashimoto, 1991; *Estimated number of assisted living facilities in the US: 1995–2000*, 2001). Many families place older members in nursing homes, where they may be more likely to experience few meaningful interactions with others. Other older people become widows and widowers during this period and live out the remainder of their lives in fairly isolated surroundings. In addition, as the ability to be mobile outside the home decreases, the chances for social interactions show a concomitant decline. These factors may decrease one's chances for meaningful interactions with other, familiar individuals. Given that such types of interactions can actually improve an older adults' level of wisdom-related knowledge to that above younger adults' (Staudinger & Baltes, 1996), modern society's tendency to isolate their elders may have negative implications for this population's development of wisdom-related knowledge.

Medical Technology Is Lagging

The inability to find increases in wisdom-related knowledge across the lifespan may be hampered by the cognitive declines that occur during old age. Although conventional measures of intelligence do not contribute a significant portion of unique variance to wisdom-related knowledge (Staudinger, Lopez, & Baltes, 1997), it is thought that a minimal level of cognitive functioning is necessary for one's level of wisdom-related knowledge to be maintained. Very old adults (i.e., those above 80 years of age) are presumed to be at risk for this less than minimal level of functioning. There is not a sufficient amount of data from adults within this age group to be able to draw any firm conclusions (Baltes et al., 1995); however, the possibility remains that if medical technology were able to develop ways to preserve cognitive abilities into the very late years of the lifespan, wisdom also would hold the possibility of being able to flourish to its full potential.

Conclusions

Considering the theoretical and empirical research that has been done on wisdom and adult age, it is difficult to believe that these two factors are directly related. A more likely relationship between wisdom and age is that wisdom holds the possibility of maintaining itself across the lifespan and older individuals are just as likely as young individuals to be amongst the "world record holders" in wisdom-related knowledge. If wisdom is indeed the Fountain of Youth, then few people discover this fountain prior to death. Regardless if one is young or old, the likelihood of possessing wisdom is low (Smith & Baltes, 1990).

There also may be factors that act as catalysts for wisdom-related knowledge, meaning that their presence at the beginning of the lifespan promotes the development of wisdom in the later years. One possible catalyst may be moral reasoning, for it has been found that those who perform above a mean level in moral reasoning also demonstrate a positive correlation between wisdom and age (Pasupathi & Staudinger, 2001). There may be many other wisdom catalysts that have yet to be identified, including level of interaction with multiple generations and the availability of other, valued individuals with whom to discuss difficult life dilemmas (Staudinger & Baltes, 1996).

If wisdom does not increase with age, does this predict a dire outlook for the aging individual? Certainly not. Given that fluid intelligence (Schaie, 1996) and physical strength decrease with age, the finding that wisdom maintains itself – or shows no relationship with age (possibly barring the very late years of the life span [Baltes et al., 1995]) is in fact quite promising. This finding demonstrates that wisdom is not dependent on other cognitive and physical abilities and can stand in the face of declines in each.

Anecdotal evidence of older individuals who have accomplished great things demonstrates that old age is not a period of the life span void of personal achievement and growth. For example, Gandhi was 61 when he made his famous 24-day protest march to the sea, Benjamin Franklin was 70 years old when he served as a signer of the Declaration of Independence, and Mother Teresa continued to work for the good of the poor until her death at the age of 87. Did these individuals possess wisdom? On the implicit level, I predict that most people would say they did; but, it is likely that their wisdom was not automatically bestowed upon them in old age. Rather, it is possible that certain factors present in early adulthood allowed wisdom to develop in middle age and prosper in the elderly years of life. Thus, old age did not bring the abilities necessary for these individuals to complete their accomplishments, nor did it noticeably hinder their progression.

What Can We Conclude about Wisdom and Age?

Can the empirical findings on wisdom and age be taken as conclusive evidence that these two variables are unrelated? They most likely cannot. For one, laboratory investigations allow one to draw only limited conclusions. Studying wisdom in a laboratory context clearly has advantages. Most notably, it allows the investigators to isolate variables to make them testable without the interference of other factors; but this isolation imposes limits on the construct being studied. These limitations can be of particular concern when studying a construct as complex and abstract as wisdom. Wisdom-related knowledge and ability may increase with age, but this relationship may not be able to be fully captured and documented through the use of laboratory paradigms.

In addition, even if older people do not exhibit advantages on measures of wisdom-related knowledge, this does not mean that wisdom does not increase across one's own lifespan. If wisdom does increase across the lifespan within individuals, its development may not be evidenced in studies conducted across cohort groups if younger cohorts have benefited from life experiences that have provided wisdom-related advantages. Such advantageous experiences may include the accessibility of higher education, exposure to multiple cultures via technology, and the ability to travel farther distances in shorter times – all factors that have increased during the last several decades. Studying the change in wisdom over time intraindividually would require longitudinal studies that track an individual's wisdom-related knowledge. Unfortunately, no such studies have yet been undertaken.

It is also possible that wisdom may not be fully understood by those who are not wise. Even a researcher with expertise in psychological inquiry may not be skilled enough to understand how to study a construct that he or she has no personal experience with. This question can be posed, but is unlikely to ever be answered.

The Questions that Remain

There are several questions that remain unanswered in the relationship between wisdom and aging. Below are those that I believe are the most significant.

Can one be robbed of wisdom? This chapter addressed factors present in the lifespan that may help wisdom develop and factors that may limit its growth. Factors that may reduce wisdom with increased age were not addressed because thus far, no research has documented a decline in wisdom across the lifespan. Wisdom repeatedly has been shown to be an ability sustained into old age (Baltes et al., 1995; Smith & Baltes, 1990; Smith et al., 1994; Staudinger et al., 1992). Even though it has been posited that wisdom may decline past the age of 80, there is no conclusive evidence for this (Baltes et al., 1995). This is a question that still requires investigation.

If it is found that wisdom does decrease during very old age, why might this be? Is it because this cohort has less exposure to meaningful social interactions (Staudinger & Baltes, 1996)? In addition, although intelligence has not been found to be predictive of wisdom-related knowledge (Staudinger et al., 1997), what specific age-related losses in cognitive functioning at the end of the life span might lead to negative effects to wisdom-related knowledge?

What can be done to help wisdom's development? Factors facilitative to wisdom-related knowledge have been identified; however, there has yet to be an intervention program designed to increase wisdom-related knowledge during adulthood. Given that wisdom is related to fundamental life knowledge (Baltes & Smith, 1990), a program that could potentially increase this knowledge would be advantageous to both physical and emotional well-being in old age. It remains unknown if wisdom is capable of being developed through an explicit invention and if it is, how long would the positive effects of such an intervention remain?

Is age a proxy for another variable? Empirical research has demonstrated that an increase in age does not lead to an increase in wisdom (Smith & Baltes, 1990; Smith et al., 1994; Staudinger et al., 1992). These findings still leave open the possibility that age is a proxy for another variable, namely, life experience. Is there any evidence available to support this possibility?

Life experience alone has not been found to be a predictor of wisdom-related knowledge (Staudinger et al., 1992). For example, it was found that when individuals identified as experts in life matters were assessed for their wisdom-related knowledge, they performed better than their nonexpert counterparts; however, within this expert population, older experts performed no better than did younger experts (Smith et al., 1994; Staudinger et al., 1992). If life experience were a predictor, then individuals who received training and practice in domains related to the conduct and meaning of life (i.e., clinical psychology) would be expected to increase their level of wisdom-related knowledge with increased training (Staudinger, et al., 1992).

It is hypothesized that this lack of variance in performance between age groups may be because of cohort effects. Young adults may have greater access and be exposed to more information on life dilemmas than were generations that preceded them. This may mean that young people do not need to experience difficult life events themselves, but can experience and gain knowledge from them vicariously. This hypothesis proposes that although individuals are growing in wisdom throughout their own lifespan, younger generations have the advantage of gaining knowledge on the fundamental pragmatics of life through simpler modes and at a faster rate, overriding the positive effects of the natural aging process. The only way to test this hypothesis would be to conduct longitudinal studies examining the development of wisdom across the lifespan of people from several generations.

The Challenges and Triumphs of Wisdom

No matter what unanswered questions on this relationship remain, one thing is clear – empirical research on wisdom should continue. Research on wisdom is costly in terms of time, human resources, and money, but it is unlikely that assessing wisdom-related knowledge can be done using traditional methodological practices. If wisdom is indeed one of the highest forms of knowledge (Clayton & Birren, 1980) and an ideal of human development (Staudinger & Baltes, 1996), then measuring wisdom must involve sophisticated methods. The behavioral approach to measuring wisdom employed by the Berlin Wisdom Paradigm is sophisticated, as well as costly, but this approach has been the only one to successfully employ empirical and behavioral methodology to measure wisdom. It also has possibly produced some of the most valuable research on this topic. Sadly, because of these challenges, this line of research is at risk of fading from the future of psychological inquiry.

Ponce de Leon devoted his life to searching for the Fountain of Youth – a mystical body of water that would retain the vitality of whomever drank from it. Perhaps psychology has found the fountain that de Leon died looking for. Wisdom has been found to maintain itself across the lifespan, neither increasing nor decreasing with age. Unlike the physical body and the mechanics of the mind, which both decline with age, wisdom fights to exist (Baltes, 1993). And as far as psychology can tell, it is winning.

References

Anderson, J. R. (1982). Acquisition of cognitive skill. *Psychological Review, 89,* 369–406.

Ardelt, M. (2000). Antecedents and effects of wisdom in old age. *Research on Aging, 22*(4), 360–395.

Baltes, P. B. (1993). The aging mind: Potential and limits. *The Gerontologist, 33,* 580–594.

Baltes, P. B., & Nesselroade, J. (1984). Paradigm lost and paradigm regained: Critique of Dannefer's portrayal of life-span developmental psychology. *American Sociological Review, 49,* 841–847.

Baltes, P. B., & Smith, J. (1990). Toward the psychology of wisdom and its ontogenesis. In R. J. Sternberg (Ed.), *Wisdom: Its nature, origins, and development* (pp. 87–120). New York: Cambridge University Press.

Baltes, P. B., & Staudinger, U. M. (2000). Wisdom: A metaheuristic (pragmatic) to orchestrate mind and virtue toward excellence. *American Psychologist, 55*(1), 122–136.

Baltes, P. B., Staudinger, U. M., Maercker, A., & Smith, J. (1995). People nominated as wise: A comparative study of wisdom-related knowledge. *Psychology and Aging, 10,* 155–166.

Berg, C. A. (2000). Intellectual development in adulthood. In R. J. Sternberg (Ed.), *Handbook of Intelligence* (pp. 117–137). New York: Cambridge University Press.

Berg, C. A., & Sternberg, R. J. (1992). Adults conceptions of intelligence across the adult life span. *Psychology and Aging, 7*(2), 221–231.

Brown, W. S. (Ed.). (2000). *Understanding wisdom: Sources, science, and society.* Philadelphia, PA: Templeton Foundation Press.

Clayton, V. P. (1975). Erikson's theory of human development as it applies to the aged: Wisdom as contradictory cognition. *Human Development, 18,* 119–128.

Clayton, V. P., & Birren, J. E. (1980). The development of wisdom across the life span: a reexamination of an ancient topic. In P. B. Baltes and O. G. Brim, Jr. (Eds.), *Life-span development and behavior* (pp. 103–135). New York: Academic Press.

Ericsson, K. A., & Smith, J. (Eds.). (1991). *Toward a general theory of expertise: Prospects and limits.* Cambridge: Cambridge University Press.

Estimated number of assisted living facilities in US:1995–2000. (2001). In *2001 Facts and Trends: The assisted living sourcebook.* Washington, DC: American Health Care Association [Producer and Distributor].

Hashimoto, A. (1991). Living arrangements of the aged in seven developing countries. *Journal of Cross-Cultural Gerontology, 6*(4), 359–381.

Heckhausen, J., Dixon, R. A., & Baltes, P. B. (1989). Gains and losses in development throughout adulthood as perceived by different adult age groups. *Developmental Psychology, 25*, 109–121.

Hira, F. J., & Faulkender, P. J. (1997). Perceiving wisdom: Do age and gender play a part? *International Journal of Aging and Human Development, 44*(2), 85–101.

Humphreys, C. (1961). *The Wisdom of Buddhism.* New York: Random House.

Kitchener, K. S., Lynch, C., Fischer, K. W., & Wood, P. (1993). Developmental range of reflective judgment: The effect of contextual support and practice on developmental stage. *Developmental Psychology, 29*, 893–906.

Kohlberg, L. (1973). Stages and Aging in moral development: Some speculation. *Gerontologist, 13*, 497–502.

Kunzmann, U., & Baltes, P.B. (2003). Wisdom-related knowledge: Affective, motivational, and interpersonal correlates. *Personality and Social Psychology Bulletin, 29*(9), 1104–1119.

Levy, B. R., Slade, M. D., Kunkel, S. R., Kasl, S. V. (2002). Longevity increased by positive self-perceptions of aging. *Journal of Personality and Social Psychology, 83*(2), 261–270.

Meacham, J. A. (1983). Wisdom and the Context of Knowledge: knowing that one doesn't know. In D. Kuhn and J. A. Meacham (Eds.), *On the Development of developmental psychology* (pp. 111–134). Basal, Switzerland: Karger.

Meacham, J. A. (1990). The loss of wisdom. In R. J. Sternberg (Ed.), *Wisdom: Its nature, origins, and development* (pp. 181–211). New York: Cambridge University Press.

Orwell, L., & Perlmutter, M. (1990). The study of wise persons: Integrating a personality perspective. In R. J. Sternberg (Ed.), *Wisdom: Its nature, origins, and development* (pp. 160–177). New York: Cambridge University Press.

Pasupathi, M., & Staudinger, U. M. (2001). Do advanced moral reasoners also show wisdom? Linking moral reasoning and wisdom-related knowledge and judgment. *International Journal of Behavioral Development, 25*(5), 401–415.

Pratt, M. W., Diessner, R., Pratt, A., Hunsberger, B., & Pancer, S. M. (1996). Moral and social reasoning and perspective taking in later life: A longitudinal study. *Psychology and Aging, 11*, 66–73.

Robinson, D. N. (1990). Wisdom through the ages. In R. J. Sternberg (Ed.), *Wisdom: Its nature, origins, and development* (pp. 25–51). New York: Cambridge University Press.

Rudolph, K. (1987). Wisdom. In M. Eliade (Ed.), *The encyclopedia of religion* (pp. 393–401). New York: Macmillan.

Schaie, K. W. (1996). *Intellectual development in adulthood: The Seattle Longitudinal Study.* New York: Cambridge University Press.

Silver, C. B. (1998). Cross cultural perspective on attitudes toward family responsibility and well-being in later years. In J. Lomranz (Ed.), *Handbook of aging and mental health: An integrative approach* (pp. 383–412). New York: Plenum Press.

Smith, J., & Baltes, P. B. (1990). Wisdom-related knowledge: Age/cohort differences in response to life-planning problems. *Developmental Psychology, 26*(3), 494–505.

Smith, J., Staudinger, U. M., & Baltes, P. B. (1994). Occupational settings facilitative of wisdom-related knowledge: The sample case of clinical psychologists. *Journal of Consulting and Clinical Psychology, 64*, 989–1000.

Staudinger, U. M. (1999). Older and Wiser? Integrating results on the relationship between age and wisdom-related performance. *International Journal of Behavioral Development, 23*(3), 641–664.

Staudinger, U. M., & Baltes, P. B. (1996). Interactive Minds: A facilitative setting for wisdom-related performance? *Journal of Personality and Social Psychology, 71*, 746–762.

Staudinger, U. M., Lopez, D. F., & Baltes, P. B. (1997). The Psychometric location of wisdom-related performance: Intelligence, personality, and more? *Personality and Social Psychology Bulletin, 23*(11), 1200–1214.

Staudinger, U. M., Maciel, A. G., Smith, J., & Baltes, P. B. (1998). What predicts wisdom-related performance? A first look at personality, intelligence, and facilitative experiential contexts. *European Journal of Personality, 12*, 1–17.

Staudinger, U. M., Smith, J., & Baltes, P. B. (1992). Wisdom-related knowledge in a life review task: Age differences and the role of professional specialization. *Psychology and Aging, 7*(2), 271–281.

Staudinger, U. M., Smith, J., & Baltes, P. B. (1994). *Manual for the assessment of wisdom-related knowledge* (Technical Report No. 46). Berlin: Max Planck Institute for Human Development and Education.

Sternberg, R. J. (1985). Implicit theories of intelligence, creativity, and wisdom. *Journal of Personality and Social Psychology, 49*(3), 607–627.

Sternberg, R. J. (Ed.). (1990). *Wisdom: Its nature, origins, and development.* New York: Cambridge University Press.

Sternberg, R. J. (1998). A balance theory of wisdom. *Review of General Psychology, 2*(4), 347–365.

Takahashi, M., & Bordia, P. (2000). The concept of wisdom: A cross cultural comparison. *International Journal of Psychology, 35*(1), 1–9.

World populations prospects population database: 2000–2020, North America [Electronic Database]. (2001). New York: Population Division of the Department of Economic and Social Affairs of the United Nations Secretariat [Producer and Distributor].

PART III

WISDOM AND THE PERSON

8

Wisdom and Personality

Ursula M. Staudinger, Jessica Dörner, and Charlotte Mickler

At first sight, the topic "wisdom and personality" seems to be straightforward and clear. Only when taking a closer look do some of the ambiguities of this theme come to the foreground: Is wisdom itself a personality characteristic or a constellation of personality characteristics, or is wisdom rather the consequence and/or correlate of certain personality characteristics? Or is it both? Extant approaches to wisdom can be subsumed under one of these two options. For instance, Erikson viewed wisdom as the pinnacle of personality development and as such considered wisdom a personality characteristic (e.g., Erikson, 1959). In contrast, the Berlin Wisdom Paradigm, one of the few performance-based approaches to the study of wisdom, considers personality characteristics as antecedents, correlates, or consequences of wisdom (e.g., Baltes, Smith, & Staudinger, 1992).

In the following chapter, we attempt to tease apart some of these intricacies of the relationship between wisdom and personality. To do so, it may be useful to distinguish between *self-related* or *personal*, on the one hand, and *general* wisdom, on the other (Staudinger, 1999, in press). This distinction is loosely related to the philosophical separation between the ontology of the first and the third person (Searle, 1992). The ontology of the first person indicates insight into life based on personal experience. The ontology of the third person, however, refers to the view on life based on an observer's perspective. In loose analogy to Searle's first-person perspective, we maintain that self-related or *personal wisdom* refers to a person's insight into his/her own life: What does a person know about himself/herself, his/her life? Analogously to the third-person perspective, we maintain that *general wisdom* is concerned with insights

TABLE 8.1. *Tentative Assignment of Extant Wisdom Approaches to Personal or General Wisdom*

Wisdom Approach	Personal Wisdom	General Wisdom
Explicit Theories		
Personality Perspective		
Erikson	X	
Loevinger	X	
Helson & Wink	X	
Labouvie-Vief	X	
Ardelt	X	
Webster	X	
Orwoll & Perlmutter	X	
Neopiagetian Perspective		
Arlin, Kitchener, Kramer		X
Expertise Perspective		
Berlin Paradigm		X
Sternberg		X
Implicit Theories		
Holliday & Chandler		X
Clayton & Birren		X

into life in general. What does an individual know about life from an observer's point of view, that is when she/he is not personally concerned? For instance, your general wisdom is tapped if a friend comes to you because *his/her* marriage is in a deep crisis and he/she is considering divorce. But it takes your personal wisdom if you search for a solution because your *own* marriage is in a deep crisis and you are considering divorce.

We would like to suggest that this distinction between personal and general wisdom might be helpful when trying to settle some of the ongoing debates in the field of wisdom research. For heuristic purposes, Table 8.1 assigns many of the extant approaches in wisdom research to either a personal wisdom or a general wisdom perspective. Please note that this categorization is sometimes difficult to make because the original authors do not describe their notion of wisdom along these lines. Consequently, the assignment is tentative and based on inferences on our behalf.

Why do we think that the distinction between personal and general wisdom may be helpful, especially when dealing with the relation between personality and wisdom? Personal wisdom approaches consider wisdom as a personality characteristic or pattern of personality

TABLE 8.2. *A Matrix Guiding the Study of the Development of Wisdom and of Wisdom and Personality*

	Life Experience	
	Self-Related/Personal	**General**
Average Level	Self-Insight	Life Insight
Highest Level	Personal Wisdom Wisdom	General Wisdom

characteristics (e.g., Erikson, 1959), whereas most of the general wisdom approaches view wisdom as a theoretical object that may crystallize on an individual but also on a societal level, such as constitutional texts (e.g., Staudinger & Baltes, 1994). Therefore, we can expect that both types of wisdom show somewhat different relational patterns with personality characteristics. We believe that it is an empirical question whether both types of wisdom always coincide in a person or not. A person can be wise with regard to the life and problems of other people and can be sought out for advice from others because of her wisdom but the very same person does not necessarily have to be wise about her own life and her own problems (see Table 8.2). This question can only be answered, however, if the two types of wisdom are conceptualized and measured independently of each other.

The two types of wisdom are usually related to different research traditions. The approaches primarily geared toward personal wisdom are usually based in the tradition of personality research and personality development. Wisdom in this perspective describes the mature personality or the endpoint of personality growth (e.g., Erikson, 1959; Helson & Wink, 1987; Helson & Srivastava, 2001). When thinking about wisdom from this vantage point clearly there are close links to research on coping (e.g., Aldwin & Sutton, 1998; Vaillant, 1993). The approaches primarily investigating general wisdom typically have a stronger connection with the historical wisdom literature and an expertise approach to the study of wisdom (e.g., Baltes, Smith, & Staudinger, 1992; Sternberg, 1998).

The distinction between personal and general wisdom also is relevant when exploring the ontogenesis of wisdom. First, there is reason to assume that it is the dynamic between personal and general knowledge and judgment about life that is at the heart of eventually attaining wisdom. Decades of research on self-regulation (e.g., Carver & Scheier, 1998; Karoly, 1993) as well as research on the therapeutical process have demonstrated that it is much more difficult to obtain insight into one's own life than into the difficulties and problems of others. Thus, we propose that general wisdom is less difficult to attain than personal wisdom and therefore the final attainment of the former may precede that of the later in ontogenesis. Certainly, in the *course* of ontogeny, that is, in working toward general and/or personal wisdom, both types may alternate in taking the lead. We do know, however, from research on the development of the self-concept that the infant appropriates general knowledge about the world before she/he is able to acknowledge the self (e.g., Harter, 1999). From research on the self later on in ontogeny, we have learned that any self-relevant piece of information seems to be processed differently than is general information. On the one hand, we do have under certain conditions better memory for self-relevant information. On the other hand, it also has been found that threatening or inconsistent self-relevant information is suppressed or modified (e.g., Greenwald & Pratkanis, 1984), which indeed may hinder the development of personal wisdom. Second, it is also conceivable that individuals who have attained personal wisdom do not have the ability and/or the motivation to think about life problems beyond their own specific circumstances or are lacking the advice-giving ability. As a consequence, we expect that wisdom encompassing both the personal and general dimension is very rare.

Table 8.2 shows that yet another distinction is relevant when discussing the relation between personality and wisdom. It is the distinction between normal levels of functioning and highest levels of functioning. By definition, wisdom is reserved to denote highest levels or ideal forms of functioning (e.g., Baltes, 1993). It may be confusing to also denote lower or average levels of functioning as wisdom (which is often done in the literature, however). It is suggested, therefore, to choose a different term for levels of functioning below the highest level. One may either call them wisdom-related (see, e.g., Staudinger, Smith, & Baltes, 1992) or as suggested in Table 8.2 even use a completely different term such as "insight." The relationship with personality may differ depending on whether average or highest levels of functioning are concerned. Very rarely, however, is the relation between wisdom and personality tested for nonlinear trends or by applying extreme-group comparisons. After this introduction of basic theoretical notions and the illustration of some gaps in research on wisdom and personality to date, we will now review evidence on the relation between personality and wisdom following the distinction between personal and general wisdom.

General Wisdom and Personality

Various approaches to general wisdom can be distinguished, one of which is the cultural–historical analysis of wisdom. Cultural–historical work concerning the origins of religious and secular bodies of wisdom-related texts has revealed a common core of defining features of wisdom that seems to reflect the notion of general wisdom more than that of personal wisdom. The common core of wisdom, as revealed in this analysis, is defined as follows (Baltes, 1993): (1) Wisdom comprises knowledge with extraordinary scope, depth, measure, and balance; (2) it addresses important and difficult questions and strategies about the conduct and meaning of life; (3) it includes knowledge about the limits of knowledge and the uncertainties of the world; (4) it represents a truly superior level of knowledge, judgment and advice; (5) it is easily recognized when manifested, though difficult to achieve and to specify. Please note that in this analysis personality characteristics are not mentioned as a defining feature common to wisdom across cultures and historical time.

Also within psychology, different approaches to general wisdom can be distinguished. Usually implicit theories, which investigate lay conceptions of wisdom (e.g., Clayton & Birren, 1980; Holliday & Chandler, 1986), are distinguished from explicit approaches such as the conceptualization of wisdom as postformal thought in the Neopiagetian tradition (e.g., Arlin, 1990; Kitchener & Brenner, 1990), or the notion of wisdom as expert knowledge in the Berlin Wisdom Paradigm (e.g., Baltes, Smith, & Staudinger, 1992). In the following, theoretical as well as empirical relations between respective conceptions of wisdom and personality characteristics are discussed.

Neopiagetian Approaches to (General) Wisdom

Informed by the Piagetian tradition of studying cognitive development, several investigators have proposed a postformal stage of adult thinking and related this stage to mature thought or wisdom (e.g., Arlin, 1990; Basseches, 1984; Irwin, 1991; Kitchener & Brenner, 1990; Kramer & Woodruff, 1986; Lee, 1991). In theories of postformal thought, wisdom is conceptualized as increasingly complex and dialectic thinking. Criteria of postformal thinking include awareness of multiple causes and solutions, awareness of paradoxes and contradictions, and the ability to deal with uncertainty, inconsistency, imperfection, and compromise. Pivotal for postformal thinking is the transcendence of the universal truth criterion that characterizes formal logic – a tolerance of ambiguity created by an acceptance of multiple truths. In this approach, little attention has been paid to the need for bounded relativity.

In Neopiagetian work very little research has been done on the relationship between postformal thought and personality. Research has examined, however, the relationship of postformal stages of development with an area at least related to the personality domain, that is, social cognition. For example, postformal thinkers demonstrated a tendency to show less of an actor–observer effect (i.e., situational causes are held responsible for one's own behavior and dispositional factors for others' behavior) and higher levels of moral reasoning than did nonpostformal thinkers (Rankin & Allen, 1991). It was also found that positive mood induction and relaxation improved postformal operations, whereas focusing attention had detrimental effects (Sinnott, 1991). In sum, we may conclude with regard to the personality–wisdom relation that "wise thinking" in the Neopiagetian sense is related to a tolerant and open-minded attitude, which is also characteristic of one of the Big Five personality dimensions, that is, "openness to experience." Plus, it seems easier to think "wisely" when one is relaxed and in a positive mood.

Sternberg's Balance Theory of Wisdom

In Sternberg's (1998) approach, wisdom is related to both practical (e.g., Sternberg, 1985), and academic intelligence. Academic intelligence provides a necessary but by no means sufficient basis to wisdom-related functioning. But wisdom also involves the application of tacit knowledge (Polanyi, 1976), which is the key aspect of practical intelligence. Tacit knowledge is action-oriented (procedural) knowledge that is usually acquired without direct help from others (rather by role modeling) and that allows individuals to achieve goals that they personally value (Sternberg, Wagner, Williams, & Horvath, 1995). In contrast to practical intelligence, however, wisdom by definition is oriented toward a balance between self-interest, the interests of others, and of other contextual interests to achieve a common good. This balancing is the key aspect of Sternberg's theory of wisdom (Sternberg, 1998). The output of wisdom typically is a piece of advice. Wisdom is assessed by presenting people with problems that involve solutions that maximize a variety of intrapersonal, interpersonal, and extrapersonal interests.

A wise person in this sense is comfortable with ambiguity (Sternberg, 1990), in contrast to a conventionally intelligent person, who considers ambiguity as something to be resolved, and in contrast to a creative person who can tolerate ambiguity, but is uncomfortable with it. Also, when managing obstacles, the wise person tries to understand the problem and its implications for self and others. The wise person endorses a judicial thinking style, that is, she/he always tries to understand why, rather than judging whether something is good or bad (Sternberg, 1990). Also related to the area of personality is the assumption that a wise person is highly motivated to seek the common good (Sternberg, 1998).

The Berlin Wisdom Paradigm

In the Berlin Wisdom Paradigm, wisdom is defined as expertise in the fundamental pragmatics of life (e.g., Baltes & Staudinger, 2000). The fundamental pragmatics of life refer to deep knowledge and sound judgment about the essence of the human condition and the ways and means of planning, managing, and understanding a good life. Wisdom is further defined through a set of five criteria (e.g., Baltes, Smith, & Staudinger, 1992). The first criterion, *factual knowledge*, concerns knowledge about such topics as human nature, lifespan development, variations in developmental processes and outcomes, interpersonal relations, and social norms. The second criterion, *procedural knowledge*, involves strategies and heuristics for dealing with the meaning and conduct of life, for example, heuristics for giving advice and ways to handle life conflicts. Additionally, a wise person should show *lifespan contextualism*, that is, to consider life problems in relation to the domains of life (e.g., education, family, work, friends, leisure, the public good of society, etc.) and their interrelations, and to put these in a lifetime perspective (i.e., past, present, future). *Relativism of values and life priorities* is another criterion of wisdom. It means to acknowledge and tolerate interindividual differences in values, as long as they are geared toward optimizing and balancing the individual and the common good. Finally, the last criterion, the *recognition and management of uncertainty*, is based on the idea that human beings can never know everything that is necessary to determine the best decision in the present, to perfectly well predict the future, or to be 100 percent sure about why things happened the way they did in the past. A wise person is aware of this uncertainty and has developed ways to manage it.

Measurement of wisdom. In the Berlin Wisdom Paradigm, wisdom-related performance is assessed by presenting individuals with fictitious life dilemmas such as the following: "Someone receives a telephone call from a good friend who says that he or she cannot go on like this and has decided to commit suicide. What might one/the person take into consideration and do in such a situation?" Participants are then asked to think out loud about the dilemma. The responses are recorded on tape and later transcribed. To quantify performance quality, a select panel of judges, who are extensively trained and calibrated in applying the criteria, evaluates the protocols of the respondents in light of the five wisdom-related criteria using 7-point scales. The reliability of this method is very satisfactory (e.g., Staudinger & Leipold, 2002).

By now, numerous studies have been conducted using the Berlin Wisdom Paradigm, which we are not able to review here because of space constraints. Areas of research have concerned the relationship between wisdom-related performance and age (e.g., Baltes, Staudinger, Maercker, & Smith, 1995; Pasupathi & Staudinger, 2001; Staudinger, 1999), the role of experiential contexts in the ontogeny of wisdom-related knowledge and judgment (e.g., Smith, Staudinger, & Baltes, 1994; Staudinger, Smith, & Baltes, 1992; Staudinger, Maciel, Smith, & Baltes, 1998), the validation of the paradigm (e.g., Baltes et al., 1995; Maercker, Böhmig-Krumhaar, & Staudinger, 1998), and the plasticity of wisdom-related performance (Staudinger & Baltes, 1996; Böhmig-Krumhaar, Staudinger, & Baltes, 2002). Personality plays an important role in the working model of the ontogeny of wisdom-related performance (e.g., Staudinger, 1989; Baltes, Smith, & Staudinger, 1992), thus a number of findings on the relation between personality and wisdom are available, which are reported next.

Wisdom-related performance and personality. In the theoretical conception of correlates of wisdom, person factors play an important role. Various categories of person factors have been distinguished: intelligence, Big Five, growth-related personality characteristics, and person features requiring the orchestrated functioning of both intelligence and personality. When considering the Big Five, it is assumed that certain mental health conditions need to be met (in the sense of a threshold model). That is, neuroticism should demonstrate normal levels. Apart from that, personality dimensions such as openness to experience are expected to contribute to the accumulation of wisdom-related knowledge and judgment (e.g., Staudinger & Baltes, 1994). The latter assumption is based on the argument that if a person remains open-minded and continues to take in new information and experiences, this person has a better chance to refine, correct, and update knowledge and insights about the fundamental pragmatics of life. And indeed, openness to experience has been found to be the most important predictor of wisdom-related performance in the personality domain for adults (Staudinger, Lopez, & Baltes, 1997; Staudinger, Maciel, Smith, & Baltes, 1998). The correlation between openness and wisdom-related performance has been found to be even higher in adolescence. Basic components of psychological functioning such as intelligence and personality appear to play a more important role for wisdom-related performance in adolescence than person characteristics that unfold their developmental peaks in midlife and later, such as growth-related personality and constructs requiring the orchestrated functioning of personality and intelligence (Staudinger & Pasupathi, 2003).

When turning to growth-related personality, it is characteristics such as psychological mindedness and personal growth that have been postulated to be of importance in the ontogeny of wisdom (Staudinger & Baltes, 1994). Psychological mindedness measures "the degree to which the individual is interested in, and responsive to, the inner needs, motives, and experiences of others" (Gough, 1964, p. 11). Personal growth refers to the degree to which a person pursues his/her personality maturation (e.g., Ryff, 1989). The significant positive but moderate relationships of both psychological mindedness and personal growth with wisdom-related performance indicate that high scorers in wisdom-related performance also have a pronounced interest in understanding the psychological functioning of others and are motivated to pursue their own personality growth (Staudinger, Lopez & Baltes, 1997). As personal growth can be viewed as an indicator of personal wisdom (see later), this finding also illustrates that, as expected, personal and general wisdom are to a certain degree related.

Finally, in the domain of personality–intelligence interface characteristics, creativity, cognitive style, and moral reasoning strongly relate to wisdom-related performance (Pasupathi, Staudinger, & Baltes, 2001; Staudinger et al., 1997). The relationship with creativity suggests that deep insight and good judgment with regard to difficult life problems require a certain degree of creative potential. And indeed, in the wisdom literature, moving beyond the given or outside of the system as defined by a given problem situation is often described as a central feature of a wise solution (e.g., Assmann, 1994). With regard to cognitive style, as measured by the Sternberg inventory (Sternberg, 1994), it was found that wisdom-related performance is positively related to a judicial style, that is, to asking why and how something happened rather than judging it as right or wrong (Staudinger et al., 1997). At the same time, wisdom-related performance is negatively related to an oligarchic style, which reflects the experience of tension and conflict between multiple goals. This fits the notion that a wise person should be able to pursue multiple goals without getting lost or losing sight of priorities. Finally, people with high wisdom-related scores did not report a cognitive style labelled as conservative – that is, adhering to existing rules, minimizing change, and avoiding ambiguous situations. Rather, such participants reported a progressive style that implies moving beyond existing rules and being tolerant of ambiguous situations. This relationship pattern suggests that wisdom-related knowledge and judgment are not, as sometimes suspected, conservative in nature (e.g., Hahn, 1991). Finally, a moderate positive relation between wisdom-related performance and moral reasoning was found (Pasupathi & Staudinger, 2001). But it also was discovered that this relationship is completely mediated through measures of personality and intelligence.

When comparing the predictive power of the personality and the personality–intelligence interface domain, the latter emerged as more important. This difference was especially pronounced when considering the unique predictive variance: Neither intelligence nor personality per se remained significant predictors (Staudinger et al., 1997) – indicating that wisdom is most closely related to the personality–intelligence interface. With regard to the ontogeny of wisdom, it is interesting to note that in adolescence – most likely because of differences in developmental status of respective predictors – a complementary picture emerges. In adolescence, it is intelligence and personality that demonstrate more unique predictive power than the personality–interface characteristics (Staudinger & Pasupathi, 2003).

Beyond structural characteristics of personality, it is also of interest to investigate process features linked to the regulation of emotion and motivation. There it was found that wisdom-related knowledge and judgment is associated with a tendency for reporting both fewer negative and fewer pleasant feelings but more feelings indexing active interest (Kunzmann & Baltes, 2003). This is in line with the wisdom literature and developmental theorizing that describes a wise person as demonstrating some emotional distance and serenity but without losing interest in what is happening (e.g., Assmann, 1994; Labouvie-Vief & Medler, 2002; Ryff, 1989). Also the results on the relationship of value orientation with wisdom-related knowledge and judgment are completely in line with expectations based on the historical wisdom literature and explicit theories of wisdom (e.g., Baltes & Staudinger, 2000; Sternberg, 1998). Wisdom-related performance is positively related to other-enhancing values (i.e., values relating to the well-being of friends, societal engagement) and to self-enhancing values as far as they are oriented toward self-actualization and insight into life in general (Kunzmann & Baltes, 2003). Very much in line with the distinction between eudaimonic and hedonistic well-being (Waterman, 1993), wise people show less orientation toward values revolving around a pleasurable life. In addition, people with higher scores in wisdom-related performance reported more respect for others and a preference for cooperative rather than domineering, submissive, or avoidant conflict strategies (Kunzmann & Baltes, 2003).

In sum, according to findings from the Berlin Wisdom Paradigm, people with higher wisdom-related performance scores seem to be open, growth-oriented, moral, creative, and do not show a conservative and judgmental thinking style. They are interested in understanding the psychological functioning of others, are socially competent, have developed some emotional serenity without losing interest in the world, and are oriented toward the well-being of others and society rather than toward their own pleasure.

Implicit Theories of (General) Wisdom and Personality

As mentioned earlier, besides explicit theories of wisdom, implicit theories of (general) wisdom can also be reviewed with regard to the evidence they provide about the relationship between wisdom and personality. In studies of implicit theories of wisdom, participants are asked to describe their concept of a person who is capable of giving wise advice, meaning a person who is insightful about the difficult problems of others. This understanding of wisdom matches our definition of general wisdom. Across a number of classical studies the following personality characteristics of a wise person emerged (Clayton & Birren, 1980; Holliday & Chandler, 1986; Sternberg, 1986; Sowarka, 1989). Wise persons are characterized as educated, intuitive and reflective, sensitive and sociable, discreet, and nonjudgmental. They display concern for others, understand people, are thoughtful, fair, peaceful, and good listeners. All in all, according to studies of implicit theories wise people exhibit excellent character, have a sensitive nature, and are intellectually capable.

Personal Wisdom and Personality

When we turn from conceptions of general wisdom to those of personal wisdom, two other notions come to mind and those are "maturity" and "personal growth." Influential conceptions of personal wisdom can be found in clinical, personality, and developmental theories. In clinical psychology, for instance, it is the work of Freud or Rogers that comes to mind. The former defines personal maturity as achieving the genital character who is able to love and work, and the latter talks about the fully functioning person who is open to experience, able to live existentially, trusts in his/her own organism, expresses feelings freely, acts independently, is creative, and lives a rich life. In personality psychology, it is, for instance, Maslow's self-actualizing individual or Allport's criteria of a wise person (e.g., extension of the sense of self, capacity for intimacy, emotional security, realistic perception, self-objectification (insight and humor), unifying philosophy of life and religion), that are often cited as references for the definition of personality growth. Within developmental psychology, Charlotte Bühler (1959) talked about motivational tendencies such as intentionality or creative expansion that play an important role in reaching personal fulfilment. And Erik Erikson (1959) linked wisdom with the final psychosocial crisis of life, that is, finding a balance between integration and despair in the face of death. These theories remain important resources until today. However, the interest in the topic has far from receded (e.g., Ardelt, 2000; Heath & Heath, 1991; Noam & Röper, 1999; Roberts, Caspi, & Moffitt, 2001; Webster, 2003; to name just a few). Obviously, it is impossible to cover all of them in this chapter. Instead, we are going to focus on four conceptions of personal wisdom (Loevinger, Ryff, Helson, Labouvie-Vief) that have integrated many of the others.

Ego Development, Personal Wisdom, and Personality

According to Jane Loevinger, human development can be described along four lines: physical, psychosexual, intellectual, and in terms of character (Hauser, 1976). She attempted to capture character development in a stage-model following the Piagetian model of cognitive development. However, although Piaget's concern was to describe the cognitive changes, Loevinger investigated character development as a means to protect the self-system (Loevinger, 1998). Loevinger conceived the stages of ego development as a successive progression toward psychological maturity, developing along the four dimensions of impulse control, interpersonal style, conscious preoccupations, and cognitive styles (e.g., Blasi, 1998; Loevinger & Wessler, 1970; Manners & Durkin, 2001). The model comprises eight stages (impulsive, self-protective, conformist, self-aware, conscientious, individualistic, autonomous, integrated) that are characterized by increasingly mature versions of the four dimensions mentioned earlier. Most people are categorized to be in the third to fifth stage, that is the conformist, self-aware, and conscientious stages. The self-aware stage is the modal stage in late adolescence and adult life (Holt, 1980; Loevinger, 1998). The eighth stage, the integrated stage, is rarely observed in random samples (Loevinger, 1998).

Ego level and other indicators of personal wisdom or personal growth. Is it indeed the case that we can consider ego level as one possible operationalization of personal wisdom? In a recent study, positive significant relations between self-related wisdom and psychometric indicators of personal growth were obtained (Staudinger, Dörner, & Mickler, 2003). Thus, it seems meaningful to consider ego level as one operationalization of personal wisdom. This conclusion is supported by findings from the Mills Study that demonstrated that it is useful to differentiate between a social and a personal type of maturity. The former is represented in the concept of competence derived from the revised California Psychological Inventory (CPI; Gough, 1987) and the latter in Loevinger's ego level (Helson & Wink, 1987). Social maturity refers to the ability to function well within society. Personal maturity indexes the degree of intrapsychic differentiation and autonomy that is independent of or even transcends social conventions (Manners & Durkin, 2001). When comparing these two notions of maturity with regard to their relation with a range of other measures, it was found that although ego level and CPI competence showed considerable overlap, both with regard to their interrelations and their relations with the other measures, remarkable differences also were found. Ego level related to the "appreciation of the other's individuality" and the individuality of the integration and conscious development of a personal philosophy of life, whereas CPI competence showed strong relations with "pursuit of harmony" and emotional security.

Ego level and personality characteristics. On the one hand, there is evidence for positive relations between ego level and highly adaptive personality characteristics such as ego resiliency, interpersonal integrity, and regulation of needs (Westenberg & Block, 1993), or mastery of socioemotional tasks and impulse control (Blanchard-Fields, 1986; Labouvie-Vief, Hakim-Larson, DeVoe, & Schoeberlein, 1989), as well as indicators of mental health (e.g., Lorr & Manning, 1978; Vaillant & McCullough, 1987). On the other hand, ego level is also positively and significantly correlated with both lifetime psychiatric visits and regular psychotherapeutic sessions (Helson & Wink, 1987; Vaillant & McCullough, 1987). It is unclear, however, from those studies whether "psychotherapy helped subjects to advance developmentally or whether later-stage capacity to see ambiguities in life increased individuals' willingness to seek psychotherapy" (Fisher, 1995, p. 11).

The latter interpretation is in line with the positive quadratic relation between neuroticism and ego level (i.e., *higher* neuroticism at low and high ego level) and a negative quadratic relation between conscientiousness and ego level (i.e., *lower* conscientiousness at low and high ego level; Einstein & Lanning, 1998; Hy & Loevinger, 1996). Openness to experience is often considered the strongest predictor of ego development. Results differ somewhat between studies but there seems to be a trend toward a positive linear relation with ego level. Finally, extraversion and agreeableness yield the highest positive correlations with ego level at least in males and in two of the available studies (Einstein & Lanning, 1998; Staudinger et al., 2003).

In sum, this pattern of results revolving around Loevinger's measure of ego development suggests that in contrast to *social maturity*, that is, mastering norms and social relations, ego development or *personal maturity* may also display maladaptive features. Moving beyond the given, seeing reality more clearly, transcending extant social norms, central features of wisdom, does not come without costs. It seems that being faced with the complexities of life in the way it is true for a person at high levels of ego development does not always lead to greater happiness but also to greater concern and doubt as well as the insight that further self-development is needed.

Psychological Well-Being as an Indicator of Personal Wisdom

It is not perceived life-satisfaction (i.e., hedonistic well-being) that is at the center of the notion of psychological well-being (PWB) but eudaimonic well-being. Eudaimonic well-being, in the sense of Aristotle's eudaimonia, refers to the distinction between the satisfaction of right and wrong desires, or following Rogers, it implies a "striving for perfection that represents the realization of one's true potential" (Ryff, 1995, p. 100). Thus, psychological well-being may actually qualify as one possible operationalization of personal wisdom. Based on developmental (i.e., Bühler, Erikson, Neugarten), clinical (i.e., Jung, Maslow, Rogers), and personality theories (i.e., Allport), six dimensions of PWB have been defined (for a detailed description see Ryff, 1995): self-acceptance, positive relations with others, autonomy, environmental mastery, purpose in life, and personal growth. In the following, we are interested in finding out whether these six dimensions can be considered as indicators of personal wisdom.

With regard to the relations between PWB and the Big Five, Schmutte and Ryff (1997) expected that PWB scales in general are positively linked with extraversion and negatively linked to neuroticism. In particular, feelings about one's self (self-acceptance) and beliefs about one's ability to control and to manage day-to-day activities (environmental mastery) were assumed to have strong emotional consequences, and thus, to exhibit the strongest correlations with extraversion and neuroticism. Positive relations with others were assumed to be facilitated by an agreeable personality and therefore to correlate with agreeableness. A conscientious life was supposed to give rise to a sense of competence and mastery (environmental mastery). Openness to experience, similarly, was assumed to be beneficial in terms of the motivation to grow and to improve across the life course (personal growth). Likewise, persons high on openness to experience were supposed to be driven by a strong sense of self-determination (autonomy).

As expected, results indicated negative links with neuroticism and positive links with extraversion for nearly all subscales (quadratic relations were not tested in this study). Environmental mastery, purpose in life, and self-acceptance showed very similar correlational patterns. The expected differential relationships were only partly confirmed. For example, openness to experience correlated with personal growth, but not with autonomy. Conscientiousness and agreeableness showed high correlations with all PWB subscales (with the exception of autonomy). This pattern of results was replicated and extended in a recent German study (Staudinger et al., 2003). In this study, interrelations between a number of indicators of personal and social maturity were explored using factor analysis. Results indicated that some of the PWB dimensions such as self-acceptance and positive relations with others associate with measures of social maturity, whereas other PWB dimensions, such as personal growth, related most highly with other indicators of personal maturity or personal wisdom. Incidentally, the age trends found for the respective PWB dimensions also support that distinction. It is the "social maturity" dimensions that show normative *increases* with age, and it is the "personal maturity" dimensions that show *stability* and/or *decline* after midlife (e.g., Ryff, 1995). The latter age-related finding is typical for indicators of personal as well as general wisdom (e.g., Blanchard-Fields, 1986; Labouvie-Vief, Hakim-Larson, & Hobart, 1987; Mickler & Staudinger, 2003; Staudinger, 1999). During adulthood,

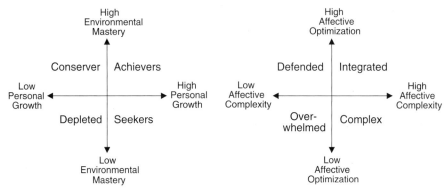

FIGURE 8.1. Two Typologies of Maturity (left panel: after Helson & Srivastava, 2001; right panel: after Labouvie-Vief & Medler, 2002).

wisdom, be it personal or general, does not come normatively with age. In sum, then, we suggest that only personal growth and possibly purpose in life can be considered as indicators of personal wisdom, whereas the other PWB dimensions are indicative of social maturity.

Two Types of Maturity: Social and Personal

Along these lines, Helson and Srivastava (2001) used two PWB dimensions, environmental mastery (EM) and personal growth (PG) to index social and personal maturity. Building on work by Helson and Wink (1987), the authors assumed that EM or effectiveness in the outer world and PG or intrapsychic development often preclude each other. And indeed EM and PG show very low correlations (Schmutte & Ryff, 1997). When crossing these two dimensions four personality types emerge (see Figure 8.1, left panel): "Those who seek the security and harmony of living in accord with social norms (high EM, low PG; Conservers), those who value social recognition and achievement (high EM, high PG; Achievers), and those who seek personal knowledge and independence in social norms (low EM, high PG; Seekers)" and those who are low on both dimensions (Helson & Srivastava, 2001, p. 995).

The two groups high on EM (Conservers and Achievers) were expected to show strength in psychosocial development, whereas the two groups high on PG (Achievers and Seekers) were expected to show strength in intrapsychic development. The California Psychological Inventory (CPI) competence scale (Gough & Bradley, 1996) and a measure of generativity (Peterson & Klohnen, 1995) were used to assess successful psychosocial development. Intrapsychic maturity was measured by

Loevinger's Ego Level (Loevinger & Wessler, 1970), and a wisdom composite based on the practical and transcendent wisdom scales (Wink & Helson, 1997) and a wisdom task modified from Baltes, Staudinger, Maercker and Smith (1995). The results correspond to the hypotheses except for the low relation between Achievement (high EM, high PG) and indicators of wisdom. A closer look at the life paths of this group revealed that the Achievers are characterized by many positive features, such as being very generative and reporting the most positive and the least negative emotions. But they also had to pay a price that was mostly related to a lack of privacy and of time to reflect. Having time to reflect certainly is crucial for making progress on the way to wisdom (e.g., Staudinger, 2001). It is the Seekers that come closest to show what we have called personal wisdom.

Personal Wisdom as Cognitive–Emotional Integration

Combining the cognitive theory of Piaget (1972) with psychoanalytic notions and ideas from adult attachment theory, Labouvie-Vief designed developmental models of self as well as of emotional understanding (Labouvie-Vief, 1982; Labouvie-Vief, DeVoe, & Bulka, 1989). Throughout life, self-representations change from being "poorly differentiated from others or social conventions to ones that involve emphasis on process, context, and individuality" (Labouvie-Vief, Chiodo, Goguen, Diehl, & Orwoll, 1995, p. 404). Building on this earlier work, Gisela Labouvie-Vief in her most recent publications focused on the development and/or maturation of self-regulation (Labouvie-Vief & Medler, 2002). In this latest approach, she has developed a notion of growth or maturity that combines Affect Optimization (AO), "the tendency to constrain affect to positive values," with Affect Complexity (AC), "the amplification of affect in the search for differentiation and objectivity" (Labouvie-Vief & Medler, 2002, p. 571). In this notion of maturity, it is crucial that the search for complexity and differentiation is combined with or better constrained by a search for optimizing positive affect in any given situation. But at the same time, the search for positive affect is guarded by the ability to experience events and other persons in an open and differentiated fashion. Again, combining the two dimensions of AC and AO results in four "personality" types that are depicted in Figure 8.1 (right panel).

Figure 8.1 also depicts the similarities between the typology introduced by Helson and Srivastava (2001) and the one presented by Labouvie-Vief and Medler (2002). Both classification systems aim to distinguish different types of maturity, one geared toward social success and happiness and the other toward insight and wisdom. Labouvie-Vief's model, however, is located at a microanalytic level of emotion regulation and Helson's model operates at the level of complex behaviors. Labouvie-Vief and Medler (2002) expected the integrated group to function best. And, indeed, high ego levels, high intelligence, and adaptive coping patterns, excluding repressive or regressive strategies, characterize the integrated group. In contrast, defended individuals, although scoring second highest on positive affect, are characterized by repressive coping styles and their intellectual ability tends to be low. Complex individuals represent a kind of mirror image of the defended group: With the lowest scores on repression, and high intelligence scores, they can be regarded as the most open and "realistic" group of the four. Finally, across the different indicators overwhelmed individuals demonstrate the lowest levels of functioning. In sum, it seems that the complex type comes closest to what we have called personal wisdom.

Self-Related Wisdom

Next, we would like to introduce a recent attempt to conceptualize personal wisdom based on the Berlin Wisdom Paradigm (Mickler & Staudinger, 2003). Our goal in this approach has been to create a measure of personal wisdom, by integrating the definition of wisdom as developed in the Berlin Wisdom Paradigm (e.g., Baltes, Smith, & Staudinger, 1992) with conceptions of personality growth (e.g., Allport, 1961; Bühler, 1959; Cloninger, 2003; Erikson, 1959; Freud, 1917; Jung, 1934; Labouvie-Vief, 1982; Loevinger, 1976; Maslow, 1968; Rogers, 1961).

We chose the Berlin Wisdom Paradigm because it is a well-established and validated performance measure of (general) wisdom. In a next step, we systematically reviewed different approaches to the conceptualization of personality growth from the developmental, clinical, and personality literature, with regard to the characteristics of a mature person in the areas of cognition, emotion, motivation, and volition. Those aspects of growth personality were then checked against the five criteria of the Berlin Wisdom Paradigm (for detailed definition, see Staudinger, Smith, & Baltes, 1994). This way self-related specifications were identified and the five new criteria of self-related wisdom were developed. At the same time, based on this review we found that the basic topics represented in the five criteria of general wisdom indeed are rather comprehensive and exhaustive.

The first criterion is *rich self-knowledge*, that is, deep insight into oneself. A self-wise person should be aware of his or her own competencies, emotions, and goals, and have a sense of meaning in life. The second criterion requires a self-wise person to have available *heuristics for growth and self-regulation* (e.g., how to express and regulate emotions or how to develop and maintain deep social relations). Humor is an example of an important heuristic that helps us to cope with various difficult and challenging situations. *Interrelating the self*, the third criterion, refers to the ability to reflect on and have insight in the possible causes of one's behavior and/or feelings. Such causes can be age-related or situational or linked to personal characteristics. Interrelating the self also implies that there is an awareness about one's own dependency on others. The fourth criterion is called *self-relativism*. People high on self-relativism are able to evaluate themselves as well as others with a distanced view. They critically appraise their own behavior but at the same time display a basic acceptance of themselves. They also show tolerance for others' values and lifestyles – as long as they are not damaging to self or others. Finally, *tolerance of ambiguity* involves the ability to recognize and manage the uncertainties in one's own life and one's own development. It is reflected in the awareness that life is full of uncontrollable and unpredictable events, including death and illness. At the same time, tolerance for ambiguity includes the availability of strategies to manage this uncertainty through openness to experience, basic trust, and the development of flexible solutions. Self-related wisdom is measured by first using a thinking-aloud and subsequently a rating procedure, developed after the Berlin (general) Wisdom Paradigm. This similarity was also kept because we wanted to be in a position to compare both measures without an intervening method confounding us.

In a first study, our measure of self-related wisdom showed good convergent validity. It was positively correlated with other measures of personality growth, such as Ryff's personal growth and purpose in life measure and Loevinger's ego development measure, as well as with benevolent values (Mickler & Staudinger, 2003) measures. With regard to discriminant validity, it was demonstrated that self-related wisdom, as to be expected for a measure of personal maturity, was uncorrelated with notions of well-being and adaptation such as life satisfaction, negative or positive emotions, and adaptive motives such as power, achievement, and hedonism. Also, self-related wisdom is not preempted by

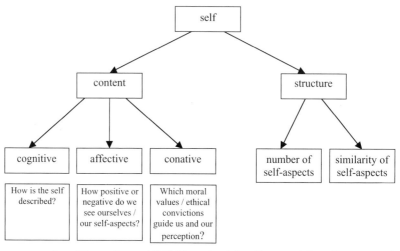

FIGURE 8.2. Dimensions of Self-Maturity (after Dörner & Staudinger, 2003).

knowing a person's intelligence. As far as the relationship with personality variables is concerned, openness to experience was the most important predictor – of the other Big Five variables none showed significant correlations with self-related wisdom. Apart from that, psychological mindedness, a concept measuring interest in thoughts and feelings of other people, was significantly correlated with self-related wisdom.

Personal Wisdom and the Mature Self

Finally, we would like to present a notion of personal wisdom that is grounded in the self-concept literature (for more detail, see Dörner & Staudinger, 2003). This definition of the mature self is based on a conceptualization of the self-concept that distinguishes between content and structure. Figure 8.2 illustrates how these two basic dimensions are further differentiated. Based on our reading of the self-concept and the personality growth literature, we first defined self-esteem as a necessary but not sufficient precondition of personality growth. Second, self-complexity, integration, and value orientation have been delineated as the other three interdependent facets of the mature self that are operationalized using basic self components (e.g., Linville, 1985, 1987; Noam & Röper, 1999; Staudinger & Baltes, 1994; Sternberg, 1998).

Self-esteem. We believe that the basic precondition for any self-growth to occur is an intermediate level of self-esteem. Clinicians have never failed to stress that personality growth is not possible without a certain amount of self-esteem (e.g., Maslow, 1968; Noam, 1998; Rogers, 1961). Only if we have enough self-esteem can we develop the courage and/or confidence to find out more about ourselves (or the world).

Self-complexity. Although being one of the most often cited and studied characteristics of self-concept development, there are few empirical investigations regarding self-complexity and its relations to maturity rather than adaptivity. The study by Labouvie-Vief and others (1995), mentioned earlier, showing a relation between affect complexity of written self-descriptions and higher ego levels, is one of the few exceptions (see also Evans & Seeman, 2000). Self-complexity can refer to content as well as affect (see Figure 8.2). Thus, a self-complex person is characterized by a wide array of self-relevant domains as well as feelings.

Integration. Even though a mature person has to be self-complex, the complexity needs to be integrated by means of a common self-descriptive core that cuts across different self-aspects. It is this common core that allows the experience of a consistent self across different self-aspects. Without integrating the self-complexity, the person lacks a sense of identity or "self-sameness" (Erikson, 1959), which has been demonstrated as a vital antecedent of psychological health and maturity (e.g., Campbell, Assanand, & DiPaula, 2003; Diehl, Hastings, & Stanton, 2001).

Value orientation. Still, integrated complexity does not yet make a mature self. Integrated complexity can be applied to achieve many things, for example, to commit the perfect crime. It is obvious therefore, that a third facet needs to be added: value orientation (e.g., Allport, 1961; Orwoll & Perlmutter, 1990). A wise person is driven by self-transcending values and by the attempt to balance self-centered and altruistic goals (e.g., Kunzmann & Baltes, 2003; Sternberg, 1998).

These indicators of self growth (measured through a modified version of Linville 1985, 1987) were related to personality measures from the trait tradition (e.g., Big Five; Costa & McCrae, 1992), as well as the growth tradition, including Ryff's measure of Psychological Well-Being (Ryff & Keyes, 1995), Loevinger's sentence-completion test for assessing ego development (Hy & Loevinger, 1996), and a newly developed measure assessing self-related wisdom (see earlier; Mickler & Staudinger, 2003). Furthermore, we included indicators of adaptivity such as past and current life satisfaction. The emerging relational pattern was such that integration, value orientation, and self-esteem showed strong relations with social maturity and adaptation, whereas complexity and value orientation related more strongly to indicators of personal maturity or personal wisdom (Dörner & Staudinger, 2003).

Personal Wisdom: Questionnaire Measures

Apart from these theoretically driven approaches, recently two more empirically oriented attempts that aim at the economical assessment of personal wisdom have been proposed: the self-assessment wisdom scale (SAWS; Webster, 2003) and the three-dimensional wisdom scale (3DWS; Ardelt, 2003). The SAWS assesses five different components of wisdom: emotional regulation, reminiscence and reflectiveness, openness to experience, humor, and experience. In line with expectations, the SAWS scores have been shown to correlate with measures of generativity ($r = .44$, $p < .01$; McAdams & de St. Aubin, 1992) and of ego integrity ($r = .23$, $p < .05$; Taft & Nehrke, 1990). Furthermore, and in accordance with other studies of wisdom, no significant age differences were found. The convergent validity data indeed indicate that the scale seems to measure something like personal wisdom. However, it remains unclear whether these relationships are mediated by standard measures of personality and intelligence and to which degree the results of the SAWS are distorted by social desirability.

The 3DWS measures three dimensions of wisdom, the reflective (i.e., ability to take multiple perspectives), cognitive (i.e., motivation and ability to attain thorough and accurate knowledge), and affective dimensions (i.e., sympathy and compassion). High scores on all three dimensions define wisdom. The 3DWS shows significant and positive correlations with mastery, subjective well-being, purpose in life, and subjective health, and negative relations with depressive symptoms, death avoidance, fear of death, and feelings of economic pressure. Education and occupation both showed significant and positive correlations with 3DWS. This correlational pattern seems to indicate that the 3DWS measures something close to social maturity rather than personal wisdom, as discussed before.

Conclusion

Wisdom and personality – what have we learned about that relationship? First and foremost, that it is not possible to speak about *the* relationship between wisdom and personality because extant conceptualizations of wisdom differ widely. For some researchers, especially the ones that are interested in *personal wisdom*, wisdom is a very special and rare personality characteristic. For others, primarily those who study *general wisdom*, certain personality characteristics are antecedents and/or consequences of wisdom because wisdom can manifest itself within an individual but also in written text (which normally is not described using personality characteristics).

Second, when interrelating different measures from the realm of personality development and adaptation, it seems that two distinct factors emerge, social and personal maturity. Social maturity is defined by measures of adaptation such as life satisfaction, environmental mastery, or positive social relations. Personal maturity, however, is indexed by openness to experience and indicators of personal wisdom such as personal growth and ego development.

Unfortunately, we could not elaborate very much on the nonlinear relations between wisdom and personality because only few studies have looked at that. Neither was it possible to investigate the relation between personal and general wisdom more closely because no data set is available yet that works with a similar measurement paradigm for both types of wisdom and thus avoids an investigation of the relationship that is confounded by measurement variance. We hope that future wisdom research cuts across different measurement paradigms and contributes to building systematic knowledge about the relation between personal and general wisdom on the one hand and between both types of wisdom and a wide variety of personality indicators on the other hand.

References

Aldwin, C. M., & Sutton, K. J. (1998). A developmental perspective on posttraumatic growth. In R. G. Tedeschi, C. L. Park, et al. (Eds.), *Posttraumatic growth: Positive changes in the aftermath of crisis. The LEA series in personality and clinical psychology* (pp. 43–63). Mahwah, NJ: Lawrence Erlbaum Associates.

Allport, G. W. (1961). *Patterns and growth in personality.* New York: Holt, Rinehart & Winston.

Ardelt, M. (2000). Antecedents and effects of wisdom in old age. A longitudinal perspective on aging well. *Research on Aging, 22,* 360–394.

Ardelt, M. (2003). Empirical assessment of a three-dimensional wisdom scale. *Research on Aging, 25,* 275–324.

Arlin, P. K. (1990). Wisdom: The art of problem finding. In R. J. Sternberg (Ed.), *Wisdom: Its nature, origins, and development* (pp. 230–243). New York: Cambridge University Press.

Assmann, A. (1994). Wholesome knowledge: Concepts of wisdom in a historical and cross-cultural perspective. In D. L. Featherman, R. M. Lerner, & M. Perlmutter (Eds.), *Life-span development and behavior* (Vol. 12, pp. 187–224). Hillsdale, NJ: Erlbaum.

Baltes, P. B. (1993). The aging mind: Potential and limits. *Gerontologist, 33,* 580–594.

214 *Ursula M. Staudinger, Jessica Dörner, and Charlotte Mickler*

4Baltes, P. B., & Staudinger, U. M. (2000). Wisdom: A metaheuristic to orchestrate mind and virtue towards excellence. *American Psychologist, 55*, 122–136.

Baltes, P. B., Smith, J., & Staudinger, U. M. (1992). Wisdom and successful aging. In T. Sonderegger (Ed.), *Nebraska symposium on motivation* (Vol. 39, pp. 123–167). Lincoln: University of Nebraska Press.

Baltes, P. B., Staudinger, U. M., Maercker. A., & Smith, J. (1995). People nominated as wise: A comparative study of wisdom-related knowledge. *Psychology and Aging, 10*, 155–166.

Basseches, M. (1984). *Dialectical thinking and adult development.* Norwood, NJ: Ablex.

Blanchard-Fields, F. (1986). Reasoning on social dilemmas varying in emotional saliency: An adult developmental perspective. *Psychology and Aging, 1*, 325–333.

Blasi, A. (1998). Loevinger's theory of ego development and its relationship to the cognitive-developmental approach. In P. M. Westenberg, A. Blasi, & L. D. Cohn (Eds.), *Personality development: theoretical, empirical, and clinical investigations of Loevinger's conception of ego development* (pp. 133–143). Mahwah, NJ: Lawrence Erlbaum Associates, Inc.

Böhmig-Krumhaar, S., Staudinger, U. M., & Baltes, P. B. (2002). Mehr Toleranz tut Not: Läßt sich wert-relativierendes Denken und Urteilen verbessern? [In need of more tolerance: Is it possible to facilitate value relativism?]. *Zeitschrift für Entwicklungspsychologie und Pädagogische Psychologie, 34*, 30–43.

Buehler, C. (1959). *Der menschliche Lebenslauf als psychologisches Problem* [The human life course as a psychological problem]. Göttingen: Dieterichsche Universitäts-Buchdruckerei.

Campbell, J. D., Assanand, S., & DiPaula, A. (2003). The structure of the self-concept and its relation to psychological adjustment. *Journal of Personality, 71*, 115–140.

Carver, C. S., & Scheier, M. F. (1998). *On the self-regulation of behavior.* New York: Cambridge University Press.

Clayton, V. P., & Birren, J. E. (1980). The development of wisdom across the life-span: A reexamination of an ancient topic. In: P. B. Baltes & O. G. Brim Jr. (Eds.), *Life-Span Development and Behavior* (Vol. 3, pp. 103–135). New York: Academic Press.

Cloninger, C. R. (2003). Completing the psychobiological architecture of human personality development: temperament, character, and coherence. In U. M. Staudinger & U. Lindenberger (Eds.), *Understanding human development: Dialogues with lifespan psychology* (pp. 159–181). Boston/Dordrecht: Kluwer Academic Publishers (Group).

Costa, P. T., & McCrae, R. R. (1992). *Revised NEO Personality Inventory (NEOPI-R) and NEO Five-Factor Inventory (NEO-FFI).* Odessa, FL: Psychological Assessment Resources.

Diehl, M., Hastings, C. T., & Stanton, J. M. (2001). Self-concept differentiation across the adult life span. *Psychology and Aging, 16*, 643–654.

Dörner, J. & Staudinger, U. M. (2003). *Personality growth from the inside: The mature self-concept.* Unpublished manuscript. International University Bremen, Bremen, Germany.

Einstein, D., & Lanning, K. (1998). Shame, guilt, ego development, and the five-factor model of personality. *Journal of Personality, 66,* 556–582.

Erikson, E. H. (1959). *Identity and the life cycle.* New York: International University Press.

Evans, D. W., & Seaman, J. L. (2000). Developmental aspects of psychological defenses: their relation to self-complexity, self-perception and symptomatology in adolescents. *Child psychiatry and human development, 30,* 237–254.

Fisher, D. (1995). *Personal and organizational development: The social science of transformational action.* Paper presented at the Academy of Management Annual Meeting, Vancouver, BC, August.

Freud, S. (1917). *Vorlesungen zur Einführung in die Psychoanalyse* [Lectures. Introduction to psychoanalysis]. Frankfurt: Fischer.

Gough, H. G. (1964). *The California Psychological Inventory.* Palo Alto, CA: Consulting Psychologists Press.

Gough, H. G. (1987). *Manual for the California Psychological Inventory.* Palo Alto, CA: Consulting Psychology Press. (First edition published 1957)

Gough, H. G., & Bradley, P. (1996). *California Psychological Inventory manual* (3rd ed.). Palo Alto, CA: Consulting Psychologists Press.

Greenwald, A. G., & Pratkanis, A. R. (1984). The self. In R. W. Wyer & T. K. Srull (Eds.), *Handbook of social cognition* (Vol. 3, pp. 129–178). Hillsdale, NJ: Erlbaum.

Hahn, A. (1991). Zur Soziologie der Weisheit [A sociology of wisdom]. In A. Assmann (Ed.), *Weisheit. Archäologie der literarischen Kommunikation* [Wisdom. Archaeology of literary communication] (pp. 47–58). München: Wilhelm Fink Verlag.

Harter, S. (1999). *The construction of self: A developmental perspective.* New York: Guilford Press.

Hauser, S. T. (1976). Loevinger's model and measure of ego development: A critical review. *Psychological Bulletin, 83,* 928–955.

Heath, D. H., & Heath, H. E. (1991). *Fulfilling lives: Paths to maturity and success.* San Francisco, CA: Jossey-Bass/Pfeiffer.

Helson, R., & Srivastava, S. (2001). Three paths of adult development: Conservers, seekers, and achievers. *Journal of Personality and Social Psychology, 80,* 995–1010.

Helson, R., & Wink, P. (1987). Two conceptions of maturity examined in the findings of a longitudinal study. *Journal of Personality and Social Psychology, 53,* 531–541.

Holliday, S. G., & Chandler, M. J. (1986). Wisdom: Explorations in adult competence. In J. A. Meacham (Ed.), *Contributions to human development* (Vol. 17, pp. 1–96). Basel: Karger.

Holt, R. R. (1980). Loevinger's measure of ego development: Reliability and national norms for male and female short forms. *Journal of Personality and Social Psychology, 39,* 909–920.

Hy, L. X., & Loevinger, J. (1996). *Measuring ego development* (2nd ed.). Hillsdale, NJ: Lawrence Erlbaum Associates.

Irwin, R. R. (1991). Reconceptualizing the nature of dialectical postformal operational thinking: The effects of affectively mediated social experiences. In

J. D. Sinnott & J. C. Cavanaugh (Eds.), *Bridging paradigms. Positive development in adulthood and cognitive aging* (pp. 59–72). New York: Praeger.

Jung, C. G. (1934). *Modern Man in Search of a Soul*. Oxford, England: Harcourt, Brace.

Karoly, P. (1993). Mechanisms of self-regulation: A systems view. *Annual Review of Psychology, 44*, 23–52.

Kitchener, K. S., & Brenner, H. G. (1990). Wisdom and reflective judgement: Knowing in the face of uncertainty. In R. J. Sternberg (Ed.), *Wisdom: Its nature, origins, and development* (pp. 212–229). New York: Cambridge University Press.

Kramer, D. A., & Woodruff, D. S. (1986). Relativistic and dialectical thought in three adult age-groups. *Human Development, 29*, 280–290.

Kunzmann, U., & Baltes, P. B. (2003). Wisdom-related knowledge: Emotional, motivational, and interpersonal correlates. *Personality and Social Psychology Bulletin, 29*, 1104–1119.

Labouvie-Vief, G. (1982). Dynamic development and mature autonomy: A theoretical prologue. *Human Development, 25*, 161–191.

Labouvie-Vief, G., & Medler, M. (2002). Affect optimization and affect complexity: modes and styles of regulation in adulthood. *Psychology & Aging, 17*, 571–587.

Labouvie-Vief, G., Chiodo, L. M., Goguen, L. A., & Diehl, M. (1995). Representations of self across the life span. *Psychology & Aging, 10*, 404–415.

Labouvie-Vief, G., DeVoe, M., & Bulka, D. (1989). Speaking about feelings: Conceptions of emotion across the life span. *Psychology and Aging, 4*, 425–437.

Labouvie-Vief, G., Hakim-Larson, J., DeVoe, M., & Schoeberlein, S. (1989). Emotions and self-regulation: A life-span view. *Human Development, 32*, 279–299.

Labouvie-Vief, G., Hakim-Larson, J., & Hobart, C. J. (1987). Age, ego level, and the life-span development of coping and defense processes. *Psychology and Aging, 2*, 286–293.

Lee, D. M. (1991). Relativistic operations: A framework for conceptualizing teachers' everyday problem solving. In J. D. Sinnott & J. C. Cavanaugh (Eds.), *Bridging paradigms. Positive development in adulthood and cognitive aging* (pp. 73–86). New York: Praeger.

Linville, P. W. (1985). Self-complexity and affective extremity: don't put all of your eggs in one cognitive basket. *Social Cognition, 3*, 94–120.

Linville, P. W. (1987). Self-complexity as a cognitive buffer against stress-related illness and depression. *Journal of Personality and Social Psychology, 52*, 663–676.

Loevinger, J. (1976). *Ego Development: Conceptions and Theories*. San Francisco: Jossey-Bass.

Loevinger, J. (1998). Completing a life sentence. In P. M. Westenberg, A. Blasi, & L. D. Cohn (Eds.), *Personality development: theoretical, empirical, and clinical investigations of Loevinger's conception of ego development* (pp. 133–143). Mahwah, NJ: Lawrence Erlbaum Associates, Inc.

Loevinger, J., & Wessler, R. (1970). *Measuring ego development. Construction and use of a sentence completion test*. San Francisco: Jossey-Bass.

Lorr, M., & Manning, T. T. (1978). Measurement of ego development by sentence completion and personality test. *Journal of Clinical Psychology, 34*, 354–360.

Maercker, A., Böhmig-Krumhaar, S., & Staudinger, U. M. (1998). Existentielle Konfrontation als Zugang zu weisheitsbezogenem Wissen und Urteilen: Eine Untersuchung von Weisheitsnominierten [Existential confrontation as one access to wisdom-related knowledge and judgment]. *Zeitschrift für Entwicklungspsychologie und Pädagogische Psychologie, 30,* 2–12.

Manners, J., & Durkin, K. (2001). A critical review of the validity of ego development theory and its measurement. *Journal of Personality Assessment, 77,* 541–567.

Maslow, A. H. (1968). *Toward a psychology of being.* New York: Van Nostrand Reinhold Company.

McAdams, D. P., & de St. Aubin, E. (1992). A theory of generativity and its assessment through self-report, behavioral acts, and narrative themes in autobiography. *Journal of Personality & Social Psychology, 62,* 1003–1015.

Mickler, C., & Staudinger, U. M. (2003). *Self-insight: Definition and measurement of self-related wisdom.* Unpublished manuscript, International University Bremen, Bremen, Germany.

Noam, G. (1998). Solving the ego development–mental health riddle. In P. M. Westenberg, A. Blasi, & L. D. Cohn (Eds.), *Personality development: theoretical, empirical, and clinical investigations of Loevinger's conception of ego development* (pp. 271–295). Mahwah, NJ: Lawrence Erlbaum Associates, Inc.

Noam, G., & Röper, G. (1999). Auf dem Weg zur entwicklungspsychologisch differentiellen Intervention [On the way to a differential developmental intervention]. In R. Oerter (Ed.), *Klinische Entwicklunspsychologie: Ein Lehrbuch. [Clinical developmental psychology: A handbook]* (pp. 478–511). Weinheim: Beltz Psychologie.

Orwoll, L., & Perlmutter, M. (1990). The study of wise persons: Integrating a personality perspective. In R. J. Sternberg (Ed.), *Wisdom: Its nature, origins, and development* (pp. 160–177). New York: Cambridge University Press.

Pasupathi, M., & Staudinger, U. M. (2001). Do advanced moral reasoners also show wisdom? Linking moral reasoning and wisdom-related knowledge and judgment. *International Journal of Behavioral Development, 25,* 401–415.

Pasupathi, M., Staudinger, U. M., & Baltes, P. B (2001). Seeds of wisdom: Adolescents' knowledge and judgement about difficult matters of life. *Developmental Psychology, 37,* 351–361.

Peterson, B. E., & Klohnen, E. C. (1995). The realization of generativity in two samples of midlife women. *Psychology and Aging, 10,* 20–29.

Piaget, J. (1972). Intellectual evolution from adolescence to adulthood. *Human Development, 15,* 1–12.

Polanyi, M. (1976). Tacit knowledge. In M. Marx & F. Goodson (Eds.), *Theories in contemporary psychology* (pp. 330–370). New York: Macmillan.

Rankin, J. L., & Allen, J. L. (1991). Investigating the relationship between cognition and social thinking in adulthood: Stereotyping and attributional processes. In J. D. Sinnott & J. C. Cavanaugh (Eds.), *Bridging paradigms. Positive development in adulthood and cognitive aging* (pp. 131–152). New York: Praeger.

Roberts, B. W., Caspi, A., & Moffitt, T. E. (2001). The kids are alright: Growth and stability in personality development from adolescence to adulthood. *Journal of Personality and Social Psychology, 81,* 670–683.

Rogers, C. R. (1961). *On becoming a person*. Boston: Houghton Mifflin.

Ryff, C. D. (1989). Happiness is everything, or is it? Explorations on the meaning of psychological well-being. *Journal of Personality and Social Psychology, 57,* 1069–1081.

Ryff, C. D. (1995). Psychological well-being in adult life. *Current Directions in Psychological Science, 4,* 99–104.

Ryff, C. D., & Keyes, C. L. M. (1995). The structure of psychological well-being revisited. *Journal of personality and social psychology, 69,* 719 – 727.

Searle, J. R. (1992). *The rediscovery of the mind.* Cambridge: Cambridge University Press.

Schmutte, P. S., & Ryff, C. D. (1997). Personality and well-being: Reexamining methods and meanings. *Journal of Personality and Social Psychology, 73,* 549–559.

Sinnott, D. K. (1991). Limits to problem solving: Emotion, intention, goal clarity, health and other factors in postformal thought. In J. D. Sinnott & J. C. Cavanaugh (Eds.), *Bridging paradigms. Positive developments in adulthood and cognitive aging* (pp. 169–201). New York: Praeger.

Smith, J., Staudinger, U. M., & Baltes, P. B. (1994). Occupational settings facilitative of wisdom-related knowledge: The sample case of clinical psychologists. *Journal of Consulting and Clinical Psychology, 62,* 989–1000.

Sowarka, D. (1989). Weisheit und weise Personen: Common-Sense-Konzepte älterer Menschen [Wisdom and wise persons: Common-sense-concepts of older people]. *Zeitschrift für Entwicklungspsychologie und Pädagogische Psychologie, 21,* 87–109.

Staudinger, U. M. (1999). Older and wiser? Integrating results on the relationship between age and wisdom-related performance. *International Journal of Behavioral Development, 23,* 641–664.

Staudinger, U. M. (2001). Life reflection: a social-cognitive analysis of life review. *Review of General Psychology, 5,* 148–160.

Staudinger, U. M. (in press). Personality and aging. In M. Johnson, V. L. Bengtson, P. G. Coleman & T. Kirkwood (Eds.), *Cambridge handbook of age and ageing.* Cambridge: Cambridge University Press.

Staudinger, U. M., & Baltes, P. B. (1994). The psychology of wisdom. In R. J. Sternberg (Ed.), *Encyclopedia of intelligence* (pp. 1143–1152). New York: Macmillan.

Staudinger, U. M., & Baltes, P. B. (1996). Interactive minds: A facilitative setting for wisdom-related performance? *Journal of Personality and Social Psychology, 71,* 746–762.

Staudinger, U. M., Dörner, J., & Mickler, C. (2003). *Self-insight: Operationalizations and plasticity.* Unpublished manuscript, International University Bremen, Bremen, Germany.

Staudinger, U. M., & Leipold, B. (2002). The assessment of wisdom-related performance. In S. J. Lopez & C. R. Snyder (Eds.), *The Handbook of positive psychology assessment* (pp. 171–184). Washington, DC: American Psychological Association.

Staudinger, U. M., & Pasupathi, M. (2003). Correlates of wisdom-related performance in adolescence and adulthood: Age-graded paths towards desirable development. *Journal for Research on Adolescence, 13,* 239–268.

Staudinger, U. M., Lopez, D., & Baltes, P. B. (1997). The psychometric location of wisdom-related performance: Intelligence, personality, and more? *Personality and Social Psychology Bulletin, 23*, 1200–1214.

Staudinger, U. M., Maciel, A. G., Smith, J., & Baltes, P. B. (1998). What predicts wisdom-related performance? A first look at personality, intelligence, and facilitative experiential contexts. *European Journal of Personality, 12*, 1–17.

Staudinger, U. M., Smith, J., & Baltes, P. B. (1992). Wisdom-related knowledge in a life review task: Age differences and the role of professional specialization. *Psychology and Aging, 7*, 271–281.

Staudinger, U. M., Smith, J., & Baltes, P. B. (1994). *Manual for the assessment of wisdom-related knowledge.* Berlin: Max-Planck-Institut für Bildungsforschung.

Sternberg, R. J. (1985). Implicit theories of intelligence, creativity, and wisdom. *Journal of Personality and Social Psychology, 49*, 607–627.

Sternberg, R. J. (1986). Intelligence, wisdom, and creativity: Three is better than one. *Educational Psychologist, 21*, 175–190.

Sternberg, R. J. (1990). Wisdom and its relations to intelligence and creativity. In R. J. Sternberg (Ed.), *Wisdom: Its nature, origins, and development* (pp. 142–149). New York: Cambridge University Press.

Sternberg, R. J. (1994). Thinking styles: Theory and assessment at the interface between intelligence and personality. In R. J. Sternberg & P. Ruzgis (Eds.), *Personality and intelligence* (pp. 169–187). New York: Cambridge University Press.

Sternberg, R. J. (1998). A balance theory of wisdom. *Review of General psychology, 2*, 347–365.

Sternberg, R. J., Wagner, R. K., Williams, W. M., & Horvath, J. A. (1995). Testing common sense. *American Psychologist, 50*, 912–927.

Taft, L. B., & Nehrke, M. F. (1990). Reminiscence, life review, and ego integrity in nursing home residents. *International Journal of Aging & Human Development, 30*, 189–196.

Vaillant, G. E. (1993). *The wisdom of the ego.* Cambridge, MA: Harvard University Press.

Vaillant, G. E., & McCullough, L. (1987). The Washington University Sentence Completion Test compared with other measures of adult ego development. *American Journal of Psychiatry, 144*, 1189–1194.

Waterman, A. S. (1993). Two conceptions of happiness: Contrasts of personal expressiveness (eudaimonia) and hedonic enjoyment. *Journal of Personality and Social Psychology, 64*, 678–691.

Webster, J. D. (2003). An exploratory analysis of a self-assessed wisdom scale. *Journal of Adult Development, 10*, 13–22.

Westenberg, P. M., & Block, J. (1993). Ego development and individual differences in personality. *Journal of Personality and Social Psychology, 65*, 792–800.

Wink, P., & Helson, R. (1997). Practical and transcendent wisdom: Their nature and some longitudinal findings. *Journal of Adult Development, 4*, 1–15.

9

The Role of Emotions in the Development of Wisdom

Mihaly Csikszentmihalyi and Jeanne Nakamura

It is with a slight sense of embarrassment that we embark on this task of writing about wisdom. Although it is clearly the case that one can be immersed in a subject without claiming kinship with it – an entomologist can write about spiders without having to be one – wisdom has an alluring aura suggesting that those who dare to write about it must be to some extent also wise. We would like to relinquish any claims to that effect at the outset, and, relieved of the burden of appearing wise, start to analyze this important and interesting phenomenon with the conceptual tools of the social sciences.

In what follows we sometimes will use the same word "wisdom" to refer to two distinct phenomena. The first refers to the *content* of wisdom, or the kind of knowledge or information that a particular culture deems wise at a given time. The second use of the term refers to an individual's *capacity* to think or act wisely. Although we usually distinguish these two usages at least implicitly, for the sake of style and space sometimes we refrain from doing so, confident that the reader will have no trouble discerning the intended meaning.

Research on the relationship between wisdom and emotions usually focuses on patterns of affective regulation that are considered to be "wise" – such as being able to recognize one's own and other people's emotions and being able to restrain oneself from inappropriate emotional responses (Lazarus, 1991; Gross, 1999). Recently, this perspective has become assimilated into the literature on "emotional intelligence" (Barrett & Salovey, 2002). Some of the studies are also concerned with how positive (Frederickson & Joiner, 2001) or negative (Parrott, 2001) emotions can complement rational decision-making processes, contributing to better outcomes.

This chapter will focus specifically on the relationship between emotions and the development of wisdom. Although, as we shall see, there is an important relationship between the two, the task of presenting the evidence is made difficult because the research literature on this point is rather scant. The development of wisdom is usually seen as a dialectic interaction between personal experience and reflection, or between affect and cognition (Berg & Sternberg, 1985; Kramer, 1990; Labouvie-Vief, 1982). In this chapter, instead of assuming that wisdom is exclusively an intrapsychic process, we look at it as the result of an interaction between persons, on the one hand, and knowledge stored in cultural values, behavior patterns, artifacts – or memes – on the other. The question then becomes, what emotional factors are implicated in the development and transmission of wisdom in this restricted sense? This is the question that the present chapter attempts to answer.

Before considering the connection between emotions and the pursuit of wisdom, we will need to set a broader conceptual stage. In doing so, we may overlap with the content of some of the other chapters in this volume. However, without providing a theoretical context, the significance of emotions for an understanding of the emergence of wisdom would remain unclear.

The broadest theoretical framework is the one provided by evolutionary theory. Thus, in the first section of this chapter, we shall apply an evolutionary perspective to what constitutes wisdom, separating the cognitive aspects from those depending more on emotion, and concluding with the question: *How does practicing wisdom feel?* This leads us to the next section, which examines the phenomenology of wisdom. Two different claims are considered: that wise people cannot be happy because they know too much about human suffering; and the opposite claim, that wisdom confers serenity and happiness. We end this section by concluding that the evidence suggests that the second claim is closer to the truth, and that in fact *wisdom generates positive emotions that are necessary to continued engagement with tasks requiring wisdom.* The emotion we focus on is the intrinsically rewarding feeling of engagement people experience when involved in the practice of wisdom – a feeling that is often indexed simply as happiness, or positive emotion. In this section, we report material from some case studies of wise individuals describing the emotional commitment to the pursuit of wisdom. Finally, the next two sections expand on *how positive emotions are implicated in the development of wisdom*, and *how the measurement of positive emotions might be used in doing research on wisdom.*

Wisdom and Knowledge: An Evolutionary Perspective

At a first glance, emotions do not seem to have much relevance to wisdom, which is generally considered to be mainly a form of cognitive calculus. But is wisdom really nothing but a form of intelligence, a particular cognitive process that can be understood within the paradigms appropriate to the study of other rational processes? The answer seems to be both yes and no, depending on how narrowly we define rationality itself. In many respects, wisdom is a concept that has been used to define mental activity that is directed by values and emotion. The limitations of reason have been well understood since ancient times. As any high school debater learns, depending on the premises chosen and what evidence is suppressed or advanced, diametrically opposite conclusions can be reached logically from the same array of facts. The concept of wisdom is usually defined in contrast with overly narrow perspectives on rationality.

Many thinkers have sounded warnings about trusting the intellect too much. In 1580, at the beginning of his *Essays*, Montaigne wrote: "For it is not for knowledge to enlighten a soul that is dark of itself, nor to make a blind man see. Her business is not to find a man's eyes, but to give, govern, and direct them, provided he have sound feet and strong legs to go upon..." (Montaigne, 1987 [1580], I, 24). More recently, Albert Einstein expressed the same idea using remarkably similar language: "We must take care not to make intellect our God. It has, of course, powerful muscles, but no personality. It cannot rule, only serve." Even though Montaigne attributes muscles to the soul, and Einstein to the intellect, both writers agree that knowledge or reason are only tools, and they need direction from somewhere else. No one stated the idea more succinctly than Martin Luther when he wrote: "The intellect is the Devil's whore" (quoted in Steigmann-Gall, 2003, p. 55). In other words, reason, intelligence, and knowledge can be used for good or for ill, and there is good reason to fear that they will be used unscrupulously, or for ends that one will later regret. An excellent illustration of this quandary is the one provided by the Manhattan Project, where some of the best minds of the last century spent years perfecting the first nuclear device, a process that their leader, Robert Oppenheimer, described in a letter to his wife as the solution to "that sweet problem" (Csikszentmihalyi,

1985). It did not take too many more years for physicists to realize that although the problem of building the A-bomb had been intellectually challenging and thus "sweet" to theoreticians, it might not have been entirely wise.

At the same time, wisdom does not refer to thinking that is irrational, or even arational. Rather, it describes a mental process that is best characterized by focusing on the most relevant variables, by considering the broadest interests, and by taking long-range effects into consideration (Csikszentmihalyi & Rathunde, 1990). Given this holistic, inclusive agenda wisdom cannot proceed with the simple elegance of self-contained symbolic systems such as mathematics, or even that of the sciences. It relies more on global judgments, intuitive leaps, and consideration of values. It is more likely to aim at satisfying than optimizing. But within the domain in which these priorities are in effect, wisdom proceeds by the rules of ordinary logic.

The reason wisdom is nowadays discounted by many people as if it were an archaic remnant of primitive thought is that contrary to more "modern" cognitive domains, it has never developed a *sui generis* symbolic system – such as those developed by logicians, mathematicians, and scientists. This is both its weakness and its strength. The strength lies in two related consequences of it being an unsystematic cognitive process: first, that it is not constrained to operate within an abstract domain isolated from the rest of reality; and second, that it does not have to cater to the self-interests of a cadre of specialists. The weaknesses of wisdom are obvious: Lacking clear rules of procedure it is difficult to separate what is truly wise from what only appears to be so; its truth may take a long time to be confirmed; there is no cadre of specialists to vouch for its veracity and promote its virtues. Nevertheless, as specialized knowledge becomes more and more molecular while the problems confronting human survival get increasingly global, it would seem that the use of wise deliberation is increasingly essential.

What differentiates a person who impresses others as being "wise" from one who is perceived to be less so? Both the reading of a variety of texts dealing with wisdom, ranging from the Bible to modern philosophers (Csikszentmihalyi & Rathunde, 1990), and the investigations of Robert Sternberg and his lab (Sternberg, 1990), permit us to identify some specific traits of wise persons that in the public eye distinguish them from people who are intelligent or creative but not necessarily wise. These traits include being able to contextualize information, to understand the limits of what is known, to be aware of ambiguities and moderating conditions, and to get at the deeper meanings beyond superficial appearances (Peterson & Seligman, 2004; Sternberg, 1990). Or, according to the conclusions of the Berlin Wisdom Project, *wisdom is integrative, holistic, and balanced knowledge oriented toward the common good* (Baltes, Glück, & Kunzmann, 2002).

We doubt that the ability to use one's mind in such ways is the result of specific brain structures. It is more likely that wisdom is the result of mental habits formed early in life that result in perceiving problems as embedded in complex matrices, and that include empathy and care for a wide circle of responsibility. Wise individuals pay attention differently than the rest of us, relying more on that "disinterested interest" Jurgen Habermas described (1972). They are objective in their assessment of reality (and thus disinterested), yet at the same time are concerned about each aspect of reality (and thus interested).

More specifically, wisdom always includes an understanding of human nature – a knowledge of its strengths and weaknesses, of its limits and its aspirations. It is for this reason that one would be reluctant to call "wise" persons who allied themselves with extremist movements such as Nazism or the Russian Soviets – both of which ignored the real needs of human beings for the sake of imaginary ideals – whereas many perfectly rational intellectuals did not hesitate to embrace such movements. In addition, wise persons know their own specific strengths and weaknesses (e.g., Meacham, 1983). This element of self-knowledge – enshrined in the words carved at the entrance of the Delphic oracle – is one of the most distinctive attributes of wisdom. Wise persons are not inclined to denial, self-aggrandizement, or wishful thinking. Nor do they feel a sense of unwarranted inferiority.

But where does this ability to think wisely originate? The habits of attention that we tend to characterize as wise – the dispassionate concern for relationships and their consequences – are more likely the result of nurture than of nature. Even more than other cognitive processes, wisdom relies on selecting relevant information from the past and on applying it to present conditions. Wisdom is definitely not "in the head," but in the relationship between an inquiring mind, and the results of the inquiries of bygone minds. Thus a person who has no access to the wisdom of the past, who is not able to separate what is relevant to the present from what is not, is not likely to be thought wise.

Every culture needs to pass on the hard-earned lessons of the past. Until recently, these were worked into myths, fireside stories, proverbs, songs, and ritual dances. Later, religious systems evolved, shrouding important advice about living in divinely inspired commandments. For most of human history, the lessons were transmitted by the medium of words, and required one-to-one communication (Csikszentmihalyi, 2000). With the advent of writing a few thousand years ago, the storage and diffusion of information became much easier and more reliable. Thus, historical writing, literature, and quite recently the human sciences began the task of sorting out and preserving thoughts deemed important for the future.

Of course, if we think of wisdom as the transmission of past experience, the question immediately arises: Who decides what is important, useful, worth remembering – that is, wise? Clearly not all individuals contribute equally to these decisions. In simple hunting–gathering societies it is likely that the myths and proverbs that survived were the ones that a majority believed and endorsed. But as hierarchical societies emerged roughly ten thousand years ago, the selection, coding, and transmission of information became increasingly centralized and controlled by the military, religious, and economic elites (Csikszentmihalyi, 1990b). Thus, it became increasingly necessary to be careful in simply endorsing traditional wisdom, for it might represent the interests of particular groups rather than the common good.

This is, of course, a problem not limited to wisdom, but to the transmission of *all* cultural material: Whether it pertains to religion or to science, to the laws or to artistic taste, all messages are to a certain extent tainted by special interests. It is for this reason that wisdom begins with the sifting of past wisdom, continues with prioritizing the messages that pass muster, and then seeks the application of past lessons to present conditions. It is in this respect that wisdom has an advantage over other forms of knowledge. When religion and science become institutionalized, they develop a strong interest in keeping control of the accumulated knowledge for their own benefit. The Catholic church claimed privileged access to the will of God, and built lavish monasteries and cathedrals with the sweat of peasants, since nothing less would be fitting to house the servants of the Lord. The scientific institutes of our days construct huge labs that once built must be staffed and maintained, whether the knowledge they produce is useful or not. Because wisdom is less dependent on organized interest groups such as churches or scientific domains (although it can be exploited by both), it is less likely to be contaminated with specious pleading.

Thus, wisdom is best understood as part of the process of cultural evolution. Like biological evolution, the cultural form is a process by which previous information is reproduced, new "mutations" are introduced by chance or by design, then the most promising mutations are selected out from the less promising ones, and finally the selected novelties as well as the surviving old matrix are transmitted to a new generation (Campbell, 1976). Unlike biological evolution, where the information is chemically coded in genes, in cultural evolution the information is coded in *memes* that must be passed on through learning (Csikszentmihalyi, 1993; Dawkins, 1976; Inghilleri, 1999). Although other cognitive processes such as scientific thinking privilege the production of new memes rather than the selection and transmission of knowledge, wisdom is primarily concerned with selecting worthwhile memes and then transmitting the selected ones to new generations.

Given this perspective, we may define the content of wisdom as information relevant to important life choices, which one is prone to pay attention to, remember, and want to transmit to others – regardless of momentary interests or specialized knowledge. Although cumbersome, this definition captures the salient aspects of what makes information wise: It is a meme believed to be useful, hence worth remembering; something that does not depend on particular conditions or special training; that is believed to help make life decisions, and is thus selected spontaneously by those who are privy to it. It follows that a wise person is someone who can provide such content.

From an evolutionary perspective, the fact that some individuals are willing to invest psychic energy in this process may seem absurd. Why spend effort acquiring disinterested knowledge that may or may not benefit the self? A person who takes the long view, who is primarily concerned with the common good, is to that extent less able to pursue his or her own interests. Thus, the logic of selection should eliminate wisdom from the repertory of human responses. But recent evolutionary thinking has been correcting the excessively individualistic interpretations of Darwinian theory. It is now becoming clearer that selfless individuals, who are taken advantage of in a competitive society, prosper in a social milieu that is less selfishly competitive. And less selfish societies – other things being equal – have an advantage over more selfish ones (e.g., Wilson, 2002). Applying this insight to wisdom we may conclude that the reason wisdom has yet to be eliminated from our conceptual repertory is that communities in which it is encouraged have some advantage over those that do not see any point in it; and in such communities wise persons may prosper despite their relative lack of selfish interests. A more proximal explanation as to why people will practice wisdom has to do with its phenomenology – with the emotions a person feels when attending to memes that contain wisdom.

The Phenomenology of Wisdom

Thus, although essentially a cognitive process, cognition is not the only aspect of wisdom that should interest psychologists. A neglected dimension of wisdom is its lived quality – the emotional experience that accompanies it. One widely held assumption is that wise individuals must pay a high price for their understanding – after all, their insights into the nature of reality must inevitably reveal the tragic elements of life. Concern for the well-being of others must exact a heavy toll when the wise contemplate the sufferings of humankind. Less wise individuals, either because they are taken in by superficial appearances, or because they ignore the suffering of others, can be happy; but that feeling must be inaccessible to the wise. This widespread sentiment was well illustrated by the answer Charles De Gaulle gave to a journalist who had asked him during an interview: *"Monsieur le President,* are you a happy man?" De Gaulle stretched his frame to its fullest height, and looking down the bridge of his formidable nose on the quivering reporter answered with another question: "What kind of a fool do you take me for?" Only fools, apparently, can afford to be happy.

Yet there is another, contrary set of beliefs that links wisdom with happiness. In an earlier paper, it was claimed – mainly on the basis of traditional accounts – that psychologists have largely ignored the claim that wise people enjoy life, both moment-by-moment, and in its entirety (Csikszentmihalyi & Rathunde, 1990). For example, Plato made the point that to get any of the rewards of life – pleasure from good health, satisfaction from fame, good use from wealth – one needs wisdom (*Meno*, 87; *Euthydemus,* 278). Similar conclusions were reached by most classical and Christian philosophers: by Aristotle in the *Nichomachean Ethics,* by St. Augustine in *De Trinitate,* and by Thomas Aquinas in the *Summa Theologica* (e.g., 1, 5; 1, 64). Montaigne asserted that "the most manifest sign of wisdom is continual cheerfulness" (*Essays,* 1, 25). Or, as the final chorus chants in Sophocles' *Antigone*: "Wisdom is the supreme part of happiness."

At this point, there is only scant empirical evidence on which to decide which of these opposing claims is closer to being true. Of the few studies, most seem to support the second conclusion, namely that wisdom induces positive emotions. For instance, Peterson and Seligman (2004) cite several studies showing a positive relationship between wisdom and psychological well-being. In Lyster's (1996) study, those with higher wisdom scores expressed less dissatisfaction with their lives than those with lower wisdom scores, which she viewed as indicating freedom from despair. More positively, in the same study, serenity – an accepting stance toward both positive and negative feelings – was the emotion conveyed by the largest percentage (52%) of those nominated as wise. Barrett and Salovey (2002) have suggested that knowing how to read, use, and manage emotions – aspects of emotional intelligence – constitutes a kind of "wisdom in feeling"; we would expect this to be associated with subjective well-being. Finally, using data from the longitudinal Berkeley Guidance Study, Ardelt (1997) concluded that the strongest predictor of life satisfaction in old age is wisdom. Still, one needs triangulation with more ecologically valid data before this important issue can be considered settled.

While waiting for further evidence, we might formulate the question on theoretical grounds: How *could* wise persons be cheerful and happy when their holistic understanding inevitably must highlight the tragic elements of life? On the face of it, such a thing should not be possible. As usual when anomalies such as these arise, their presence suggests some interesting and possibly important breakthrough in understanding. In this case, there are both ancient and contemporary clues as to how it is possible to be wise and happy at the same time. In the writing of Christian philosophers, for instance, the argument is made that all of creation is God's work and hence good. Evil and suffering only come about when the will of God is purposefully thwarted. From this perspective the wise person, although regretting the presence of evil introduced by sinful individuals, rejoices in identifying with God's creative vision, confident that eventually a blessed harmony is bound to prevail. An identification with the universe as a whole, an acceptance of the mysterious presence of evil as a minor theme in the scheme of things, and hope in a better future tend to be ways in which wisdom has been linked to happiness East and West through the centuries.

For example, Viktor Frankl, the Austrian psychiatrist who described his confinement in the Nazi extermination camps, writes: "The prisoner who had lost faith in the future – his future – was doomed. With his loss of belief in the future, he also lost his spiritual hold; he let himself decline and became subject to mental and physical decay" (Frankl, 1985, p. 95). But how were prisoners to believe in their personal future when comrades were dying left and right each day because of the dehumanizing, hopelessly brutal conditions of the camps? Frankl suggests that despite the painful reality, some individuals were able to keep hope and dignity to the end, because "they were able to retreat from their terrible surroundings to a life of inner riches and spiritual freedom" (Frankl 1985, p. 55). The "inner riches" Frankl refers to are not something encoded in the genes, or acquired by chance. They are the result of the cultivation of past wisdom. Only those individuals who become carriers of the evolving culture – those who recognize and select the best memes of the past, who remember them and transmit them to others – only those persons can feel that they have a role in preserving a livable world.

In other words, past memes that are wise serve as bridges to the future. Christian theologians as well as Jewish psychiatrists know that the worst sting of suffering can be eased by the knowledge that one is responsible for preserving what is best about humankind. Thus, it is possible to be hopeful, and perhaps joyful, even under the worst adversity.

These considerations also explain why a person would spend energy in being wise (i.e., in attending to, selecting, improving on, and transmitting memes that are unlikely to result in any practical personal advantage). If it is true that acting as an agent of cultural evolution provides a positive experience in the moment, the nagging question: Why be wise? would be answered. In other words, wisdom is one of the activities that we do because they are intrinsically rewarding.

Most things we do need to be motivated by the expectation of *extrinsic* rewards, because there are no other reasons for doing them. We study, work, commute, groom, eat, and sleep because we have to. We need external rewards or threats to keep investing scarce psychic energy in them. And then there are activities like singing or dancing, playing or exploring, that are so rewarding in and of themselves that we do them even without any stick or carrot to motivate us. These are activities that provide *intrinsic* rewards (Csikszentmihalyi, 1975, 1990a; Nakamura & Csikszentmihalyi, 2002).

But whether one feels rewarded intrinsically does not depend only on the nature of the activity. Enjoyment is both a *state* (that is, it depends on parameters of the activity or the environment), and a *trait* (it depends also on the habits and attitudes of the person). Some people seem to be able to transform almost everything they do into an enjoyable activity. For such "autotelic" individuals even study, work, and the routines of everyday life can be rewarding intrinsically. So we suggest that the possession of wisdom is rewarding in itself, and that wise persons find joy and serenity in pursuing wisdom.

The Development of Wisdom

How do emotions affect the development of wisdom? This question would not be important if all it took to be wise was to accumulate enough varied experiences as one aged. Although popular opinion generally attributes wisdom to older individuals, assuming that we grow wiser with time, the empirical evidence is inconclusive. Cross-sectional studies generally find no correlation between wisdom and age. After reviewing the latter literature on the subject, Ursula Staudinger (1999) concluded: "Between 20 and 75 years, age has been demonstrated to show a zero relation with wisdom-related knowledge and judgment" (p. 641). After age 75, wisdom suffers from the same decrement as other cognitive functions, but perhaps somewhat less than, for instance, memory does (Baltes & Staudinger, 2000).

A different perspective on wisdom and development is the one proposed by Meacham (1990). Here wisdom is seen not as the possession of cognitive skills or knowledge *per se* but as a particular attitude toward knowledge: a critical balance between knowing and doubting. The assumption is that "all people are wise to begin with, as children," and tend to lose their critical attitude as they age (Meacham, 1990, p. 198).

Whether one conceives of wisdom as the acquisition of certain kinds of information, or as a specific way of processing information, leads to different developmental predictions, and to different approaches to intervention. If wisdom relies mainly on content, it would make sense to expect that it will increase with age; if it involves cognitive strategies that may be adversely affected by too much information, as Meacham suggests, then one might expect a decline with time.

It bears noting that recent longitudinal studies provide some evidence in support of the popular belief that wisdom increases with age (Hartman, 2000; Wink & Helson, 1997). The jury, thus, is still out. Because age in any case is what developmental psychologists have sometimes called an "empty" variable, a marker of age-associated processes that remain to be understood, we turn now to thoughts about the underlying developmental processes. As we have stated earlier, in our opinion the essence of wisdom consists in acting as a bridge between valuable past experience and its future reproduction. This involves the relatively rare inclination and ability to manage a dialectic: the willingness to turn to cultural tradition for answers, and simultaneously the willingness to question traditional answers in light of personal experience – and to enjoy doing both.

Which pole of this dialectic is privileged may vary in different cultures at different times. Acquiring wisdom in a traditional culture may involve substantially different processes than it does in contemporary society. The more slowly a society changes, the more readily succeeding generations might perceive traditional wisdom as being relevant to experience. In collectivist cultures, or in current fundamentalist religious subcultures, the emphasis is on the replication of past memes, and questioning their wisdom with reference to personal experience is frowned on or actually punished. In individualistic cultures and subcultures, such as the academic enclaves of postmodernism, traditional wisdom is suspect, whereas personal experience and current perspectives are privileged. Perhaps reflecting this, Western psychological theories of wisdom may preserve the dialectic but cast it in exclusively individualist terms, portraying it as the personal growth that occurs through the interplay between the lessons of the *personal* past and the individual's current experience. The subculture of science also tends to discount the past in favor of the present and the future: On the door of many undergraduate physics or chemistry departments one could read slogans such as: "The knowledge of the past generation is no longer true."

When the dialectic tilts too far in one or the other direction, the result can hardly be called "wisdom" any longer. There can be legitimate variation in emphasis between past and present and still remain within the bounds of what might be allowed as wisdom. Our perspective suggests, however, that any developmental model, or any educational intervention, must take into account both aspects of the dialectic: the concern for sifting among the memes of the past, and the concern for transmitting the best to the future. Any human group that forgot the record of past life choices and their consequences would have to rediscover the most elementary rules for how to live, and painfully recapitulate literally tens of thousands of years of cultural evolution.

In the lay view, wisdom develops as a result of experience. Surely this is not the complete story, however. One certainty is that it is possible to grow old without growing wise. Nor is an eventful life a guarantee of wisdom, any more than having led a quiet life precludes the growth of perspective – one thinks of the life of Emily Dickinson. Empirical research is beginning to suggest a picture that recognizes the importance of a person's attitude toward, and response to, his or her life experiences. If it is not enough to have long or extensive experience, how does wisdom develop? Two key and dynamically interrelated factors appear to be openness to experience and a capacity to reflect on experience to make sense of it.

Kramer (2000) reviewed the empirical research and concluded that openness to experience is the most common personality predictor of wisdom. It encompasses both psychological-mindedness, or openness to one's *inner life*; and curiosity about the *outer world*, including openness to other perspectives – not the least of which, we suggest, are "culture carriers" such as wise people, books, the arts, and traditional belief systems.

Openness is paired with a reflective stance about experience. Lyster (1996), for example, examined a host of factors and concluded that wisdom develops in midlife "through the dynamic interplay between openness and critical reflection" (p. iv). An individual makes sense of experience through life review, the process of coming to terms with past choices; reflecting on rather than avoiding past life experiences; and critically evaluating lessons drawn from the past, both individual and collective.

Despite promising recent research, a number of questions about the ontogeny of wisdom continue to remain virtually untouched. First and most fundamentally, in the absence of the kind of interventions currently being explored by Sternberg (2002), *why* does a person develop wisdom – what sets a person on this path and what subsequently keeps him or her on it? In our terms, how does a person form the habit of attending to the domain of life choices? One possible answer is that a person's life experience – for example, some tragedy or stress – demands this focus of attention. The idea has the ring of truth, and researchers have examined negative life events, and stressful life events, as possible antecedents of wisdom. The findings have been mixed. Lyster (1996), for example, interviewed individuals nominated as wise and found that contrary to her expectations, wisdom was associated with identifying *positive* life events as the turning points in personal development.

A second possibility, equally plausible from an evolutionary perspective, is that people might be drawn (rather than driven) to invest their psychic energy in thinking about life matters because of the positive emotions that accompany the process. We have suggested that possessing wisdom may bring with it happiness rather than despair. It may seem still more dubious that the *pursuit* of wisdom would be intrinsically rewarding, enjoyable, or undertaken for its own sake. After all, several models of development reviewed by Kramer (2000) characterize the process as "long and arduous," "often painstaking," and dependent upon the "active exertion of will." But our interviews with leaders in a variety of fields, many of whom qualify as "wise" in their own domain of achievement and also more broadly, lead us to wonder. The futurist and economist Hazel Henderson provides an example of someone who recalls sheer delight at reflecting on the domain of life, from early child-hood on. She explained:

[People] should really enjoy contemplating themselves, and figure out, you know, "What am I doing here on this planet?" Enjoy the wonder of that question. Which I know I had when I was *five* ... where you just open your eyes and you look around and say, *"Wow, what an incredible trip this is! What the hell is going on? What am I supposed to be doing here?"* You know. And I've had that question in me all my life. And, I love it! Because it makes every day very fresh.... [I]f you can keep that question fresh and remember what that was like when you were a child and you looked around and you looked at, say, trees, and you forgot that you knew the word "tree," ... when you wake up, it's like the dawn of creation. (Unpublished interview, Creativity in Later Life Study)

People who become wise may thus resemble individuals animated by an intense interest in domains of other kinds, such as the naturalist fascinated by flora and fauna so vividly described by E. O. Wilson in his autobiography (Wilson, 1994).

A child's family and community may meet and satisfy this joyful cu-riosity, or perhaps extinguish it, for instance, by socializing the child into a religious or other tradition that provides ready-made, authoritative an-swers to life's questions. In contrast, Henderson's parents catalyzed a lifelong search, modeling a path of openness and critical scrutiny carved out between the unquestioning acceptance of traditional wisdom on the one side, and the unquestioning rejection of traditional wisdom, on the other. If most people tilt toward the guidance of either personal ex-perience or else toward tradition as they acquire wisdom, Henderson illustrates the former process:

I think that one of the advantages I had as a child was that my parents were strict atheists. And so I didn't have any religious code stamped on me. And so ... what I would later describe as the spiritual inquiry was quite urgent.... I would come home from school when I was five years old, you know – I remember vividly – or six, and say to my mother, "Well, we learned all about the little Lord Je-sus today." And she'd say, "What rubbish!." ... "Wow, what am I supposed to do with *that?*" ... it both makes you very open, and you don't reject anything, but you also – everything is subject. And you allow yourself to perceive an aw-ful lot and you don't reject anything automatically, but neither do you accept anything automatically. So you're constantly in a very active mode of evalu-ation and critical reasoning. (Unpublished interview, Creativity in Later Life Study)

We have suggested that the acquisition of wisdom entails turning to memes embedded in culture carriers – books, people, art, and so on – in a quest to make sense of the problems of life. The importance of books or other sources of the culture's accumulated wisdom might be revealed through chance events, as exemplified by Malcolm X's discovery of books while in prison; or through normative experiences, for example, years of socialization within the family of origin. Another participant in the Creativity in Later Life Study, the writer Madeleine L'Engle, illustrates how the early family environment may model and encourage the valuing of culture as a legitimate source of insight:

> I lived in a house full of books. A story was not an unusual thing in my household as it is in some households. My parents read aloud to each other, every night of their lives, a story. So I lived in an atmosphere where story was honored, not considered suspect. . . . I understood [as a child] that when you want to find out what life is about, you turn to story, not encyclopedias. Those are for facts. Facts are thin . . . they don't carry you very far. (Unpublished interview, Creativity in Later Life Study)

It may make sense to understand the turn toward culture, like the immersion in exploration of life matters, as intrinsically rewarding or enjoyable for at least some people "at risk" for wisdom. L'Engle's enduring respect for story (versus mere "facts") extended to culture carriers more generally. She explicitly recognized the role of the wise individuals in her own life, as well as the role of story, as bridges between past and future:

> story is not "looking behind." It's the rock which gives us the impetus to spring forward into the future. And we need wise old women; we need wise old men; we need wise older people. I've been very lucky in my life. This is really the first time in my life where I'm not young enough to have wise older friends. They've been very important to me . . . people who had lived a lot longer and knew a lot more and had accumulated a lot of wisdom and humility. (Unpublished interview, Creativity in Later Life Study)

Finally, we have argued that developing wisdom depends on a dynamic interplay between openness and reflection, and on a turn toward carriers of culture that enables the individual to draw on the wisdom of the past to solve problems in the present. The development of wisdom, and the desire to transmit the yield of the cultural and personal past to future generations, would seem to depend additionally on a concern for others beyond oneself. At this stage in our understanding of the ontogeny of wisdom, we can only speculate about possible sources.

One possibility is that a concern for others is a positive impetus beginning early in life, much like the lifelong curiosity about the world that Hazel Henderson professed. A related possibility is that a sense of care transcending the boundaries of the self may arise if a person is led to universalize some dilemma he or she has personally encountered. The notion of a *discovered life theme* describes a person's formulation of an experienced dilemma in universal terms, thereby permitting it to be addressed through a culturally provided solution (Csikszentmihalyi & Beattie, 1979). Finally, consistent with the notion of developmental tasks that succeed one another over the life course, the generativity concerns normatively associated with the middle years might explain the hypothesized growth of wisdom in the second half of life (Hartman, 2000). In all these cases, investment of psychic energy in goals that transcend the individual self, or generativity, may be intrinsically enjoyable. That is, like the devotion of psychic energy to life matters, and like the turn to culture, caring for future generations is sometimes motivated by the experiential rewards that it provides (e.g., Colby & Damon, 1992). In a rare study of wisdom that addressed this question, several participants reported that "generative interactions were experienced as fulfilling, satisfying, or enriching suggesting that the interactions were intrinsically motivating" (Lyster, 1996, p. 129).

In the cases of both Hazel Henderson and Madeleine L'Engle, this expansion of the boundaries of the self was evident in maturity, at the time of their participation in the Creativity in Later Life Study. For example, L'Engle explained:

First comes the enjoyment of the activity – but I am responsible for what I write. I know that I influence a lot of people. And therefore, I have to have a certain concern that what I write is not destructive.... I don't like hopeless books.... I don't think I could write hopeless books. I think I would just not do it. Books that make you think, "Life's not worth living." I want to finish a book thinking, "Yeah, this endeavor is difficult but it is worth it, and it is ultimately joyful." (Unpublished interview, Creativity in Later Life Study)

Henderson reached backward, explicitly recalling a strong early identification with humanity and the natural world:

... one of my resolutions was my connection with the biosphere and nature. And the order that I've always felt in nature, and the beauty of nature, and the fact that everything in nature is so perfect.... So ecological theory has always been a very important way of understanding these contexts, and that ... the human race is a family, wherever you find people there's much more the same about them than there is different about them. (Unpublished interview, Creativity in Later Life Study)

Whereas Henderson and L'Engle represent individuals whose wisdom, although solidly grounded in tradition, tilts toward the critical evaluation of the past based on personal experience, other persons who also can be called wise are more deeply immersed in the past and take traditional cultural memes – religious or otherwise – more for granted. In a recent study of responsible and socially conscious business leaders, for instance, it was quite surprising to find how deeply influenced by early religious training such individuals were (Csikszentmihalyi, 2003). For example, the founder of one of the largest advertising companies specializing in ethnic markets said:

Black culture is founded on the belief – a religious foundation – that good things will come. In my generation, they have. I mean, I admire my forefathers because they persevered when there didn't seem to be much opportunity. . . . But we have an obligation to work hard. . . . I think religion is a very strong element in going forward. (Csikszentmihalyi, 2003, p. 157)

In this case the memes for perseverance in the face of difficulty, and for the necessity of working hard, were carried in the "cultural phenotype" of a religious context. The CEO of a large real-estate investment group described his personal philosophy as follows:

It's a faith that there is some overall purpose or plan to life, and that you and I occupy some place in that plan. My faith gives me that context so everything I see, I see in that context . . . and I feel like I'm on the Lord's errand, and he has an interest in what I'm doing. (p. 159)

Although each business leader claimed to have evaluated his or her early beliefs and accepted them in adulthood because they jibed with lived experience, at present it is impossible to know how much critical evaluation is needed before the acceptance of past memes can be considered wise.

For example, in the documentary *Bowling for Columbine*, Charlton Heston, a spokesman for the National Rifle Association, defended the Second Amendment – "the right to bear arms" – on the grounds that if it was good for the wise ancestors who had founded this country, it was good enough for him. Here the meme of the right to bear arms was accepted by Heston without questioning whether "arms" at the time of muzzle-loading muskets, and the automatic machine guns now available to teenagers, are actually the same things. Regardless of what one might feel about this issue, the ahistorical, decontextualized acceptance of traditional memes cannot be called wise.

Although case studies can be very illuminating, systematic research on this topic requires more easily quantifiable measures. Yet, the ability to recognize worthwhile options for the investment of psychic resources – or wisdom – is arguably the most difficult personal trait to measure. In terms of the conceptual model developed here, wisdom consists in finding out which goals are worth investing psychic energy in, and then actually doing so. This process should result in the best possible outcomes for both the individual and for the environment in which he or she lives. In other words, being wise should be enjoyable for the wise person and helpful to society.

The Measurement of Wisdom

Even though most theories of wisdom attribute a great deal of importance to life experiences, up to now researchers have endeavored to measure wisdom mainly by means of vignettes that require the person to solve a dilemma bearing on some crucial life decision. For instance, the laboratory of Paul Baltes at the Max Planck Institute for Human Development in Berlin adopted five criteria to assess "wisdom-related performance." These are (a) factual and (b) procedural knowledge; (c) understanding of the basic contexts of life and their interrelations; (d) acknowledgment and tolerance for a diversity of values; and (e) recognition and management of uncertainty. These five criteria are assessed by responses to fictional life problems presented in the context of an interview. Transcripts of the tape-recorded protocols are then coded by trained judges (Baltes & Staudinger, 2000). Robert Sternberg (2002) uses similar dilemmas including conflict resolution problems, moral judgment problems, and personal dilemma problems to assess wisdom-related thought processes of students.

In line with our preference for measuring experience and behavior in ecologically valid real-life settings, we suggest that the following approaches based on assessing more emotionally based dimensions may complement previous approaches:

Assessing attention and commitment to the past. We have argued that a wise person is like a link, joining the achievements of the past with those of the future – an agent of cultural evolution. Thus, perhaps the most important thing to find out about a person is not whether he or she can reason wisely, but whether the person is interested in acquiring valuable information from the past to resolve fundamental questions about human life. Is the person interested in what the cultural tradition has to say about differentiating true from false, good from bad, the beautiful from the ugly?

Assessing belief in and commitment to the future. Wise people are characterized by hope for the future, and commitment to it. They aspire to transmit their accumulated wisdom to others and to put it in the service of a future that is larger than their own. Is that interest discernible in plans to invest their energies in goals that include a wide circle of responsibility, rather than in goals that are more self-serving (Schmuck & Sheldon, 2001)?

Assessing how people use their time and the habits they form. However, it is not enough to know what attitudes toward the past are held by a person – nor what goals the person embraces. Equally important, if not more, is what people actually do. Is a concern for life matters discernible in the way time is spent? Is interest in lessons of the past reflected in actual investment of psychic energy in thinking, talking, and reading about what others have thought or written about the good life? Is avowed commitment to the future manifested in devotion of psychic energy to the pursuit of self-transcendent goals, whether mentoring, grandparenting, environmental conservation, civic life, or something else?

For instance, a record of actual time use can be obtained with the Experience Sampling Method (ESM) or diary method (e.g., Csikszentmihalyi & Schneider, 2000). This would begin to indicate whether a person invests his or her time in these ways, or in others – for example, passive leisure (e.g., television viewing) or contentious interpersonal interactions. This method also may reveal to what extent the person is developing habits of action and attention that may lead to life-choices consistent with wisdom. Habits, as the early psychologists recognized, are among the most distinctive and powerful determinants of the quality of life. So, for instance, when George Vaillant (2002, p. 208) reports in the follow-up to the Harvard Study of Aging that whereas 64 percent of men who drank little and smoked little were free of physical disabilities between 75 and 80 years of age, but only 24 percent of those who drank little but smoked heavily were hale and hearty at that age, it is not too difficult to conclude that starting to smoke early is not a wise life choice.

Assessing the quality of subjective experience. Most important, the ESM could be used to provide a measure of the person's quality of experience in the context of everyday life. Thus, it would be possible to see whether the patterns identified earlier are associated with active enjoyment when thinking about, talking about, and taking action in the domain of life choices. In addition, it would be possible to measure that capacity to regulate both inner life and interpersonal experience that is widely attributed to wise persons. Finally, it would be possible to explore whether these patterns are associated with overall serenity or other forms of positive affect – whether the habitual pursuit of wisdom brings enduring happiness.

Conclusions

In this chapter we have argued that the *content* of wisdom is best defined as those memes – or units of information learned from the culture – that are perceived as being most helpful in making choices leading to a happy, or at least to a satisfied life. The *trait* of wisdom therefore refers to the ability to search for and recognize such memes, to evaluate their applicability to current conditions, to implement them in one's life, and then to transmit the information to future generations.

The proximal reason wisdom exists, we have argued, is that its pursuit and possession are intrinsically rewarding. The joy of discovering a valid truth provides some of the most memorable moments in life, and dedication to wisdom leads to a serene existence that few other achievements can match. Of course, not all persons are equally equipped to pursue wisdom. Whether because of genetic differences or early experiences, some individuals appear to mistrust or be disinterested in traditional wisdom. Others are too ready to accept memes from the past without distinguishing the ones that are still valid from those that are not.

These considerations suggest that wisdom can be learned. The prerequisites for it – such as openness to experience, exposure to past wisdom, and the ability to evaluate tradition critically – are to some extent teachable. How to do this well is one of the priorities for our time.

Like other valued human attributes – such as beauty, virtue, or creativity – wisdom is time- and space-specific. Polynesian obesity is not considered particularly beautiful these days, nor Spartan virtue very desirable. Much of what our ancestors rightly thought was wise can no longer pass muster. The worldview of Confucius fragmented into fortune cookies has little chance to enhance our life choices. Nevertheless, at any given time some memes strike enough people as valid distillations of experience to merit the label "wise," and no culture can exist for long without the belief that it can distinguish what is wise from what is foolish. Even though it may not affect the majority's behavior, the belief in wisdom is by itself sustaining. For this reason if for nothing else, facilitating the growth of wisdom and the capacity for cultivating it remain priorities even in our age of increasing specialization.

In this endeavor it is essential to remember that the pursuit of wisdom, and its deployment, thrive on joy. The best recipe for the spread of wisdom is the encouragement of curiosity, respect for the best accomplishments of the past, coupled with a burning desire for improving on them; and all of this within a conception of self that extends to other people, the planet, and beyond. When these elements are in place, a joyful immersion in the complexity of life is likely to ensue – an openness to experience, a willingness to delve deep into issues of concern to self and others. If such an attitude develops far enough then understanding life becomes increasingly rewarding in itself. The person will be seen as wise, and his or her actions also will be considered wise.

References

Ardelt, M. (1997). Wisdom and life satisfaction in old age. *Journal of Gerontology (Psychological Sciences), 52B*, 15–27.

Baltes, P., & Staudinger, U. (2000). A metaheuristic (pragmatic) to orchestrate mind and virtue towards excellence. *American Psychologist, 55*, 122–136.

Baltes, P. B., Glück, J. & Kunzmann, U. (2002). Wisdom: Its structure and function in regulating successful life-span development. In C. R. Snyder & S. J. Lopez (Eds.), *Handbook of positive psychology* (pp. 327–347). New York: Oxford University Press.

Barrett, F. L., & Salovey, P. (Eds.). (2002). *The wisdom in feeling: Psychological processes in emotional intelligence*. New York: Guilford Press.

Berg, S. A., & Sternberg, R. J. (1985). A triarchic theory of intellectual development during adulthood. *Developmental Review, 5*, 334–370.

Campbell, D.T. (1976). Evolutionary epistemology. In D.A. Schlipp (Ed.), *The library of living philosophers* (pp. 413–463). La Salle, IL: Open Court.

Colby, A., & Damon, W. (1992. *Some do care: Contemporary lives of moral commitment*. New York: Free Press.

Csikszentmihalyi, M. (1975). *Beyond boredom and anxiety*. San Francisco: Jossey-Bass.

Csikszentmihalyi, M. (1985). Reflections on enjoyment. *Perspectives in Biology and Medicine, 28*(4), 469–497.

Csikszentmihalyi, M. (1990a). *Flow: The psychology of optimal experience*. New York: Jossey-Bass.

Csikszentmihalyi, M. (1990b). Literacy and intrinsic motivation. *Daedalus, 119*(2), 115–140.

Csikszentmihalyi, M. (1993). *The evolving self: A psychology for the third millennium*. New York: HarperCollins.

Csikszentmihalyi, M. (2000). The mythic potential of evolution. *Zygon, 35*(1), 25–38.

Csikszentmihalyi, M., & Beattie, O. (1979). Life themes: A theoretical and empirical exploration of their origins and effects. *Journal of Humanistic Psychology*, *19*, 45–63.

Csikszentmihalyi, M., & Rathunde, K. (1990). The psychology of wisdom: An evolutionary interpretation. In R. J. Sternberg (Ed.), *Wisdom: Its nature, origins, and development* (pp. 25–51). Cambridge, England: Cambridge University Press.

Dawkins, R. (1976). *The selfish gene.* New York: Oxford University Press.

Frankl, V. E. (1985 [1946]). *Man's search for meaning.* New York: Pocket Books.

Frederickson, B. L., & Joiner, T. (2001). Positive emotions trigger upward spirals toward emotional well-being. *Psychological Science, 13*, 172–175.

Gross, J. J. (1999). Emotion regulation: Past, present, future. *Cognition and Emotion, 13*, 551–573.

Habermas, J. (1972). *Knowledge and human interests.* Boston: Beacon Press.

Hartman, P. S. (2000). *Women developing wisdom: Antecedents and correlates in a longitudinal sample.* Unpublished doctoral dissertation, University of Michigan.

Inghilleri, P. (1999). *From subjective experience to cultural evolution.* New York: Cambridge University Press.

Kramer, D. A. (1990). Conceptualizing wisdom: The primacy of affect-cognition relations. In R. J. Sternberg (Ed.), *Wisdom: Its nature, origins, and development* (pp. 279–313). Cambridge: Cambridge University Press.

Kramer, D. A. (2000). Wisdom as a classical source of human strength: Conceptualization and empirical inquiry. *Journal of Social and Clinical Psychology, 19*, 83–101.

Labouvie-Vief, G. (1982). Dynamic development and mature autonomy: A theoretical prologue. *Human Development, 25*, 161–191.

Lazarus, R. S. (1991). *Emotion and adaptation.* Oxford: Oxford University Press.

Lyster, T. (1996). *A nomination approach to the study of wisdom in old age.* Unpublished doctoral dissertation, Concordia University, Montreal, Canada.

Meacham, J. A. (1983). Wisdom and the context of knowledge: knowing that one doesn't know. In D. Kuhn & J. A. Meacham (Eds.), *On the development of developmental psychology* (pp. 111–134). Basel, Switzerland: Karger.

Meacham, J. A. (1990). The loss of wisdom. In R. J. Sternberg (Ed.), *Wisdom: Its nature, origins, and development* (pp. 181–211). Cambridge: Cambridge University Press.

Montaigne, M. E. (1987 [1580]). *The essays.* Chicago: The Encyclopedia Britannica Inc.

Nakamura, J., & Csikszentmihalyi, M. (2002). The concept of flow. In C. R. Snyder & S. J. Lopez (Eds.), *Handbook of positive psychology* (pp. 89–105). New York: Oxford University Press.

Parrott, W. G. (2001). Implications of dysfunctional emotions for understanding how emotions functions. *Review of General Psychology, 5*, 180–185.

Peterson, C., & Seligman, M. E. (2004). *Character strengths and virtues.* New York: Oxford University Press.

Schmuck, P., & Sheldon, K. M. (2001). *Life-goals and well-being.* Gottingen: Hogrefe & Huber.

Staudinger, U. (1999). Older and wiser? Integrating results on the relationship between age and wisdom-related performance. *International Journal of Behavioral Development, 23*, 641–664.

Steigmann-Gall, R. (2003). *The holy reich.* New York: Cambridge University Press.

Sternberg, R. J. (1990). Wisdom and its relations to intelligence and creativity. In R. J. Sternberg (Ed.), *Wisdom: Its nature, origins, and development* (pp. 142–159). Cambridge: Cambridge University Press.

Sternberg, R. J. (2002, October 4). *Wisdom, schooling, and society.* Paper presented at the First International Positive Psychology Summit, Washington, DC.

Vaillant, G. (2002). *Aging well: Surprising guideposts to a happier life from the landmark Harvard Study of Adult Development.* Boston: Little, Brown.

Wilson, D. S. (2002). *Darwin's cathedral: Religion and the nature of society.* Chicago: University of Chicago Press.

Wilson. E. O. (1994). *Naturalist.* Washington, DC: Island Press.

Wink, P., & Helson, R. (1997). Practical and transcendent wisdom: Their nature and some longitudinal findings. *Journal of Adult Development, 4*, 1–15.

PART IV

WISDOM IN SOCIETY

10

Morality, Ethics, and Wisdom

Joel J. Kupperman

A prelude to determining the role (if any) of wisdom in ethics and morality is to gain some sense of what wisdom might be. Ideally, this would be based on evidence that would satisfy the requirements of experimental psychology. However, experimental psychology is usually at its best when there is a clear and reasonably precise idea of what is being tested. Until we have a clear and reasonably precise idea of wisdom, we may have difficulty in determining, for example, which of a group of subjects could be considered to be wise. It may be that "wisdom" falls (along with such concepts as "freedom" and "democracy") in the territory of what W. B. Gallie (1964) termed "essentially contestable." If so, the difficulty can persist.

To say this is consistent with the thought that our discourse about wisdom, along with what are contained in what a great many people take as sources of wisdom, does converge on a general characterization of the kind of thing that wisdom is. This is one of the conclusions to be argued for in this chapter. Rival ways of thinking, each of which satisfies the general characterization of what wisdom is, can then differ about whether certain choices or ways of life are (or are not) wise.

In arriving at any general characterization of wisdom, and of its relations with morality and ethics, we may have to look at forms of evidence that are somewhat tentative. These include psychological research that relies on judgments (that may or may not be entirely reliable) that certain people or certain choices are wise. There also will be evidence that perhaps is inferior to that provided by experimental psychology. Reports (including self-reports) of people's lives can seem illuminating, even if one would very much like more independent confirmation than is available.

Even jokes can be suggestive. One group of jokes includes versions of something like the following. A seeker after truth climbs a mountain to ask the guru at the top what the secret of the universe is. The answer is "everything converges on oneness." The climber replies "Surely you are kidding." "You mean it doesn't?" the guru asks. Even if the leveling impulse in jokes that portray a supposedly "wise" person as a fool is obvious, they may tell us something useful: about what wisdom in our ordinary sense is not.

Forms of Knowledge

It may help the reader to have an outline of the argument that runs through this section. It is as follows:

> Wisdom is primarily a form of knowing-how.
>
> It is portrayed in "wisdom literature" most fundamentally as knowledge of how to live. The knowledge that wisdom represents must be exhibited in the wise person's life.
>
> Hence, actual lives fill out the meanings of what are presented as wise pronouncements, which by themselves may be cryptic.
>
> All of this is compatible with the thought that humans are imperfect, and even someone who is wise will perform better in some areas than in others.
>
> Sternberg's (1998) Balance Theory accords (with some qualifications) with what has traditionally been thought of as wisdom, in ordinary discourse, and also as central to what has been called "wisdom literature." The qualifications emerge depending on whether one looks at wisdom in terms of a whole life, or as embodied in specific judgments.

A fundamental distinction, which was a staple of analytic philosophy in the middle third of the 20th century, is between knowing-how and knowing-that (Ryle, 1945–1946). Both sides of the distinction are more complex and varied than at first one might think. Knowing-that can be a matter of mastery of isolated facts, so that one can give a correct answer to a specific question. At the opposite extreme, it can involve a sophisticated theory and understanding both of it and of virtually everything that is relevant to it. Knowing-how can involve specific skills, such as knowing how to ride a bicycle. More complex forms include knowing how to sustain satisfying human relationships, and (even more broadly) knowing how to live.

Furthermore, like so many distinctions, this one is not as sharp as it might look. There is room for gray areas and for mixed forms of knowledge. Knowing higher mathematics, which looks at first like a form of knowing-that, requires knowing how to complete proofs and solve problems in higher mathematics. Knowing how to sustain satisfying human relationships would be impossible for someone who does not know that it is stupid to treat with contempt people who are close to you.

Nevertheless, this basic distinction is a start. The first, most obvious, point then is that wisdom includes a large element of knowing-how. A naive person who thinks that really important knowledge must have a pronounced intellectual dimension, and hence can be captured in a formulation, might miss this point. The joke in which the supposedly wise person explains the secret of the universe, and looks like a fool, capitalizes on this. It illuminates a common mistake: that (one might think) the core of wisdom consists of a concise gem of knowing-that. But any relevant knowing-that is almost meaningless (and can be shaky or worthless) except in the context of a pervasive pattern of knowing how to live well.

This is a point that is made repeatedly in virtually all of the classics of Indian and Chinese philosophy, works that often are placed in the category of "wisdom literature." Zen Buddhism (much of whose literature comes from China, where it was known as Chan Buddhism) especially ridicules people who think that wisdom can consist of intellectualized formulas. There is the story of Tokusan, a scholarly monk, who one day stops for tea while carrying his commentary on the Diamond Sutra. The tea lady asks what it is, and then says, "I read that sutra which says 'The past mind cannot be held, the present mind cannot be held, the future mind cannot be held.' You wish some tea and refreshments. Which mind do you propose to use for them?" Tokusan, shaken, asks her if she knows a good teacher; and another story shows him (after his mind is opened) burning his commentaries on the sutras (Reps & Senzaki, 1985, pp. 142–143). One point of the story is that scholarly learning is much less important than a basic change in one's personal outlook, and that scholarly learning can actually get in the way of this basic change. A somewhat similar (but more moderate) turn of thought shows up in Plato's *Republic*, in the insistence that at the highest level of knowledge the knower becomes the known: " ... the virtue of wisdom more than anything else contains a divine element which always remains, and by this conversion is rendered useful and profitable ... " (Plato, trans. 1937, 518, vol. 1, pp. 518).[1]

Plato makes it clear, in the *Republic* and elsewhere, that wisdom centers on knowledge of The Good (Plato, 506–509, vol. 1 pp. 767–771). Hence, it must be exhibited in knowing how to live, which includes good choices and also high-quality states of one's soul. Again, there is a similar insistence running through virtually all of the classics of Indian and Chinese philosophy, although in some cases the general point would be put in somewhat different terms.

Because of this, recommendations of what is said to be a wise way to live inevitably point beyond the words to an actual life or lives. It is no accident that two leading examples, the *Dialogues* of Plato and the *Analects* of Confucius, contain what amount to biographical portraits of Socrates and Confucius. The *Analects* of Confucius, which was compiled during the generations after Confucius' death by his students and their students, illustrates a related point. It consists of a large number of short entries, which together have been widely regarded as a major source of wisdom. But at first reading almost all of it seems both bland and cryptic. Because of the central concern with how to live, brief statements of purported wisdom usually do seem cryptic (absent a strong sense of the kind of life that accords with them), and often seem merely high-minded and bland.

Arriving at a sense of the meaning of the *Analects* requires a kind of lateral integration, in which patterns in the mosaic of its entries begin to emerge. It is possible to reconstruct an integrated philosophy, including a pattern of implicit argument (Hall & Ames, 1987; Kupperman 2001, chap. 4). But the descriptions of Confucius as a human being play a part in this.

Reading the *Analects* also requires an ability to relate short remarks to one's personal experience and observation. The meaning has to be filled out from one's own resources. This fits Confucius' remark (Confucius, trans. 1938, Book VII, 8) that the student he prefers is one who, presented with one corner of a subject, will come back with the other three.[2]

The crucial fact here is that much of what is encompassed in being a wise person has aspects that cannot be captured in formulations. This

---

[1] All references to Plato's *Dialogues* are from Jowett (1937).
[2] Confucius passages are from Waley (1938).

has implications for the nature of the wisdom, taking us back to the point that it is primarily a form of knowing how to live. It also suggests that some intellectualized ways of acquiring wisdom would not be effective, and that a role model – preferably one with whom one could interact – would normally be crucial.

In a variety of accounts, both Asian and Western, the process of acquiring wisdom is presented as – first and foremost – a transformation of self. Education of the emotions often plays a major role in this. Kramer (1990) has commented on the reciprocal interaction of cognitive and affective development in the production of wisdom-related skills or processes. This certainly fits the philosophical literature that claims to portray wisdom.

It might seem that the image of wisdom to be gained from this literature verges on perfection. It is true that much of it centers on figures (such as Socrates, Confucius, Buddha, Daoist eccentrics, or gurus of various sorts) whose lives are supposed to exhibit the form of wisdom that is being endorsed; and often not much time is devoted to revealing flaws or imperfections in these figures. But there are certainly exceptions. Confucius presents an exceptionally clear picture of a purportedly wise person who was keenly aware of personal fallibility, and who recommended strongly that you be alert to the possibility of suboptimal performance (and learn from the people around you).

Confucius (Book V, 26) makes it clear that he thinks it important to take seriously one's own faults, but says that it is rare to find someone who takes this very seriously. He represents himself (Book VII, 1, 2, and 3) as disquieted by his shortcomings. He was anxious to get to know people with different views (Book XVIII, 5 and 7). There is one report (Book XVII, 20) of what, from his general point of view, might have seemed suboptimal behavior: He is deliberately rude and instructs someone to tell a lie. (He had a messenger [from a man who had disgraced himself] told that he was in ill health.) When the messenger was leaving, he took up his zithern (a stringed instrument) and sang loudly. It may well have been though that these deviations from his normal style of behavior would have seemed, in the context of everything else, refreshing.

A paradox of wisdom is that someone who thinks he or she is wise is likely to be overpositive, obstinate, and egotistic – and hence is very unlikely to be wise. Confucius (trans. 1938, Book IX, 4) is described in the *Analects* as taking nothing for granted when he was not sure, and is said never to have been over-positive, obstinate, or egotistic. "Do I regard myself as a possessor of wisdom?," he asks (Book IX, 7). "Far from it. But if even a simple peasant comes in all sincerity and asks me a question, I am ready to thrash the matter out, with all its pros and cons, to the very end."

The discussion thus far suggests that wisdom is a kind of practical knowledge. Furthermore, it is not equivalent to the practical knowledge or prudence associated with ordinary self-seeking behavior, although some elements of this may fall out from wisdom. The altruistic dimension of wisdom emerges in Sternberg's (1990) account of sagacity, especially in the element of concern for others. This is certainly an important part of what distinguishes wisdom from mere cunning. Orwoll and Perlmutter (1990) put the point well in speaking of the "ability to transcend the self, that is, to move beyond individualistic concerns to more collective or universal issues." Clearly there are moments at which wisdom is displayed in ways in which a person can act for her or his own good, but we would normally not term a person wise who did not also act for the good of others and of society in a way that reflected superior knowledge (Staudinger, 1996).

The relation between wisdom and prudence is complex. Living wisely is widely agreed to be (at least usually) on the whole personally advantageous. It follows that pursuing a wise life will in general meet the standards of prudence, although much of what we call prudence is quite separate from wisdom. (Philosophers as different from one another as Plato, Confucius, Bishop Joseph Butler [1726/1983], and David Hume [1739/1978] have held that the merely cunning person who lacks due concern for others will actually miss important values, and hence will not meet the standards of prudence.)

The territory of wisdom – where it is displayed – is difficult choices. As Baltes and Smith (1990) point out, "wisdom involves good judgment and advice about important but uncertain matters of life" (p. 95). Let me suggest that important but uncertain matters of life include (a) determining what is morally acceptable or obligatory in cases of a nonstandard sort, (b) arriving at a strategy for attaining various goals when there is some degree of ambiguity or uncertainty in relevant factors, (c) arriving at a good sense of desirable goals in one's life, (d) deciding decent and helpful ways to behave in relation to other people, or (e) deciding how to advise others in any of these areas. The know-how in these cases includes and requires forms of knowing-that. These include knowledge of what has high, low, or negative value, and of how people normally react to events in their lives, of how things tend to play out in the long run, of risks, of what one's own emotional responses in certain situations tend to be, and of which ways of treating other people are conducive to satisfactory relationships. These forms of knowing-that typically require experience, usually over a considerable period of time.

It might be nice to end this section with a definition of wisdom. But any philosopher of a Wittgensteinian bent will be skeptical of the ability of even a reasonable definition or a good theory to capture fully the meaning of a word or phrase. We can say more about what wisdom is in the course of commenting on Sternberg's (1998) Balance Theory.

This theory has many features that, in effect, this chapter's discussion already has endorsed. It centers wisdom on "tacit knowledge," viewing it as primarily a form of knowing how, and focuses on wisdom as inherent in the interaction between an individual and a situational context. Wisdom further is "defined as the application of tacit knowledge as mediated by values toward the goal of achieving a common good . . . " (Sternberg, 1998, p. 353).

This seems very right if wisdom is viewed (as traditional "wisdom literature" does) primarily in a whole-life perspective. In fact though, wisdom is commonly spoken of in two different contexts. One is when a person is spoken of as wise or unwise. Here it seems to me that the Balance Theory is entirely right. The other is when choices or policies are spoken of as wise or as unwise. Here qualifications are necessary.

Examples may help. It is wise not to plan projects entirely in terms of "best case" scenarios: There should be tolerances or fallback strategies to deal with glitches, unexpected impediments, and so on. It is unwise, if there are tense relations with an angry and volatile group of people, systematically to humiliate them. It often would be unwise for a professional who has congenial working relations to accept a position at a somewhat more prestigious institution at which prospective colleagues are troubled and deeply divided. It is often wise, by contrast, not to allow cooperative and helpful instincts to go so far as to drain away most of the time needed for one's own projects.

In all of these cases, the decision maker's primary focus is on her or his well-being. How does wisdom differ here from ordinary practical intelligence? Part of the answer is that there is no sharp difference in terms of thought processes that can be made explicit. We tend to use words like "wise" and "unwise" when the good solutions require something beyond routine calculation, when they demand a broader perspective derived from considerable experience of life. But still the focus is on "What would benefit *me* in the long run?"

The Balance Theory still does have a kind of indirect bearing. We could consider a counterfactual: What if the decisions that benefit me would cause real damage to a number of other people? If it were to turn out to be that they would cause real damage, we would not term the self-interested decisions "wise," but would use some other word, such as "clever" or "cunning." So there is an implicit "balance" constraint, even when (because nothing suggests a threat of harm to others) there is no reason to worry about anything other than one's own interests.

Ethics and Morality

The argument that runs through this section and the following one will be that reliably good performance in the choices that fall within morality, or more broadly in ethics, requires what amounts to wisdom.

The words "ethics" and "morality" have ordinary meanings, but they also are philosophers' terms of art. Not surprisingly, different philosophers use them differently. What follows will develop one use of "ethics" and "morality" that seems to do justice to much that is contained in the ordinary meanings. It will be a use in which "ethics" emerges as a broad term that includes morality. This will prepare us to consider, first, the role of wisdom in relation to morality, and then secondly, the role of wisdom in parts of ethics outside of morality.

Ethics has sometimes been presented as the study of morality. This has been especially congenial to philosophers who wished to assume that philosophical accounts of morality could be and should be morally neutral. This assumption was attacked by Iris Murdoch (1957) early on, and was later undermined by the work of philosophers such as John Rawls (1971). It is no longer the dominant view.

An alternative account is to regard morality as a specialized region within a more general picture of how we should behave in life. What makes morality special? One possibility is that it centers on a sense of "wrong," such that we tend to think that someone who chooses what is "wrong" in this sense should be punished (see Mill, 1861/1979, chap. V, para. 14, p. 47–48). The "punishment" could consist of informal social pressures or a sense of guilt.

This would not be a common response to someone who chooses the wrong fork with which to eat the salad course. But that is a different sense of "wrong." The moral sense of "wrong" is very common in relation to murderers, torturers, and more generally those who wantonly harm innocent people. Such acts are immoral; using the wrong fork is not, nor is foolishly drinking into the night before taking an important exam.

Given this usage of "immoral" and "morally wrong," one might think of morality as a zone of high pressure recommendations and judgments within ethics (Strawson, 1961; see also Kupperman, 1983, chap. 1). Ethics includes a range of judgments, not only about how we should behave, but also about the kind of life that is most rewarding for a human being. Aristotle's *Nicomachean Ethics*, for example, begins with a careful and judicious examination of what is most worth seeking in a human life. The *Analects* of Confucius is generally viewed as presenting Confucius' ethics, but relatively few of the judgments presented are of what we would normally consider moral issues. There is no sharp line drawn between, on one hand, issues involving serious mistreatment of innocent people, and, on the other, insensitive or disrespectful treatment of family members or more generally crude and tasteless behavior.

It is a commonplace among scholars of classical Chinese philosophy, as among many scholars of classical Greek philosophy, that there is no category name that is a good translation of our word "morality." That does not mean, of course, that there are not matters considered by philosophers such as Confucius and Aristotle that we would regard as moral issues. Indeed such matters tend to be treated with especial seriousness by the philosophers.

A slightly different model of what morality is would view it as concerned with obligations taken as especially demanding (Williams, 1985, chap. 10). We have obligations to respond to invitations, and instructors may feel obligated to erase the blackboard at the end of class. But neither of these normally qualifies as moral obligation. The obligation to save someone (whom you easily could rescue) from drowning normally does.

Many moral determinations can look quite easy to arrive at. As children we are taught a collection of broad, general rules that prohibit killing innocent people, rape, torture, theft, and so on. There is no logical requirement that such rules be so broad and general; but it is extremely useful, in the teaching of small children and in forming adult mindsets and inhibitions, that they be so (Kupperman, 2002). Judgment of the normal case of murder, rape, or theft as a result requires very little thought.

Aristotle's treatment of the mean in Book II of the *Nichomachean Ethics*, though, is designed to focus on judgments (some of them, judgments that we would consider moral) that are not so easy to make. What counts in Aristotle's account as following the mean is in fact a case-sensitive way of adjusting one's conduct to the particular factors of the present situation. There is also a Confucian *Doctrine of the Mean*, according to tradition written by Confucius's grandson; it was translated under that title by James Legge (1870), and recently again (as *Focusing the Familiar*) by Hall and Ames (2001).

Both the foolhardy person and the coward, to give an example, have a consistency of behavior: One always advances into danger, and the other always avoids it. The courageous person's behavior, in contrast, depends on her or his judgment of whether there is a goal in prospect that is worth the risks. If the answer is no, the courageous person on that occasion makes the same sort of decision as the coward; if the answer is yes, the decision is like that of the foolhardy person.

Some of these "hard cases" will involve moral issues. Generosity is a mean between being too free with money and being stingy; there are serious moral issues of whether or not one should help someone who badly needs help. Similar issues occur in relation to moral rules that generally are reliable but may well have exceptions. Any reader can easily think of cases in which, under certain peculiar circumstances, it might not be easy to decide whether stealing something is morally justified. For those readers who balk, there is Lawrence Kohlberg's (1981) example of a man whose only chance of saving his dying wife is to steal a drug from an extortionate pharmacist. We can see that moral issues, which in the most familiar examples usually look fairly easy, can be quite difficult.

A natural thought is that some superior powers of judgment, which might be related to wisdom, are relevant here. This is essentially the answer suggested by both Aristotle and the Confucians. Aristotle in fact says, in relation to matters of the noble and the pleasant, that the good man is "as it were the norm and measure of them" (Barnes 1984, p. 1113a).[3]

This is a very preliminary case for regarding wisdom as playing a major role in making possible really good moral judgment. How about the rest of ethics? One contrast between Aristotle and Confucius is this. There are long discussions of friendship here and there in Aristotle, but for the most part his discussion of that portion of interpersonal relations in which the decisions are not what we would normally term "moral" is rather schematic. The bits and pieces of Confucius's *Analects* add up to a much larger treatment of how interpersonal relations can be conducted well or badly, and more generally of the values of everyday life.

---

[3] Aristotle passages are from the edition by Barnes (1984).

Confucius' position is that what is required to conduct interpersonal relations well is not an isolated set of skills, but rather is connected to the nature of one's self. If we think of a child as having a nature, then someone who has learned to conduct interpersonal relations well has in effect constructed a second nature, becoming a more refined sort of person. This is a difficult educational process. A running theme in the Confucian literature is that it must be gradual, requiring sustained attention.

Confucius' great (4th century B.C.) follower Mencius makes this point in a joke about a farmer from Sung who comes home exhausted, telling his family that he has been working hard to make the plants grow. When the family members go to look at the results, they discover that his tugging has pulled the plants out of the ground (Mencius, trans. 1970, Book 2, A.2). [4] The message is that to expect transformation of one's personhood to be rapid is unwise and counterproductive.

Much of the *Analects* in fact is devoted to examination of the ways in which someone, starting out with what in broad outline are good tendencies, can develop into someone whose interpersonal relations are of a high order. Nuance, style, and the underlying attitude expressed in behavior are crucial. In the treatment of aged parents, for example, it is "the demeanor that is difficult" (Book II. 8).

The personal freedom and spontaneity that develop when an effective style of personal interactions becomes second nature are very gratifying. Social interactions (including what we would term moral choices) then become a species of what Csikszentmihalyi (1990) has called "flow."

This suggests a thesis about the values that might be sought after in a life. The most persistent and secure ones are those involved in recurring activities of a high quality. Only the sage-like person who has achieved these values, through constructing an appropriate second nature, will know this. In effect, wisdom is required to know what is most important in life.

The values that the average person most desires (money, property, prestige, etc.) are sometimes fleeting, and in general depend heavily on the attitudes and behavior of others. Because of this, Confucius holds that the average person tends to look for luck, and is anxious and insecure. Only someone who knows what is important, and has developed the right sort of second nature, can really enjoy life and be serene. There

---

[4] Mencius passages are from Lau (1970).

can be other rewards: Mencius (Book 2, A.2) specifically mentions a high energy level.

Such a person also will be comfortable with ambiguity, partly because the sage-like person can deal with ambiguity and partly because values known to be really important will usually not be at stake. This connects with Sternberg's finding (1990) that the wise person is comfortable with ambiguity and "can be serene in the face of challenges that would distress the less wise" (p. 155).

Aristotle advances a thesis somewhat similar to that of Confucius: that only someone who has developed and exercises virtues (which include "intellectual" virtues as well as virtues in personal interactions) can have a high degree of *eudaemonia* (usually translated as happiness or as well-being, and clearly requiring both), and that this high degree of *eudaemonia* is relatively secure. In the survey (in Book I of the *Nicomachean Ethics*) of competing views of what *eudaemonia* is, it is clear that inadequate views lead to inadequate lives. Something very like wisdom enables one to know what *eudaemonia* is, and the person who has this is in a position to have a life of high quality.

These comments on Confucian philosophy and on Aristotle can be taken as pointing to a *prima facie* case for holding that wisdom is a major factor in (and perhaps is required for) both a very good pattern of moral choice, and also more broadly a sense of what the most important values to aim for in life are. Views of this sort are the norm in classical Greek philosophy (including Plato's and also stoicism and epicureanism), and also in classical Indian and Chinese philosophy, even though what is considered to be wisdom varies from philosophy to philosophy.

It may be useful briefly to outline this for three other traditions: the Indian tradition that centers on the *Upanishads* and the *Bhagavad Gita*, that of Buddhist philosophy, and that of Chinese Daoism (Taoism). In the first of these, true wisdom centers on really knowing the identity of the personal innermost self (*atman*) with the entire universe (Brahman). The knowledge required here goes far beyond being able to give the right answer. True knowledge is not intellectual or formulaic, but rather requires seeing and responding to the world in terms of this identity, which amounts to seeing through the illusion of an individual personal nature.

A long process of personal reshaping is required for this. As a result, meditational practices and more general techniques for enlightenment (yoga) developed in this tradition. The wisdom that results is assumed to guarantee acceptable moral choice, and also will include knowledge of what is really most valuable in life (i.e., the fulfillment and release brought by thorough awareness of the identity). This is first and foremost the position of the *Upanishads*. Nothing in the *Bhagavad Gita* conflicts with this, but the *Gita* adds an elaborate account of alternative routes to the wisdom of impersonality. (For an expanded account of the philosophical arguments here, and of the cultural roots, see Kupperman, 2001, chaps 1 and 3.)

The wisdom that Buddha regards as crucial follows from the doctrine of *anatman* (that there is no *atman*). In the light of this wisdom, desires wither away. If there is no substantial "me" (whether its nature is irreducibly individual or not), desires lose their point. Good (altruistic and compassionate) moral choice naturally follows from this, and wisdom must lead to a sense of what is important in life: a detached, mildly compassionate set of attitudes that includes peacefulness and some inner joy (see Collins, 1982).

The wisdom that Daoism purports to offer does not have a single central thesis, but rather consists of a radical openness of thought and emotion (rejecting fixed categories and required responses), which makes possible a harmonious existence in the face of continuous change in the world. Does this contribute to moral judgment? The great 4th-century (B.C.) Daoist text the *Chuang Tzu* (*Zhuangzi*) seems to suggest a limited skepticism of morality: An excessive or artificial virtue is portrayed as toxic.

The warmth of the sun might be taken as analogous to virtue. *Chuang Tzu* refers to the old Chinese myth about the ten suns, which used to take turns (in the old 10-day week) rising above the earth. One day they all came up at once, scorching the earth and threatening to destroy life. The world was saved when a superhero archer shot out nine of the suns (Christie, 1968, p. 62).

Much of the *Chuang Tzu* is sardonic or downright joky. Confucius, the ultimate socially responsible do-gooder, is repeatedly parodied, usually being satirized as someone who is trying to get the hang of Daoism. Hence when (Graham 1981, chap. 2) the legendary emperor Shun is represented as saying "Formerly ten suns rose side by side and all the myriad things were all illumined, and how much more by a man in whom the Power is brighter than the sun," this must be taken as heavily ironic. In the Daoist view, anyone who tries too strenuously to change the world is dangerous to know.

Nevertheless, there is an idea in the Daoist texts of something like good moral behavior. It is low-key, unobtrusive, and does not try to dominate events. (A view that is not entirely dissimilar is suggested when the Confucian philosopher Mencius cautions against "trying to dominate people through goodness" [Lau, 1970, Book 4.B.].) Daoist wisdom enables one to know how to behave in this naturally decent way. It also is presumed to enable us to realize that what is most important in life is the kind of spontaneity and emotional freedom that the rejection of fixed categories and required responses makes possible.

Much of this also was incorporated into Zen Buddhism, which includes other elements as well, including Buddha's prohibition of any taking of life. How such wisdom works its way into actual practice, especially within a larger community, is a separate matter (typically involving selective willingness to be influenced), which lies outside of the scope of this paper. Here is an example, though, of selective willingness to be influenced. The medieval samurai were known for a casual attitude to taking human life, but some of them (under the influence of Zen) became vegetarians (see Frederic, 1972, p. 73).

It should be clear that there are many competing systems of wisdom. Furthermore, they do not all have exactly the same form. Arguably all of them assign some role to personal experience and also to reflective thought. But some (e.g., Buddha's) place great emphasis on reflective thought leading to some general principles; Confucius, in contrast, places the greatest emphasis on creative immersion in a cultural tradition, buttressed by personal experience. In Daoism, the emphasis is on disciplined stripping away of required responses and conformist attitudes: "The Way is gained by daily loss" (Blakney, 1955, Poem 48). Despite the differences, it is possible to think that more than one system of wisdom has considerable merit, and someone might, to a degree, combine elements of two or more in one's life. It is often said that for centuries many educated Chinese combined Confucianism and Daoism in their lives.

Wisdom and Morality

Let us for the sake of argument assume that something like one or another of the models of wisdom that have been outlined (or some amalgam of models) is valid. It still may be wondered how important this can be for morality. Surely anyone can be virtuous, without necessarily possessing wisdom?

One influential view is that moral judgments must always be made on the basis of principle. Indeed, we commonly speak of virtuous people as "women (or men) of principle." Once one locates or remembers the appropriate principle, it provides (in this view) what amounts to an algorithm for moral judgment. Of course, there are disagreements about how principles are to be formulated or employed. One might, because of these, think of, say, Kantians and utilitarians as like providers of rival morality software systems.

Given this story of what morality is, one might well think that wisdom is irrelevant and unnecessary in relation to morality. All that is needed is a steady good will in following good principles. Virtually everyone can be presumed to know what is morally right and what is morally wrong, so that the emphasis will fall on the steady good will.

This story of what morality is, however, is far too simple. Kant (1785/1981, p. 3) points out very early in the *Grundlagen* that morality requires judgment to relate cases to principles. In the second part of the *Metaphysics of Morals*, Kant (1797/1996) emphasizes the role of casuistry, when interpretation of principles is required. If Kantian morality is thought of as a kind of morality software, then we need to add that it cannot itself interpret, into the language of the software, the cases to be judged.

Beyond this, the rigorism (the insistence that general rules do not have exceptions) that is often associated with Kant's ethics is no longer considered by many reflective people to be acceptable. Most of us think that there are occasions on which it is quite right to lie or not to keep a promise, and that there could be situations in which stealing would be justified. The morality system by itself cannot readily tell us when these occasions would be. One might hope to arrive at formulations of exceptions; but in practice what is to be formulated turns out to be too complex, multifaceted, and slippery. Further, it looks as if a morality that includes such formulations will be so prolix and hard to retamorein that it will fail to fulfill many of the normal functions of a moral order.

Legal scholars often distinguish between "hard cases" and ordinary cases in the law. The former typically involve conflicts or tensions between precedents or accepted principles. A mark of a hard case is that no solution will seem obviously, unproblematically right to an unbiased person. In much this way, we might distinguish between hard cases and easy cases in morality. Easy cases are ones in which a reasonable solution is readily apparent to anyone who has learned the traditional moral rules. We all know that you should not take the opportunity to kill a neighbor just because he or she is disagreeable. If someone implements the wrong solution, it is usually assumed that the cause is weakness of will rather than lack of knowledge of what is right.

An adage among legal scholars is that "hard cases make bad law," and for similar reasons hard moral cases are very difficult to integrate into a moral code. Kohlberg's case of the man who could save his wife's life only if he steals the necessary medicine is an example. My sense, for what it is worth, is that Kohlberg radically under-describes his case – there is more one would like to know before accepting Kohlberg's view of it – but at the least it suggests the possibility of hard cases, ones that many people would judge constitute exceptions to the rule. There is no reason to assume that we can arrive at a precise formulation that would enable us to judge these cases with assurance. Contemporary debates about whether it might be acceptable to torture terrorists if this seemed the only way to obtain information that would be likely to save numbers of lives provide another example of this difficulty.

There is an insistence running through much of classical Greek, and also Confucian, philosophy that genuine virtue requires reliably good performance across the range of serious decisions that justify societal involvement (the ones that we would term moral decisions). Someone whose performance is reliably good only in easy cases, or only when not subject to disorienting pressures or temptations, would not in this view count as really virtuous. In favorable (e.g., prosperous, stable, and secure) circumstances, one might get the impression that most people are morally virtuous. But the view running through Confucianism and much of classical Greek philosophy is that this is a mistake.

This is because morally acceptable behavior is usually not so demanding, at least for most people in a prosperous, stable, and secure society. How much effort has the reader devoted in the last few months to not murdering, raping, torturing, or stealing? For many of us, a normal pattern of generally morally acceptable behavior represents passing a rather easy test.

In a well-regulated society, most of us early on get in the habit of following the major rules. It is true that this habit sometimes can be broken if a temptation is sufficiently alluring. But also the habit may not serve us well in situations that seem so different from the normal that it may look as if the familiar rules do not apply. In such cases, someone can become genuinely convinced that the sort of thing that used to be considered morally wrong now is (in the changed circumstances) quite acceptable.

The psychologist Stanley Milgram (1974) cleverly constructed a situation in which groups of people might think that normal rules of behavior did not apply. Experimental subjects were instructed to administer electric shocks of increasing severity to someone (who they thought was another experimental volunteer, but actually was a stooge) on the other side of a glass partition if he failed in certain learning tasks. The man on the other side of the partition (deliberately) kept failing, leading the subjects to administer what they thought were shocks of increasing voltage. Any subject who, moved by the man's apparent distress, questioned the procedure was told, "The experiment must go on." More than 60% did go on, past the point at which the shocks were supposedly dangerous.

Because of their perceptions of lapses under pressure, neither Plato nor Aristotle or Confucius would have been disturbed by the results of the Milgram experiment. They all thought that genuinely virtuous people represented a small minority of the population. The vast majority, in their view, would behave well or badly depending on circumstance. In the Confucian texts this comes out in Mencius' remark (Book 6, A.7) that in good years the young men are mostly lazy, and in bad years are mostly violent. Confucius (Book VIII, 9) had said that the vast majority of people can be made to follow the Way, but not to understand it.

A similar view emerges in Plato's *Republic*, especially at three points. The most familiar is the Myth of the Cave, which begins Book VII. This is an image of the great majority of the human race as confined to perceiving only indirect reflections of reality. The implication is that only a few have a direct image of reality, including real goodness.

There is also in Book II (359) the story of the shepherd who discovers a ring that can make its wearer invisible. We might assume that he previously had behaved virtuously; but it does not take him long to realize that, armed with the ring, he can get away with anything, and in the end he commits serious crimes and becomes a tyrant. The insinuation is that virtually everyone would in the end succumb to this temptation, but the reader is meant to think that someone like Socrates (because of what he values in life) would not. Finally, there is the story in Book X (614–621) of the man who has a near-death experience in which he sees the souls in Hades choosing new lives. One of these, who has previously behaved virtuously as a citizen of a well-ordered community, chooses the glittering, evil, and ruinous life of a tyrant. Perhaps this might be surprising, but the comment is that his previous "virtue" (619) was a matter of habit and not philosophy. Any reader who thinks that the view that only a minority of people who usually behave virtuously have genuine virtue is limited to ancient philosophy might be referred to Mark Twain's (1899/1985) story "The Man That Corrupted Hadleyburg."

In circumstances that are different from those of the familiar, "normal" case, one has to make a judgment call. Perhaps the special circumstances of the case at hand call for something different from what had been one's normal behavior? Sometimes, especially given hindsight, we realize that the answer was no. Most of Milgram's subjects made what amounted to a moral mistake. So have those who, under great pressure (and thinking perhaps that there was a new social reality, with different standards), collaborated with dictatorial regimes. During the rule of the Thirty Tyrants in Athens, five citizens including Socrates were ordered to arrest one Leon of Salamis (who one presumes was an innocent man) and bring him to justice. The risks of defying the order would have been obvious. Everyone except Socrates complied. Socrates simply went home, and as luck would have it was not punished (*Apology*, 32). We now would regard it as obvious that Socrates made the right moral choice, and the others made the wrong one.

By contrast, sometimes the answer is yes. It may be that, in changed circumstances, one can do a great deal of good (and little harm) by behaving differently from one's norm. It is because of such cases that Confucius (Book XVIII, 8) said that he had no inflexible "thou shalt or thou shalt not." The person who refuses can emerge as narrow and rigid. Perhaps some would reach for such a verdict if the husband, in Kohlberg's example, refused to steal the medicine to save his wife's life, or if parents treated a teenage daughter who had "sinned" in the punitive and thoroughly unsympathetic way that is said to have been more common a hundred years ago.

It is in part because of such possibilities, I think, that Confucius (Book XVII, 13) remarked that "the 'honest villager' spoils true virtue." A standard interpretation of this is the one provided by Mencius (Book 7, B.37): The honest villager is motivated too strongly by desire for approval, and hence acts with the wrong attitude. In the condensed Confucian style, though, it is possible to mean two or more things in the same utterance. Confucius may have been saying that the honest villager has the wrong attitude (and because of this, will make conformist choices in circumstances in which they are not at all appropriate), and *also* that the honest villager's judgment in difficult cases will be highly flawed (so that he will self-righteously do something that is rigid and intolerant).

Aristotle and the Confucians agree on the importance, in cases many of which we would regard as involving moral judgment, of finding the mean. They agree that what is crucial in such cases includes sensitivity to the particular circumstances (as opposed to merely following a general rule). It also is plausible for each to suppose that awareness of the particular circumstances will include a sense of what the likely consequences would be of various possible courses of action.

There are subtle differences between the two positions. There is more emphasis in the *Analects* on the importance of taking other people's views and responses seriously as possible indicators of one's own mistakes (see Book IX. 4; see also IX. 7, IX. 24, XIV. 32, XV. 29). It is clear that in Confucius's view wise choices can benefit from discussion and dialogue (see Sternberg, 1985; Baltes & Staudinger, 1996; Staudinger, 1996).

These two philosophies outline a strong case for regarding forms of intelligent judgment that are reflective and experience-based as crucial to many difficult moral decisions. It seems reasonable to think, as many leading ancient philosophers did, that someone who is not capable of these forms of intelligent moral judgment does not meet the high standards of genuine moral virtue. (Some lower form of praise might be appropriate, such as "Will behave virtuously in situations that are not disorienting and as long as things are going reasonably well.")

Furthermore, the forms of intelligent moral judgment that are required in the Aristotelian and Confucian models amount to what would generally be considered wisdom. (John Kekes [1983] has before me emphasized the way in which judgment of hard cases requires wisdom.) The judgment required goes well beyond mere intelligent awareness of what particular situations are like. Implicit in both the Aristotelian and Confucian models is an agent's personal commitment to doing what is best, and a notion of what is best that includes the concern for others is incorporated in Sternberg's (1990) recent formulation of sagacity. To be a morally good person in difficult or disorienting circumstances, in short, requires more than habits of behaving well and more than intelligence of an ordinary sort. It requires a kind of wisdom.

Wisdom and the Rest of Ethics

Ethics earlier was characterized as the study of how best to live, including what the major features would be of a rewarding life. This leaves room for a heterogeneous collection of questions that for various reasons do not meet the threshold level of social urgency required for something to be a moral issue or decision. We can label these as the zone of the "submoral." Behavior toward others that is crude, insensitive, and/or somewhat selfish would not normally be termed immoral, although many ethical philosophies would advise against it. Being a "jerk" does not violate morality. Foolishness and lack of care in pursuing personal projects also do not rise to the level of immorality. In the early modern period, sometimes – especially in puritan societies – laziness was treated as a kind of immorality; but it has long since crossed the line into the territory of the undesirable-but-not-immoral. The portion of ethics outside of morality also includes the question of what is most important in a rewarding life, a central concern for Plato, Aristotle, and most ancient Indian and Chinese philosophers.

As we will see, a case can be made for assigning wisdom a crucial role in any superior performance in any of these areas. There may be some initial doubts in relation to the second of the three, that concerned with the success of personal projects. Surely, it may be thought, this is a matter of prudence, and there is a sharp difference between prudence and wisdom. Clearly there is a difference, but the argument will be that at very high levels of prudence the difference is not at all sharp.

The argument in relation to submoral matters of interpersonal relations parallels the one already given in relation to morality. There the main point was that there are important cases in which a simple stance of rule-following might well be inadequate. Good choices in such cases typically require sensitivity to the features of the particular case, and judgment of what is appropriate. This judgment in turn requires wide experience of a variety of situations, and the way in which choices often play out, all of this guided by concern for (and sensitivity to) the interests of others as well as one's own. The superior level of judgment and sensitivity involved in good decisions in such hard cases amounts to what would normally be called wisdom.

All of this often applies to what is involved in very good performance (i.e., in producing mutually satisfactory and harmonious connections) in submoral matters of interpersonal relations. Indeed, the wisdom factor tends to be even more pronounced in this area. Here is the reason: Style, nuance, and evidence of personal attitude are factors that often have little weight in the high-pressure decisions of morality. If what is at issue is whether to kill, torture, steal from, or break promises to someone, it normally hardly matters what the style of the performance is. If the killer sneers at the victim, this may make us loathe the killer even more; but after all, the important thing is, "Should you kill or not?" Add to this the fact that the great majority of moral decisions concern behavior toward people with whom one has hardly any personal relationship to speak of, so that in these cases the after-effects of style and attitude are very often not important.

The style and attitude of someone's behavior, in contrast, will have a major effect on her or his personal relationships. It is true that sometimes the broad nature of what one chooses to do can make a real difference, and reasonably can inspire gratitude or resentment. Above and beyond such highlights, though, a relationship can be deeply affected by the characteristic style of behavior as much as by specific decisions between sharply discrete alternatives. The attitude that comes through will have a major effect on the quality of the relationship. Recall Confucius' observation that in the treatment of parents, "it is the demeanor that is difficult."

Qualities of style and of the attitude that is conveyed are not easy to monitor or to control. Friends can play a crucial role, both in monitoring and in efforts to change, which is one reason why David Hume (1739/1978) spoke of "mirroring fellow minds" in the development of character. A self-critical attitude helps (Sternberg, 1996). In the end, a very good style of personal interaction and desirable manifestations of attitude will normally require becoming a certain kind of person: a person for whom the very good style has become second nature, and who genuinely has the desirable attitudes and feels comfortable with them. This is central to the Confucian ideal.

Good styles of personal interaction also have a feature that makes them difficult to talk about. It is possible adequately to formulate many choices in life, including the vast majority of moral choices, by means of verbal formulas. The choice, that is, will be between this and that; and the "this" and the "that" can be pretty well spelled out in words. No doubt one could also speak of a choice between serving food to one's aged parents in a surly way or in a manner that expresses warmth and gratitude for what they have done. But the style and attitude involved in the huge number of continuous bits of behavior toward friends, family, coworkers, and so on often do not lend themselves to crisp formulation. Differences can be subtle and elusive, and yet be cumulatively felt.

In some sense all of this, because it largely consists of voluntary behavior, is a matter of choice. But by and large, it cannot be a matter of conscious choice, especially in that conscious choice would usually have difficulty in finding the verbal formulations of alternatives that would give it traction. Because so many of the choices are very difficult to talk about, the excellences they call for (and what might lead to them) also are difficult to talk about. This is one of the reasons why the Confucian program of educating oneself to be sage-like is so subtle, and is indicated in such oblique ways.

Our present concern though is with what is required for superior performance in this area. The point to be made is this. It already has been argued that because of the "hard" cases involved in finding the mean, an intellectualized reliance on a set of verbal formulas is hardly sufficient for superior moral performance. It inevitably will be flawed, and sometimes will lead to serious mistakes. What we have seen of submoral matters of personal relations, though, makes the prospects for any intellectualized reliance on a set of verbal formulas look even worse – much worse – in this area. Try learning from a book about how to be a charming, spontaneous person who makes others (when not inappropriate) feel good about themselves.

What is needed is a deeply internalized kind of knowing-how that normally does not require pauses and time to think. This knowing-how must be responsive to the moods, needs, and responses of the persons with whom one interacts. There must also be some experiential sense of how various kinds of interaction play out in the long run. All of this approximates one kind of what normally would be considered wisdom. Furthermore, in this area, there is little competition from intellectualized formulas, which might be thought of as a clumsy cousin of wisdom.

What, then, about the submoral choices related to the success of personal projects, and more broadly to self-interest? Most of these seem matters of prudence, although not all: There is ample room for doubt as to whether the successful conduct of risky or self-destructive projects can be subsumed under this heading. Many submoral choices centering on personal projects do call for something that resembles wisdom in one or two features, especially in sensitivity to local conditions and awareness of how things generally play out in the long run.

It is clear that what – seen across a person's life – we consider wisdom cannot merely be sheer self-interest, and that in some matters due weight given to the interests of others must be a prominent element. There is a widespread and arguable assumption, though, that some of our submoral decisions, including ones crucial to our success in life, either do not have a corresponding importance for other people or (alternatively) will be beneficial for them if they are beneficial for us. In such cases there can be a kind of wisdom in sensitivity to local conditions and awareness of how things normally play out. We would tend not to call it wisdom though (downgrading it to cunning or mere prudence) if other people's interests became salient and the agent nevertheless did not give them due weight.

There also is an argument, developed by the early-18th-century philosopher Bishop Joseph Butler (1726/1983) and then endorsed by Hume (1739/1978), that enlightened self-interest actually requires altruism. The core of the argument is that it makes no clear sense to speak of self-interest except in relation to a variety of things that an agent cares about. Someone who is guided almost entirely by direct calculations of self-interest will (in this self-referential personal world) have an impoverished range of possible satisfactions. Caring about other people greatly expands the range of possible satisfactions.

There also is the obvious point that the submoral choices involving general considerations of self-interest are best made if one chooses a long-term stance of cooperativeness and moderate altruism. This also would hold for submoral choices in relation to the success of personal projects, to the degree to which this success might depend on other people's cooperation or restraint in interfering. At the highest level of skill this would require a fine sense of how to keep other people happy, how to balance their interests against one's own so that in the long run everyone would be happy, and the ability not to go for immediate advantages at the cost of long-term deterioration in personal relations (and long-term disadvantages). All of this seems very like what we would normally term "wisdom."

Finally, the realm of the submoral includes the element of judgment of values. Much of what we have been discussing arguably is related to this element. It also is indicated by John Kekes's (1983) claim that the knowledge involved in wisdom concerns the means to good ends. What constitutes good ends is a matter that requires judgment of values.

Certainly, reliable moral judgment in disorienting circumstances or in the face of temptation is facilitated by an appropriately strong sense of what is really important in life. Plato plainly believed that, whatever the rest of us might do, Socrates would not employ the ring of invisibility for selfish ends. Given what he considered valuable in life, he would hardly imagine any genuine use for it. Also the wise policy of considering the wishes and interests of those involved in one's projects (as well as one's own interest) is not likely to be available to someone who does not realize the value of the psychological rewards of continuous harmonious and cooperative relations with others.

Judgments of values are often difficult to make. Happiness contains an implicit positive value judgment of one's life, but such a judgment all the same is corrigible. If someone, as a result of an accident, has a right-side frontal lobotomy and then is happy as a clam, we need not conclude that this is a wonderful life; on the contrary, we are usually sorry for the person. If someone is very happy as a result of completing a collection of bottle caps, or finally having visited all 50 state capitals (both of these attainments that most of us would think of as fairly trivial), a normal response would be "Get a life." A running theme in much ancient philosophy, including that of Plato, Aristotle, and Confucius, is that most people lack appreciation of what is most important in life.

Experience makes a difference. I have argued elsewhere (Kupperman, 2003) that, much as being an eyewitness puts someone in a better position to know whether something happened (although not all eyewitness reports will be correct), having experienced something puts one in a better position to know whether it has value. In addition, there is an implicit comparative element in judgments of value. David Hume (1742/1985) contends that no one who has not read great poetry is in a position to know how very good a poem is. In much this way, some experience of unusually deep values that are possible in life will enable someone to have perspective on the wide variety of available values.

Conclusion

Depth of personal experience and the ability to have appropriate perspective are important elements in what we normally think of as wisdom. There is a running argument in a great deal of ancient philosophy (Greek, Chinese, and Indian) that the sense of what is important that the depth and perspective contribute to will inform personal projects and the general conduct of life. Wisdom, in these views, is primarily a form of knowing-how. Most fundamentally, it is a matter of knowing how to live. Because of this, the knowledge that wisdom represents must be exhibited in the wise person's life. Someone who wishes to acquire wisdom therefore is well-advised to find good role models whose lives provide a full sense of what wisdom can be like.

Some "wisdom literature," especially the philosophy of Confucius, strongly recommends a habit of self-criticism. Wisdom, in this view, is incompatible with smugness and complacency. There is a paradox of wisdom that follows from this: Anyone who thinks that he or she is wise very probably is not.

Wisdom implies a general concern, as Sternberg's (1998) Balance Theory claims, for the common good. This concern, however, is not necessarily triggered in every decision that we would term "wise." Often such decisions are purely ones of self-interest, except for the side-constraint that if others' interests *were* seriously damaged this would have to be taken into account.

Wisdom has an important role in relation to morality because of hard cases, ones in which disorientation or extreme pressure or temptation are major factors. (Someone with good habits who lacks wisdom can make virtuous choices in easy cases. Plato, Aristotle, and Confucius all argued though that genuine virtue requires wise choices in hard cases.)

Wisdom also is required for optimal decisions about the values that are worth aiming for in a life. These values underlie a wide range of personal decisions, and a number of philosophers have argued that it is impossible to live well if one lacks an adequate sense of what is truly important and what is not important. There also are a wide range of choices, including most of those involved in social relations, that can matter to the quality of a life even though they do not involve the social urgency characteristic of moral choices. These "submoral" choices are best if they are informed by the range of experience and the sensitivity to detail that are characteristic of wisdom.

References

Baltes, P. B., and Smith, J. (1990). Toward a psychology of wisdom and its ontogenesis. In R. J. Sternberg (Ed.), *Wisdom: Its nature, origins, and development* (pp. 87–120). Cambridge: Cambridge University Press.

Baltes, P. B., and Staudinger, U. (1996). Interactive minds in a life-span perspective: prologue. In P. Baltes and U. Staudinger (Eds.), *Interactive minds: Life-span perspectives on the social foundation of cognition* (pp. 1–32). Cambridge: Cambridge University Press.

Barnes, J. (Ed.) (1984). *The complete works of Aristotle* (vol. 2). Princeton, NJ: Princeton University Press.

Blakney, R. B. (Trans.) (1955). *The way of life (Daodejing)*. New York: Mentor.

Butler, (Bishop) J. (1726/1983). *Five sermons*. Indianapolis, IN: Hackett.

Christie, A. (1968). *Chinese mythology*. London: Hamlyn.

Collins, S. (1982). *Selfless persons*. Cambridge: Cambridge University Press.

Csikszentmihalyi, M. (1990). *Flow: The Psychology of Optimal Experience*. New York: Harper and Row.

Frederic, L. (1972). *Daily life in Japan at the time of the samurai,1185–1603*, (Eileen M. Lowe, Trans.). New York: Praeger. (Original work published 1967).

Gallie, W. B. (1964). *Philosophy and the historical understanding*. London: Chatto and Windus.

Graham, A. C. (Trans.) (1981). *The seven inner chapters and other writings from the book Chuang Tzu*. London: Geo. Allen & Unwin.

Hall, D., & Ames, R. (1987). *Thinking through Confucius*. Albany: SUNY Press.

Hall, D., & Ames, R. (2001). *Focusing the familiar.* Honolulu: University of Hawaii Press.

Hume, D. (1739/1978). *Treatise of human nature,* 2nd ed. (L. A. Selby-Bigge, Ed.; P. H. Nidditch, Rev.). Oxford: Clarendon Press.

Hume, D. (1742/1985). On the standard of taste. In Eugene Miller (Ed.), *Hume's essays* (pp. 226–249). Indianapolis: Liberty Fund.

Jowett, B. (Trans.). (1937). *The Dialogues of Plato* (2 vols.). New York: Random House.

Kant, I. (1785/1981). *Grounding of morality* (James Ellington, Trans.). Indianapolis: Hackett.

Kant, I. (1797/1996). Metaphysical principles of the doctrine of virtue, Part II of *The metaphysics of morals* (Mary Gregor, Trans.). Cambridge: Cambridge University Press.

Kekes, J. (1983). Wisdom. *American Philosophical Quarterly, 20,* 277–286.

Kohlberg, L. (1981). *The philosophy of moral development: Moral stages and the idea of justice.* San Francisco: Harper and Row.

Kramer, D. (1990). Conceptualizing wisdom: The primacy of affect-cognition. In R.J. Sternberg (Ed.), *Wisdom: Its nature, origins, and development* (pp. 279–313). Cambridge: Cambridge University Press.

Kupperman, J. J. (1983). *The foundations of morality.* London: Geo. Allen & Unwin.

Kupperman, J. J. (2001). *Classic Asian philosophy: A guide to the essential texts.* New York: Oxford University Press.

Kupperman, J. J. (2002). A messy derivation of the categorical imperative. *Philosophy, 77,* 485–502.

Kupperman, J. J. (2003). *The epistemology of intrinsic value,* Duke/University of North Carolina Workshop on Intrinsic Value.

Lau, D. C. (Trans.). (1970). *Mencius.* Harmondsworth: Penguin Books.

Legge, J. (Trans.). (1870). Doctrine of the mean, in *Chinese Classics, vol. 1.* New York: Hurst & Co.

Milgram, S. (1974). *Obedience to authority.* London: Tavistock.

Mill, J. S. (1861/1979). *Utilitarianism.* G. Sher (Ed.). Indianapolis, IN: Hackett.

Murdoch, I. (1957). Metaphysics and ethics. In D. F. Pears (Ed.), *The nature of metaphysics* (pp. 99–123). London: Macmillan.

Orwall, L., & Perlmutter, M. (1990). The study of wise persons: Integrating a personality perspective. In R. J. Sternberg (Ed.), *Wisdom: Its nature, origins, and development* (pp. 160–177). Cambridge: Cambridge University Press.

Rawls, J. (1971). *A theory of justice.* Cambridge, MA: Harvard University Press.

Reps, P., & Senzaki, N. (Eds). (1985). *Zen flesh, zen bones.* Boston: Tuttle.

Ryle, G. (1945–6). Knowing how and knowing that. *Proceedings of the Aristotelian Society* XXXXVI, 1–16.

Staudinger, U. (1996). Wisdom and the social-interactive foundation of the mind. In P. B. Baltes & U. Staudinger (Eds.), *Interactive minds* (pp. 276–315). Cambridge: Cambridge University Press.

Sternberg, R. J. (1985). Implicit theories of intelligence, creativity, and wisdom. *Journal of Personality and Social Psychology, 49,* 607–627.

Sternberg, R. J. (1990). Wisdom and its relations to intelligence and creativity. In R. J. Sternberg (Ed.), *Wisdom: Its nature, origins, and development* (pp. 142–159). Cambridge: Cambridge University Press.

Sternberg, R. J. (1996). Styles of thinking. In P. B. Baltes & Ursula Staudinger (Eds.), *Interactive minds* (pp. 347–365). Cambridge: Cambridge University Press.

Sternberg, R. J. (1998). A balance theory of wisdom. *Review of General Psychology*, 2, 347–365.

Strawson, P. F. (1961). Social morality and individual ideals. *Philosophy, 36*, 1–17.

Twain, M. (1899/1985). The man that corrupted Hadleyburg. In J. Kaplan (Ed.), *Mark Twain's short stories* (pp. 400–442). New York: Signet.

Waley, A. (Trans.). (1938). *The analects of Confucius*. New York: Vintage.

Williams, B. (1985). *Ethics and the limits of philosophy*. London: Fontana.

Wittgenstein, L. (1953). *Philosophical investigations*, (G. E. M. Anscombe, Trans., with parallel German text). London: Macmillan.

11

Crossing Boundaries to Generative Wisdom

An Analysis of Professional Work

Jeffrey L. Solomon, Paula Marshall,
and Howard Gardner

In a famous 1837 address, Ralph Waldo Emerson exhorted "professionals" – including the "American scholars" of his audience – to undertake their work wisely.[1] By this, Emerson meant looking beyond both remote matters and minutiae to become "the world's eye" and "the world's heart." Such professionals should "resist the vulgar prosperity that retrogrades ever to barbarism, by preserving and communicating heroic sentiments, noble biographies, melodious verse, and the conclusions of history." In today's world, Emerson's call for professionals to aspire to the lofty goal of societal stewardship is likely to sound both naive and decidedly out of character with the nature of contemporary professions. After all, the professions of the early 21st century – medicine, accounting, law, and the like – are beset by unprecedented economic, ethical, and technological challenges that were unimaginable in Emerson's day.

Despite these challenges, however, there are individual professionals who embody an Emersonian type of commitment to advancing the well-being of society, and, in particular, to establishing the conditions for successive generations to flourish. In our research on "good work" we have identified professionals whose work has the qualities of what we call *generative wisdom*; that is, particular products, outcomes, or initiatives that are geared toward enhancing the welfare of generations to

[1] "The American Scholar." Originally delivered in 1837 at Harvard University and published in 2000 in *The Essential Writings of Ralph Waldo Emerson*. New York: The Modern Library. The professions as we know them did not exist in Emerson's time; he was referring to the educated classes of society who influenced various realms of work and society as a whole.

come. These professionals' work is marked by a concern for creating what Csikszentmihalyi (1993) calls "harmonious" conditions for humanity writ large (future descendents included). This type of wisdom is *generative* in the sense in which Erikson used the term: "a concern in establishing and guiding the next generation" (1963, p. 267).

Professionals develop generative wisdom by adhering to three mental models of *boundary crossing*. They go beyond conventional understanding or knowledge, they see beyond the here and now, and they undertake work that goes beyond traditional professional boundaries.[2] Using this cognitive triptych as a starting point, our purpose in this chapter is to establish a model for explaining generative wisdom and to provide detailed examples of professionals who exhibit it.

Going beyond conventional understanding or knowledge is the most obvious part of what generatively wise professionals do. This expansion of purview actively entails creating novel ideas or products, asking new questions about phenomena, viewing things in a different light, or developing alternative professional identities. Each of these means of going beyond conventional understanding or knowledge represents a divergence from established ways of conducting professional work. Novel ideas or products represent outcomes hitherto unimagined and/or unattainable and point to new conceptualizations about the applications of professional work. Asking new questions about phenomena, as well as viewing things in a new light, points to alternate approaches to problems and other important matters germane to one's professional focus. Developing alternative professional identities refers to a recasting of how professionals regard the purpose and meaning of what they do. In all of these cases, going beyond conventional understanding or knowledge is a step toward creating paradigm shifts in the professions (Gardner, 1993; Kuhn, 1970).

Seeing beyond the here and now entails the capacity to link one's work with consequences that will become apparent beyond one's own lifetime. Although generatively wise professionals certainly hope that

---

[2] Simonton's (2000) concepts of "crosstraining" and "cross-talk" among creative professionals overlap with our boundary-crossing framework. Simonton notes that "expertise must be wide and diverse rather than narrow and specialized" among those who are creative. He further adds that "some discussions of the creative process have underlined the importance of cross-talk between separate projects, including projects that may have no apparent connection with each other" (p. 288). Other scholars who have dealt with these ideas include Gruber, 1974; Hargens, 1978; Root-Bernstein, Bernstein, & Garnier, 1993; Simon, 1974; and Tweney, 1990.

their work has direct applications they might themselves witness, they recognize that the problems addressed in their work are complex and deep-rooted enough that true solutions must be given adequate time to take root and develop. Wise professionals undertake their work with the expectation that successive generations will reap the benefits of their endeavors.

Undertaking work that goes beyond traditional professional boundaries stems from the recognition that adhering to the established methods and epistemologies associated with one profession might be limiting and not necessarily effective in helping one to achieve desired goals. This type of boundary-crossing is related to developing alternative professional identities. The difference, however, is that going beyond professional boundaries concerns transcending the widely agreed-on methods and mechanisms of a domain of work, whereas developing new identities has more to do with how generatively wise professionals conceive of what it means to be a professional in the broader sense. Because these professionals view the problems they are addressing as the result of multiple, complex and, at times, conflicting causes, it is perhaps not surprising that the solutions they espouse are an assemblage of methods and conceptual frameworks.

What, then, is a professional? We adhere to a broad definition, based on the one proffered by Gardner, Csikszentmihalyi, and Damon (2001). In this view, professionals are the "individual practitioners [who] define the specific knowledge, skills, practices, rules and values that differentiate them from the rest of the culture" (p. 21). In some cases professional domains are sharply drawn, meaning that professionals employ skills and knowledge that are highly specialized and for very specific purposes. The practice of clinical medicine is the classic example of such domain specialization: Physicians have specialized knowledge of the human body, as well as skills put to use specifically for the diagnosis and treatment of illness.

Some domains are more loosely demarcated. In these cases, there are relatively broad conceptualizations of what constitutes professional work. In journalism, for example, what counts as "journalistic" includes the daily reporting of events, investigative reporting, news analyses, editorials, talk television/radio, and essays. Professionals in journalism and other loosely demarcated domains tend to bring to their work a wide range of experiences and skills; one need not obtain a degree in journalism, for instance, to become a journalist. Still, journalists are quite judgmental about individuals who claim to be journalists but who, like Matt Drudge, do not authenticate rumors one person reports; and they expel from their ranks individuals like Jayson Blair, a reporter who fabricated stories and who plagiarized from other publications.

Literature on Wisdom

The concept of generative wisdom overlaps with an epistemological orientation found in the scholarly literature. More specifically, boundary-crossing is conceptually related to definitions of wisdom emphasizing seeing, knowing, or understanding dimensions of experience that are not readily apparent. For example, Labouvie-Vief (1990) describes wisdom as the result of integrating two modes of knowing (translate *logos* and *mythos*) commonly assumed to be incompatible. Baltes and Smith (1990) conceptualize wisdom as "exceptional insight into human development," especially concerning "important but uncertain matters of life" (p. 87). Orwoll and Perlmutter (1990) note that wisdom entails developing a "deep understanding of philosophical and epistemological issues" and a "transcendence of conventional levels of self-absorption" (p. 162). In these examples, as well as others (see, for instance, Arlin, 1990; Kramer, 1990; and Meacham, 1990), wisdom is framed as a means of seeing beyond common understandings or as having unusual degrees of insight into a particular realm of good life.

A second area of overlap between our framework and the literature concerns viewing wisdom as the by-product of an ongoing engagement with particular contexts. The professionals in our research must gauge their thoughts and actions against the continually shifting contexts of world events, their professions writ large, the narrower confines of their day-to-day work environments, and their personal life experiences. As an example of the theoretical foundation for such psychological gauging, Sternberg (1998) posits a "balance theory of wisdom," which is premised on the notion that wisdom is "inherent in the interaction between an individual and a situational context." He goes on to explain that one must balance:

multiple intrapersonal, interpersonal, and extrapersonal interests . . . in order to achieve a balance among responses to environmental contexts: adaptation to existing environmental contexts, shaping of existing environmental contexts, and selection of new environmental contexts. (p. 353)

Csikszentmihalyi and Rathunde (1998) draw on a Piagetian framework to construct a person–environment interaction theory of wisdom development. Wise people, they argue, have the "capacity to move toward optimal experiences by understanding the dynamic relation of self and environment," involving "the need to accommodate to avoid anxiety and disorder, and the need to assimilate to avoid boredom and stagnation" (pp. 662–663). There is no end state to the process of accommodation and assimilation; rather, it is ongoing, arising from shifting environmental conditions and personal needs.

Our conceptual framework diverges from previous wisdom scholarship in two important ways. First, we focus on specific contexts of professional work. Although, as we have noted, some scholars emphasize the importance of context in developing wisdom, their work is primarily theoretical. In this chapter we move beyond a theory of context to examine how wisdom plays out in actual professional situations.

Second, our analysis of wisdom is based on open-ended, in-depth interviews with professionals (read on for specifics), whereas most other research has entailed eliciting subjects' responses to questionnaires and other more close-ended prompts in controlled settings (cf. Baltes & Smith, 1990; Chandler & Holliday, 1990; Kitchener & Brenner, 1990). Our view is that open-ended interviews allow subjects a high degree of flexibility to address subjectively salient matters (the emic perspective). The more we can understand what is relevant to subjects' lived experiences, the greater our analytical powers become for making sense of how wisdom manifests itself in people's lives.

Theoretical Framing

Wisdom is a distinct way of knowing, or an epistemological "take" on life. Goodman (1978) refers to such epistemological realms like art, science, politics as "worlds," and he makes the important point that not only are various worlds permeable, but they are themselves built up out of the elements of other worlds. Goodman refers to the process of constructing worlds as "worldmaking," and he states that "worldmaking as we know it always starts from worlds already on hand; the making is the remaking" (p. 6). Our view is that wisdom is a world that is predicated on elements from other worlds.

Goodman outlines several possible worldmaking paths, the most relevant for our purposes being "composition and decomposition." Goodman explains this process as follows:

Much but by no means all worldmaking consists of taking apart and putting together, often conjointly: on the one hand, of dividing wholes into parts and partitioning kinds into subspecies, analyzing complexes into component features, drawing distinctions; on the other hand, of composing wholes and kinds out of parts and members and subclasses, combining features into complexes, and making connections. (1978, pp. 7–8)

Worldmaking is relevant for understanding boundary crossing, as each of the three types can be considered key "parts" out of which the "whole" of generative wisdom is constructed. Wise professionals continuously mix and match boundary crossings, variously drawing on some types but not others in response to changing circumstances. In essence, worldmaking is an ongoing and iterative process.

Boundary crossing is the defining cognition that shapes generative wisdom; however, there are other contexts that wise professionals draw on that support the framework of generative wisdom. Such contexts include unique personal circumstances, childhood influences, one's personality, the state of one's professional domain, institutional cultures, and broader social/global events.

But how do professionals go about worldmaking? Lévi-Strauss's (1966) concept of *bricolage* offers a useful framework for understanding the type of human agency underlying worldmaking and, ultimately, generative wisdom. Bricolage refers to the tendency of people to solve problems or create products in an iterative, nonlinear, and fluid manner. The defining feature of a *bricoleur* (literally "handyman" in French) is that he or she integrates various ideas and materials from diverse contexts that, on the surface, might appear unrelated and even inherently incompatible, and yet, when combined, represent novel ways of responding to and shaping social contexts. As Lévi-Strauss explains:

[The bricoleur's] first practical step is retrospective. He has to turn back to an already existent set made up of tools and materials, to consider or reconsider what it contains and, finally and above all, to engage in a sort of dialogue with it and, before choosing between them, to index the possible answers which the whole set can offer to his problem. He interrogates all the heterogeneous objects of which his treasury is composed to discover what each of them could 'signify' and so contribute to the definition of a set which has yet to materialize but which will ultimately differ from the instrumental set only in the internal disposition of its parts. (1966, p. 18)

Professionals, then, are bricoleurs in their own right. They continuously draw on the "tools" at their disposal in varying combinations to work toward meeting their professional goals.

The Research Study

The data for our model come from a multiyear national study of the professions called the Good Work Project. Since 1995, investigators at

Harvard, Stanford, Claremont Graduate Universities, and the University of Chicago have been researching how professionals in a wide range of domains carry out work that is at once high in quality and embodies principles of social responsibility. Through in-depth, face-to-face interviews lasting roughly·two hours, researchers have so far proved how nearly 1,000 high-achieving professionals in a wide range of domains – including journalism, genetics, higher education, medical education, philanthropy, law, and business, among others – strive to do "good work."[3] The interviews have focused on subjects' professional goals and values, their formative influences, challenges confronting their work, and the nature and extent of support for their work (emotional, structural, financial), among other topics.

Our study of good work was not designed initially to investigate generative wisdom. Instead, we selected subjects' interview transcripts for inclusion in our analysis retrospectively, based on their widely known leadership in shaping the direction of their professional domains and their tendency to integrate diverse professional and disciplinary perspectives into their work. We then undertook a qualitative analysis that entailed identifying common themes and patterns across subjects' work lives, as reported both in their transcripts and in what is publicly known about them. In other words, our conceptualization of generative wisdom as a phenomenon, *sui generis*, grew out of drawing on evidence from both *etic* (objectively known) and *emic* (subjective perceptions) sources of data.

Examples of Generative Wisdom

We now turn to examples of generative wisdom, drawn from the lives of six professionals. In keeping with our framework, we divide the examples into three types of boundary-crossing: going beyond conventional understanding or knowledge, seeing beyond the here and now, and going beyond traditional professional boundaries. We wish to emphasize that the types of boundary-crossing are interdependent, although we separate them throughout this chapter for purposes of analysis.

Going beyond Conventional Understanding or Knowledge

Albert Bloom's work as the president of Swarthmore College represents an example of going beyond conventional understandings of

---

[3] The principal investigators of the Good Work Project are Howard Gardner, Mihaly Csikszentmihalyi, and William Damon. For more information on the research, see *Good Work: When Excellence and Ethics Meet* (2001), *Making Good* (2004), and http://www.goodworkproject.org.

what an institution of higher learning can be. In essence, by drawing on the Quaker tradition of Swarthmore as well as gathering support from others, Bloom's leadership has helped to redefine the identity of a college, thereby providing a potential model to be emulated by other institutions.

The place to start understanding Bloom's work is his vision for Swarthmore. Bloom's objective is to make the college a place where, as he says, through "rigorous intellectual pursuit," American society is viewed as existing in an inescapable and complex global web. He has encouraged this view through curricular reforms (teaching non-Western perspectives on literature and economics, for example) and various programs that provide students with opportunities to translate classroom learning into "shaping a better world." By this latter point Bloom means building on the values of "intellectual seriousness" and "ethical responsibility" that are "anchored in [Swarthmore's] Quaker tradition" so that students can take their "training and actually use it in a socially relevant way while they are here." Such experiences provide students with opportunities to "ground . . . theories in practice" and "see how complex the reality is compared to . . . parsimonious theories and come up with an appreciation for the complexities of that kind of work."

An example of a program that strives to achieve these objectives places engineering, biology, and theater students in a remote region of Poland that is facing serious environmental and social problems. The engineering and biology students collaborate with their Polish counterparts to figure out strategies for translating academic ideas into practical solutions for restoring the integrity of a local river. Their task is made all the more difficult because of the challenges of navigating a foreign language and culture. The theater students work with Polish colleagues to produce works designed to encourage innovative thinking about abiding social maladies and, ultimately, to act as a "spur to economic and social development of communities that have been . . . left to deteriorate in a world where Warsaw has all the investment and the small communities in Poland are . . . remote and not touched by that."

Fully realizing Bloom's vision of Swarthmore has entailed refashioning the organization – and, ultimately – the identity of the college. In the fall of 2001 Bloom, backed by the board of trustees, announced the disbanding of the football program. At first glance this action might not appear terribly bold, especially at a place known for its academic rigor, not its athletic accomplishments. And yet, the decision proved to be highly contentious and divisive. Sports programs have come to be viewed as a natural part of the collegiate experience, not just by students, but by parents, administrators, and perhaps most important, by alumni. Therefore, it is in the context of strong opposition by key constituents that Bloom's decision must be understood.

Bloom came to realize that the high cost of maintaining a football program – despite its popularity – drained resources from his vision of the college as a place devoted to the kind of intellectual inquiry that would sustain innovative programs like the one in Poland. As he noted:

> There were two choices. Either you [accept to Swarthmore] more kids for athletic talent as opposed to other kinds of talents, in addition to being intellectually engaged and exciting and ethically responsible because that's the base of anyone we take. But in addition to that you want to take some kids who are interested in music and other kids who are interested in engineering and other kids who have a lot of experience in social change in poor communities. And they do overlap some, but they don't overlap as much as would allow you to fill your athletic teams with leadership unless you recruit specifically taking athletic talent into account.

In adhering to his view that "education excellence . . . requires [institutional] change in order to preserve that mission," Bloom has helped to mold a new collegiate identity that goes beyond conventional understandings of what compromises higher learning. In an era when many institutions devote millions of dollars to football programs, and pay coaches high salaries (often at the expense of library and other core academic budgets), Bloom's action appears path-breaking.[4]

For Bloom, going beyond conventional understandings of what comprises an institution of higher learning is informed by the worlds of the two other types of boundary-crossing. He sees beyond the here and now by aligning the mission, structure, and culture of Swarthmore to achieve projected future goals that will help ensure institutional distinctiveness (and therefore viability) for the next generation. Furthermore, Bloom's work strives to make Swarthmore a place where students (and faculty) undertake work that goes beyond traditional disciplinary boundaries. As an example, the program in Poland is structured to provide students with exposure to a different language and culture, as well as to types of problems – and proposed methods (collaboration with Polish colleagues) – they are unlikely to have encountered before.

---

[4] Bowen and Levin (2003) note that even at selective liberal arts colleges, which typically do not provide athletic scholarships, student athletes do less well academically than their nonathlete peers, because of the all-consuming nature of sports.

But Bloom's vision is not all his own. As he acknowledges, he draws on the traditional Quaker values of Swarthmore to frame and legitimate his ideas. Convergence between Bloom's personal views and the culture of the college – even if not complete – is essential to satisfy the board of trustees, alumni, and students, and, ultimately, to be successful in his work.

A second example of going beyond conventional understanding or knowledge can be found in the work of Charles Ogletree, a Harvard law professor and practicing defense attorney.[5] Ogletree's work represents a shift away from the traditional lawyer's objective of winning individual cases to redressing overlooked and misunderstood discrepancies in the legal system. To understand Ogletree's mission, a bit of background is necessary.

The prevailing attitude among both politicians and the public at large is that the inequities that once so glaringly afflicted U.S. society have been sufficiently addressed. A common refrain is that the Civil Rights Act is the crowning legislative achievement to ensure that African Americans and other disenfranchised groups are protected by the rule of law to the same extent as other segments of the population. Because many Americans view this measure as adequate, a widespread argument is that social relations should be organized according to "laissez-faire" (or meritocracy-based) principles, rather than through further tinkering with systemic or legislative mechanisms.

The problem Ogletree (and others) have recognized is that despite laws "on the books," and espoused principles of equal justice before the law, the actual workings of the legal system tend to disadvantage African Americans. Ogletree adheres to a strict commitment to ensure that all his clients receive what he calls "zealous" representation. He accomplishes his mission by adhering to a twofold strategy. First, Ogletree works to ensure that legal procedures and principles are adhered to for his disadvantaged clients to the same extent as for the rest of the populace. He does so by pointing out cases when key players in the legal system, such as police officers, attorneys, or judges, apply different, and therefore compromised, standards to particular groups of people (racial profiling being just one example).

---

[5] After this chapter went to press we learned that Charles Ogletree, by his own admission, inadvertently did not attribute a passage in his most recent book to the proper source. Despite this well-publicized professional lapse, our view remains that Ogletree exhibits generative wisdom in the areas of his work that are the focus of our discussion.

Ogletree's second strategy for zealous representation is what he calls a "client-centered approach." In addition to rigorous legal representation, Ogletree's philosophy is that lawyers should tend to the full range of human needs presented by their clients. He explains his view:

> If we really want to talk about helping clients, [lawyers should] help them think about changing their lives, their goals and objectives, and give some meaningful help. We have to be not just lawyers, but counselors, social workers, psychologists, ministers, and any other number of roles to provide true comfort and support to clients.... You can represent somebody and get an acquittal, but that gives you little opportunity to talk about what brought the person there: poverty, despair, depression, anxiety, neglect, abuse.... I [explain to students]: "Don't just look at the result, but try to figure out how this person found himself in this position."

For Ogletree, his commitment to zealous representation ensues from his "steadfast [belief] in defending the indefensible, the unpopular, the despised. Because I think that we can't have a just system unless we are willing to defend those that many people criticize and despair."

Because of the inherently adversarial nature of the legal system (prosecutors versus defense attorneys), lawyers have traditionally focused on winning individual cases to establish an impressive track record. Ogletree, too, shared this mentality earlier in his career. He notes:

> [My] goals have changed over time. I think originally [my] interest was in winning and the philosophy of: "It's us against the world."... I have matured in my thinking about what I do as a lawyer. When I was a young lawyer winning case after case, I always looked forward to celebrating the win. And as I moved forward in my life, the celebration was less important to me.... My goal now is ... [doing] more [systemic] reform so that I don't have to try to win a case [to begin with]. Can I change the system? ... I understand that no matter how many cases I win, if the system is still broken, then these are hollow victories.... It's not that I don't like winning.... It's that it's an incomplete exercise, as far as I am concerned.

Ogletree spent "half his career making a very modest salary for clients who couldn't afford to pay" and representing clients regardless of race or economic status. To this day, he continues to apply the same standard of representation to those in need. Over the years, however, his circumstances have changed. Through the visibility afforded him as a Harvard professor, and through his deliberate attempts to represent high-profile clients[6] as a means of focusing public attention on universal injustices,

---

[6] Ogletree has represented many clients, from Anita Hill to the reparation movement.

that is, racial discrimination, profiling, and so on, Charles Ogletree offers an example of a defense attorney whose work has shifted from the more narrow and traditional role of striving to win, to the less well-understood realm of cracks in the legal system. In essence, Ogletree is striving to ensure that the rights of a democratic society are extended to all of its inhabitants for generations to come.

Ogletree's professional convictions are rooted in the world of experiencing discrimination during childhood. He explains:

> As a young child growing up in Merced, California, I am very familiar with the criminal justice system. From an early age I witnessed police treat people differently based on race and class. If you were poor or black you had fewer rights and very little respect from law enforcement authorities. And so I was primarily interested in criminal law as a means of changing the way the police respond to people who are poor or black.

During college, Ogletree became riveted by the trial of the wrongfully indicted political activist Angela Davis. His attendance at the trial reinforced his convictions about racial inequities in the legal system and led to his decision to become a lawyer. Furthermore, when Ogletree formed a student organization to lobby for Davis's release, she personally encouraged him to broaden the mission of the group to encompass injustices writ large, instead of focusing on her particular case. Davis's push to look broadly at inequities made an indelible mark on Ogletree.

Clearly, Ogletree's vision of going beyond conventional understandings is influenced by his ability to see beyond the here and now. By shifting his attention from individual cases to a reformation of the justice system, Ogletree is striving to create a more equitable society for future generations.

At the same time, Ogletree goes beyond traditional professional boundaries by practicing a type of law that he understands to be embedded in larger social structures. The individual client – the traditional focus for lawyers – is emblematic of a greater whole.

Seeing beyond the Here and Now

Worldwide hunger is an urgent matter of the here and now. As Frances Moore Lappé has striven to convey, however, the causes are complex and therefore do not lend themselves to being rectified in the short term. Lappé is a social activist, critic, and writer, as well as founder of organizations that address social injustices and inequities. She has played a pivotal role in shaping attitudes and beliefs regarding the causes of global hunger and the bases for socially responsible and healthy eating. In her influential book, *Diet for a Small Planet*, as well as in subsequent books, projects and organizations, Lappé has shown that lack of food is not the result of outright scarcity. Lappé has gone beyond traditional understandings of the causes of hunger (what she calls a prevalent "myth") to show that there is an abundance of food in the world, and yet, because of various political arrangements, adequate supplies often do not end up in those countries most in need of it.

It is a cruel irony that what many people need most today they are unlikely to receive, not only today, but within their lifetimes. Lappé acknowledges that the benefits of her work – shedding light on obstacles to alleviating hunger – will most likely be experienced by successive generations. As she explains:

> I've just always assumed all my life that what I'm working on is larger than my lifetime.... I really believe that if you want to do something that is truly significant you can't expect to see the rewards for a long time.... The extreme deprivation, the ill health of society, is a result of patterns of thought and behavior in systems that have been put in place over hundreds and hundreds of years.... It's just completely illogical to me to think that in one short lifetime – or certainly one short adult lifetime – you could see the impact in the systemic sense. You could just hope... to be as strategic as possible in moving history, in having a historical impact over strains that are developing way beyond your own individual life.

In addition to recognizing that resolving global hunger is a mission that will extend beyond her lifetime, Lappé, like the other professionals who exhibit generative wisdom, has an appreciation for the history of the problem she has chosen to confront. Note her reference to "patterns of thought and behavior in systems that have been put in place over hundreds and hundreds of years" as an acknowledgment of the historical dimension of hunger. Being attuned to history, we argue, is an important foundation – for Lappé and others – for appreciating the lengthy time scale needed to address complex problems.

Lappé's capacity to see beyond the here and now can be traced to the world of her childhood, and especially the influence of her parents. Although living in a conservative region of Texas, Lappé's parents founded a racially integrated Unitarian church in the segregated society of the 1950s. Her parents' commitment to resolving deep-rooted social problems permeated the household and imprinted itself on Lappé. Her bedroom was down the hallway from the kitchen, where her parents and their friends weighed in on "what I thought of as the adults talking about the big important things." She goes on:

And even though I didn't know exactly what they were talking about, I found those memories of that intensity of their involvement, of their caring about what was happening in the society at large [influential]. . . . It all had to do with democracy, in effect. It all had to do with inclusivity, and the democratic process was the core of it – what was fair, what was just. . . . One wanted to have a life that had some meaning, that you were aligning yourself with something that was better than what had been.

Lappé's understanding of the complexity of social problems, as well as their historical basis, deepened when she arrived for her first year of college, at the height of the divisiveness erupting around the Vietnam War. Despite their liberal leanings, her parents supported the war. But the influence of the Quaker college she attended, plus her own reading of the facts behind the war, led her to realize that "my government was, in effect, lying to me." This experience, she noted:

was the first break to see [that] what's wrong is much deeper than just cleaning things up around the edges. And it was very, very traumatic because it was a break with my parents. . . . That was my beginning of pulling away the layers to try to understand what is the root of the problem, and how do I align myself, my life, with something better: with a solution, with a direction.

It is precisely this sensibility to the complex and historical dimensions of problems that Lappé has carried through to this day to her work on global hunger and various other initiatives concerning democracy.

By building on the influences of her childhood and her capacity to see beyond the here and now, Lappé has not so much gone beyond traditional boundaries as created a new professional sphere of work. She describes herself as a synthesizer of information from disparate sources, all the while holding to her core values concerning social injustices.

Les Kaufman's work is predicated on seeing beyond the here and now. As a conservation biologist, Kaufman's research has shown that natural environments have the potential – if maintained properly by people over time – to regenerate themselves in the aftermath of damaging events. He has alerted fellow scientists, fishermen whose interactions most directly impact ecological niches, and the public at large (through public television and museum projects) to an important insight: that there is a chance of saving threatened natural environments crucial to the well-being of the planet if human beings take corrective actions. In recent years, Kaufman has devoted most of his energies to restoring the health of Lake Victoria, in Kenya, for the benefit both of the species that inhabit it and the local human communities whose welfare depends on the vitality of the lake.

Although one could certainly argue that the raison d'être of biological conservation is to improve conditions for the environment and humanity for generations to come, Kaufman's goals are based on an especially broad view of history and what it implies for scientists' roles in society. As Kaufman explains:

> there used to be shamans who did this stuff. There used to be people in society whose job it was to stand at the edge of the woods and make sure nature didn't step on us. They did this not in a confrontational way, but by romancing nature and dancing with it, and understanding what was going on as well as they could, and anticipating changes. That function has been pretty much lost in the hubris of Western society, in which it's assumed that we are in control of everything so we don't need anybody out there watching. The basic idea is to, at the community level, put the watchers back. It should give a new role to ecologists and socio-economists similar to the ones that we now reserve for doctors and judges. Basically, they're liaisons with a large, complex, and bewildering world. But in order for this to work the common populous has to be better educated and more receptive to these bits of information which are often pretty scary and require personal sacrifice to address.

In this passage Kaufman blends a sweeping historical view with a reconfigured vision of the modern-day scientist, all in the service of regenerating fragile ecological niches for long-term sustainability. He looks beyond the traditional research boundaries of scientists' work and recognizes that Western society lacks the "watcher" role accorded to shamans in times (and cultures) past[7] but yet does not provide the professional mechanisms to fill this gap. Part of the solution, Kaufman suggests, is to imbue scientists with the same kind of authority and trust granted to physicians and lawyers. This new role for scientists is to help society make sense of the limited "bits of information," or what is often called "sound bites," that come out of politically charged debates about how people should respond to information they are receiving about the environment.

Kaufman's perspective is grounded in a combination of what he has learned through his research and what he observed in his childhood.

---

[7] Shamans can still be found in some cultures, but their role has diminished as the popularity of Christianity and other organized religions have surged. (*New York Times* Web Site, 10/14/03: http://www.nytimes.com/2003/10/14/international/africa/14CHUR. html).

As noted earlier, Kaufman has gone beyond conventional scientific knowledge by showing that nature can, to a certain extent, regenerate itself in the aftermath of damaging events. He has come to understand, that, for example:

> The accumulation of coastal pollution, deforestation, poorly planned development, [and] all the things people do on beaches . . . don't actually destroy coral reefs, seagrass beds, or mangrove forests outright so much as create conditions in which they would be incapable of regenerating from a subsequent insult.

This perspective is a far more subtle and interdependent account of human actions and environmental effects than that assumed by scientists and the public at large. As a result of his view, Kaufman looks not only ahead to the future (scientists serving as entrusted professionals) but to societal roles of the past (scientists in the mold of shamans, qua watchers).

Kaufman's sensibility to the effects of human behavior on the environment first emerged when he was 8 years old. On moving from Brooklyn to his new home in Queens he noticed that:

> they were just putting up a lot of housing developments and reclaiming a lot of marsh land. There was a mass exodus of creatures from the marsh into the fringing communities. My memory of it is of a virtual parade of snakes, terrapins, and orphan birds, and all kinds of coastal animals . . . like refugees streaming from the marsh and walking across our front yard and off to oblivion. I became fascinated with this and began spending a lot of time in the marsh.

Perhaps the reason Kaufman took note of the displacement of animals to begin with is because of a preexisting fascination with them nurtured by his father. His father, he notes, "was interested in critters, and brought turtles and frogs home at a time when ectotherms actually occurred through much of New York and could be found in vacant parking lots." As is the case with Lappé, early childhood experiences, and especially parental modeling, played a pivotal role in the development of Kaufman's professional views.

Going beyond Traditional Professional Boundaries

The complex and historically rooted problems that generatively wise professionals confront spur them to incorporate methods and ways of knowing from multiple domains of work. John Gardner, an early subject in our study who died in 2002, is a case in point. Gardner (no relation to Howard Gardner) had a highly successful career as a public servant.

He assembled an original career path comprised of several equally important and prominent positions. Gardner exemplified going beyond the traditional single-career track. He served as the secretary for Health, Education, and Welfare (HEW) during the Johnson administration, was the president of the influential Carnegie Corporation for 10 years during one of the most notable periods in its history, and helped to found and lead Common Cause and the Independent Sector, among many other equally important professional initiatives.

Over the course of his long and fruitful career, Gardner held firmly to his guiding principle of serving society and improving it for the present and for future generations. He integrated the methods and ways of knowing associated with various domains (and worlds) into his professional repertoire, all for the purpose of realizing his goal of public service. While president of Carnegie, for example, Gardner funded initiatives that opened up new pathways for shedding light on the human condition, including Jerome Bruner's early work in cognitive science, pioneering books by economist John Kenneth Galbraith and the establishment of the influential Russian Studies Centers, first at Harvard and subsequently at other universities. Gardner drew on his training as an academic – a psychologist, in fact – to identify the ideas of others that held the greatest promise for gaining insight into humanity.

During his tenure at HEW, Gardner oversaw the launching of Medicare, a key element of Lyndon Johnson's historic Great Society program. He also helped establish the Corporation for Public Broadcasting. Both of these initiatives were rooted in Gardner's convictions concerning the need for the populace at large and the government to band together for the common good. More than possessing convictions, however, Gardner learned how to apply leadership skills and political acumen to the complex role of serving on the president's cabinet. (Interestingly, although serving a Democratic president, Gardner was a lifelong Republican.)

After leaving formal politics, Gardner founded Common Cause in 1970. Uniting the skills and experiences he accrued in his other professional roles and his commitment to public service, Gardner's newest initiative gave citizens an organized forum for pressuring the U.S. government to be more open and accountable. In this capacity he also brought attention to campaign finance reform, a matter that continues to be of great concern to this day.

The roots of Gardner's assembling multiple professional roles around a common theme can be found at the very beginning of his professional life. While stationed in Italy during World War II (and already an academic psychologist), he had a breakthrough. As he explains:

> It occurred to me that two times my whole career had been turned over by outside events: the Depression and the war. I had paid no attention to this. I had paid the attention an informed citizen pays, but not the attention that an active mind ought to pay. So I wrote my family and asked them to send me some books, and I set out to try to understand things beyond my own field. I was very well read, so it was an easy transition. But when I came back [from the war] I was determined to find work that exposed me to a broader range of social issues, social problems, the way the world functioned.

The key ingredients Gardner employed at this point in his career, and on which he would continue to draw, are a strong interest in the underlying causes of social and human behavior (understanding "outside events" of great import), monitoring his knowledge base (realizing he hadn't paid attention to a trend), the capacity to identify how his skills could be used to advance understanding ("I was very well read, so it was an easy transition"), and renewing his commitment to a broad cause ("I was determined to find work that exposed me to . . . social issues, social problems").

Gardner frames the idea of role switching in what he calls *self-renewal*. This concept, which also is captured in an eponymous book, speaks to the importance of continually seeking new challenges and avoiding the complacency associated with established solutions that lapse into obsolescence. As Gardner notes, many of us have:

> [the] impulse to stay by proven methods, methods that were appropriate to the earlier iteration of the problem [even when] the objective situation [has] moved on. [Yet] the methods are still sacred after the changes in outer circumstances would suggest changing the methods.

Without his belief in the importance of self-renewal, it certainly is conceivable that limiting himself to one realm of endeavor would have resulted in a notable career. And yet, it is clear that Gardner's principle of striving to take on new challenges and look for new solutions was at the heart of his varied accomplishments.

Bernard Lown's work as a physician points to a different manner of going beyond professional boundaries. Lown won the Nobel Peace Prize for his work on organizing physicians in opposition to nuclear proliferation. He also has founded or played an important contributing role in efforts to institute universal health care in Massachusetts, and to harness satellite and computer technology to enhance health care in impoverished regions of the world.

Although John Gardner adhered to an abstract ideal of public service and undertook a variety of projects that loosely fit under this canopy, Lown has identified himself first and foremost by his primary professional affiliation – as a physician – and as one who integrates a diverse range of initiatives into his expansive notion of what it means to be a doctor. For Lown, being a physician means attending to the individual patient in the fullest possible sense, working to institute access to health care for at-risk and disenfranchised populations, and organizing colleagues to address matters of urgent public health.

All of these, and various related projects undertaken by Lown, fit under his expressed sentiment that "I wanted to do good [and] doctoring was a way to do [so]." The concept of doing good, he says, can encompass various degrees of scale, whether the "scale is focused on a person or focused beyond the individual." In Lown's view, the individual and the social are not two separate entities that both happen to be of interest to him. Instead, these two degrees of scale are inherently intertwined. The health and safety of the community at large impacts the well-being of the person, and vice versa. Viewing medicine as having the broadest possible reach – and acting on this conviction – has pushed Lown's work beyond the traditional physician's focus on individual patients.

Lown's philosophy has driven him to contribute to the creation of many initiatives, such as Physicians for Social Responsibility, International Physicians for the Prevention of Nuclear War (hereafter IPPNW), and the Ad Hoc Committee to Defend Health Care. His views also have influenced how he leads established organizations. For example, in 1985 he reached the conclusion that the "developing world will define the future for humankind." In his capacity as co-chair of IPPNW, Lown steered the organization in "that direction with a lot of opposition," and ultimately settled on the idea of "vaccinating the world's children." Members of IPPNW did not understand the relationship between the "antinuclear struggle" and vaccination. And yet Lown, drawing on his expansive view of what it means to be a physician, argued that "we will never have legitimacy in the developing world unless we address problems that are cogently painful and relevant to them, far more than whether white people are going to incinerate each other with nuclear bombs." This project concerning vaccination ultimately led Lown to undertake other programs to improve health care in the developing world, including using satellites to send medical information to various countries. The ultimate result was creation of another organization, called SateLife.

Lown's commitment to health and social welfare can be traced to the worlds of his childhood and early adult years. Having been born poor and Jewish in Lithuania imprinted on Lown a set of convictions and values that influence his life today. As he explains:

> My grandfather and great grandfather were rabbis in a small community, and these were rabbis of a different time. The rabbi was really a social worker for a community; the do-gooder in an abundance of poverty, where people were desperate and were oppressed in a way it's hard for us to imagine. Seeing that, no doubt, [was] a role model. It was a certain contempt for money – money was the root of evil [in that] mentality. To be happy you don't need much money, but you do need the good regard of other human beings. I'm sure these values cascaded when I was a youngster.

Lown's sensitivity to social injustices sharpened when he arrived in Baltimore to start medical school at the Johns Hopkins University. He had been living in Maine since arriving in the United States, where he had only seen one African American person in the several years he spent there. The segregation of Baltimore had a major impact on his sense of the world. He elaborates:

> What hit me was here we are fighting a war against fascism [WWII]. And, I felt it very deeply being Jewish, having come from Lithuania. Suddenly I realized that [Johns Hopkins] was the most racist place I'd ever been to. No black students, no black teachers, no black nurses. . . . It was appalling to me.

Interestingly, both Lown and Gardner cite World War II as key points in their professional development. The difference, however, is that for Lown the "war against fascism" tied into personal experiences and convictions regarding injustice. This experience, in turn, led to his adapting his role as a physician to rooting out injustices. For Gardner, the war led him to realize the limitations of his chosen profession (psychology) and develop a broader interest in serving the public in various professional guises.

Our profiles of professionals illustrate that generative wisdom develops in response to various contexts and ways of knowing – what Goodman calls worlds. Whether it be influences from childhood, happenings in one's profession, broader social/global events, or the culture of an institution, generative wisdom is a phenomenon constructed over time. For example, Albert Bloom's decision to abolish the football program at Swarthmore was made possible by appealing to the abiding

Quaker values of the college. Charles Ogletree's focus on systemic reform is built on his previous and more traditional emphasis on winning individual cases. Frances Moore Lappé's commitment to social change can be traced back to the hum of political discourse in her parents' kitchen. And John Gardner's calling as a public servant came about because of insights gleaned during World War II.

When viewed from an even broader angle, these professionals are *bricoleurs* in their own right. They draw together experiences, values, and methods in ever shifting combinations to serve their broader goal of enhancing the welfare of succeeding generations. We now consider how our analysis of good work might aid professionals in training.

Implications for Teaching Generative Wisdom
The well-being – and the viability – of humanity will always rest on the ability of certain extraordinarily resourceful people in the present to make strides in resolving complex problems that will enable future generations to adapt successfully to the circumstances of their time. Generatively wise professionals, as we have seen, play an important role in this respect. Are there ways, though, to help ensure that future *professionals* develop generative wisdom? In other words, can generative wisdom be taught in schools of professional education? Evidence from our research suggests it is possible.

As an example of how generative wisdom might be taught, we will draw from our recent research on "good work" in medical education.[8] Although medical education undoubtedly is distinct from other forms of professional education, there are, we believe, potential models for teaching generative wisdom that can be carried over to other realms of training. Our discussion of medical education is organized according to overlaps we identified between the teaching strategies mentioned by physicians and the three types of boundary-crossing.

Going beyond conventional understanding or knowledge. Since the middle of the 20th century, medicine has been associated with remarkable technological innovations. In fact, the advent and use of magnetic resonance imaging, non-invasive surgery, and powerful

---

[8] This research has been funded by the Robert Wood Johnson Foundation. Schools were selected as follows. We assembled a panel of physicians and asked them to nominate up to five medical schools that, in their professional estimation, adhere to principles of good work. We provided criteria of good work in advance. We also requested the physicians nominate schools in terms of geographic and institution type diversity.

pharmaceuticals, among many other developments, are often viewed by both physicians and patients as what medicine does, what its very purpose is. "Medicine-qua-technology" has become the conventional understanding of what defines the profession.

The physicians we interviewed, however, discussed the need to go beyond this conventional understanding. In their teaching they convey to students that technology should be regarded as but one means of diagnosing and treating illness, not the sole foundation of practicing medicine. In this view, the doctor–patient relationship remains at the heart of medical care. One physician, who has developed an influential course for first-year students, stressed that methods of diagnosis and healing are (and always have been) variable; what endures is the support, listening, and comfort a physician can provide to a patient. In her course students read, critique, and discuss medical research studies, as well as other pertinent literature, to understand how the doctor–patient relationship can be harnessed to promote desired patient outcomes. Students also participate in structured group activities that provide them the opportunity to reflect on how their personal perspectives and experiences can shape their approach to doctoring.

Physicians also talked about informal strategies for imparting new understandings of what it means to practice medicine. Many mentioned using clinical experiences to teach medical residents about the importance of the doctor–patient relationship. Such teaching typically entails role modeling interactions with patients and their families and debriefing after clinical encounters to reflect on what went well and what needs improvement (either with individual residents or with groups of residents). Physicians commented that even residents who have taken introductory courses about the doctor–patient relationship benefit from this type of teaching. Putting into clinical practice the abstract principles learned in the lecture hall is a complex, challenging process.

Going beyond traditional professional boundaries. Many of the physicians we interviewed explained that reconceptualizing what it means to be a doctor entails going beyond traditional professional boundaries. Students are taught that two skills sets must be mastered to be considered a good physician. First, they need to master scientific realms of knowledge. A thorough grasp of anatomy and physiology, chemistry, and biology, as well as various medical techniques, is essential. Second – and this is the realm that goes beyond traditional boundaries – students are expected to understand the psychological dimensions of practicing medicine. This means teaching students to develop a repertoire of interpersonal skills that will lead to successful relationships with patients, such as empathic listening, asking open-ended questions, responding in a nonjudgmental and nonauthoritarian manner, and sitting at a patient's bedside (instead of standing). Physicians explain to students that the sum total of these skills is an expression of respect for patients. Patients who are treated respectfully, physicians reported to us, are more likely to have successful outcomes.

Seeing beyond the here and now. In both courses and informal teaching situations, physicians convey to students the importance of looking beyond the here and now of the immediate clinical encounter. Students are encouraged, instead, to adopt a systemic understanding of patient care. A systemic understanding is one that takes into account the multiple and overlapping contexts in a patient's life that influence the course of illness and healing. These include economic circumstances (and therefore access to levels of care), social environments, the history and dynamics of family and personal relationships, religious and political affiliations, employment status/circumstances, and mental health, among other factors. One physician discussed teaching medical residents to evaluate general guidelines for treatments against patients' ability to afford or comply with them. She works with residents, when necessary, to devise alternate treatment plans that patients will be able to pay for and/or adhere to. Such close work with residents increases their sensitivity to factors impacting health care beyond the here and now.

Conclusion

When looked at together, the new models of teaching medical students and the examples of boundary-crossing among the six professionals indicate that generative wisdom is itself the outcome of others' generative actions. By all accounts medical education has undergone significant shifts in recent years, due in no small measure to the recognition that developing good physicians in the full sense of the term cannot be left to chance. Medical schools have recognized that students need direct instruction and guidance in their development, whether it be through formal lectures or on the spot "teachable moments" that emerge in clinical settings.

Most of the six professionals we have profiled explicitly refer to other people or environments that provided guidance and support for their professional development. Parents, community figures, and institutional values figure prominently in their accounts. Although John Gardner does not cite specific people with whom he interacted, he points to the importance of reading others' ideas in shaping his new understanding of the world and his role in it.

Our analysis suggests, then, a range of strategies for helping to develop generative wisdom. Whether we are parents, colleagues, teachers, or fellow citizens, we can encourage others to go beyond conventional understanding, see beyond the here and now, and go beyond traditional boundaries. As our analysis reveals, examples of boundary-crossing are readily available as models to be emulated by the next generation of professionals.

On a more theoretical level, the professionals we have profiled show the dynamic and subtle interplay between boundary-crossing and diverse contexts, ranging from uniquely personal circumstances to broader institutional or cultural factors. This framework raises two important questions for further research. First, do professionals from various other fields not considered in this chapter indicate contextual influences (in both a constraining and enabling manner) particular to their domains of work? Second, what is the applicability of our model of generative wisdom to those who do not work in the elite professions? Do generatively wise K–12 teachers, for example, adhere to the models of boundary-crossing we have outlined? These questions suggest the rich array of research pathways open to future investigators of generative wisdom.

References

Arlin, P. K. (1990). Wisdom: The art of problem finding. In R. Sternberg (Ed.), *Wisdom: Its nature, origins, and development* (pp. 230–243). New York: Cambridge University Press.

Baltes, P., & Smith, J. (1990). Toward a psychology of wisdom and its ontogenesis. In R. J. Sternberg (Ed.), *Wisdom: Its nature, origins, and development* (pp. 87–120). New York: Cambridge University Press.

Bowen, W., & Levin, S. (2003). Revisiting "The game of life": Athletics at elite colleges. *The Chronicle Review*, September 19, pp. 12–14.

Chandler, M., and Holliday, S. (1990). Wisdom in a postapocalyptic age. In R. Sternberg (Ed.), *Wisdom: Its nature, origins, and development* (pp. 121–141). New York: Cambridge University Press.

Csikszentmihalyi, M. (1993). *The evolving self*. New York: HarperPerennial.

Csikszentmihalyi, M., & Rathunde, K. (1998). The development of the person: An experiential perspective on the ontogenesis of psychological complexity. In W. Damon (Ed.), *Handbook of childhood psychology* (Vol. 1). New York: John Wiley and Sons.

Erikson, E. (1963). *Childhood and society*. New York: W. W. Norton & Company.

Fischman, W., Solomon, B., Greenspan, D., & Gardner, H. (1994). *Making good: How young people cope with moral dilemmas at work*. Cambridge, MA: Harvard University Press.

Gardner, H. (1993). *Creating minds*. New York: Basic Books.

Gardner, H., Csikszentmihalyi, M., & Damon, W. (2001). *Good work: When excellence and ethics meet*. New York: Basic Books.

Goodman, N. (1978). *Ways of worldmaking*. Indianapolis: Hackett Publishing Company.

Gruber, H. (1974). *Darwin on man: A psychological study of scientific creativity*. New York: Dutton.

Hargens, L. (1978). Relations between work habits, research technologies, and eminence in science. *Sociology of Work and Occupations, 5*, 97–112.

Kramer, D. (1990). Conceptualizing wisdom: The primacy of affect–cognition relations. In R. J. Sternberg (Ed.), *Wisdom: Its nature, origins, and development* (pp. 279–316). New York: Cambridge University Press.

Kuhn, T. (1970). *The structure of scientific revolutions*. Chicago: University of Chicago Press.

Labouvie-Vief, G. (1990). Wisdom as integrated thought: Historical and developmental perspectives. In R. J. Sternberg (Ed.), *Wisdom: Its nature, origins, and development* (pp. 52–86). New York: Cambridge University Press.

Lévi-Strauss, C. (1966). *The savage mind*. Chicago: University of Chicago Press.

Meacham, J. (1990). The loss of wisdom. In R. J. Sternberg (Ed.), *Wisdom: Its nature, origins, and development* (pp. 181–211). New York: Cambridge University Press.

Orwoll, L., & Perlmutter, M. (1990). The study of wise persons: Integrating a personality perspective. In R. J. Sternberg (Ed.), *Wisdom: Its nature, origins, and development* (pp. 160–180). New York: Cambridge University Press.

Root-Bernstein, R., Bernstein, M., & Garnier, H. (1993). Identification of scientists making long-term, high-impact contributions, with notes on their methods of working. *Creativity Research Journal, 6*, 329–343.

Simon, R. (1974). The work habits of eminent scientists. *Sociology of Work and Occupations, 1*, 327–335.

Simonton, D. (2000). Creative development as acquired expertise: Theoretical issues and an empirical test. *Developmental Review, 20*, 283–318.

Sternberg, R. J. (Ed.). (1990). *Wisdom: Its nature, origins, and development*. New York: Cambridge University Press.

Sternberg, R. J. (1998). A balance theory of wisdom. *Review of General Psychology, 2*, 347–365.

Tweney, R. (1990). Five questions for computationalists. In J. Shrager & P. Langley (Eds.), *Computational models of scientific discovery and theory information* (pp. 471–484). San Mateo, CA: Kaufman.

12

Wisdom in Public Policy

Lloyd S. Etheredge

A problem that strikes one in the study of history, regardless of period, is why man makes a poorer performance of government than of almost any other human activity. In this sphere, wisdom . . . is less operative and more frustrated than it should be.

– Barbara W. Tuchman (Tuchman, 1980)

1. Definitions and Examples

Wisdom in public policy is good judgment about important matters, especially embodying a genuine commitment to the well-being of individuals and to society as a whole. In international politics wisdom is the core of statesmanship, extending a commitment to the well-being of peoples of other nations, and often restructuring the international system to work better for future generations.

If political wisdom can be engaged there is a growing potential to create a better world. Social science may contribute to the growth of wisdom for public policy: Most problems are similar across cultures and centuries. The advance of physical science and the levels of wealth and education in advanced countries and some underdeveloped countries provide new resources that could, for the first time, be used to meet basic needs of all people (Etheredge, 1981, 1992).

Tuchman's contrast (quoted earlier) between rates of progress in government and other fields suggests that we can learn to improve the wisdom of public policy. Yet one possible lesson of history in the Western intellectual tradition is that the attractive dream to marry political power and wisdom should trigger a psychological alarm. In Tolkien's mythological *The Lord of the Rings* the wise answer is *not* to seek political power, even for good. Frodo and a coalition of good hobbits, men, and other creatures of Middle Earth seek to destroy the Ring that grants dominion to its possessor. On the other side (evil) are the Dark Lord and others who seek to possess the Ring of Power for themselves and to use it; and *also* from the race of men, on the side of good, are those who are drawn by the power of the Ring and too weak to do what must be done. In the classic Western spiritual tradition one of Satan's three temptations to Christ was dominion over the earth and all of its peoples; and the right answer was no.

Yet in the political life of Washington, DC, people still compete to possess the Ring (or to be the National Security Adviser). Believing *they* will use power wisely. The reader is forewarned.

The Western political tradition drew consequential lessons about wisdom before any reader of this chapter was born. The earliest choices to trust political power to (or acquiesce to dominance by) divine Kings, Sons of Heaven, and Holy Fathers were changed, along with the plausible theory (that turned out to have limited practicality) that improving the individual virtue of rulers and humankind was the most reliable path to mitigate the evils of the world. Spiritual/philosophical wisdom is no longer the only wisdom required for public policy. Political processes have created new human-designed systems of remarkable size and complexity (e.g., democracies, market economies, a nonprofit sector) and partly reassigned ultimate control to free and educated people who are – by various mechanisms – supposed to keep the world and their own lives on track.

Today, wisdom is more intellectually challenging: A wise leader must provide intellectual *and* political leadership and answer four questions: What is the Good? What works? What comes next? How do we get it (the next step) done? Yet an elected democratic leader is not a king or queen who can solve problems in his or her own head and give orders. Ultimately, progress will require that wiser policies be adopted in a democracy and this is no simple task in America (Smith, 1992, 2002).

The plan of this chapter is, first, to discuss definitions and examples of wise leaders and wise policies. Second, I will review two traditions in philosophy (supernatural guidance and secular philosophy) and then discuss the expanded repertoire of ideas contributed by social science. Next I will discuss political wisdom as an individual trait and the experiment to create professional identities; and then wisdom

> **Box 12.1** *Examples of Wise Leaders*
> Pericles
> Marcus Aurelius
> Ashoka
> Charlemagne
> Founding Fathers (US)
> Franklin Delano Roosevelt
> Mikhail Gorbachev
> Nelson Mandela

about the functioning of two of the invented systems (democracy and markets) on which American society relies. I will conclude with three recommendations.

1.1. Wise Leaders

Box 12.1 provides examples of historical political leaders who supplied notably beneficial leadership. (It is based on a list by the historian Barbara Tuchman.)[1] The list includes Pericles, who governed democratic Athens at the height of its Golden Age; Marcus Aurelius, who ruled the Roman Empire at the height of its Golden Age and the Roman Peace – the period, in the judgment (at the end of 18th century) of the historian Edward Gibbon, "during which the condition of the human race was most happy and prosperous" (Gibbon, 1946, p. 61); the remarkable Ashoka, whose humanitarian achievements in India (c. 250 B.C.) remain a standard against which many modern leaders and governments can still be judged; Charlemagne, who (in Tuchman's words) "was able to impose order upon a mass of contending elements, to foster the arts of civilization no less than those of war and to earn a prestige supreme in the Middle Ages . . . "; and the American Founding Fathers ("fearless, high-principled, deeply versed in ancient and modern political thought, astute and pragmatic, unafraid of experiment,

---

[1] I have removed Julius Caesar, included in Tuchman's list, because his rule was brief (46–44 B.C.) before his assassination: I do not believe we know how wise a ruler he would have been. Historical lists are affected by many factors, including whether the candidates were articulate communicators whose work was preserved (e.g., the funeral oration of Pericles, the writings of Marcus Aurelius and Julius Caesar, the U.S. Founding Fathers), or who had capable publicists (Charlemagne; the achievements of Ashoka were recognized in the modern world only after discoveries of large, inscribed stone monuments recording the accomplishments).

and . . . convinced of man's power to improve his condition through the use of intelligence" and who, "to a degree unique in the history of revolutions, applied careful and reasonable thinking" (Tuchman, 1980).[2] Waiting 50 years before adding names to this list may be prudent, but Mikhail Gorbachev's change of domestic and international policies in the former USSR and Nelson Mandela's leadership to end apartheid in South Africa make them likely candidates.

None of these historical leaders embodies an idealized Hollywood image of wisdom. They are not people with unassailable identities, nor were they always virtuous, right, or successful. Nor would the enemies in their political battles be likely to agree with their inclusion. However, I think that they are illustrative of the best that has been achieved, and perhaps of the best that we can expect until further problems (discussed in this chapter) can be solved.

We might develop related lists of: (a) leaders and key advisers who, working together, produced wise policies (e.g., Elizabeth I and Lord Salisbury); (b) people whose wisdom influenced public policy without holding political power (e.g., Confucius, John Maynard Keynes, Gandhi, Martin Luther King Jr.); (c) leaders at the opposite extremes, without any beneficial accomplishments or who (like Hitler or Pol Pot) were evil and genocidal; (d) leaders who were wise about specific challenges in specific historical circumstances but appear unwise in other respects (e.g., Churchill's leadership during World War II contrasted with his views toward Gandhi and the end of the British Empire; or Richard Nixon's openness to China contrasted with the Watergate break-in and his impeachment); (e) leaders of extraordinary political and military accomplishments who were not wise, and perhaps never intended to be: Alexander the Great, for example; and (f) messianic visionaries and revolutionaries who thought they were wise but whose visions for a better world ultimately failed (e.g., Marx, Lenin, Mao).

1.2. Wise Policies

Wisdom is an attribute of policies (although it also can be an attribute of individuals). Wise policies can be identified by a balance sheet of effects (good, nil, and evil) distributed across populations and time.

---

[2] I also include Franklin Delano Roosevelt for his leadership to bring America into World War II and lay the groundwork for a more permanent peace than was achieved after World War I.

> **Box 12.2** *Eight Values for Human Betterment*
> Power
> Enlightenment
> Wealth
> Well-Being
> Skill
> Affection
> Rectitude
> Respect

For this discussion, I will use eight values (which have been useful for the study of human rights) to define wise policies (Box 12.2, from the work of Harold Lasswell) (Brewer & De Leon, 1983; Lasswell & McDougal, 1991; see also Fogel, 2000; Rokeach, 1973; Sen, 2000). Of the eight values, "enlightenment" means education, although (as we will see) it also refers to a special kind of personal growth that may be possible; "well-being" refers both to physical and mental well-being.

Box 12.3 provides examples of wise public policies, with an emphasis on the United States (see also Light, 2002; Montgomery & Rondinelli, 1995). Some recent achievements are remarkable by any historical standard (e.g., the end of the Cold War and of apartheid). Several entries are *wiser* policies, but I do not intend an ultimate endorsement. For example, free markets are *relatively* wise, especially by contrast with the failures of national socialism in the 20th century in the USSR, Eastern Europe, and China. Their balance sheet also contains many negative entries: Underregulated and amoral capitalism does great damage, and political conflict throughout the 20th century was required to mitigate the damage. (For example: unionization, worker safety, and child labor laws; product safety; truthful advertising; laws to safeguard competitive practices; financial disclosure; regulation of environmental damage.)

Wise public policies often originate outside government. They also may require social movements – organizing, participation, leadership, and election victories. Even when presidents play essential or catalytic roles, the groundwork (e.g., the end of the US–China and US–USSR Cold Wars) often has been laid across many years. The peaceful end of apartheid in South Africa required unique leadership by Nelson Mandela but also involved collaboration by leaders, and many other people, on both sides (Waldmeir, 1997).

Box 12.3 *Examples of Wise Policies*
Trial by jury
Democratic government
Separations of church and state
Joint-ownership stock companies (corporations)
Due process and conflict of interest rules
Elimination of slavery
Civil and human rights
Universal public education
Public libraries
Private tax-exempt foundations; nonprofit institutions
Wide availability of higher education, with access by merit
Substantial investment (public & private) in scientific research
Market capitalism
Regulation of market capitalism
Settlement of WWII (incl. Marshall Plan) vs. settlement of WW I
United Nations
European Common Market
Medicare
End of apartheid (South Africa)
End of the Cold War (US–China; US–Russia)

---

2. Two Traditions of Political Philosophy

Two philosophical traditions have shaped thinking about wisdom in
public policy: supernatural guidance and secular philosophy.

2.1. Supernatural Guidance

Most governments, before the invention of democracy, were a story
of the creation, management, and (sometimes) revolt against male-
dominated hierarchies. Rulers claimed a supernatural or divine source
of legitimacy. Pharaohs or emperors were gods or Sons of Heaven; kings
ruled by divine right and the sanctification of priests. Further guidance,
if needed, was sought by prayer, magic, divination, or the consulting of
oracles; and after the invention of writing, by the written record of divine
revelation and the interpretation of its true prophets (Finer, 1999, p. 316).

The early gods (including the Greek and Roman gods) did not have
moral codes for their own behavior nor did they expect moral behavior
of mortals. Later, with the development of large agrarian societies, new

deities and the great enduring religions with moral codes emerged – Catholicism, Judaism, Islam, Buddhism, and others (Lenski & Nolan, 1998). These began, and continue, to shape public policy with the idea that a better collective life will be achieved by greater individual virtue as defined by their codes. For example, the Catholic catechism teaches that wisdom and, by extension wise policy, will grow from the four cardinal virtues of prudence, justice, fortitude, and temperance, of which the guiding virtue is prudence (*auriga virtutum*, the charioteer of the virtues), which disposes "practical reason to discern our true good in every circumstance and . . . choose the right means of achieving it" (United States Catholic Conference, 1995, p. 496).

In religious traditions the deepest and most unsettling question about public policy is the remarkable persistence of evil (Neiman, 2002). In *The City of God,* Saint Augustine imagined two cities: "In the one, the princes and the nations it subdues are ruled by the love of ruling; in the other, the princes and subjects serve one another in love, the latter obeying, while the former takes thought for all" (St. Augustine, 1950, p. 477). But the saints in this world are few and the fallen nature of the vast majority of the children of God, who determined the politics and moral tone of their societies, meant that only limited progress would be possible. The virtuous few in 21st-century America (and beyond) are destined to live in societal (and public policy) Babylons across the centuries until Judgment Day.

The Judeo-Christian legacy includes a theory of *resistance to wisdom*, of an inherent design flaw in human nature that limits, and even works against, good. The observations that religious thinkers tried to explain by a theory of Original Sin certainly want for a good explanation. We might *picture* the arrival of wisdom as a political leader with a calm, assured, and noble bearing – conveying a sense of an unassailable identity – briefly articulating the essential issues to guide a decision. His words bring a moment of silence, and then universal assent. By contrast, across the centuries and today, *every* advance in wise public policies is strenuously resisted (Box 12.3). Wise leaders can be assailed, marginalized, or assassinated by political enemies. (Socrates, called the wisest of men by the Delphic Oracle, was condemned to death in democratic Athens; Jesus was crucified; recent examples of assassinations include Rev. Martin Luther King, Gandhi, President John Kennedy and his brother Robert Kennedy, Anwar Sadat, and former Prime Minister Rabin of Israel.) Nelson Mandela spent years in prison. Confucius, whose thought and moral example shaped the governance of China for

2,500 years, was considered too independent and ethically candid by the power holders of his day; he never had a permanent civil service position, and faced periods of loneliness, starvation, poverty, and even physical danger.

Today, looking back, it is almost impossible to imagine that wise policies were opposed. Yet it required extraordinary political work and conflict to end slavery, and to secure the right of women to vote, regulations for safe and healthy food and working conditions, and the prohibitions against child labor (Gamson, 1986). It is as though a divided human nature always was in political combat with itself when faced with any change for the good, or that the modern democratic electorate is initially divided almost evenly between progress and opposition, or good and evil.

Christian thinkers also believe that *selfishness* partly explains the evil of the world (Mansbridge, 1990). Selfishness, in a society of wolves and lambs, makes wise policies for the common good impossible: The wolves do not have any self-interest in change, even if they claim it. This simple model (assuming an analogous distribution of personality traits in political behavior) could explain much of the political history of the world.

Christian virtue and preaching, and the other great ethical religions, did produce wiser policies. One reason for their early spread, in competition with a wide range of pagan religions, was that these new religions delivered. In poor societies without welfare systems and with indifferent governments, they were not merely an opiate of the masses: The early Christians, Muslims, Jews, and Buddhists cared, and they provided charity and community (Dodds, 1991).

2.2. Secular Philosophy

A second tradition is the use of human reason and secular philosophy to provide guidance for wise public policy. The tradition begins with the birth of democracy in Greece – whose gods gave no specific guidance – and especially in Athens whose patron goddess, Athena, was the goddess of wisdom. In Ancient Greece *philo* + *sophia*, the love of and inquiry about wisdom, was coterminous with psychology. The first philosophers asked questions about every topic, and they thought the power of reason should change private lives and public policy. They wanted to teach people to grow beyond being creatures of impulse or habit or living in a passive stimulus–response relationship to circumstances – for example, to examine their unhappiness, caused by exaggerated ideas or fears, by the light of their powers of reason; and they prescribed thinking, dialogues with philosophers, and meditative and other practices for personal growth (Hadot, 1995, 2002). They were the Abraham Maslows, Tony Robbinses, and Landmark Corporations – the theorists, clinicians, and self-help writers of Athens. And, at times, its in-your-face performance artists: When Diogenes (d. circa 320 B.C.) walked with a lighted lamp in broad daylight looking for an honest man he was making a point to his society. (Diogenes also lived without material possessions and slept in public buildings to dramatize a philosophical discovery that a happy and fulfilled life need not depend on material possessions or social conformity.) The population of free male adults in Athens in the Golden Age was only 30,000 to 45,000 (Finer, 1999, p. 341); its philosopher/psychologists, the advocates of *philosophia*, were a part of its civic life – so much so that Socrates eventually was condemned to death by a jury of 500 of his fellow citizens (for explanations, see Brickhouse & Smith, 2002; Ober, 2001, p. 167).

An example of Greek secular philosophy – and the most influential passage about wisdom ever written by a philosopher – occurs in a dialogue of Socrates recorded later in Plato's *Republic* (Book VII) (Plato, 1991): It uses the picture of an ascent toward sunlight by some members of a tribe that lives in an underground cave filled with shadows and echoes; and tells of a confusing and hard journey for the few members who are freed to walk the upward path.[3] The dialogue proposes that there is a higher, enlightened sense of reality that can change politics for the better. The achievement of this enlightenment is the goal of educating students who will become Philosopher–Guardians of the state and it can be achieved by specific methods (Socratic dialogues to stimulate independent, analytical reasoning) that awaken and encourage the potential of the individual. The ideas shape Western education: Any modern student in the West who is assigned two contrasting authorities and asked to think for him-/herself and "contrast and compare" – rather than being given a work by a learned authority and assigned to "memorize and recite" a received wisdom – is participating in a unique and Western theory of civic education and wisdom articulated here.

Plato's unitary Good – appearing as the blazing light of the sun after ascent from a cave, to all enlightened people – is a true source of ethical

---

[3] Plato was a student of Socrates and founded a school to continue his methods. I follow convention by attributing the views in this section of *The Republic* to both Plato and Socrates.

illumination and knowledge of excellence in public policy, gymnastics, or drama, or architecture or teaching or friendship (etc.). This Good is not the nonviolence of Gandhi or a benign ethics in all circumstances: Plato saw the right conduct of guardians being "kind to friends and fierce to enemies" (Plato, 1961, p. 1153). When necessary (but not otherwise), the enlightened Guardians would lie to less enlightened citizens to achieve the best interests of the State: For example, the people were to be told that marriages were arranged by lot, but officials would manipulate lots to assure favorable breeding (Plato, 1961, p. 1154).

The global political influence of Plato increased because of the British Empire. The elites of Victorian England pictured themselves as the heirs of Athens and (especially the enlightened graduates of Oxford and Cambridge, who became the upper class and civil servants) to be the Guardians for their country and the peoples of the British Empire. The self-image was enhanced by the personal example and conviction of the kind and gifted Benjamin Jowett, master of Balliol College, who translated Plato into the beloved and recognizable cadences of the King James Bible and who readily interpreted Plato's Good as the early pagan equivalent of the teachings of Christ and the values of the Church of England and the playing fields of Eaton (Turner, 1981, pp. 431, 414–446). "Man is a creature who makes pictures of himself, then comes to resemble the picture," observes Iris Murdoch (Murdoch, 1999a, p. v). The picture of Plato's Guardians continues in the democratic governments, educated elites, and civic culture of their subjects after independence.

Plato envisioned a more demanding path than did recent American psychological growth theorists such as Abraham Maslow. Plato taught that the attachments and defining illusions and behaviors that human beings conventionally rely on for security, respect, affection, social identity, and other needs must be questioned and abandoned in their original form, whereas Maslow's view apparently was that the meeting of such needs (by whatever mechanism) was sufficient (Maslow, 1987, 1998; for Jung's view of struggle and individuation, Odajnyk, 1973, p. 146).

The theory of personal growth, guided by philosophically defined virtue, as the foundation for wise public policy also developed independently in China with the leadership of Confucius (551 B.C.–479 B.C.), the most influential political philosopher and teacher in Chinese history. Confucius believed that, through education, each man could shape his destiny; he envisioned a better world built and maintained by the education, self-cultivation, and leadership of a fellowship of scholarly noblemen (*chün-tzu*). (The abilities that he developed and his moral excellence, not birth or current wealth or status, fitted a man for this leadership.) Confucius felt that innovations (including radical or revolutionary changes) in formal institutions were much less important than was the renewal of spiritual energy and humanity that social and political institutions (beginning with the family) always required. Noblemen would govern wisely, with a harmonious relation of above and below, primarily by moral suasion and the example of the spirit and humanity of their conduct, especially their *i* (righteousness) and *jen* (benevolence). The higher the rank of the official, the more consequential his example. The methods for such self-cultivation were different from Plato's (or Maslow's) and included *inter alia* mastery of six arts – music, ritual, calligraphy, archery, charioteering, and arithmetic – which required many years to achieve. Although several of these arts are, in part, practical skills for an emperor and higher civil service, the awakening sensibilities required for their mastery also make them an education to (in the conception of Chinese culture) *become* human – exercises for inner growth whose closest Western analogy might be an advanced and refined Gestalt therapy. Thus, calligraphy and archery are prized for self-cultivation in China in part because they develop artistic and aesthetic sensitivity, which permits experience of different underlying and unifying forces and energy in the human body, society, and the physical universe (*qi* or *ch'i* and its two fundamental aspects, *yin* and *yang*). Their relations (e.g., the creation and relaxation of tension, assertion and receptivity, inertia, aliveness, conflict, balance, and harmony) also shape and explain human behavior and even physical health (e.g., Kuriyama, 2002).[4] Although this sensibility shaped the political philosophy and governance of China for 2,500 years, the existence of *qi* (*yin* and *yang*) forces and energy is not confirmed by Western physical science or social

[4] The sense of a deep ontological unity that informs Chinese discussions of wisdom is such that, when a supernova disturbed the Heavens, or there was a period of drought, it was appropriate for an emperor to retire and reflect on the disharmonies of his own mind that might be causal (Huang, 1981, pp. 11, 119). Thus, simple translations of words can be misleading. True, in the West, the image of a collective psychology was used to legitimate hierarchical rule (thus, the assertion that the natural and wisest practice was for the king or emperor, as the "head" of the state, to do the thinking and for others to obey). However, in Western political thought the linkage of the individual human body and the body politic (as "a person writ large") was almost always only an analogy rather than an assertion about the constitutive unity of reality. It was common to the 17th century when it lost favor to a defining analogy of a social contract (Hale, 1973). For a Freudian analysis of wisdom and power in the political "head," see Brown, 1990.

science.[5] Such cultivation of the self in a co-humanity with others was the essential policy foundation of personal health and inner harmony, of social order, of political stability, of good (righteous and benevolent) government, and of universal peace (Creel, 1960; Jaspers, 1962).

Confucian education for the civil service, widely open and based on merit and competitive examination, was compatible with many religious beliefs, and within several centuries it supplanted hereditary aristocracy and became the foundation for Chinese public administration. Like Christianity, there were gaps in implementation and selective adoption of different elements.

2.3. Limits of Religion and Moral Philosophy

The strategy of maximizing individual morality to achieve the collective Good may seem obvious. It required many centuries to recognize the limitations of the assumption.

– The original theory that the moral leadership of the Catholic Church and mankind's slowly increasing Christian virtue ("onward and upward by 2% a century" one critic remarked) could be relied on to bring a better world lost credibility after 1,500 years. In a pattern that recurs in history, institutions tend to become corrupt and to serve their own self-interests rather than the goals and people they were created to serve. The potential for corruption increases as institutions become powerful and the wrong people are thereby drawn by new temptations ("Power tends to corrupt and absolute power corrupts absolutely" in the phrase of the historian and Catholic intellectual, Lord Acton) (Himmelfarb, 1952, p. 203). Even popes became corrupt, added false interpretations of the teachings of Christ, and invented the sale of indulgences to divert wealth from local charities in impoverished medieval Europe to build St. Peter's in Rome and to support a lavish worldly lifestyle for the princes of the Church. The Protestant Reformation and Counter-Reformation ignited horrific wars and persecutions throughout Europe. In the West, the improved design of a more secular modern world, with the separation of church and state, the terminated doctrine of the divine right of kings, and the change to democracy, was born of this violent crisis.

– A second attack on the strategy of increasing individual virtue came from Machiavelli, who observed the violent and treacherous Italian politics in the early 16th century. He rejected (i.e., even if it could be

---

[5] The psychoanalyst Wilhelm Reich used a similar idea about a unitary life energy to shape the radical Freudian Left sexual-politics movement: (Robinson, 1990).

achieved) the ideal of Christian piety for rulers (loving, and beloved by, their subjects) – and even the obedience to law. In *The Prince* he wrote a prescription for a realistic ruler who could survive and do good for his subjects: "learn how to do evil" – the cold realism, cunning, dissembling, and pragmatic use of spies, bribery, and violence required of a ruler in a world of hardball politics, facing unprincipled people who wished his favor or to seize his power or small kingdom by violence; and subjects who were themselves more selfish than virtuous (Machiavelli, 1977). Machiavelli invoked the Italian virtue of *virtu* – the strength, cunning, wisdom of realism, and ruthlessness of Vito and Michael Corleone in *The Godfather*. As part of his advice he dismissed the preaching that wise rulers should rely upon the love of their subjects, just as Michael Corleone explains the danger that he faces at one point: "Our people are businessmen. Their loyalty is based on that."

– A third attack on the guidance of moral philosophy to fashion a better world came from Nietzsche, who proposed a new path of liberation and truth-telling on behalf of realizing a stronger and wiser human being than any who had previously existed. He would be a man who would be master of his own destiny, a man who could give and keep his word in the face of changing circumstances: an animal who could promise. A man whose spirit and speaking could – in reality, and not just in Wagnerian opera – encompass and soar above the turbulent cacophonies of the world.

Nietzsche's "beyond good and evil" redefinition of the question held that civilization and moral philosophy were an entrapment that suppressed humanity's powers (just as animals are domesticated) inside a slave mentality (see also Freud's theory of civilization and neurosis: Freud, 1961).[6] Nietzsche challenged do-good democratic theorists and reform movements to improve civilization: "the universal green-pasture happiness ... with security, lack of danger, comfort, and an easier life for everyone; the two songs and doctrines which they repeat most often are 'equality of rights' and 'sympathy for all that suffers' – and suffering itself they take for something that must be abolished!" (Nietzsche, 1966, p. 54). In his reanalysis of Greek culture, Nietzsche identified the source of health, power, and aliveness as the Dionysian spirit (versus the Apollonian rational-talk, rational-talk, and more rational-talk spirit

---

[6] See also Rousseau's theory that man (innately good) is corrupted by society and civilization, which become more harmful as they become more sophisticated (Ritter & Bondanella, 1987).

of Plato) – the joyful power and the instinct for growth and durability of
the choruses of amoral satyrs in Greek drama – a life force, the human
unity "behind all civilization" (from *The Birth of Tragedy* Bluhm, 1971,
p. 530).

Nietzsche also rejected Plato's idealistic view of a harmony of Good.
He saw a world with masks and evasion, cruelty behind the highest
human achievements: The competitive glory for the few in the winner's
circle was the agony of defeat for losers (e.g., Conroy, 2002). Societies
"feign contrition" about their problems (Safranski, 2002, p. 75). The intellectual achievements of Plato, Socrates, et al. were a lifestyle conducted
atop a slave economy – slaves who (presumably) served the wine but
who do not participate, and are seldom mentioned, in these dialogues.

3. Beyond Philosophy to Social Science

Next, the development of social thought and social science created a new
dimension and cornucopia of new ideas for thinking about wise policy.
A recognition of *social structure and structural variables* – the opportunity
to design institutions and systems to produce better outcomes without
greater individual human virtue – liberated policy analysis from philosophical arguments. The higher *levels of analysis* to describe and analyze
the causal features of social organization and complex systems became
the basis for new social sciences alongside psychology. I will discuss
several examples and a modern critique of the potential limits of reason
and social science to solve conflicts involving "isms."

3.1. Collective Good from Self-Interested Behavior

It is easy to illustrate the importance of structure and social design. A
system with one simple rule can turn personal selfishness into a simula-
tion of Golden Rule behavior: The first child cuts the cake, the other child
gets to select the piece. (See also Axelrod, 1997; Ostrom, 1991.) Modern
market economies make use of individuals who pursue selfish ends to
create the moral reversal of efficient production, economic growth, and
material abundance for society (beyond the dreams of utopian writers
in earlier centuries, albeit unequally distributed).[7]

– Similarly, as the *Federalist Papers* (especially number 10) explain, the
American Constitution designed a new kind of government that used

---

[7] Most people pursue their own *good*, and that of their families (etc.). The arguments about
capitalism and sin require a refined moral and psychological analysis.

ambition to check ambition by a mechanism of checks and balances. Today ("a government of laws and not men") the social realities of laws (Friedman, 1986), roles and institutions, informal rules, and accountability processes for the executive branch, judiciary, and Congress in a federalist system are extensive and embody many theories of how to design better systems and institutions to produce better policy.

I will return to an assessment of both markets and democracy in a later section. Although they are major forward steps, neither has been completely satisfactory.

3.2. *The Search for Synergistic Policies: Explaining the Rise and Fall of Civilizations*

How do we improve the performance of *systems*? Researchers began to study the societal characteristics, policies, and causal pathways that produce desirable outcomes across many cultures (e.g., the eight values in Box 12.2). For example: Toynbee's *A Study of History* analyzed the rise and fall of 26 civilizations (Toynbee, 1961; Fernandez-Armesto, 2001; Montagu, 1956). The research question is compelling – and the cycles of rise and fall challenge simple evolutionary/sociobiological ideas. As he traveled the world, Toynbee saw the ruins of many past civilizations. But surely, today, there is about the same human genetic material as during the times of past glory. What went right – and wrong? Could we bring the same chemistry together, today, anywhere that we wish? Athens, with 30,000–45,000 male adults, was no larger than many small cities around the world – who may await their date with destiny. . . .

To summarize the 12 volumes briefly: Toynbee found that civilizations rose by responding creatively to challenges, with new leadership supplied from minority groups. They exhibited an unusual energy and spiritual force as a component of a collective psychology; their religion played a sustaining role (secular philosophies did not achieve an equivalent cultural and political power [Toynbee, 1956, pp. 73–74]). Civilizations declined when new establishments (as they did usually, but not inevitably) ceased to respond creatively, became despotic tyrannies, and succumbed to sins of nationalism and militarism. (For a vision of quantitative psychohistory influenced by Toynbee, see Asimov, 1986.)

The research traditions are alive and vigorous and a great deal needs to be sorted out: (McClelland, 1961, 1971; Murray, 2003; Simonton, 1994, 1999; Huntington & Harrison, 2001; Melko & Scott, 1987; Bok, 1997; Fernandez-Armesto, 2001). And there are other data that might contribute to an answer. We know (for example) that some of the 50 states in the United States are more progressive and create policies that later become accepted as wise in other states and for national policy (Walker, 1969) – but what makes them leaders for wisdom?

– Today, most ideas about public policy have been shaped by the growth of social theory and social science since the Enlightenment (Deutsch & Markovits, 1986; Nisbet, 2003). The term "statistics" (from the Latin *statisticus* = "of politics" and the German *Statistik* = "study of political facts and figures") was created in 1770 to designate the emerging science of national social measurement (serving the policy goals of governments) that grew during the 19th century. Each of the eight values (Box 12.2) has (in the language of economists) a "production function," although only the wealth outcomes are yet measured and modeled rigorously. However, a survey of the 50 most successful innovations in American government since 1950 shows the wide use of national statistics to measure problems and progress, with benefits for government policy, administration, budgeting, and democratic accountability (Light, 2002).

3.3. *The Limitations of Social Science?*
But did we reach the limits of human rationality and social science in the 20th century? The fascist and communist quests for a better world (alongside other "isms" that also were visions of Good for different groups) killed hundreds of millions of people in the 20th century, equal to 10% of the world's population in 1900. At the end of the 20th century the political philosopher Isaiah Berlin expressed his despair that he could not – despite his youthful dream – see any method to dissuade such movements or solve political conflicts by reason or evidence-based argument, as he had hoped would be true after reading Plato's vision of a higher unifying Good. He quoted Immanuel Kant's view as his own: "Out of the crooked timber of humanity, no straight thing was ever made" (Berlin, 1997, p. 16).

Berlin may prove to be right, but a pessimistic conclusion is premature. The great messianic "isms" of the 20th century were tested – albeit in the real world, rather than by academic methods. They (except capitalism) became widely viewed as failures, and they were abandoned, or destroyed when, like Hitler, they became pathologies. The experiments were too costly and no historical learning process is guaranteed – but the human race did learn from these mistakes.

Box 12.4 *In Plato's Cave: Vivid Higher Images and Emotional/ Ideological Reactions Higher Image*

Distance from Self	Controlling & Hostile	Benevolent
Close	Authoritarian	Quiescent, blessed
	Rebellion	Liberal activism
Distant	Underground	Anomie, despair
(Clinical dimension)	(Paranoid)	(Dependent)

Also, it is premature to draw despairing lessons from the recent political impasse and recycling ideological arguments in American domestic policy. In history simple ideological schema often have been at loggerheads. Concerning the plague, for example: Conservatives emphasized contamination from foreign sources and favored quarantine; liberals held a "miasmatic" theory of a disease bred in the foul air of low-lying and unsanitary sites, especially along the waterfronts, inhabited by the poor. Finally, when science *was* applied, researchers could evaluate elements of truth in the recycling arguments, determine the true causes of the plague, and eliminate it (Cooper, 1989).

There may be a similar hopeful role for social science in engaging current ideological impasses. There is a similarity between ideological systems of thought and entrapments studied by clinical psychology (Box 12.4). For example, three characteristic responses are invoked by a higher image that dramatizes actual or potential hostility and domination: (a) close identification (law-and-order authoritarians); (b) active rebellion to restrict or weaken it, or overthrow it and seize its power; and (c) withdrawal into a subjective and diffuse underground, with government a unitary and impersonal "They" or "It," up there, somewhere – hostile and to be avoided.

Three characteristic syndromes also can be observed when a vivid, higher image dramatizes actual or potential benevolence: (a) the quiescent citizens trust their benevolent welfare-state government and live in the faith that its leaders already are wise; (b) activists who experience a partially benevolent government power above, whose (welfare-state) potential *can* meet needs within its purview to be cared about, nurtured, and protected – the poor, underdeveloped countries, those without health insurance, the environment; (c) at furthest removed are citizens who have lost any hope of higher benevolence: disillusioned, anomic, abandoned, living lives of quiet desperation here on the barren windswept landscape of modernity (Etheredge, 1982a, 1982b, 1986, 1990).[8,9]

A full discussion of the potential benefits of such a clinical psychological framework for evidence-based discussions of ideological assumptions is beyond the scope of this review, but it implies that Plato may have been right about conventional, inside-the-box entrapments. And there *might be* a genuine ultimate agreement about the Good that unites apparently irreconcilable political opposites – that is, emotion-charged zealotry notwithstanding, all ideological combatants actually may value and desire strong, secure, and healthy individuals. Once they step *outside* the cave of (different) conventional realities, enlightened activists may find a new basis of agreement and progress if they study the causes of this outcome scientifically.[10]

4. Wisdom as an Attribute of Individuals; the Political Profession

In both the Western and Eastern traditions the highest priority has been the problem of bringing the wisest people into positions of power, and, even more urgently, the associated problem of how to keep the wrong people (e.g., with sharp elbows or knives or guns) from getting into power and operating unchecked.

It is likely that people have always believed that the personal characteristics of leaders determined success (including, too, whether they were favored by the gods). The rule of primogeniture solved practical problems, but it also was a theory that the ability of a remarkable ruler could be retained by his bloodline – that is, by the heirs closest to him, the eldest son and his issue. (Modern genetics has discovered what only became apparent slowly through dynastic rule – namely that unusual inherited abilities show a regression toward the mean so that, after several generations (and especially with inbreeding among royalty), this early

---

[8] The same dramas and reparative responses can be observed when the higher image is God. See also Lakoff, 2002; Tomkins, 1963. Vivid hierarchical images may involve physiological mechanisms which can be investigated.

[9] The first column entries are what Bion/Klein in the clinical tradition call "fight/flight" or "paranoid" relations to hostile higher objects; the second column describes "dependent" relationships. At full intensity, the fight/flight drama produces a fear-inhibited or paranoid personality; and the dependent entrapment a manic-depressive or suicidal despair response.

[10] To clinical psychologists (or Plato) the answer may be "all of the above/none of the above" – that is, one must honor, but also dissolve, the entrapments.

theory produced a decline in the mean ability of dynastic rulers, with egregious historical results.)

"Every politician has something missing," the columnist George Will once wrote. The study of personality and leadership, and of ideal leaders and decision processes, is one of the most important topics in the study of personality and politics (Barber, 1992; Burns, 2003; Etheredge, 1976, 1979; Renshon, 2003; Janis, 1982, 1989; Post, 2003). Of the many issues that might be discussed I will focus on a requirement for political wisdom that may be *sui generis*: The job can require the use of violence, and a capacity to recognize and deal with ambitious, immoral, deceptive, and (sometimes) violent people. The resulting dilemma of selecting effective leaders on the basis of personality is illustrated by President Richard Nixon, who was admired by a majority of voters for *Realpolitik* acumen in elements of his foreign policy but who was rightly impeached for using a modest degree of this operating style against his domestic political enemies.

Especially before democratic mechanisms for peaceful change, political power (even attempting to be a wise political leader) was a dangerous job. Even Roman emperors who were decreed by the Senate to be gods lived in fear that ambitious and gifted military commanders like Julius Caesar would cross the Rubicon – and, often, they did. For the list of wise rulers (Box 12.1) before democracy, the effective use of violence, and successful defense against violence, were essential: Pericles spent most of his adult life with the rank of general, living with war and the threat of war; Ashoka gained the power to convert India to Buddhism by military conquest; even Marcus Aurelius, the only serious philosopher to rule an empire, who loathed war as an expression of human folly, spent most of his reign commanding Roman legions against barbarians on the northern frontiers and suppressing internal revolt. The American Founding Fathers had to risk their lives, and they won freedom and the right to author a Constitution only by a successful, violent revolution. Since Franklin Roosevelt, every American president has decided to give orders that he knew would kill people.

William James, who saw the American Civil War, addressed the possibility of identifying one ideal type of person but thought the answer depended on the requirements of circumstances and specific roles. The issue of violence was decisive. Saints made a vital contribution as their "leaven of righteousness" could draw the world "in the direction of more prevalent habits of saintliness." Yet in a world with "beaked and taloned graspers," the fate of these good men and women was death and martyrdom. They were like "herbivorous animals, tame and harmless barn-yard poultry" (James, 1997 [1902], pp. 294–297).

The most important fresh idea has been to improve on the options provided by personality-based behavior in a new (invented) psychology of professional identities, aided by graduate programs for professional training. The idea of a *profession of politics* received its most articulate early formulation by the sociologist Max Weber in Munich, in 1919 (Muir Jr., 1977; Weber, 1994) and professionalism has become a widespread American experiment to improve public and other institutions. Today, most successful democratic leaders are (to a degree) professionals: Former Secretary of State Colin Powell is an example of a decent man and a political professional, who (in a previous role as a military professional) had the lead responsibility to plan and kill many enemy soldiers in the Persian Gulf War. British Prime Minister Tony Blair, also an advocate of the Iraq War of 2003, is another example. Whether Weber's ideal (which included ends–means rationality, a subjective distance from personal vanity, passion, a recognition of the ubiquity of unjustified suffering, and honesty with oneself) will be achieved, or whether educational institutions will produce a nightmare world of socialized, emotion-dissociated technocrats (as Nietzsche might warn) remains unclear.

5. Wisdom about Systems

The United States already has bet its future on two systems, democracies and markets, combined with other institutions and professional identities in a free society. Wiser public policy will require improved social science to understand how these two systems work, how they impact people's lives, how they can be improved, and how all of the elements can work well together. A review of these issues is beyond the scope of this chapter, but several comments may be useful.

5.1. Democracies

– The fate of ordinary men and women is undoubtedly better in democracies than their fate under the divine kings and oligarchies of earlier periods. There is vigorous and often justified criticism about each element of American democracy. Yet how well the many recommended solutions will work is unclear. Democracy is a civil religion and there are untested beliefs about civic virtues that will, the more closely we approximate them (e.g., well-informed voters who participate actively; an improved news media, etc.), bring utopia. These injunctions, like preaching more Christian virtue as a cure for the world (above), may not be practical, and social science may identify more powerful and realistic ways to improve performance.

– The beginning of political wisdom is to recognize that American government was *not* designed to be wise; nor to learn; nor to be efficient; nor to reform society or improve the world (Hamilton, Madison, & Jay, 1999 [1788]). It can be *used* for these purposes, but does not achieve them automatically. There also are important, higher-order issues about the wise role of government and the design of public policy: (a) in a free society with limited government, (b) with limited knowledge about consequences (Lindblom, 1965), and (c) managing the programs in a $2.2 trillion annual budget impacting a $10 trillion/year, complex economy and pluralist society (Smith, 1992, 2002).

– A revealing observation, whether of patients in a clinical setting or a democratic political system, is what is *not* being discussed. Politicians have two jobs: (a) to identify a wiser policy; and (b) the applied psychology of democracy: listening and eventually securing the consent of the governed. When Egyptian President Anwar Sadat said that 90% of the problem of achieving peace in the Middle East (and *his* problem) was psychological, he spoke aloud what most democratic politicians, in most circumstances, also believe. In late 2004, 40-plus million Americans were without health insurance – yet a discussion was not on the agenda: (a) the 40-plus million people had not organized themselves to give voice to this fact as a political issue; and (b) politicians who cared about this problem had not found a way to talk about the problem that connected emotionally to voters. Like clinical work, until people are *ready*, or you *bring them along*, facts will not produce a public policy (Mayhew, 2002; Searles, 1979).

Athenian democracy admired *rhetoric*, the capacity to engage fully (both reason and emotion) an audience (Ober, 1989; Worthington, 1994). If we are seeking new resources for wisdom in democracies, they may reside in a way of speaking that – by comparison with recycling ritualistic and dull political rhetoric that fills the silences when nobody is ready to act – enrolls people and begins to bring a future to life.

5.2. *Markets*

Modern societies are shaped by historical lessons and political battles to create partially independent realms: the separation of church and state; the separation of power among branches of government (and federalism); removing government control of the press and from (to a substantial degree) the private lives of free individuals; and the partial removal of government from most of the daily operation of the economy (Ginzberg, 2002; Yergin & Stanislaw, 1998).

However, the moral arguments concerning market capitalism in the 17th and 18th centuries, before its triumph, were prescient (Hirschman, 1997). The use of man's rational capacities to maximize selfish benefits sanctioned (and celebrated) by the mathematical theorists of the market was, to Christian theologians, a sin of avarice. Avarice is a *capital* sin, defined as a sin that creates further sin and induces people to be accomplices with one another in sin (United States Catholic Conference, 1995, pp. 509–510). Catholic theology was right: The joint stock corporations of capitalism created great human (and environmental) damage and required many laws and regulations, passed in the 20th century, to limit their predatory amorality. Battles to achieve a better balance between benefits and costs – and for civic responsibility over selfishness – are not over, and still define important policy agendas in most countries.

Market economies also produce psychological benefits and costs, which are only partly understood. They permit people to cooperate, even on a global scale, without liking each other or agreeing on values. They free ambitious people to build global empires without violence – an outlet for ambition that, in early centuries, could have been channeled into revolt.[11] They reward certain types of behavior and penalize others. Nearly all social problems also are affected by the behavior of markets and their psychological impacts may increase depression: (Lane, 1991, 2000; Muller, 2002, pp. 141–142). Without economic growth (driven today by scientific progress) politics will default to what it has been for most of history – distributional politics – which is more conflict-prone. Better models are needed (Easterly, 2001).

6. Conclusions

Man in his natural state, it has been said, is a bunch of chimpanzees sitting around, eating bananas, and picking lice off each other. Everything

---

[11] The (wise) government and corporate investment in R&D have made capitalism a more benign social force than the ideas about profit, in earlier centuries, that used government armies for colonization and trade advantages and that enjoined the lowest possible wage to a workforce.

else has to be created. I suggest three conclusions about the next steps for wise public policy.

6.1. Walk the Chosen Path

Our already chosen future is to follow Plato's path – individual freedom, education, and the growth of humankind's higher faculties. The need for Plato's enlightened Guardians is shared by both market-based (conservative) and government-based (liberal) ideological solutions. Market-based solutions depend ultimately on the motivation and wise choices of consumers. Government-based solutions depend ultimately on the motivation and wise choices of voters. The populations of consumers and voters substantially overlap: The world needs strong and enlightened individuals who, apart from any specific role, can initiate and participate in discussions and help to steer.

6.1.1 The Lower Half. As Iris Murdoch writes: "The details of what happens in the cave are to be studied seriously; and the 'lower half' of the story is not just an explanatory image of the 'upper half' but is significant in itself" (Heidegger, 2002; Murdoch, 1999b, p. 389). American society, creating freedom for individuals, *de facto* weakens authority and pressures of social conformity which social psychologists have documented as among the powerful mechanisms for conventional social control (e.g., Milgram, Asch). A relatively free and unstructured society can increase anomie, regression, and many social pathologies if people are unprepared (De Grazia, 1948; Merton, 1968) and clinical psychologists have a role in prevention and treatment. Public policy must be haunted by E. R. Dodds's study of self-dampening cosmopolitan freedom and the unexpected decline of Athens – psychological regression induced by a lack of structure and growing fear (Dodds, 1983, pp. 236–269).

6.1.2 The Upper Half. In the upper half, can more people complete a path to Enlightenment? One scientific strategy is to ask: *Is there a belief-independent process of spiritual growth?* Is it possible that many theorists and observers from many traditions have, like blind men describing an elephant, been calling attention to the same phenomenon? Aldous Huxley perceived similar ideas about this human potential from widely different cultures and historical periods and called it a "perennial philosophy" (Huxley, 1990; see also Andresen & Forman, 2002; James, 1997 [1902]; Wilber, 1998, 2002; Wulff, 2000). *The Republic* makes a testable claim – that a certain set of mental exercises, conducted by a qualified teacher, will produce enlightenment. The psychologist Abraham Maslow reported that his most developed "self-actualized" subjects had altered ("Being cognition") perceptions or "peak" experiences that might be similar to the reports of Plato and others (Maslow, 1964, 1998; Wulff, 2000, pp. 422–424).[12]

Deciding this question solely from written texts probably is impossible. There is wide agreement that the experiences are ineffable (one reason that the term "mystical" is applied both to the states and to the writers themselves) and the subjects report a post-verbal knowledge that has a clarity (e.g., visual and auditory clarity), depth, and authority "unknown to the discursive intellect" (James, 1997 [1902], pp. 299–300; Wulff, 2000, p. 400). By contrast with elusive texts, a recent film depicting the process of attaining enlightenment and wisdom based on reliving the same day while retaining memories and *karma* of earlier lives (Harold Ramis's *Groundhog Day*), could serve as a touchstone to catalyze research.

Although not all religious practices are the same (Gross & Muck, 2003), it does appear that similar outcomes across different traditions might be produced by similar methods. For example, a Buddhist teaching process does not depend on beliefs (and includes a "twinkle in the eye" test that distinguishes Enlightened teachers from people at the level of televangelists). The methods ("skillful means") recognize sequences of growth and use "pattern interrupts" directed at a student's identity, attachments, and stimulus–response mechanisms. A student who is drawn to material possessions may be enjoined to take a vow of poverty; if attached to hedonism and sexuality, then plain food, sparse accommodations, and chastity; if verbal sociability, then the vow of silence; if rational analysis and right answers, then "What is the sound of one hand clapping?" and "If the tree falls in the forest and there is no one there to hear it, is there a sound?"; if an active life, then sitting and following one's breathing for hours per day. However, it now seems clear that none of these spiritual practices (silence, poverty, chastity, meditative exercises) are, as it might appear to an outside observer, ends in themselves or the *essence* of higher spiritual evolution. ("Skillful means" are the raft to cross the river, not a raft to cling to.)

---

[12] This unconcealment/"unhiddenness" theory of truth contrasts with a correctness theory of truth that has characterized Western logical/analytic philosophy (Heidegger, 2002). It is unclear how much the psychological studies of moral reasoning are a part of this discussion. Plato's claim was that all Guardians will agree, having directly experienced the unifying (postlinguistic) higher light of Good. But do the subjects at Kohlberg and Gilligan's highest stages agree (Gilligan, 1993; Rest, Navaez, Bebeau, & Thomas, 1999)?

If there *is* authentic spiritual growth, it could be important for wise public policy: Genuine spiritual and moral leaders (e.g., Confucius, Buddha, Jesus, Gandhi, Nelson Mandela) have had powerful, uplifting effects on political systems (see also Burns, 2003). And because right-wing fundamentalist politics and right-wing fundamentalist religious sects are drawn to each other and energize political conflict. If the actual potential is for *belief-independent* spiritual growth, future violent polit-ical/religious battles that brought Isaiah Berlin to despair in the 20th century might be diminished in favor of a common exploration.[13]

6.2. Identify Half-Truths That Work Fairly Well

The second lesson derives from Alfred North Whitehead: "We live per-force by half-truths and get along fairly well as long as we do not mis-take them for whole-truths, but when we do mistake them, they raise the devil with us" (Whitehead, 1954, p. 243). Unless there is a crisis (Wilson, 1966), Plato's tribe of prisoners in America always may live inside a moderately comfortable conventional reality, on the edge of an ambivalent choice between accepting the routine "things are going fairly well" status quo or continuing another kind of journey. Thus, a useful step (for individuals and political institutions) would be to de-sign a good mechanism to recognize the (partially satisfying) half-truths of public policy. A new network of evidence-based policy centers could be established by the National Science Foundation through competi-tive grants. The centers would receive research questions from anybody with a plan to use the answer – from state and local officials; from civic groups; and from individual citizens (including the nation's scientists, in their capacity as citizens). Public advisory committees would rank the questions and publish the rankings on the Internet. The centers would develop the research designs and begin to answer them. Such a national mechanism also could advance a wise idea by the late Donald Campbell and his collaborators, that we treat government policies, at all levels of government, as theories and experiments (Cook & Campbell, 1979).

6.3. Improve Accountability Systems

One lesson of history ("Put not your faith in Princes") is that there al-ways will be Establishments. Juvenal's question "Sed quis custodiet

---

[13] This inquiry may introduce a new level of explanation of behavior. The damage of capitalism, for example, may not be inherent in capitalism if *enlightened* business leaders behave differently.

ipsos custodes?" ("But who will guard the guardians?") is as alive to-day as when he asked it during the Roman Empire. Once any institution gains power there is a risk that the wrong people will obtain the top positions. And a wider number of the people who obtain power, money, and status – even in institutions that they operate on behalf of ordinary men and women – will become comfortable, institutionally self-absorbed, lose a sense of urgency, and forget why they are there. (Even Mao Zedong never found a solution, although he closed all of the schools in China in 1966 and unleashed the power of idealistic young people in the Great Cultural Revolution against China's new Establishment that his earlier revolutionary success had created [Lieberthal, 1997].)

To this traditional problem, the modern Western solution adds the complexity of responsibility for public policy that is limited, shared, and/or diffused across many institutions and individuals. We are just beginning to design better *accountability* systems, domestically, to measure and improve performance in public education. There are similar needs to improve the quality of health care (Etheredge, 2002; Millenson, 1997) – and in almost every other area.

The need to design accountable systems that respond to human needs is especially strong beyond the water's edge. Nation-state democracies are not designed to care about people beyond their borders or to provide wise global leadership – that is, foreigners cannot vote. The result should not surprise us. If we want statesmanship, a significant percentage of voters in many countries must serve as representatives for the interests of people in other lands. This, in turn, also may depend on the enlightenment of individuals – for example, how rapidly people are learning to develop and manage their own lives and (in Chinese terms) the supreme virtue of *ren-yi*, co-humanity with others.[14]

Author's Note

Preparation of this chapter was supported by the Government Learning Project of the Policy Sciences Center Inc., a public foundation in New

---

[14] The Chinese character *ren* designates the supreme virtue and is composed of the graph for human being and for the number 2. An extension of the idea in the concept of empathy, *shu*, combines the graphs for the mind/heart with the meaning "to be like." See (Dainian & Ryden, 2002, p. 286; Fingarette, 1972). Although the earliest battles of Western philosophers for wisdom emphasized reason – to liberate people from being only creatures of passion or social conditioning – emotions also contribute to empathy, intelligence and wisdom (Nussbaum, 2001). Concerning empathy, see also Muir Jr. (1982).

Haven, CT. Earlier research by the author was supported by the National Science Foundation. I wish to thank many people for discussions of these issues, especially Lynn Etheredge and David Smith. Correspondence may be sent to lloyd.etheredge@yale.edu.

References

Andresen, J., & Forman, R. K. C. (2002). Methodological pluralism in the study of religion: How the study of consciousness and mapping spiritual experiences can reshape religious methodology. In J. Andresen & R. K. C. Forman (Eds.), *Cognitive models and spiritual maps: Interdisciplinary explorations of religious experience* (pp. 7–14). Charlottesville, VA: Imprint Academic.

Asimov, I. (1986). *Foundation trilogy* (Reprint ed.). New York: Del Ray.

Axelrod, R. (1997). *The complexity of cooperation.* Princeton, NJ: Princeton University Press.

Barber, J. D. (1992). *The presidential character: Predicting performance in the White House* (4th ed.). Englewood Cliffs, NJ: Prentice Hall.

Berlin, I. (1997). The pursuit of the ideal. In H. Hardy & R. Hausheer (Eds.), *The proper study of mankind: An anthology of essays* (pp. 1–16). New York: Farrar, Straus and Giroux.

Bluhm, W. T. (1971). *Theories of the political system: Classics of political thought and modern political analysis* (2nd ed.). Englewood Cliffs, NJ: Prentice Hall.

Bok, D. (1997). *The state of the nation: Government and the quest for a better society,1960–1995.* Cambridge, MA: Harvard University Press.

Brewer, G. D., & De Leon, P. (1983). *Foundations of policy analysis.* New York: International Thompson Publishing.

Brickhouse, T. C., & Smith, N. D. (Eds.). (2002). *The trial and execution of Socrates: Sources and controversies.* New York: Oxford University Press.

Brown, N. O. (1990). *Love's body* (Reprint ed.). Berkeley, CA: University of California Press.

Burns, J. M. (2003). *Transforming leadership.* Boston, MA: Atlantic Monthly Press.

Conroy, P. (2002). *My losing season.* New York: Doubleday.

Cook, T. D., & Campbell, D. T. (1979). *Quasi-experimentation: Design and analysis issues.* Boston: Houghton-Mifflin.

Cooper, R. N. (1989). International cooperation in public health as a prologue to macroeconomic cooperation. In R. N. Cooper & B. J. Eichengreen & C. R. Henning & G. Holtham & R. D. Putnam (Eds.), *Can nations agree? Issues in international economic cooperation* (pp. 178–254). Washington, DC: Brookings Institution.

Creel, H. G. (1960). *Confucius and the Chinese way.* New York: Harper Torchbooks.

Dainian, Z., & Ryden, E. (2002). *Key concepts in Chinese philosophy* (E. Rhyden, Trans.). New Haven, CT: Yale University Press.

De Grazia, S. (1948). *The political community: A study of anomie.* Chicago: University of Chicago Press.

Deutsch, K., & Markovits, A. S. (1986). *Advances in the social sciences 1900–1980.* New York: University Press of America.

Dodds, E. R. (1983). *The Greeks and the irrational.* Berkeley: University of California Press.

Dodds, E. R. (1991). *Pagan and Christian in an age of anxiety: Some aspects of religious experience from Marcus Aurelius to Constantine* (Rep. ed.). New York: Cambridge University Press.

Easterly, W. (2001). *The elusive quest for growth: Economists' adventures and misadventures in the tropics.* Cambridge, MA: MIT Press.

Etheredge, L. S. (1976). *A world of men: The private sources of American foreign policy.* Cambridge, MA: MIT Press.

Etheredge, L. S. (1979). Hardball politics: A model. *Political Psychology, 1*(1), 3–26.

Etheredge, L. S. (1981). Government learning: An overview. In S. Long (Ed.), *Handbook of political behavior* (Vol. 2, pp. 73–161). New York: Plenum Press.

Etheredge, L. S. (1982a). *The liberal activist case* (Xerox. Archived at http://www.policyscience.net).

Etheredge, L. S. (1982b). *Political behavior within imaginative forms* (Xerox. Archived at http://www.policyscience.net).

Etheredge, L. S. (1986). *Measuring hierarchical models of political behavior: Oedipus and Reagan, Russia and America* (Xerox. Archived at http://www.policyscience.net).

Etheredge, L. S. (1990). *A proposal for a study of leadership, motivation, and economic growth.* Discussion paper prepared for the Commission on Social and Behavioral Sciences and Education, National Academy of Sciences/National Research Council (Xerox. Archived at http://www.policyscience.net). Swarthmore, PA: Swarthmore College.

Etheredge, L. S. (1992). Wisdom and good judgment in politics. *Political Psychology, 13*(3), 497–516.

Etheredge, L. S. (2002). *A breakdown crafted by silences: Scientific mismanagement and national policy error* (Xerox. Archived at http://www.policyscience.net).

Fernandez-Armesto, F. (2001). *Civilizations: Culture, ambition, and the transformation of nature.* New York: Free Press.

Finer, S. E. (1999). *The history of government from the earliest times: I. Ancient monarchies and empires* (Vol. 1). New York: Oxford University Press.

Fingarette, H. (1972). *Confucius: The secular as sacred.* New York: Harper and Row.

Fogel, R. W. (2000). *The fourth great awakening and the future of egalitarianism.* Chicago: University of Chicago Press.

Freud, S. (1961). Civilization and its discontents (1930). In J. Strachey (Ed.), *The standard edition of the complete psychological works of Sigmund Freud* (Vol. 21, pp. 64–145). London: Hogarth Press.

Friedman, L. M. (1986). *A history of American law* (2nd ed.). New York: Touchstone Books.

Gamson, W. (1986). *The strategy of social protest* (Rep. ed.). New York: Dorsey Press.

Gibbon, E. (1946). *The decline and fall of the Roman Empire* (Vol. 1). New York: Heritage Press.

Gilligan, C. (1993). *In a different voice: Psychological theory and women's development.* Cambridge, MA: Harvard University Press.

Ginzberg, E. (2002). *Adam Smith and the founding of market economics*. New Brunswick, NJ: Transaction Publishers.

Gross, R. M., & Muck, T. C. (Eds.). (2003). *Christians talk about Buddhist meditation. Buddhists talk about Christian prayer*. New York: Continuum International Publishing Group.

Hadot, P. (1995). *Philosophy as a way of life: Spiritual exercises from Socrates to Foucault* (M. Chase, Trans.). London: Blackwell.

Hadot, P. (2002). *What is ancient philosophy?* (M. Chase, Trans.). Cambridge, MA: Harvard University/Belknap Press.

Hale, D. G. (1973). Analogy of the body politic. In P. P. Wiener (Ed.), *Dictionary of the history of ideas: Studies of selected pivotal ideas* (Vol. 1, pp. 67–70). New York: Charles Scribner's Sons.

Hamilton, A., Madison, J., & Jay, J. (Eds.). (1999 (1788)). *The federalist papers*. New York: Mentor.

Heidegger, M. (2002). *The essence of truth: On Plato's cave allegory and Theaetetus* (T. Sadler, Trans.). New York: Athlone Press.

Himmelfarb, G. (1952). *Lord Acton: A study in conscience and politics*. Chicago, IL: University of Chicago Press.

Hirschman, A. O. (1997). *The passions and the interests: Political arguments for capitalism before its triumph* (20th anniversary ed.). Princeton, NJ: Princeton University Press.

Huang, R. (1981). *1587, a year of no significance: The Ming dynasty in decline*. New Haven, CT: Yale University Press.

Huntington, S. P., & Harrison, L. E. (Eds.). (2001). *Culture matters: How values shape human progress*. New York: Basic Books.

Huxley, A. (1990). *The perennial philosophy* (Reissue ed.). New York: HarperCollins.

James, W. (1997 (1902)). *The varieties of religious experience: A study in human nature*. New York: Simon and Schuster.

Janis, I. L. (1982). *Groupthink: Psychological studies of policy decisions and fiascoes* (2nd ed.). Boston: Houghton Mifflin.

Janis, I. L. (1989). *Crucial decisions*. New York: Free Press.

Jaspers, K. (1962). *Socrates, Buddha, Confucius, Jesus, the paradigmatic individuals*. New York: Harcourt, Brace and World.

Kuriyama, S. (2002). *The expressiveness of the body and the divergence of Greek and Chinese medicine* (Rep. ed.). New York: Zone Books.

Lakoff, G. (2002). *Moral politics: How liberals and conservatives think* (Second ed.). Chicago: University of Chicago Press.

Lane, R. E. (1991). *The market experience*. New York: Cambridge University Press.

Lane, R. E. (2000). *The loss of happiness in market democracies*. New Haven, CT: Yale University Press.

Lasswell, H. D., & McDougal, M. S. (1991). *Jurisprudence for a free society*. Boston, MA: M. Nijhof.

Lenski, G., & Nolan, P. (1998). *Human societies: An introduction to macrosociology* (Eighth ed.). New York: McGraw Hill.

Lieberthal, K. (1997). *Governing China: From revolution through reform*. New York: W. W. Norton.

Light, P. C. (2002). *Government's greatest achievements: From civil rights to homeland security*. Washington, DC: Brookings Institution.

Lindblom, C. E. (1965). *The intelligence of democracy*. New York: Free Press.

Machiavelli, N. (1977). *The prince*® (M. Adams, Trans.). Norton Critical Edition. New York: W. W. Norton.

Mansbridge, J. (1990). The rise and fall of self-interest in the explanation of political life. In J. Mansbridge (Ed.), *Beyond self-interest* (pp. 3–24). Chicago: University of Chicago Press.

Maslow, A. H. (1964). *Religions, values and peak-experiences*. Columbus: Ohio State University Press.

Maslow, A. H. (1987). *Motivation and personality* (3rd ed.). Boston, MA: Addison-Wesley.

Maslow, A. H. (1998). *Toward a psychology of Being* (3rd ed.). New York: John Wiley and Sons.

Mayhew, D. R. (2002). *Electoral realignments: A critique of an American genre*. New Haven, CT: Yale University Press.

McClelland, D. C. (1961). *The achieving society*. Princeton, NJ: Van Nostrand Reinhold.

McClelland, D. C. (1971). *Motivating economic achievement*. New York: Free Press.

Melko, M., & Scott, L. R. (Eds.). (1987). *The boundaries of civilizations in space and time*. Lanham, MD: University Press of America.

Merton, R. K. (1968). *Social theory and social structure* (Enlarged ed.). New York: Free Press.

Millenson, M. L. (1997). *Demanding medical excellence: Doctors and accountability in the information age*. Chicago: University of Chicago Press.

Montagu, A. (Ed.). (1956). *Toynbee and history: Critical essays and reviews*. Boston, MA: Porter Sargent.

Montgomery, J. D., & Rondinelli, D. A. (Eds.). (1995). *Great policies: Strategic innovations in Asia and the Pacific basin*. Westport, CT: Praeger.

Muir Jr., W. K. (1977). *Police: Streetcorner politicians*. Chicago: University of Chicago Press.

Muir Jr., W. K. (1982). *Legislature: California's school for politics*. Chicago: University of Chicago Press.

Muller, J. Z. (2002). *The mind and the market: Capitalism in modern European thought*. New York: Alfred A. Knopf.

Murdoch, I. (1999a). *Existentialists and mystics: Writings on philosophy and literature*. New York: Penguin.

Murdoch, I. (1999b). The fire and the sun: Why Plato banned the artists. In P. Conradi (Ed.), *Existentialists and mystics: Writings on philosophy and literature* (pp. 386–463). New York: Penguin.

Murray, C. A. (2003). *Human accomplishment: The pursuit of excellence in the arts and sciences, 800 B.C. to 1950*. New York: HarperCollins.

Neiman, S. (2002). *Evil in modern thought: An alternative history of philosophy*. Princeton, NJ: Princeton University Press.

Nietzsche, F. (1966). *Beyond good and evil: Prelude to a philosophy of the future* (W. Kaufman, Trans.). New York: Vintage.

Nisbet, R. A. (2003). Social science. *Encyclopædia Britannica*. Retrieved April 7, 2003, from http://www.britannica.com/eb/article?eu=117534.

Nussbaum, M. (2001). *Upheavals of thought*. New York: Cambridge University Press.

Ober, J. (1989). *Mass and elite in democratic Athens: Rhetoric, ideology, and the power of the people*. Princeton, NJ: Princeton University Press.

Ober, J. (2001). *Political dissent in democratic Athens: Intellectual critics of popular rule* (Reprint ed.). Princeton, NJ: Princeton University Press.

Odajnyk, W. (1973). The political ideas of C. J. Jung. *American Political Science Review, 67*, 142–152.

Ostrom, E. (1991). *Governing the commons: The evolution of institutions for collective action*. New York: Cambridge University Press.

Plato. (1961). Timaeus (B. Jowett, Trans.). In E. Hamilton & H. Cairns (Eds.), *The collected dialogues of Plato including the letters* (Vol. LXXI, pp. 1153–1211). Princeton, NJ: Princeton University Press.

Plato. (1991). *The republic: The complete and unedited Jowett translation* (B. Jowett, Trans.). New York: Vintage.

Post, J. M. (Ed.). (2003). *The psychological assessment of political leaders: With psychological profiles of Saddam Hussein and William Jefferson Clinton*. Ann Arbor, MI: University of Michigan Press.

Renshon, S. (Ed.). (2003). *Good judgment in foreign policy: Theory and application*. Lanham, MD: Rowman and Littlefield.

Rest, J. R., Navaez, D., Bebeau, M. J., & Thomas, S. J. (1999). *Post-conventional moral thinking: A neo-Kohlbergian approach*. New York: Lawrence Erlbaum.

Ritter, A., & Bondanella, J. C. (Eds.). (1987). *Rousseau's political writings* (Norton critical ed.). New York: W. W. Norton.

Robinson, P. A. (1990). *The Freudian Left: Wilhelm Reich, Geza Roheim, Herbert Marcuse* (Reissue ed.). Ithaca, NY: Cornell University Press.

Rokeach, M. (1973). *The nature of human values*. New York: Free Press.

Safranski, R. (2002). *Nietzsche: A philosophical biography* (S. Frisch, Trans.). New York: Knopf.

Searles, H. F. (1979). Unconscious processes in relation to the environmental crisis. In H. F. Searles (Ed.), *Countertransference and related subjects: Selected papers* (pp. 228–242). New York: International Universities Press.

Sen, A. (2000). *Development as freedom*. New York: Anchor Books.

Simonton, D. K. (1994). *Greatness: Who makes history and why*. New York: Guilford Press.

Simonton, D. K. (1999). *Origins of genius: Darwinian perspectives on creativity*. New York: Oxford University Press.

Smith, D. G. (1992). *Paying for Medicare: The politics of reform*. New York: Aldine de Gruyter.

Smith, D. G. (2002). *Entitlement politics: Medicare and Medicaid 1995–2001*. New York: Aldine de Gruyter.

St. Augustine. (1950). *The city of God* (M. Dods, Trans.). New York: Random House.

Tomkins, S. (1963). Left and Right: A basic dimension of ideology and personality. In R. W. White (Ed.), *The study of lives* (pp. 388–411). New York: Atherton.

Toynbee, A. J. (1956). *An historian's approach to religion*. New York: Oxford University Press.

Toynbee, A. J. (1961). *Reconsiderations* (Vol. XII). New York: Oxford University Press.

Tuchman, B. W. (1980, May). An inquiry into the persistence of unwisdom in government. *Esquire, 93*, 25–27,29–31.

Turner, F. M. (1981). *The Greek heritage in Victorian Britain*. New Haven, CT: Yale University Press.

United States Catholic Conference. (1995). *Catechism of the Catholic church*. New York: Doubleday.

Waldmeir, P. (1997). *Anatomy of a miracle: The end of Apartheid and the birth of the new South Africa*. New York: W. W. Norton.

Walker, J. L. (1969). The diffusion of innovation among American states. *American Political Science Review, 63*(3), 880–899.

Weber, M. (1994). The profession and vocation of politics. In P. Lassman & R. Speirs (Eds.), *Weber: Political writings* (pp. 309–369). New York: Cambridge University Press.

Whitehead, A. N. (1954). *Dialogues of Alfred North Whitehead as recorded by Lucien Price*. New York: New American Library.

Wilber, K. (1998). *The marriage of sense and soul: Integrating science and religion*. New York: Random House.

Wilber, K. (2002). Waves, streams, states and self: Further considerations for an integral theory of consciousness. In J. Andresen & R. K. C. Forman (Eds.), *Cognitive models and spiritual maps: Interdisciplinary explorations of religious experience* (pp. 145–176). Charlottesville, VA: Imprint Academic.

Wilson, J. Q. (1966). Innovation in organization: Notes toward a theory. In J. D. Thompson (Ed.), *Approaches to organizational design* (pp. 193–218). Pittsburgh, PA: University of Pittsburgh Press.

Worthington, I. (Ed.). (1994). *Persuasion: Greek rhetoric in action*. New York: Routledge.

Wulff, D. M. (2000). Mystical experience. In E. Cardena & S. J. Lynn & S. Krippner (Eds.), *Varieties of anomalous experience: Examining the scientific evidence* (pp. 397–440). Washington, DC: American Psychological Association.

Yergin, D., & Stanislaw, J. (1998). *The commanding heights: The battle between government and the marketplace that is remaking the modern world*. New York: Simon & Schuster.

PART V

THE ABSENCE OF WISDOM

13

Foolishness

Robert J. Sternberg

Western societies place a great deal of emphasis on educating students to make them "smart." But what do we mean by smart? I recently received an e-mail from an individual who indicated that he was intending to become the smartest person in the world by reading and committing to memory everything in the *Encyclopedia Britannica.* Is this a smart way to spend his time, or a foolish one? This conception of what it means to be smart is not limited to one individual on the Internet.

Many countries have television quiz shows that test people's knowledge of obscure facts. The United States once had a program, *College Bowl*, which pitted undergraduate students from various universities against each other to determine which university had the smartest students, in much the same way that the universities competed in football. The United States had other programs, such as *The Sixty-four Thousand Dollar Question*, for which the stakes were so high that the producers decided to rig the games, causing a nationwide scandal when the fraud was discovered. Today, in the United States as in other countries, there are spelling bees, and there even is a current movie, *Spellbound*, that documents the lives of youngsters memorizing the spellings of thousands of words to compete nationally to be the spelling champion. Is memorizing thousands of obscure spellings, or, for that matter, pi to thousands of digits, the road to smartness, or to foolishness? More important, can a person be smart, in the sense of knowing all the facts he or she needs to know and then some, and at the same time be foolish in some sense?

Examples of foolish behavior in smart people abound. Bill Clinton, a graduate of Yale Law School and a Rhodes Scholar, compromised his presidency by his poor handling of a scandal involving Monica Lewinsky and other women from his past. More recently, the administration of George W. Bush (who himself was also a Yale graduate) seems to have gotten itself into a war with Iraq in the absence of any preformulated coherent and workable plan for postwar reconstruction and governance. The antics of Silvio Berlusconi, one of the richest men in the world and the prime minister of Italy, at times seem to defy belief (or at least, my own), such as his denial that Mussolini was responsible for any of the deaths of his countrymen but rather only sent some Italians "on vacation." And lest all this seem recent, we only need to go back to Neville Chamberlain and his slogan of "peace in our time" as a means to appease Hitler to realize that smart people can act very foolishly, or so it seems.

Such behavior is not limited to politicians. Some of the world's smarter and better-educated businessmen orchestrated the scandals and fiascoes that led to the bankruptcies of or debacles in major U.S. corporations such as Adelphia, Arthur Andersen, Enron, Tyco, WorldCom, and others. Such scandals are not, of course, limited to the United States or any other single country.

If there is one conclusion that seems clear, it is that smart people can be foolish. If foolishness is in some sense the opposite of wisdom, it means that intelligence is no protection against foolishness. No one would question whether Clinton, once the most powerful man in the United States, or Berlusconi, currently the most powerful man in Italy, is smart. Indeed, one might argue that the people who are most likely to be foolish are those who are not very bright, because they are not very bright, and those who *are* very bright, because they think they are somehow immune to foolishness.

The Traditional View of Smartness and Why It Does Not Protect Us from Foolishness

Daniel Gilbert (1991) has suggested an interesting distinction between what he refers to as Cartesian and Spinozan forms of reality. The Cartesian view is that when we hear true information we accept it, and when we hear false information we reject it. Our minds are computational devices that in one way or another enable us to distinguish the true from the false, or at the very least the credible from the incredible. The Spinozan view is that our minds are primed more or less to accept whatever we hear. To reject what we hear, we must initiate an extra step of thinking. We need actively to reject information that is untrue, rather than our minds simply automatically rejecting it. On this view, people may hear something that is untrue or incredible, and have the capacity to reject it, but fail to reject it because they do not take the additional step. Gilbert argues that there is a preponderance of evidence for the Spinozan view.

Compounding the problem of people's failure actively to reject low-credibility information is people's demonstrated lack of skills in accurately remembering source information (Johnson, Nolde, & DeLeonardis, 1996; Johnson, Hashtroudi, & Lindsay, 1993). That is, people are much more likely to remember what they heard than where they heard it. So if they do not immediately take the extra step and tag the information as wrong or not credible, they later may fail to tag it as such because they simply have forgotten where they heard it.

Is it possible that people's minds could operate at what would seem to be so basic or even base a level? The popularity of supermarket tabloids and numerous tabloid TV shows, all of highly doubtful veracity, suggests that the answer is affirmative. Indeed, this popularity suggests that people may even welcome such simplistic thinking because it feels comfortable and does not challenge them. A number of theorists, such as Seymour Epstein (1998), have suggested that people have two systems of thinking, a more cognitively logical and rational one, and a more associatively illogical and arational one. The evidence in favor of such dual processing is quite good. For many of the problems we face in everyday life, we fall back on the associative system. We accept the foolishness of advertisements – on which advertisers dish out a small fortune – because they appeal to our associative thinking, even if they do not appeal to our rational thinking.

When we are educated to rely on our memories rather than our critical thinking, we become susceptible to committing a whole variety of everyday inductive fallacies. Consider just a few examples of fallacies routinely committed by intelligent people (see Kahneman & Tversky, 1971, 1979; Sternberg, 1986; Tversky & Kahneman, 1973).

Fallacies of Informal Reasoning

Fallacies of Relevance. Fallacies of relevance are committed when the premises of an argument have no bearing on its conclusion, when the conclusion is irrelevant to the line of reasoning that led up to it. Arguments of this type are referred to by the Latin names *non sequiturs* (from the Latin phrase meaning "it does not follow") and *ignoratio elenchi* (which translates to "irrelevant conclusion").

Ad Hominem Arguments. Ad hominem inferences (meaning "against the person" in Latin) attempt to discredit a claim by attacking its proponents instead of providing a reasoned examination of the claim itself. There are four different types of ad hominem arguments.

Ad hominem abusive arguments attack a person's individual characteristics – age, character, family, gender, ethnicity, appearance, socioeconomic status, professional, or religious or political beliefs. In other words, arguments of this type imply that there is no reason to take a person seriously – the argument is against the person rather than against the person's position on an issue.

Guilt by association arguments (also known as *poisoning the well* arguments) attempt to repudiate a claim by attacking not the claimer himself or herself, but the company he or she keeps (or doubting the reputation of those with whom the claimer shares opinions).

Tu quoque ("you too") arguments are constructed to refute a claim by attacking the claimer on the grounds that he or she has shown questionable conduct. The argument in this case attempts to show that behavior of the person making the claim is hypocritical or demonstrates a double standard.

Vested interest arguments attempt to dispute a claim by stating that its proponents are motivated by the desire to take advantage of a situation.

Straw Man Arguments. Straw man arguments attempt to refute a claim by replacing it with a less plausible statement (the straw man) and then attacking the weaker claim rather than dealing with the original claim. An interesting aspect of this argument is that it may contain good reasons against the weaker claim, but these reasons will be irrelevant to the original claim.

Representativeness. The *representativeness* heuristic is used in making a judgment regarding the probability of an uncertain event according to (a) how obviously the event is similar to or representative of the population from which it is derived, and (b) the degree to which the event reflects the salient features of the process by which it is generated (such as randomness).

Ad Baculum Argument (Appeals to Force, Appeals to the Stick). *Ad baculum* arguments attempt to establish a conclusion by threat or intimidation. This type of reasoning error does not require much information and can be easily spotted.

Ad Verencundiam Argument (Appeal to Authority). *Ad verecundariam* arguments occur when we accept (or reject) a claim merely because of the prestige, status, or respect we have for its proponents (or opponents). The pattern of the fallacy of appeal to authority is to argue that a claim is true because Authority X supports it. An argument that appeals to authority is a fallacy whenever that authority is not suitable to give evidence. Note that the fallacy is not in appealing to authority, but in appealing to authority that is not credible for a particular argument.

Argumentum ad Populum (Appeal to Popularity). *Ad populum* arguments occur when we infer a conclusion merely on the grounds that most people accept it. The reasoning behind *argumentum ad populum* is, "If everyone else thinks this way, it must be right." The essence of this fallacy lies in our need to conform to popular views and conclusions.

Argumentum ad Misericordium (Appeal to Pity). In this form of fallacy, an appeal to pity is invoked. This type of argument asks us to excuse or forgive an action on the grounds of extenuating circumstances; it seeks clemency for breaches of duty or sympathy for someone whose poor conduct or noncompliance with a rule is already established.

"Should" Statement (Appeal to Duty). "I must do this," "I should feel that," and "They should do this" are examples of "should" statements. Such statements are irrational when they are used as the sole reason for behavior.

Argument from Ignorance (Appeal to Ignorance). This fallacy is committed whenever it is argued that something is true simply because it has not been proven false, or that it is false simply because it has not been proven true. Moreover, the fallacy of appeal to ignorance can be spotted when the same argument is used to support two different conclusions (e.g., we cannot prove that ghosts do not exist nor can we prove that they do exist; therefore, this "lack of knowledge" can be used in the arguments of both believers and disbelievers in ghosts).

Of course, there are many other fallacies (see Sternberg, 1986). But perhaps the point is made that someone could know a lot, but think quite poorly with the knowledge he or she has.

What is perhaps most disturbing is that an individual could score quite well on intelligence or achievement tests, and yet be quite susceptible to these and similar fallacies. Perhaps we need a broader ideal, such as that of the critical thinker.

A Review of Theories of Foolishness

Sternberg (2002) edited a book on "why smart people can be so stupid." This section reviews theories presented in that book. Although the book used the term *stupid*, the thinking and behavior illustrated in the book might better be captured by the word *foolishness*.

Dweck (2002) suggested that one form of foolishness arises when people have false beliefs about their own intelligence, for example, that their intelligence is fixed rather than malleable. These people believe that effort demonstrates incompetence rather than intelligence. Because they believe that their intelligence is fixed, they may fail to utilize opportunities to raise their level of intellectual performance, and as a result, start to under-perform relative to people who believe in the malleability of intelligence, and therefore fail to take advantage of opportunities to increase their level of intellectual functioning.

Wagner (2002) noted that many managers behave in foolish ways because of biases in the acquisition of information, processing of that information, and responses to the information. The biases noted by Wagner (pp. 46–48) are, for acquisition, (a) overestimating the frequency of highly salient events and underestimating the frequency of less salient ones; (b) giving too much weight to information acquired early in a decision-making or problem-solving process; (c) difficulties in conceptualizing problems that go beyond their own level of experience; (d) discovering what they expect to discover; (e) emphasizing total number of successes rather than the ratio of successes to failures; and (f) overemphasizing concrete information at the expense of abstract information; for processing, (a) applying criteria of evaluation inconsistently; (b) holding on to old opinions even after those opinions have obviously become out-of-date; (c) failing to see nonlinear relations; (d) continuing to use a course of action that has worked in the past but that clearly no longer is working; (e) overestimating the stability of data based on small samples; and (f) making decisions relative to an anchor point without asking whether the anchor point is a sensible one; and, for responses, (a) engaging in wishful thinking; and (b) succumbing to the illusion of control.

Wagner also cites the work of Lombardo, Ruderman, and McCauley (1988) on failed managers, citing eight consistent attributes of failed managers: (a) inability to build a cohesive team; (b) over- or under-management; (c) being overly ambitious; (d) being unsupportive or overly demanding of subordinates; (e) being overly emotional; (f) being insensitive, cold, or arrogant; (g) maintaining poor relations with staff; and (h) having overriding personality defects.

Perkins (2002) has suggested that all of us are susceptible to folly. He suggests several mechanisms by which people display folly: (a) impulsiveness, (b) neglect, (c) procrastination, (d) vacillation, (e) backsliding, (f) self-indulgence, (g) overdoing things, and (h) walking the edge (whereby one skirts around an issue rather than confronting it directly.

Ayduk and Mischel (2002) have suggested that a major source of foolishness is an inability to delay gratification. People take smaller rewards to get the rewards sooner, rather than waiting for the larger rewards that would be available to them if they were willing to wait. The result is that they compromise on their own successful outcomes.

Halpern (2002) has analyzed the Clinton–Lewinsky scandal in an effort to understand how someone so smart (Clinton) could behave so foolishly. She identified several errors in Clinton's processing of information: (a) failure to learn from past experience (in that Clinton had been extramaritally involved a number of times before without learning the costs of his involvements); (b) machismo; (c) failure to recognize the changing nature of evidence (e.g., with DNA analysis, "he said, she said" no longer always leads to inconclusive results, as Clinton discovered from the stains he left on Monica Lewinsky's dress); (d) failure to recognize growing public intolerance for his behavior; and (e) underestimating the almost unlimited powers of the independent counsel.

Stanovich (2002) suggested that intelligent people can be susceptible to what he refers to as "dysrationalia" – violations in rational thinking despite their intelligence. He believes that being smart provides little protection against fallacies of thinking that anyone else can commit. He cites numerous theorists who have proposed dual-process models of thinking, whereby people who are perfectly good thinkers can resort to a kind of associative, experiential thinking that leads them to conclusions that are ill thought-through.

Grigorenko and Lockery (2002) have suggested that heuristics such as those described above are implicated in foolish thinking. These heuristics include, among others, the (a) base-rate fallacy, (b) part–whole fallacy (assuming that what is true of the whole must be true of each part), (c) differential reasoning (whereby one has different standards for one's friends and one's enemies), (d) hasty generalization, and so forth.

Austin and Deary (2002) suggested that poor thinking on the part of smart individuals may stem from personality problems. Most notable are the personality disorders, which any person, smart or not so smart, is susceptible to, including schizoid, schizotypal, antisocial, borderline, histrionic, narcissistic, avoidant, dependent, and obsessive–compulsive personality disorders. They also suggest that inability properly to deal with anger can be a major source of poor thinking on the part of smart individuals.

Moldoveanu and Langer (2002) drew on the construct of *mindlessness* as a source of much poor thinking. Mindlessness, according to these researchers, occurs when an individual responds to a situation based on a frozen previous understanding of that situation, without regard to the subtle ways in which the situation might have changed or by which it may look different from different perspectives (p. 214). They note that schools often encourage mindless behavior.

My own view draws on an imbalance theory of foolishness (Sternberg, 2002). It starts with five fallacies of foolishness.

Five Fallacies of Foolishness

Foolish behavior, I suggest, is due largely, although certainly not exclusively, to five fallacies in thinking. These fallacies resemble those we might associate with adolescent thinking (Elkind, 1967, 1985), because they are the kind of thinking often seen in adolescents.

The Five Fallacies

The what-me-worry (unrealistic optimism) fallacy. This fallacy, named after *Mad Magazine* protagonist Alfred E. Neuman's favorite line and renamed by Jennifer Jordan as the "unrealistic-optimism fallacy," occurs when one believes one is so smart or powerful that it is pointless to worry about the outcomes, and especially the long-term ones, of what one does because everything will come out all right in the end – there is nothing to worry about, given one's brains or power. If one simply acts, the outcome will be fine. Clinton tended to repeat behavior that, first as governor and then as president, was likely to come to a bad end. He seemed not to worry about it.

The egocentrism fallacy. This fallacy arises when one comes to think that one's own interests are the only ones that are important. One starts to ignore one's responsibilities to other people or to institutions. Sometimes, people in positions of responsibility may start off with good intentions, but then become corrupted by the power they yield and their seeming unaccountability to others for it. A prime minister, for example, might use his office in part or even primarily to escape prosecution, as has appeared to happen in some European countries in recent years.

The omniscience fallacy. This fallacy results from having available at one's disposal essentially any knowledge one might want that is in fact knowable. With a phone call, a powerful leader can have almost any kind of knowledge made available to him or her. At the same time, people look up to the powerful leader as extremely knowledgeable or even close to all-knowing. The powerful leader may then come to believe that he or she really is all-knowing. So may his or her staff, as illustrated by Janis (1972) in his analysis of victims of groupthink. In case after case, brilliant government officials made the most foolish of decisions, in part because they believed they knew much more than they did. They did not know what they did not know.

The omnipotence fallacy. This fallacy results from the extreme power one wields, or believes one wields. The result is overextension, and often, abuse of power. Sometimes, leaders create internal or external enemies to demand more power for themselves to deal with the supposed enemies (Sternberg, 2003). In the United States, the central government has arrogated more power than has been the case for any government in recent history on the grounds of alleged terrorist threats. In Zimbabwe, Robert Mugabe has turned one group against another, as has Hugo Chavez of Venezuela, each with what appears to be the similar goal of greatly expanding and maintaining his own power.

The invulnerability fallacy. This fallacy derives from the presence of the illusion of complete protection, such as might be provided by a large staff. People and especially leaders may seem to have many friends ready to protect them at a moment's notice. The leaders may shield themselves from individuals who are anything less than sycophantic.

Examples of the Fallacies

If we return to the earlier examples, we can see the five fallacies at work. Take, for example, a corrupt business executive at a company such as Enron, the former monolith that went bankrupt because of mismanagement and corruption. The what-me-worry fallacy is exemplified by the formation and execution of code-named schemes to sequester assets that would have embarrassed all but the most brazen of scamsters. The egocentrism fallacy was exemplified by the executives' demonstration of a complete disregard for anyone but themselves in their unending attempts to enrich themselves at the expense of employees, stockholders, and consumers. The omniscience fallacy was shown by them acting like they had financial acumen and genius that they clearly did not have. The omnipotence fallacy was shown by their belief that the assets of the corporation were their own personal piggy bank with which they could do whatever they chose. And the invulnerability fallacy was shown by their confidence that they could behave in utterly outrageous ways and not get caught.

Of course, these same patterns of behavior have been shown in many outside the corporate world. The list is long. Charles Taylor in Liberia or Idi Amin in Uganda make the corporate thieves look like Boy Scouts, and both managed to get asylum in countries that, for one reason or another, perhaps financial, were willing to forget their multitudinous sins. Saddam Hussein is said to have squirreled away billions of dollars. As has been said: If one murders one person, one goes to jail for life; if one murders a million, one gets political asylum.

Two Senses of Foolishness

Foolishness can be viewed in two senses. What are they?

Foolishness and Practical Intelligence. One kind of foolishness derives from lack of practical intelligence, or common sense. Suppose you take a trip to low-lying rural areas of a country such as Kenya. You go without anti-malarial protection. You then contract malaria, a disease that in all likelihood would have been avoidable had you taken prophylactic pills. This kind of foolishness is based on a lack of practical intelligence. With more advance preparation, you could have had a much better trip than you had. Practical intelligence seems to go beyond traditional hierarchical notions of intelligence. That is, it is not just another skill embedded under a general factor (cf. Carroll, 1993; Cattell, 1971; Horn, 1994; Jensen, 1998). Nor is it quite equivalent to what Gardner (1983) has referred to as the personal intelligences.

According to my triarchic theory of successful intelligence, practical intelligence is one of three aspects of intelligence that are needed to negotiate the environment (Sternberg, 1997, 1999). (The other two are analytical and creative intelligence.)

Many scholars have studied practical intelligence (see Sternberg et al., 2000, for a review). Consider some examples.

Carraher, Carraher, and Schliemann (1985) (see also Ceci & Roazzi, 1994; Nuñes, 1994; Nuñes, Schliemann, & Caraher, 1993) studied a group of children that is especially relevant for assessing intelligence as adaptation to the environment. The group was of Brazilian street children. Brazilian street children are under great contextual pressure to form a successful street business. If they do not, they risk death at the hands of so-called death squads, which may murder children who, unable to earn money, resort to robbing stores (or who are suspected of resorting to robbing stores). The researchers found that the same children who are able to do the mathematics needed to run their street businesses are often little able or unable to do school mathematics. In fact, the more abstract and removed from real-world contexts the problems are in their form of presentation, the worse the children do on the problems. These results suggest that differences in context can have a powerful effect on performance. For these children, lacking practical skills would be foolish, as it puts their life at risk. Lacking academic skills may be perceived as less foolish or not foolish at all, if the children do not see a future based on these academic skills.

Such differences are not limited to Brazilian street children. Lave (1988) showed that Berkeley housewives who successfully could do the mathematics needed for comparison shopping in the supermarket were unable to do the same mathematics when they were placed in a classroom and given isomorphic problems presented in an abstract form. In other words, their problem was not at the level of mental processes but at the level of applying the processes in specific environmental contexts.

Ceci and Liker (1986; see also Ceci, 1996) showed that, given tasks relevant to their lives, men would show the same kinds of effects as were shown by women in the Lave studies. These investigators studied men who successfully handicapped horse races. The complexity of their implicit mathematical formulas was unrelated to their IQ. Moreover, despite the complexity of these formulas, the mean IQ among these men was only at roughly the population average or slightly below. Ceci also subsequently found that the skills were really quite specific: The same men did not successfully apply their skills to computations involving securities in the stock market. For men making large amounts of money handicapping races, their practical math skills may be worth much more than academic ones would be.

Let us return to the earlier example of malaria. Indigenous people who live in malarial regions cannot afford expensive antimalarial medications. Rather, they rely on natural herbal medicines. For them, not being foolish means knowing how to protect themselves from malaria using the medications available.

In a study in Usenge, Kenya, near Kisumu, we were interested in school-age children's ability to adapt to their indigenous environment. We devised a test of practical intelligence for adaptation to the environment (see Sternberg et al., 2001). The test of practical intelligence measured children's informal tacit knowledge for natural herbal medicines that the villagers believe can be used to fight various types of infections. Children in the villages use their knowledge of these medicines an average of once a week in medicating themselves and others. Thus, tests of how to use these medicines constitute effective measures of one aspect of practical intelligence as defined by the villagers as well as their life circumstances in their environmental contexts. Middle-class Westerners might find it quite a challenge to thrive or even survive in these contexts, or, for that matter, in the contexts of urban ghettos often not far from their comfortable homes.

We measured the Kenyan children's ability to identify the medicines, where they come from, what they are used for, and how they are dosed. Based on work the researchers had done elsewhere, they expected that scores on this test would not correlate with scores on conventional tests of intelligence. To test this hypothesis, we also administered to the 85 children the Raven Coloured Progressive Matrices Test, which is a measure of fluid or abstract-reasoning-based abilities, as well as the Mill Hill Vocabulary Scale, which is a measure of crystallized or formal-knowledge-based abilities. In addition, they gave the children a comparable test of vocabulary in their own Dholuo language. The Dholuo language is spoken in the home, English in the schools.

We did indeed find no correlation between the test of indigenous tacit knowledge and scores on the fluid-ability tests. But to our surprise, we found statistically significant correlations of the tacit-knowledge tests with the tests of crystallized abilities. The correlations, however, were *negative*. In other words, the higher the children scored on the test of tacit knowledge, the lower they scored, on average, on the tests of crystallized abilities. Many children drop out of school before graduation, for financial or other reasons, and many families in the village do not particularly value formal Western schooling. There is no reason they should, as the children of many families will for the most part spend their lives farming or engaged in other occupations that make little or no use of Western schooling. These families emphasize teaching their children the indigenous informal knowledge that will lead to successful adaptation in the environments in which they will really live. Children who spend their time learning the indigenous practical knowledge of the community generally do not invest themselves heavily in doing well in school, whereas children who do well in school generally do not invest themselves as heavily in learning the indigenous knowledge – hence, the negative correlations. Because of the importance of freedom from parasitic and other diseases in the unforgiving climate of rural Kenya, practical skills may be more important than academic ones. The foolish person may be the one who lacks practical skills, just as the foolish person in the United States might be one who walks through a dangerous environment (such as an urban ghetto) at night without having taken any means for protection.

Foolishness and Wisdom. Foolishness also can be associated with a lack of wisdom. There have been many psychological approaches to studying wisdom (Sternberg, 1990). Perhaps the best known is that of Paul Baltes.

For example, Baltes and Smith (1987, 1990) gave adult participants life-management problems, such as "A 14-year-old girl is pregnant. What should she, what should one, consider and do?" and "A 15-year-old girl wants to marry soon. What should she, what should one, consider and do?" This same problem might be used to measure the pragmatics of intelligence, about which Baltes has written at length. Baltes and Smith tested a five-component model of wisdom on participants' protocols in answering these and other questions, based on a notion of wisdom as expert knowledge about fundamental life matters or of wisdom as good judgment and advice in important but uncertain matters of life (Baltes & Staudinger, 2000).

Three kinds of factors – general person factors, expertise-specific factors, and facilitative experiential contexts – were proposed to facilitate wise judgments. These factors are used in life planning, life management, and life review. Wisdom is in turn then reflected in five components: (a) rich factual knowledge (general and specific knowledge about the conditions of life and its variations), (b) rich procedural knowledge (general and specific knowledge about strategies of judgment and advice concerning matters of life), (c) lifespan contextualism (knowledge about the contexts of life and their temporal [developmental] relationships), (d) relativism (knowledge about differences in values, goals, and priorities), and (e) uncertainty (knowledge about the relative indeterminacy and unpredictability of life and ways to manage). An expert answer should reflect more of these components, whereas a novice answer should reflect fewer of them. The data collected to date generally have been supportive of the model. These factors seem to reflect the pragmatic aspect of intelligence but go beyond it, for example, in the inclusion of factors of relativism and uncertainty.

Who, then, would a foolish person be in terms of Baltes's theory of wisdom? Someone who lacks the five attributes that are viewed as keys to wisdom might be viewed as foolish. The person would combine lack of factual and procedural knowledge with an ignorance of the extent to which cultures differ in terms of their values, goals, and priorities;

someone who is quite certain of himself or herself without proper doubts regarding his or her knowledge and beliefs. It is frightening when individuals in charge of governments feign knowledge they do not have of foreign countries, and then make decisions, such as going to war, based on erroneous beliefs and imagined threats.

Wisdom is defined elsewhere (Sternberg, 1998, 2001) as the application of successful intelligence, creativity, and experience as guided by values toward the achievement of a common good, through a balance among (a) intrapersonal, (b) interpersonal, and (c) extrapersonal interests, over the (a) short and (b) long terms, to achieve a balance among (a) adaptation to existing environments, (b) shaping of existing environments, and (c) selection of new environments (Sternberg, 1998, 2001).

Foolishness, when it results from a lack of wisdom, is characterized by the faulty acquisition or application of successful intelligence, creativity, and experience knowledge as guided by values away from the achievement of a common good, through an imbalance among (a) intrapersonal, (b) interpersonal, and (c) extrapersonal interests, of the (a) short and (b) long term, resulting in a failure in balance among (a) adaptation to existing environments, (b) shaping of existing environments, and (c) selection of new environments. Foolishness, in this case, is an extreme failure of wisdom.

If we return to our earlier examples, we see how imbalance functions in foolish decisions. In his involvement with Monica Lewinsky, Clinton obviously put his own interests well above those of his wife, family, or country (of which he was serving as chief executive). He also placed the short-term gratification of the situation above the potential long-term consequences. But, of course, he did not expect to be caught, feeling relatively omniscient, omnipotent, and invulnerable from the threats that would face others engaging in the same behavior. And his shaping of the situation was deficient by any almost standard: Few people found credible his hair-splitting definitions of what he did and did not do.

Similarly, Nixon, in his cover-up, placed his own self-interest and perhaps the interests of his co-involved cronies well above the interests of the country. His attempt to shape the situation, too, was distorted by semantic hair-splitting. Eventually, having lost whatever little constituency he might once have had, Nixon resigned the presidency of the country.

Thus, wisdom is not just about maximizing one's own self-interest, but about balancing various self-interests (intrapersonal) with the interests of others (interpersonal) and the interests of other aspects of the context in which one lives (extrapersonal), such as one's city or country. Foolishness is about an imbalance in these elements. The imbalance is usually not subtle. Rather, the combination of feelings of omniscience, omnipotence, and invulnerability leads people to believe that they will not be caught in a trap of their own making.

Wisdom is different from practical intelligence. When one applies practical intelligence, one deliberately may (although will not necessarily) seek outcomes that are good for oneself and bad for others. In wisdom, one certainly may seek good ends for oneself, but one also will seek good outcomes for others. If one's motivations are to maximize certain people's interests and minimize other people's, wisdom is not involved. In wisdom, one seeks a common good, realizing that this common good may be better for some than for others. An evil genius may be academically intelligent; he or she may be practically intelligent; he or she cannot be wise.

Foolishness can involve seeking bad outcomes for others. A New York State judge became involved in an ill-fated affair. When he was jilted, the judge tried to do everything in his power to cause harm to the woman who jilted him. Eventually, he was found out and imprisoned. The judge gained little from his attempts to hurt his former lover, except perhaps some perverse kind of personal satisfaction. In putting this satisfaction over the interests of the woman, his career, and the judiciary system that he was supposed to represent, he sacrificed a great deal. Once again, a sense of omniscience, omnipotence, and invulnerability undermined the good judgment that the judge had shown in past dealings, at least in other domains. Many of us have experienced enemies who attack us seemingly solely for the pleasure of bringing about our downfall rather than for any rational purpose that serves their own or others' interests.

I refer in this discussion to "interests," which are related to the multiple points of view that are a common feature of many theories of wisdom (as reviewed in Sternberg, 1990). Diverse interests encompass multiple points of view, and thus the use of the term "interests" is intended to include "points of view." Interests go beyond points of view, however, in that they include not only cognitive aspects of divergences, but affective and motivational divergences as well. Sometimes differences in points of view derive not so much from differences in cognitions as from differences in motivations. For example, executives in the tobacco industry for many years have defended their products. Their point of view may be divergent from those of many others, but the motivation of maintaining a multimillion dollar business may have more to do with the divergences in points of view than do any kinds of cognitive analysis. Economic interests no doubt motivate these executives to adopt a point of view favorable to the continued use in society of tobacco products. As the lawsuits mount, the behavior of these executives seems increasingly foolish. They have failed to balance the long-term interests of other people and of society against the short-term interests of their companies.

Problems requiring wisdom always involve at least some element of each of intrapersonal, interpersonal, and extrapersonal interests. For example, one might decide that it is wise to go to college, a problem that seemingly involves only one person. But many people are typically affected by an individual's decision to go to college – parents, friends, present or future significant others and children, and the like. And the decision always has to be made in the context of what the whole range of available options is. Similarly, a decision about whether to have an abortion requires wisdom because it involves not only oneself, but the baby who would be born, others to whom one is close, such as the father, and the rules and customs of the society.

Foolishness always involves interests going out of balance. Usually, the individual places self-interest way above other interests. But not always. Chamberlain may truly have believed he was doing the best for Great Britain. But in ignoring the interests of all the other countries that were being crushed under Hitler's brutal rein, Chamberlain was ignoring the common good, and, as it turned out, the long-term good of his own country.

Similarly, occasionally people sacrifice everything for another individual, only to be crushed by their own foolishness. The "classic" case is that of the prolonged war between Greece and Troy. Was Helen of Troy worth the war? Many wars have started over slights or humiliations, and the interests of the slighted or humiliated have taken precedence over the interests of the thousands who have then been sacrificed to avenge the slight. There are those who believe that the war in Chechnya resulted in part from the humiliation suffered by the Russian army in the earlier war in Chechnya. Certainly events post–World War I contributed to Germany's humiliation after that war.

Wisdom involves a balancing not only of the three kinds of interests, but also of three possible courses of action in response to this balancing: adaptation of oneself or others to existing environments; shaping of environments to render them more compatible with oneself or others;

and selection of new environments. In adaptation, the individual tries to find ways to conform to the existing environment that forms his or her context. Sometimes adaptation is the best course of action under a given set of circumstances. But typically one seeks a balance between adaptation and shaping, realizing that fit to an environment requires not only changing oneself, but changing the environment as well. When an individual finds it impossible or at least implausible to attain such a fit, he or she may decide to select a new environment altogether, leaving, for example, a job, a community, a marriage, or whatever.

Foolishness results in action that represents poor use and balance of these processes. Wars are examples of shaping of the environment that often have proved to be of little avail. What, for example, did the Hundred Years' War have to show for itself in the end? Or, for that matter, the more recent Cold War? National leaders shaped environments in ways that caused great harm, suffering, and distress. In much of the world, they continue to do so.

Foolishness does not only derive from inappropriate shaping of the environment. One can adapt to a tyrannical environment to save one's own skin, only to find oneself paying the ultimate price. An example of this principle is shown in the quotation by Pastor Martin Niemöller:

> In Germany first they came for the communists
> and I did not speak out –
> because I was not a communist.
> Then they came for the Jews
> and I did not speak out –
> because I was not a Jew.
> Then they came for the trade unionists
> and I did not speak out –
> because I was not a trade unionist.
> Then they came for the Catholics
> and I did not speak out –
> because I was a Protestant.
> Then they came for me –
> and there was no one left
> to speak out for me.
>
> – Pastor Martin Niemöller

Selection also can be foolish, as when old individuals leave good or at least acceptable marriages for much younger partners whose main goal appears to be to share the financial success of their newly found partner. The selection can be with respect to environments rather than

people. An individual may love the idea of living in a place, move to the
place, and then find that the reality bears little resemblance to the ideal.
An American living abroad commented to me somewhat bitterly that
the reasons one moved to the country in which he lived were inevitably
different from the reasons for which one stayed. Those who continued
to hope to find what they came for almost inevitably went back to the
United States, because they never found it.

Processes of Wisdom and Foolishness. Wisdom manifests itself
as a series of processes that are typically cyclical and can occur in
a variety of orders. These processes are related to what I have referred to as "metacomponents" of thought (Sternberg, 1985), including
(a) recognizing the existence of a problem, (b) defining the nature of
the problem, (c) representing information about the problem, (d) formulating a strategy for solving the problem, (e) allocating resources to
the solution of a problem, (f) monitoring one's solution of the problem, and (f) evaluating feedback regarding that solution. In deciding
whether to leave a spouse, for example, one first has to see both staying and leaving as viable options (problem recognition); then figure out
exactly what staying or leaving would mean for oneself (defining the
problem); then consider the costs and benefits to oneself and others of
staying or leaving (representing information about the problem); and so
forth.

In foolishness, the problem-solving process is defective. Most often, I
believe, one misdefines the problem one faces. Clinton perhaps defined
his relationship with Lewinsky as a harmless flirtation. Nixon perhaps
defined the Watergate cover-up as the withholding of information that
was no one else's business. It is interesting to compare Nixon's definition of the situation to that of others who have more successfully
negotiated similar situations. When the Johnson & Johnson Company
faced a disaster over the poisoning of extra-strength Tylenol, the top
executives quickly decided to remove the product from the marketplace. The disaster quickly passed. The top executives of A. H. Robbins,
in contrast, tried to hide the damage caused by a birth-control device, the Dalkon Shield, ultimately resulting in the bankruptcy of the
company.

The balance theory suggests that wisdom is at least partially domain
specific, in that tacit knowledge is acquired within a given context or set
of contexts. It is typically acquired by selectively encoding new information that is relevant for one's purposes in learning about that context;
selectively comparing this information to old information to see how the
new fits with the old; and selectively combining pieces of information

to make them fit together into an orderly whole (Sternberg, Wagner, & Okagaki, 1993).

Foolishness often results from knowledge acquisition gone awry or poorly utilized. The history of malevolent dictators like Hitler shows that they rarely stop until they are stopped. Genghis Khan was not satisfied with what he would have perceived as half a loaf. Usually, the information is there to be had. The individual avoids seeking or fully processing the information that is so readily found, in what Moldoveanu and Langer (this volume) refer to as "mindlessness."

As noted earlier, however, our research has found significant correlations on scores of tacit knowledge across domains. For example, we have found that scores on tests of tacit knowledge for academic psychology and management correlate significantly (Wagner & Sternberg, 1986), as do scores on tests of tacit knowledge for management and military leadership (Sternberg et al., 2000). Thus, although one's development of wisdom might be somewhat domain specific, the tacit knowledge one learns in one domain might potentially extend to other domains. At the same time, the wise individual necessarily would have to know the limits of his or her own tacit knowledge. Wisdom also may show some correlations across domains, although such correlations have yet to be shown empirically.

I suspect that actualized foolishness, as opposed to the potential for foolishness, shows some degree of domain specificity. People who are foolish in one domain certainly possess the potential to be foolish in others. The question is whether they are able to find the incentive to do so. Foolishness results when people let down their guard because of feelings of omniscience, omnipotence, and invulnerability. People who let down their guard in one domain may well do so in other domains, but only if there is a reason to do so.

Unfortunately, one domain can be enough. The enormous financial chicanery of the Yeltsin administration in Russia, the Mobutu administration in Zaire, or the Abacha administration in Nigeria was enough to send whole countries into soaring debt and near ruin. How many domains of foolishness were necessary for great harm to be done? In each of these cases, the foolishness of the leaders showed up in multiple domains, but one domain was largely enough to cause great harm to their countries.

The costs of foolishness can be very high. To reduce it, we first need to understand it. Such an understanding can be achieved by viewing foolishness as poor thinking that results from the fallacies of what-me-worry, egocentrism, omniscience, omnipotence, and invulnerability.

References

Austin, E. J., & Deary, I. J. (2002). Personality dispositions. In R. J. Sternberg (Ed.), *Why smart people can be so stupid* (pp. 187–211). New Haven, CT: Yale University Press.

Ayduk, O., & Mischel, W. (2002). When smart people behave stupidly: Reconciling inconsistencies in social-emotional intelligence. In R. J. Sternberg (Ed.), *Why smart people can be so stupid* (pp. 86–105). New Haven, CT: Yale University Press.

Baltes, P. B., & Smith, J. (1987, August). *Toward a psychology of wisdom and its ontogenesis.* Paper presented at the Ninety-Fifth Annual Convention of the American Psychological Association, New York, New York.

Baltes, P. B., & Smith, J. (1990). Toward a psychology of wisdom and its ontogenesis. In R. J. Sternberg (Ed.), *Wisdom: Its nature, origins, and development* (pp. 87–120). New York: Cambridge University Press.

Baltes, P. B., & Staudinger, U. M. (2000). Wisdom: A metaheuristic (pragmatic) to orchestrate mind and virtue toward excellence. *American Psychologist, 55,* 122–136.

Carraher, T. N., Carraher, D., & Schliemann, A. D. (1985). Mathematics in the streets and in schools. *British Journal of Developmental Psychology, 3,* 21–29.

Carroll, J. B. (1993). *Human cognitive abilities: A survey of factor-analytic studies.* New York: Cambridge University Press.

Cattell, R. B. (1971). *Abilities: Their structure, growth and action.* Boston: Houghton Mifflin.

Ceci, S. J. (1996). *On intelligence: A bioecological treatise on intellectual development* (expanded ed.). Cambridge, MA: Harvard University Press.

Ceci, S. J., & Liker, J. (1986). Academic and nonacademic intelligence: an experimental separation. In R. J. Sternberg & R. K. Wagner (Eds.), *Practical intelligence: Nature and origins of competence in the everyday world* (pp. 119–142). New York: Cambridge University Press.

Ceci, S. J., & Roazzi, A. (1994). The effects of context on cognition: Postcards from Brazil. In R. J. Sternberg & R. K. Wagner (Eds.), *Mind in context: Interactionist perspectives on human intelligence* (pp. 74–101). New York: Cambridge University Press.

Dweck, C. S. (2002). Beliefs that make smart people dumb. In R. J. Sternberg (Ed.), *Why smart people can be so stupid* (pp. 24–41). New Haven, CT: Yale University Press.

Elkind, D. (1967). Egocentrism in adolescence. *Child Development, 38,* 1025–1034.

Elkind, D. (1985). Egocentrism redux. *Developmental Review, 5,* 218–226.

Epstein, S. (1998). *Constructive thinking: The key to emotional intelligence.* Westport, CT: Praeger.

Gardner, H. (1983). *Frames of mind: The theory of multiple intelligences.* New York: Basic Books.

Gilbert, D. T. (1991). How mental systems believe. *American Psychologist, 46,* 107–119.

Grigorenko, E. L., & Lockery, D. (2002). Smart is as stupid does: Exploring bases of erroneous reasoning of smart people regarding learning and other disabilities. In R. J. Sternberg (Ed.), *Why smart people can be so stupid* (pp. 159–186). New Haven, CT: Yale University Press.

Halpern, D. F. (2002). Sex, lies, and audiotapes: The Clinton-Lewinsky scandal. In R. J. Sternberg (Ed.), *Why smart people can be so stupid* (pp. 106–123). New Haven, CT: Yale University Press.

Horn, J. L. (1994). Theory of fluid and crystallized intelligence. In R. J. Sternberg (Ed.), *The encyclopedia of human intelligence* (Vol. 1, pp. 443–451). New York: Macmillan.

Janis, I. L. (1972). *Victims of groupthink.* Boston: Houghton Mifflin.

Jensen, A. R. (1998). *The g factor: The science of mental ability.* Westport, CT: Praeger/Greenwood.

Johnson, M. K., Hashtroudi, S. & Lindsay, D. S. (1993). Source monitoring. *Psychological Bulletin. 114*(1), 3–28.

Johnson, M. K., Nolde, S. F. & DeLeonardis, D. M. (1996). Emotional focus and source monitoring. *Journal of Memory & Language, 35*(2), 135–156.

Kahneman, D., & Tversky, A. (1971). Subjective probability: A judgment of representativeness. *Cognitive Psychology, 3,* 430–454.

Kahneman, D., & Tversky, A. (1979). On the interpretation of intuitive probability: A reply to Jonathan Cohen. *Cognition, 7*(4), 409–411.

Lave, J. (1988). *Cognition in practice: Mind, mathematics, and culture in everyday life.* New York: Cambridge University Press.

Lombardo, M. M., Ruderman, M. N., & McCauley, C. D. (1988). Explanations of success and derailment in upper-level management positions. *Journal of Business & Psychology, 2*(3), 199–216.

Moldoveanu, M., & Langer, E. (2002). When "stupid" is smarter than we are: Mindlessness and the attribution of stupidity. In R. J. Sternberg (Ed.), *Why smart people can be so stupid* (pp. 212–231). New Haven, CT: Yale University Press.

Nuñes, T. (1994). Street intelligence. In R. J. Sternberg (Ed.), *Encyclopedia of human intelligence* (Vol. 2, pp. 1045–1049). New York: Macmillan.

Nuñes, T., Schliemann, A. D., & Carraher, D. W. (1993). *Street mathematics and school mathematics.* New York: Cambridge University Press.

Perkins, D. N. (2002). The engine of folly. In R. J. Sternberg (Ed.), *Why smart people can be so stupid* (pp. 64–85). New Haven, CT: Yale University Press.

Stanovich, K. E. (2002). Rationality, intelligence, and levels of analysis in cognitive science: Is dysrationalia possible? In R. J. Sternberg (Ed.), *Why smart people can be so stupid* (pp. 124–158). New Haven, CT: Yale University Press.

Sternberg, R. J. (1985). *Beyond IQ: A triarchic theory of human intelligence.* New York: Cambridge University Press.

Sternberg, R. J. (1986). *Intelligence applied: Understanding and increasing your intellectual skills.* San Diego, CA: Harcourt Brace Jovanovich.

Sternberg, R. J. (Ed.). (1990). *Wisdom: Its nature, origins, and development.* New York: Cambridge University Press.

Sternberg, R. J. (1997). *Successful intelligence.* New York: Plume.

Sternberg, R. J. (1998). A balance theory of wisdom. *Review of General Psychology,* 2, 347–365.

Sternberg, R. J. (1999). The theory of successful intelligence. *Review of General Psychology, 3,* 292–316.

Sternberg, R. J. (2001). Why schools should teach for wisdom: The balance theory of wisdom in educational settings. *Educational Psychologist, 36*(4), 227–245.

Sternberg, R. J. (Ed.). (2002). *Why smart people can be so stupid.* New Haven, CT: Yale University Press.

Sternberg, R. J. (2003). A duplex theory of hate and its development and its application to terrorism, massacres, and genocide. *Review of General Psychology, 7,* 299–328.

Sternberg, R. J., Forsythe, G. B., Hedlund, J., Horvath, J., Snook, S. Williams, W. M. Wagner, R. K., & Grigorenko, E. L. (2000). *Practical intelligence in everyday life.* New York: Cambridge University Press.

Sternberg, R. J., Nokes, K., Geissler, P. W., Prince, R., Okatcha, F., Bundy, D. A., & Grigorenko, E. L. (2001). The relationship between academic and practical intelligence: A case study in Kenya. *Intelligence, 29,* 401–418.

Sternberg, R. J., Wagner, R. K., & Okagaki, L. (1993). Practical intelligence: The nature and role of tacit knowledge in work and at school. In H. Reese & J. Puckett (Eds.), *Advances in lifespan development* (pp. 205–227). Hillsdale, NJ: Lawrence Erlbaum Associates.

Tversky, A., & Kahneman, D. (1973). Availability: A heuristic for judging frequency and probability. *Cognitive Psychology, 5,* 207–232.

Wagner, R. K., & Sternberg, R. J. (1986). Tacit knowledge and intelligence in the everyday world. In R. J. Sternberg & R. K. Wagner (Eds.), *Practical intelligence: Nature and origins of competence in the everyday world* (pp. 51–83). New York: Cambridge University Press.

Wagner, R. K. (2002). Smart people doing dumb things: The case of managerial incompetence. In R. J. Sternberg (Ed.), *Why smart people can be so stupid.* (pp. 42–63). New Haven, CT: Yale University Press.

Discussion

Seven Pillars of the House of Wisdom

Warren S. Brown

> Wisdom has built her house,
> she has hewn her seven pillars.
> (Psalms 9:1)

If wisdom has built a house, it is indeed a complex structure. The chapters of this *Handbook of Wisdom* testify to the wide variety of embodiments of wisdom and the many perspectives from which it can be studied. Even greater variety is apparent when this volume is viewed along with other recent edited works on wisdom (Brown, 2000a; Sternberg, 1990). This variety of types of wisdom and perspectives on its study requires that the problem be broken down into smaller segments for adequate comprehension, focus, and discussion.

Therefore, I will organize this discussion around a sevenfold typology of wisdom of my own creation – the seven pillars of the house of wisdom, if you will. I am not suggesting that this typology is inherent in the concept of wisdom, nor that this typology is exhaustive of the topic (i.e., not "the" seven pillars). However, it provides a way to organize, describe, and discuss what has been presented regarding the complex house of wisdom.

The seven pillars of the house of wisdom that I will discuss are:

Appreciative wisdom
Discernment
Common behavioral wisdom
Uncommon behavioral wisdom

Communal wisdom
Transcendent wisdom
Virtue

Pillar One: Appreciative Wisdom

To study wisdom, one must first be able to recognize behavior as being either wise or unwise. In ordinary life, we judge things people do or statements they make as wise, unremarkable, unwise, or foolish. In these ordinary contexts, wisdom is an appreciative judgment where the criteria being applied are tacit, rather than explicit. At times this judgment is made retrospectively with respect to a particularly good outcome. We may not have noticed the wisdom of the idea or decision at the time, but its wisdom becomes apparent in its consequences.

By way of example, consider the committee meeting where an important issue is being discussed. One member of the committee makes a statement that provides an as-yet-unrecognized frame to the problem, or suggests a novel solution. How would the other members of the committee decide if the suggestion or idea were wise or not? Would they recognize wisdom when they see or hear it? What is necessary both individually and corporately for the appreciative recognition of wisdom? Etheredge (Chapter 12) points out how every significant advance in wise public policy has been strenuously resisted. Obviously some folks did not appreciate the wisdom of the policy.

The problem with appreciative wisdom is that it takes a certain amount of wisdom to recognize wisdom in the statements and actions of others (Johnston, 2000). In this sense, appreciative wisdom may be like artistic taste – some people can distinguish good art from bad art, and some people cannot. Implicit theories of wisdom, as discussed in this volume by Bluck and Glück (Chapter 4) and by Jordan (Chapter 7) help us understand what commonly held associational (semantic) networks surround the word "wisdom." However, this research does not necessarily tell us what people actually see in the behavior of others that would cause them to label behavior as wise, nor whether wisdom can be equally well recognized by everyone or in every situation.

The problem is particularly important for research on wisdom. When we study wisdom we must have an explicit (operational) definition to differentiate what is wise from what is not wise. *Theories* of wisdom help us know what to look for, and provide a basis for formulating operational definitions. But these operational definitions may still not be robust and useful in identifying true instances of wisdom. Part of the problem is that wisdom is contextually defined – what is wise in one context may not be wise in another. Thus, recognition of wisdom must be appreciative of the interrelationships between a wide range of variables. In addition, there is the problem of tautology – that is, defining wisdom in a certain way setting up criteria for measurement based on this definition, and then finding support for the definition in the results. Thus, appreciative operational definitions of wisdom useful for social science research are difficult to formulate.

The need for appreciative wisdom comes to the fore in research protocols that rely on nominations for study of particularly wise persons (Kunzmann & Baltes, Chapter 5; Csikszentmihalyi & Nakamura, Chapter 9). What criteria should be used to insure that the nominators are wise enough to recognize wisdom? Similarly, what criteria should be used to choose individuals who will rate the responses of research participants as either wise or unwise? Kunzmann and Baltes circumvent this problem to a degree by training raters to recognize certain aspects of problem-related narratives theoretically predetermined to be critical characteristics of wisdom. However, if appreciating wisdom is anything like appreciating art, one might ask whether it would be possible to train persons on five specific criteria of good art and thereby ensure that they will be able to adequately differentiate good art from bad art. Appreciations are notoriously context dependent and tacit. Jordan (Chapter 7) describes the nature of this difficulty well in saying, "Even a researcher with expertise in psychological inquiry many not be skilled enough to understand how to study a construct that he or she has no personal experience with. This question can be posed, but is unlikely to be answered." For social science research to go forward, we need to understand the appreciation of wisdom.

Pillar Two: Discernment

Discernment is the form of wisdom involved in seeing an issue in a uniquely insightful way – a way that has potential to lead to a solution to the problem at hand, or that frames the problem in a way that makes the issue clear. Discernment is different from appreciative wisdom in that the focus of discernment is on understanding the nature of a problem or situation, whereas appreciative wisdom recognizes the quality of the actions of others. It is also distinct from behavioral wisdom (descriptions to follow) in that it is possible to see a problem in a wise (unique and insightful) way, without knowing how to act or being able take appropriate action.

McKee and Barber (1999, as quoted by Birren & Svensson, Chapter 1) understand wisdom as "seeing through an illusion." Bluck and Glück (Chapter 4) remind us that the Indo-European root of the word "wisdom" means "to see" or "to know." Osbeck and Robinson (Chapter 3) present an extensive account of the idea of intuition that is consistent with the concept of wisdom as discernment. Intuition is variously described as a direct apprehension and a "clear and distinct perception" (a quotation from Descarte). Plato had the idea of an irreducible insight as a basis for reason. According to Osbeck and Robinson, more recent formulations of intuition have emphasized automatic and preattentive cognitive processes that are based on implicit memories of extensive prior experience. These authors note that "intuition is a capacity at once so ordinary that it grounds our action and adaptation," and yet it also forms "the basis of our most developed and 'highest levels' of knowledge."

However, running counter to the notion of the immediacy of intuition is the emphasis placed by many writers on the importance of conscious reflection as an important part of wisdom and discernment. The relative contributions of intuition and reflection to discernment highlight an important future direction for research into the nature of wisdom.

In their discussion of wisdom in adolescents, Richardson and Pasupathi (Chapter 6) provide support for a separation between discernment and behavior in our understanding of wisdom. These authors make a relevant and critical distinction between "wisdom-related knowledge" and "wisdom-related action." "This distinction allows for a consideration of characteristics that may open the door for wisdom-related knowledge, but not necessarily lead to wise action, and also permits us to identify those whose astute insight is not necessarily evident in their own behavior." Discernment (wisdom-related knowledge) and behavioral wisdom (wisdom-related action) may not always be strongly coupled.

The discussion by Richardson and Pasupathi (Chapter 6) of the knowledge-action differentiation in adolescent development is relevant to a discussion of wisdom as related to brain damage that I presented elsewhere (Brown, 2000b). Studies of individuals with damage to the orbital frontal cortex of the brain show a disconnection between wisdom-related knowledge (i.e., preserved ability to give a reasonable verbal account of the wise thing to do) and wisdom-related action (i.e., a foolish capriciousness manifested in their behavior). Such frontal lobe control of behavior is still developing in younger adolescents. Thus, their behavior has some similarity to the behavior of individuals with frontal lobe brain damage in a disconnection between wisdom-related knowledge and wisdom-related action.

Wisdom literature is not discussed much in this volume. One of the contributions of wisdom literature is that it preserves in a useful way insightful views on common life issues (see *Section I: The Sources of Wisdom*, in Brown, 2000a). When we read the book of Proverbs in the Bible (for example), we find perspectives on life issues that we might not have thought about. These perspectives are formulated as pithy sayings that are memorable. An applicable and useful proverb helps us to discern the nature of the problem and suggests issues to be considered in taking further action. Thus, wisdom literature contributes to our powers of discernment.

Pillar Three: Common Behavioral Wisdom

Behavioral wisdom is that which is embodied in action. It is the "wisdom-related action" differentiated by Richardson and Pasupathi (Chapter 6). It is also useful to differentiate the common, everyday variety of wisdom-related action from the uncommon forms that we encounter in studies of gifted and accomplished people (as described by Gardner, Solomon & Marshall in Chapter 11). Common behavioral wisdom is not common in that everyone possesses it or most actions reflect it. Rather, it is common in that it is encountered in the "everyday pragmatics of life" (Baltes & Smith, 1990). This common variety of wisdom is what Takahashi and Overton (Chapter 2) refer to in the Japanese expression "a sack of grandma's wisdom" – the lifetime accumulation of common domestic wisdom. The lack of common behavioral wisdom is well described by Sternberg (Chapter 13) as a "lack of practical wisdom, or common sense."

Thus, a study of common behavioral wisdom would consider the insightful and effective forms of action taken by many (most?) individuals at infrequent times, or taken somewhat more regularly by the few individuals that are wiser than the average (e.g., by the grandmas who have a sack full of wisdom). Examples of common behavioral wisdom would typically involve effective management of difficult and complex issues of everyday life, such as handling well an interpersonal conflict, making a decision that takes into account the complexity of multiple influences on an institutional issue, or distributing one's financial resources well between household, savings, investments, charity, and entertainment. There is nothing remarkably outstanding or exceedingly rare about such commonly wise behaviors, but they are considered wise because they are behaviors that are not seen in everyone or at all times, yet they are effective in the midst of uncertainty and complexity.

Common behavioral wisdom is the sort of wisdom that is of most interest to social science. What is peculiar about everyday behavior that is or is not wise? What factors lead to wisdom in everyday behavior? How can wisdom be learned and fostered? What contexts encourage its occurrence or inhibit its expression?

According to the authors of this volume, the capacities that come together to allow for wisdom would include a rich store of relevant knowledge, expertise in the domain of the issue at hand (procedural knowledge), reasoning and problem-solving ability, cognitive meta-control, an adequate understanding of the limits of one's knowledge (metacognition), behavioral regulation at a high level (metabehavior), and appropriate values (an adequate world view). In a similar vein, the Berlin Wisdom Paradigm denotes five attributes that interact to enhance the emergence of common behavioral wisdom: rich factual knowledge, rich procedural knowledge, lifespan contextualization, value relativism, and ability to manage uncertainty (Baltes & Smith, 1990; Kunzmann & Baltes, Chapter 5).

An important question to consider is whether behavioral wisdom is an emergent property or continuously distributed. If it is emergent, then it only occurs when all of the components are working together optimally, and it has a threshold of emergence below which the resulting action is not wise. In this case, wisdom is both very rare in the average individual and only likely to occur with any frequency in a unique subgroup of people (see "uncommon behavioral wisdom" to follow). However, if wisdom is a more continuously distributed phenomenon (both within and between people), then wise actions, adequate behavior, and foolishness are markers along a single continuum – a continuum resulting from various levels of adequacy in the processes of reflection, insight, judgment, and expertise, as well as by the outcome of the particular behavior.

The discussion of the development of wisdom in adolescents by Richardson and Pasupathi (Chapter 6) seems to imply a more continuously distributed quality of wisdom that is progressively approximated in the behavior of adolescents and young adults. Kunzmann and Baltes (Chapter 5), by way of contrast, believe that few persons achieve wisdom (implying an emergent character of wisdom). However, Kunzmann and Baltes also suggest a more continuous distribution in talking of "wisdom-near" persons. Is "wisdom-near" below a critical threshold of emergence, or is it a lesser degree of the same phenomenon?

Pillar Four: Uncommon Behavioral Wisdom

Although some forms and degrees of wisdom are attributed to many individuals at some times, there is also a meaning of "wise" that is reserved as a designation of very rare persons. Kunzmann and Baltes (Chapter 5) suggest that, "high levels of wisdom-related knowledge are rare. Many adults are on the way toward wisdom, but very few people approach a high level of wisdom-related knowledge." In their research context, uncommon behavioral wisdom denotes the characteristics of those unusual persons who are noted for being unusually wise, or having done outstandingly wise things.

Solomon, Marshall, and Gardner (Chapter 11) also emphasize this form of wisdom in their analysis of "generative wisdom." By this they mean the particular characteristics of persons who are widely noted for doing what is deemed to be "good work," resulting in "products, outcomes, or initiatives that are geared toward enhancing the welfare of generations to come." Solomon and colleagues characterize this form of wisdom as involving "boundary crossing" – "creating novel ideas or products, asking new questions about phenomena, viewing things in a different light, or developing alternative professional identities."

Uncommon behavioral wisdom has been seen as something rare and relatively new in human affairs. When coupled with concepts from evolutionary theory, it has been thought by some to be the next step in human evolution. Thus, wisdom is viewed as an ability that is evolving and that, like intelligence, is more present in some individuals than in others. Csikszentimihalyi and Nakamura (Chapter 9; also Csikszentimihalyi & Rathunde, 1990) view the content of wisdom in such an evolutionary manner. They believe that the cultural content of wisdom undergoes a process of evolution, such that new concept "mutations" (new "memes") are preserved and passed on based on their value in promoting wisdom.

Jeffery Schloss (2000) also views wisdom from an emergent, evolutionary perspective. Referring to the work of Plotkin (1997), Schloss considers wisdom to be a forth-order (quaternary) adaptive heuristic (the other heuristics identified by Plotkin being genetic adaptation, learning, and culture). Thus, for Schloss, wisdom is a "meta-cognitive adaptation to both the rapidly changing and biologically uncoupled cultural heuristic, and the need to integrate multiple representations of the world by different but cognitive modules" (p. 168). In Schloss's view wisdom is a form of meta-evaluative process with respect to culture, allowing a wise person to differentiate what in culture leads to human flourishing, and what does not.

Generative wisdom, as studied by Solomon, Marshall, and Gardner (Chapter 11), seems difficult to differentiate from creativity. This form of wisdom also seems to be easily contaminated by success or public acclaim, that is, it is tempting to choose as examples of "generative wisdom" individuals who happen to have been afforded some level of popular distinction. Public notoriety of a successful career or important contribution may not reflect wisdom so much as happenstance, publicity, or the public image of the person involved. Thus, some care needs to be taken in the study of the uncommon wisdom of noteworthy persons (such as studied in the Good Works Project described by Solomon, Marshall, & Gardner in Chapter 11).

There is a significant danger, when designating outstandingly wise persons, of promoting a form of social elitism. Equally uncommonly wise people may have operated in a context that is less publicly visible. There is the hazard of introducing into such studies a bias that may distort our understanding of wisdom. Consider the example of "Nate Shaw," an illiterate Southern Black Alabama sharecropper whose verbal history and musings were recorded and published by Rosengarten (1974). Wendell Berry (1990), in his essay "A Remarkable Man," summarizes the profound wisdom of Nate Shaw – wisdom of discernment, behavior, and virtue. Shaw not only attained noteworthy success in the pragmatics of life as a sharecropper, but also had the virtue to risk it all in the defense of the civil rights of a neighbor, and the deep discernment to talk in an insightful and measured way about the lessons of life he had learned through it all. The Nate Shaws of the world deserve inclusion if such work is to be representative of outstandingly wise persons. However, Nate Shaw would have been unlikely to ever be included in a study of such persons. Thus, an embodiment of uncommon wisdom would typically go missing from our research.

Pillar Five: Communal Wisdom

An important issue with respect to wisdom is the degree to which it is a trait found in persons versus a characteristic of communities. Much of the discussion within this volume has presumed wisdom to be primarily an individual trait, as if wisdom were independent of the social context or of social learning. For example, both the balance theory of wisdom (Sternberg, 1998) and the Berlin Wisdom Paradigm (Baltes & Smith, 1990) are models of the nature of wisdom in individual persons. Staudinger, Dörner, and Mickler (Chapter 8) give particular emphasis to individual aspects of wisdom as they are tied to personality, considering the contributions to the understanding of wisdom of such phenomena as self-actualization, ego development, psychological health, and personal and social maturity. Csikszentimihalyi and Nakamura (Chapter 9) point out that although Western psychological theories of wisdom differentiate between the cultural and personal aspects of wisdom, these theories cast cultural wisdom "in exclusively individualist terms, portraying it as the personal growth that occurs through the interplay between the lessons of the personal past and the individual's current experience."

But what is the role of communities in embodying and fostering wisdom? Perhaps wisdom is not something that can ever exist except as a form of social interaction. That is, wisdom may be present in the characteristic ways that certain local groups interact more than it is in the individuals that compose these groups. Both Kunzmann and Baltes (Chapter 5) and Jordan (Chapter 7) summarize the studies by Staudinger & Baltes (1996) that demonstrate the value of real or imagined interactive minds in promoting greater wisdom. Regarding this research Jordan writes, "Because wisdom is a socially developed construct (one cannot be wise in situations void of other people), it is understandable that wise decision-making or wisdom-related knowledge would be enhanced by the presence of and/or consultation with another individual." Others writing about the development of wisdom emphasize the important role of mentors.

There are at least four communal/societal aspects of wisdom that are rather obvious: (1) wisdom must be developed within the context of societal relationships (parents, families, teachers, mentors, peer groups, etc.); (2) the culture of a society preserves wisdom to be passed on to younger individuals (via language usage, world view, habits of social interaction, stories, literature, frequently used proverbs and metaphors, and other cultural memes); (3) most wisdom is exercised within some form of community process; and (4) consultation with other members of a community enhances the likelihood of a wise decision.

Andy Clark (1997) has argued for the importance of social scaffolding in the development and maintenance of human intelligence.

Scaffolding refers to all of the ways that an organism relies on external supports for augmenting mental processing. He writes, "We use intelligence to structure our environment so that we can succeed with less intelligence. Our brains make the world smart so that we can be dumb in peace! . . . It is the human brain *plus* these chunks of external scaffolding that finally constitutes the smart, rational inference engine we call mind" (p. 180). It would seem even more likely that wisdom is scaffolded within the social contexts of individuals. Thus, much of ordinary life draws on wisdom that is embedded in our culture and not a unique personal attribute of single individuals.

The philosopher Alasdair MacIntyre (1999) presents a clear understanding of the relationship between wisdom (what MacIntyre calls the ability to be a good "independent practical reasoner") and the manner of interaction with one's community. MacIntyre argues that the virtues of "acknowledged dependence" are prerequisite to becoming an independent practical reasoner. According to MacIntyre, it is only through acknowledgement of our dependence on others (i.e., the community in which we live) that we become open to the learning that might lead us to wisdom. MacIntyre's argument is reminiscent of the frequent association of wisdom with humility.

Both the wisdom and the foolishness of communities are graphically illustrated in the discussion by Etheredge (Chapter 12) of wisdom in public policy. The communal embodiment of wisdom is most necessary in democratically run states and organizations, but so often absent. The fallacies of informal reasoning enumerated by Sternberg (Chapter 13) are most interesting to consider in light of the frequent use of such foolish forms of reasoning in debates over public policy. If only there were a law (a public policy) against such foolish arguments in discussions of public policy. There are many important things that need to be learned about wisdom through greater attention to interactions between individuals and communities, and through attention to the presence or absence of wisdom in the processes of public debate.

Pillar Six: Transcendent Wisdom

In any discussion of wisdom, it is hard to ignore the fact that wisdom has been tied to religious traditions for most of human history. Wisdom in religious traditions is generally understood as living one's life within the perspectives of religious faith. This is a *transcendent* form of wisdom in that it is the reflection in the life of the individual or community of a grander (more "meta") perspective on life, other persons, communities, the physical world, etc.

Religion itself is not much discussed in this volume. Birren and Svensson (Chapter 1) review briefly the understanding of wisdom in both Eastern and Western religions. Takahashi and Overton (Chapter 2), in transitioning from a Western to an Eastern understanding of wisdom, move from the rational philosophic traditions of the West to the religious traditions of the East. These authors have much to say of the potential contributions of the perspectives of Eastern religions to our understanding of wisdom. Religious points of view have been important both in philosophical discussions of wisdom (Osbeck & Robinson, Chapter 3) and in ethics (Kupperman, Chapter 10). Other authors in this volume also consider the contribution of a transcendent worldview in the development of wisdom. There does seem to be agreement that, to be wise, one must have a broader view of life that transcends the concerns of the self.

Much of the world's religious literature is focused on wisdom, both in the form of the promotion of a wisdom-enhancing transcendent perspective, and in the form of specific teachings regarding wise insights into various common life issues. The Hebrew and Christian scriptures, as well as the Qur'an and the teachings of Buddhism, Hinduism, and Confucianism, are dedicated to perspectives on life that purpose to develop wisdom in the reader.

Religion may also strengthen wisdom through a particular form of community. Good religious communities should add to a person's wisdom by providing continual grounding in teachings about a good and well-lived life, opportunities for community discernment about the critical decisions and events of one's life, continual reinforcement regarding the significance (and insignificance) of one's place in the cosmos and in the immediate community, and a moral structure that helps to define virtue.

The psychologist Jerome Bruner (1962) describes the power of a "preemptive metaphor" in shaping thinking and behavior. Religion provides a preemptive metaphor that typically leads to a more transcendent perspective on life and helps the person or group differentiate what is important from what is not. For example, the classic Hebrew / Christian statement about wisdom is, "The fear of [or reverence for] the Lord is the beginning of wisdom." (Proverbs 1:7) The fundamental point of this verse is that the transcendent perspective of knowledge of the divine puts one's life on a different footing. In this respect, a religious worldview will shape the "meta" part of meta-cognition and meta-behavior.

Transcendence as a subjective experience is sought through religion via practices such as meditation, prayer, and worship. These religious disciplines and practices reinforce a larger perspective and diminish the relative importance of the exigencies of one's immediate life. Sometimes it is the transcendent experience itself that provides the preemptive metaphor for wiser living.

Obviously much foolishness has also been tied up with religion. This provides one of the very interesting problems within the study of wisdom – when and why does religion sometimes foster wisdom, yet sometimes provides the framework for foolishness or even malfeasance? Despite the prevalence of religion and its emphasis on a transcendent perspective, Kupperman remarks (Chapter 10) that a "running theme in much ancient philosophy, including that of Plato, Aristotle, and Confucius, is that most people lack appreciation of what is most important in life." Nevertheless, Etheredge (Chapter 12), commenting on the outcome of religiousness in Western public policy, remarks that "Christian virtue and preaching, and the other great ethical religions, did produce wiser policies."

I would speculate that one critical variable in the relationship between religiousness and wisdom is whether or not religious *organizations* have become diverted to other agendas (such as social status, group control, economic advantage, ethnic paranoia and stereotypes, nationalism, mindless ritualism, etc.). Etheredge believes that all institutions, including religious organizations, "tend to become corrupt and to serve their own self-interests rather than the goals and people they were created to serve" (Etheredge, Chapter 12). I would also speculate that the forms of religion that lead to wisdom are those practiced by individuals and communities with a strong sense of humility with respect to our place in a transcendent universe.

However, as Birren and Svensson (Chapter 1) argue, "The role of religion and spiritual quests in their many forms in strengthening wisdom appears to be a subject on the horizon for further research." Certainly, in the study of wisdom, a more nuanced understanding of religion needs to replace the all too prevalent knee-jerk presupposition that religion is synonymous with authoritarianism that is rigid and stifles creativity. By contrast, one would wonder if a "belief-independent spirituality" (see Etheredge, Chapter 12) is not, on closer inspection, an oxymoron.

Pillar Seven: Wisdom as Virtue

It is likewise difficult to speak of wisdom without a strong link to virtue. Behavior that does not reflect an intention to realize a positive value (i.e., does not include an element of virtue) would not be judged as wise in anyone's definition. Behavior might be crafty, cunning, prudent, skilled, and so on, but would not be called wise if it did not promote some identifiable good. Behavior that is blatantly self-serving is never considered wise.

The original Greek concept of *sophia* implied a combination of virtue and refined intelligence (Osbeck & Robinson, Chapter 3). In more modern formulations of wisdom, values are given an important role. For example, Sternberg's definition of wisdom within his balance theory emphasizes values. Sternberg defines wisdom as "the application of successful intelligence, creativity, and experience as guided by values toward achievement of a common good . . . " (Sternberg, Chapter 13; and Sternberg, 1998). Bluck and Glück (Chapter 4) include "concern for others" as a component consistently found in their summary of studies of wisdom. Even Kunzmann and Baltes (Chapter 5), who argue for the importance of "value relativism" as a critical component of wisdom, nevertheless believe that wisdom must include the values of selecting goals and means that are "desirable in human development" and "do not violate the rights of others and co-produce collective resources."

I would argue that consistency in virtue is, itself, a form of wisdom. Would we not judge a consistently virtuous life to be a reflection of wisdom, even when many of the other components of wisdom are not obviously apparent? Would Mother Teresa be judged wise because of some noted skill or sagacity, or because of the consistency of moral virtue apparent in her lifelong commitment to serving the desperately poor people of Calcutta? Would not the persistent commitment to the values of racial justice and nonviolence demonstrated in the life of Martin Luther King be, in itself, suggestive of wisdom?

Wisdom as virtue needs some nuance, of course. Virtue is not self-righteousness nor is it rigid moralism. Rather, virtue that would be deemed wise needs to be coupled with a sense of humility – "acknowledge dependence" in the terms of Alasdair MacIntyre. The concept of humility also helps us reconcile the "value relativism" required in the operational definition of wisdom set forward in the Berlin wisdom paradigm (Baltes & Smith, 1990; Kunzmann & Baltes, Chapter 5), with the idea that virtue is a pillar of wisdom. On the surface, value relativism and virtue seem contradictory. If values are relative then virtue is meaningless. By contrast, virtue presumes a deep commitment to values not deemed relative. However, there is a reality somewhere in between. Truly wise and virtuous persons have the humility to know that their commitments do not have to be the commitments of others, that their perspective may need to be modified by experience, and that important and lasting values can come into conflict, forcing some negotiation and accommodation. Thus, wisdom as virtue combines a persistent commitment to values held as fundamentally important with the humility to understand the imperfections of one's own knowledge and perspective, and a sense of modifiability of one's values as one matures. However, the modification of critical values is more likely to occur around the edges than at the core. Kupperman points out (Chapter 10) that when we are concerned about "value relativism" as a property of wisdom, "values known to be really important will usually not be at stake."

Finally, Etheredge (Chapter 12) describes a helpful distinction presented by Weber (1994) between the "ethics of principled conviction" and the "ethics of responsibility for consequences." Both forms of ethical consideration would tap the same fundamental values that contribute to wisdom. Wise expression of values in principles for living must always reckon with values as applied to the consequences of one's principled actions. The pillar of wisdom that is virtue must be some amalgam of these two ethical forms.

Do the Seven Pillars Make One House?

Do the pillars of the house of wisdom actually make up a single, integrated structure? That is, do we have a conglomeration of positive aspects of human behavior grouped under a single abstract term, "wisdom"? Or, is wisdom a property of human nature that expresses itself in a variety of ways, but is nevertheless singular? Are these seven pillars isolated and only occasionally connected, like the pillars of Stonehenge, where one must use one's imagination to see them as a single structure? Or, are these pillars well integrated into a robustly singular building like the Temple of Athena on the Acropolis of Athens, Greece?

The table of definitions provided by Birren and Fisher (1990; reprinted in Chapter 1) suggests a wide variety of sometimes disconnected ideas about wisdom. This variety seems to be heavily influenced by the philosophical view of human nature dominant at a particular time and place.

For the ancient Hebrews, for example, wisdom was explicitly tied to religion. For the ancient Greeks, wisdom was the ability to discern the underlying universal forms. During the Enlightenment, wisdom was linked to human rationality, with a heavy emphasis on human intelligence and conscious reflection. The modernism of most current social science research favors a pragmatic and individualistic view of wisdom, at the expense of paying less attention to the communal aspects of wisdom. Modernism is also explicitly secular, setting aside, at least until very recent years, the issues involved in transcendence and religiousness. The postmodernism of the Berlin Wisdom Paradigm, with its emphasis on value relativism and uncertainty, deconstructs virtue, transcendence, and communal wisdom into the individualism of idiosyncratic resolutions of relativity and uncertainty. Although Eastern understandings of wisdom are more transcendent and communal, they do not encompass the same sorts of pragmatics of daily living (particularly the importance of individual cognition and action) that are deemed important in Western thinking about wisdom. Thus, there is much to suggest that we have a Stonehenge rather than a Temple of Athena.

The challenges for future study of wisdom are clear, at least at the meta-level of this review. Some of the pillars have been ignored in recent discussions of wisdom and need closer attention. The very short recent history of social science research into wisdom still leaves much to be learned even within those areas that have received relatively more attention. However, covering the entire field is the need for a clearly encompassing definition of wisdom that can be conceptually and empirically differentiated from other properties of human nature. At present, like Stonehenge, the gestalt of the house of wisdom demands some imagination to see.

References

Baltes, P. B., & Smith, J. (1990). The psychology of wisdom and its ontogenesis. In R. J. Sternberg (Ed.), *Wisdom: Its nature, origins, and development* (pp. 87–120). Cambridge: Cambridge University Press.

Berry, W. (1990). A Remarkable Man. In W. Berry, *What are people for?* (pp. 17–29). San Francisco: North Point Press.

Birren, J. E., & Fisher, L. M. (1990). The elements of wisdom: Overview and integration. In R. J. Sternberg (Ed.), *Wisdom: Its nature, origins, and development* (pp. 317–332). Cambridge: Cambridge University Press.

Brown, W. S. (Ed.). (2000a). *Understanding wisdom: Sources, science, & society.* Philadelphia, PA: Templeton Foundation Press.

Brown, W. S. (2000b). Wisdom and human neurocognitive systems: Perceiving and practicing the laws of life. In W. S. Brown (Ed.), *Understanding wisdom: Sources, science, & society* (pp. 193–213). Philadelphia, PA: Templeton Foundation Press.

Bruner, J. S. (1962). *On Knowing: Essays for the left hand*. Cambridge, MA: Harvard University Press.

Clark, A. (1997). *Being There: Putting Brain, Body, and World Together Again*. Cambridge, MA: Bradford Books.

Csikszentimihalyi, M., & Rathunde, K. (1990). The psychology of wisdom: An evolutionary interpretation. In R. J. Sternberg (Ed.), *Wisdom: Its nature, origins, and development* (pp. 317–332). Cambridge: Cambridge University Press.

Johnston, R. K. (2000). It takes wisdom to use wisdom wisely. In W. S. Brown (Ed.), *Understanding wisdom: Sources, science, & society* (pp. 193–213). Philadelphia, PA: Templeton Foundation Press.

MacIntyre, A. (1999). *Dependent rational animals: Why human beings need the virtues*. Chicago: Open Court.

McKee, P., & Barber, C. (1999). On defining wisdom. *International journal of aging and human development*, 49, 149–164.

Plotkin, H. (1997). *Evolution in mind: An introduction to evolutionary psychology*. Cambridge, MA: Harvard University Press.

Rosengarten, T. (1974). *All God's dangers: The life of Nate Shaw*. New York: Alfred A. Knopf.

Schloss, J. P. (2000). Wisdom traditions as a mechanism for organismal integration: Evolutionary perspectives on homeostatic "Laws of Life." In W. S. Brown (Ed.), *Understanding wisdom: Sources, science, & society* (pp. 193–213). Philadelphia, PA: Templeton Foundation Press.

Staudinger, U. M., & Baltes, P. B. (1996). Interactive minds: A facilitative setting for wisdom-related performance. *International Journal of Behavioral Development*, 26, 494–505.

Sternberg, R. J. (Ed.). (1990). *Wisdom: Its nature, origins, and development*. Cambridge: Cambridge University Press.

Sternberg, R. J. (1998). A balance theory of wisdom. *Review of General Psychology*, 2, 347–365.

Weber, M. (1994). The profession and vocation of politics [Politics as a professional]. In P. Lassman & R. Speirs (Eds.), *Weber: Political writing* (pp. 309–369). New York: Cambridge University Press.

Author Index

Achenbaum, W.A., 33, 43, 45, 46, 99
Adams, C., 38, 49, 98
Adler, M.J., 5
Albert, R.A., 149
Albino, A., 146
Aldwin, C.M., 193
Allen, J.L., 196
Allport, G.W., 202, 204, 208, 211
Ames, R., 248, 254
Amin, I., 340
Anderson, B.J., 150
Anderson, J.R., 166
Andresen, J., 319
Aquinas, T., 7, 227
Ardelt, M., 23, 45, 51, 85, 130, 177, 202, 212, 228
Aristotle, 5, 22, 66, 68, 70, 72, 73, 74, 75, 76, 78, 79, 227, 253, 256
Arlin, P.K., 44, 140, 195, 275
Arnett, J.J., 144, 146
Asahara, Shoukou, 41
Ashoka (Indian leader), 299, 315
Asimov, I., 311
Aspinwall, L.G., 111
Assanand, S., 211
Assman, A., 33, 34, 35, 110, 199, 200
Aurelius, M., 299, 315
Austin, E.J., 337
Axelrod, R., 310
Ayduk, O., 337

Bacon, F., 9, 10
Baltes, M.M., 127

Baltes, P.B., 20, 33, 44, 45, 52, 84, 85, 86, 96, 98, 101, 102, 110, 111, 114, 115, 116, 117, 118, 121, 122, 123, 124, 126, 127, 128, 129, 130, 131, 139, 140, 141, 144, 146, 150, 151, 154, 161, 163, 164, 165, 166, 167, 168, 170, 171, 172, 173, 174, 175, 176, 177, 178, 179, 181, 182, 184, 185, 191, 193, 194, 195, 197, 198, 199, 200, 201, 207, 208, 210, 211, 224, 230, 237, 250, 263, 275, 276, 343, 357, 361, 365
Bandura, A., 141, 148
Barber, C., 22, 86, 98, 356
Barber, J.D., 315
Barclay, C.R., 147
Barenboim, C., 147
Barnes, J., 254
Baron, 100
Barrett, F.L., 220, 228
Barrett, W., 35
Basseches, M.A., 43, 195
Bates, C.A., 3, 6, 7, 9, 10, 25
Beattie, O., 235
Berg, C.A., 163, 166, 170, 171
Berg, S.A., 221
Berlin, I., 312, 321
Berlusconi, S., 332
Bernstein, M., 90
Berry, W., 360
Birren, J.E., 15, 20, 33, 38, 87, 93, 95, 96, 103, 104, 110, 113, 115, 139, 145, 161, 163, 164, 167, 169, 171, 176, 178, 185, 195, 201, 366
Blakeny, R.B., 258

Taft, L.B., 212
Takahashi, M., 33, 39, 40, 41, 46, 85, 164, 167, 169, 171
Takayama, M., 38, 39
Taranto, M.A., 21
Tarule, J.M., 26
Taylor, C., 340
Taylor, S.E., 131
Tertullian, 74
Tolkein, J.R.R., 298
Toynbee, A.J., 311
Tuchman, B.W., 297, 300
Turbin, M.S., 146
Turiel, E., 141, 147
Turner, F.M., 306
Tversky, A., 333
Twain, M., 261

United States Catholic Conference, 318

Vachon, R., 143
Vaillant, G.E., 193, 203, 238
Valdez, J.M., 39
Van Buren, A., 162
van Lieshout, C.F., 145
Vandenberg, B., 44

Wagner, R.K., 196, 336, 349
Waldmeir, P., 301
Ward, S.L., 143
Waterman, A.S., 201
Waynryb, C., 147
Weaverdyck, S., 49
Weber, M., 316, 366
Webster, J.D., 85, 202, 212
Wehr, P., 88, 97

Wessler, R., 202, 207
Westenberg, P.M., 203
Whitehead, A.N., 321
Wiese, B.S., 127
Wilber, K., 319
Wilde, O., 160
Will, G., 315
Williams, B., 253
Williams, W.M., 196
Wilson, E.O., 226, 233
Wilson, J.Q., 321
Winfrey, O., 97
Wink, P., 45, 110, 114, 130, 193, 203, 206, 207, 230
Winner, E., 46
Wittgenstein, L., 78
Wolman, B.B., 13
Wood, J., 34
Wood, P., 147, 179
Wood, P.K., 146
Woodruff, D.S., 195
Woodruff-Pak, D.S., 33
World populations prospects population database, 2000–2020, 163
Worthington, I., 317
Wulff, D.M., 319, 320

Yagananda, P., 48
Yalom, I.D., 44
Yang, S., 38, 39, 41
Yee, C., 52
Yergin, D., 318
Yutang, L., 9

Zeno (philosopher), 75
Zubek, J.M., 145

Subject Index